D0089247

Table of Contents

I. Essence of Mexico

II. Some Things to Do

III. Going Your Own Way

IV. In the Shadows

V. The Last Word

TRAVELERS' TALES

MEXICO

TRAVELERS' TALES

MEXICO

Collected and Edited by

JAMES O'REILLY AND LARRY HABEGGER

Travelers' Tales, Inc.
Editorial Offices: 10 Napier Lane, San Francisco, CA 94133

Distributed by
O'Reilly & Associates, Inc., 103 Morris Street, Suite A, Sebastopol, CA 95472

La verdad padece pero no perece.
Truth suffers but never perishes.

— Mexican Proverb

TRAVELERS' TALES

We are all outsiders when we travel. Whether we go abroad or roam about our own country, we often enter territory so unfamiliar that our frames of reference become sorely inadequate. We need advice not just to avoid offense and danger, but to make our experiences richer, deeper, and more fun.

Traditionally, travel guides have answered the basic questions: what, when, where, how, and how much. A good guidebook is indispensable for all the practical matters that demand attention. More recently, many guidebooks have added cultural and experiential insight to their standard fare. But something important is still missing: guidebooks don't really prepare you, the individual with feelings and fears, hopes and dreams, goals.

This kind of inner preparation is best achieved through travelers' tales, for we get our landmarks more from anecdote than information. Nothing can replace listening to the experience of others, to the war stories that come out after a few drinks, to the memories that linger and beguile. For millennia it's been this way: at watering holes and wayside inns, the experienced traveler tells those nearby what lies ahead on the ever-mysterious road. Stories stoke the imagination, inspire, frighten, and teach. In stories we see more clearly the urges that bring us to wander, whether it's hunger for change, adventure, self-knowledge, love, curiosity, sorrow, or even something as prosaic as a job assignment or two weeks off.

But travelers' accounts, while profuse, can be hard to track down. Many are simply doomed in a throwaway publishing world. And few of us have the time anyway to read more than one or two books, or the odd pearl found by chance in the Sunday travel section. Wanderers for years, we've often faced this issue. We've always told ourselves when we got home that we would prepare better for the next trip—read more, study more, talk to more people—but life always seems to interfere and we've rarely managed to do so to our satisfaction. That is one reason for this series. We needed a kind of experiential primer that guidebooks don't offer.

Another path that led us to *Travelers' Tales* has been seeing the enormous changes in travel and communications over the last two decades. It is no longer unusual to have ridden a pony across Mongolia, to have celebrated an auspicious birthday on Mt. Kilimanjaro, or honeymooned on the Loire. The one-world monoculture has risen with daunting swiftness, weaving a new cross-cultural rug with it: no longer is it surprising to encounter former headhunters watching All-Star Wrestling on their satellite feed, no longer is it shocking to find the last guy at the end of the earth wearing a Harvard t-shirt and asking if you know Michael Jordan. The global village exists in a rudimentary fashion, but it is real.

In 1980, Paul Fussell wrote in *Abroad: British Literary Traveling Between the Wars* a cranky but wonderful epitaph for travel as it was once known, in which he concluded that "we are all tourists now, and there is no escape." It has been projected by some analysts that by the year 2000, tourism will be the world's largest industry; others say it already is. In either case, this is a horrifying prospect—hordes of us hunting for places that have not been trod on by the rest of us!

Fussell's words have the painful ring of truth, but this is still our world, and it is worth seeing and will be worth seeing next year, or in fifty years, simply because it will always be worth meeting others who continue to see life in different terms than we do despite the efforts of telecommunication and advertising talents. No amount of creeping homogeneity can quell the endless variation of humanity, and travel in the end is about people, not places. Places only provide different venues, as it were, for life, in which we are all pilgrims who need to talk to each other.

There are also many places around the world where intercultural friction and outright xenophobia is increasing. And the very fact that travel endangers cultures and pristine places more quickly than it used to calls for extraordinary care on the part of today's traveler, a keener sense of personal responsibility. The world is not our private zoo or theme park; we need to be better prepared before we go, so that we might become honored guests and not vilified intruders.

In *Travelers' Tales*, we collect useful and memorable anecdotes by country—because that's how people travel—to produce the kind of sampler we've always wanted to read before setting out. These stories will show you some of the spectrum of experiences to be had or avoided in each country. The authors come from many walks of life: some are teachers, some are writers, some are scientists, all are wanderers with a story to tell. (Where we've excerpted books, we urge you to go out and read the full work, because no selection can ever do an author justice.) These stories won't help you be an insider as many travel books promise—but they will help you to deepen and enrich the experience that you will have as an outsider.

Each *Travelers' Tales* is organized into five simple parts. In the first, we've chosen stories that reflect the ephemeral yet pervasive essence of a country. Part Two contains stories about places and activities that others have found worthwhile. In Part Three, we've chosen stories by people who have made a special connection between their lives and interests and the people and places they visited. Part Four shows some of the struggles and challenges facing a country, and Part Five, "The Last Word," is just that, something of a grace note or harmonic to remind you of the book as a whole.

Our selection of stories in each *Travelers' Tales* is by no means comprehensive, but we are confident it will prime your pump, and make your use of regular guidebooks more meaningful. *Travelers' Tales* are not meant to replace other travel guides but to accompany them. No longer will you have to go to dozens of sources to map the personal side of your journey. You'll be able to reach for *Travelers' Tales*, and truly prepare yourself before you go.

—JAMES O'REILLY AND LARRY HABEGGER

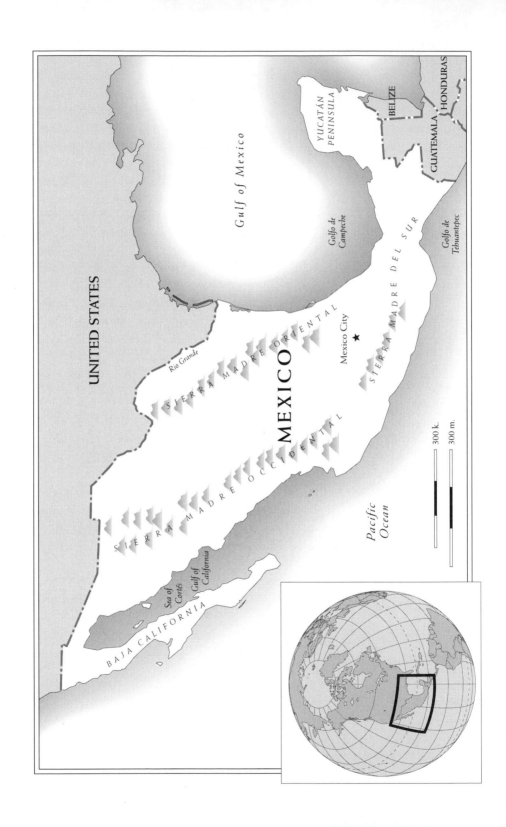

Mexico: An Introduction

Mexico, so prone to stereotyping, is one of the most deceptively complex countries in the world. "Melting pot," a phrase more often applied to the United States, is applicable in a deeper way to Mexico's towering and ancient layering of civilizations, which continues to this day in a swirling crosscurrent of indigenous peoples, multiple languages, dialects, riotous art and music, religions behind religions, hidden cosmologies, uncounted ruins, and secret knowledge. We forget just how old Mexico is. We forget, for instance, that Teotihuacán, the ancient city just north of Mexico City, was larger than Rome in its imperial heyday.

And yet, Mexico is so simple, her people so lovely. Families and children are at the core of life, as is music, food, hard work. Every town has a patron saint and a square, or *zócalo*, where the pulse of the community can be witnessed and sometimes shared. There are so many festivals in Mexico you would have to spend a lifetime sampling them. (One town even has a festival that runs 365 days a year—every year.) The most famous *fiesta* of course is the Day of the Dead, during which the dead are remembered, and in a sense, brought back to life by honoring and savoring their lives through photographs, favorite foods, and of course, stories. Life in Mexico is hard, but the hard life here has a richness it doesn't always have in other places. Mexicans are friendly and remote, shy and gregarious, and usually generous to a fault.

Mexico is deeply Catholic, but in many places, behind the façade of Rome, there lies a different landscape of shamanism, ritual, superstition, mystical labyrinths thousands of years old. You can go to a great Mexican beach, have a wonderful time, and be back in a week, but getting to know Mexico is the work of years and repeated visits.

There are many Mexicos: resorts lush enough for anyone, colonial silver cities, stunning desert beauty, jungles, brooding ruins, modern cities, murals the likes of which you won't see anywhere else. It's a disturbing place too, with serious pollution, official corruption, and population problems, but disturbing also in the best sense: you can't go there and remain the same—unless, as many do, you go only to a hermetically sealed resort—and even then....

Any discussion of Mexico must also include its love-hate relationship with the United States, the giant to the north which both beguiles and torments Mexico. Mexico's problems spill over the border like quicksilver and American culture oozes south to erode traditional Mexican family life. Solutions are as elusive as the vast no-man's land that separates the two countries, so interlinked by conquests of different sorts, ever more linked by commerce and immigration.

But one fact remains: Mexico's future is North America's future. It is worth getting to know.

A Note on Exchange Rates and a Warning on Other Matters that Affect the Traveler

This is not a travel guide in the ordinary sense, in which prices and accuracy of exchange rates figure prominently. Consequently, we have not tried to convert figures used by authors to current exchange rates as long as they are in a ballpark with admittedly ill-defined borders. However, in most cases we *have* changed prices where mentioned into new peso figures. The new peso was established January 1, 1993, to simplify currency exchange and bring the peso closer to parity with other currencies. The new peso is worth 1,000 old pesos.

We do not endorse products used, trips made, or services featured in the stories in this book. We urge every traveler to consult not just one, but two or three other guidebooks on Mexico, and make careful inquiries about the safety of travel to remote areas. Check with your physician about any health issues that you might face. When in doubt about anything, be a good ambassador.

Above all, talk to people who've been where you want to go or who've done the things you want to do. There is no better source, no travel habit more worth cultivating.

PART I

Essence of Mexico

Serenading the Future

*Mexicans are nothing if not passionate and musical—qualities that endure the
ravages of time and imports from the north.*

Mexicans know that a party has been outstandingly successful if at the
end of it there are at least a couple of clusters of longtime or first-
time acquaintances leaning on each other against a wall, sobbing
helplessly. The activities one normally associates with a party—flirting
and conversation, and even the kind of dancing that leads to an amnesiac
dawn in a strange bed—are considered here mere preludes to or distrac-
tions from the ultimate goal which is weeping and the free, luxurious
expression of pain. A true celebrant of the Mexican *fiesta* will typically
progress along a path that leads from compulsive joke-telling to stubborn
argumentativeness to thick-tongued foolery, all in pursuit of a final,
unchecked absolving wash of tears, and a casual observer of this voluptuous ritual might conclude that the essential Mexican *fin de fiesta* cannot
happen without alcohol. Not so. It cannot happen without *ranchera*
music. People may cry admirably with little help from booze, but a
drunk who begins to whimper without the benefit of song produces only
mediocre tears. He cries out of self-pity. The man or woman who, with a
few tequilas packed away, bursts into tears to the strains of a *ranchera*
hymn—"Let My Bed Be Made of Stone," for example—weeps for the
tragedy of the world, for a mother, for a father, for our doomed quests
for happiness and love, for life. Sorrow on such a magnificent scale is in
itself redeeming, and—an added benefit—its glory leaves little room for
embarrassment the morning after.

Now that Mexico is carpeted with Kentucky Fried Chicken,
Denny's, and McDonald's outlets, and Coca-Cola is the national drink;
now that even low paid office workers are indentured to their credit
cards and auto loans; now that the North American Free Trade
Agreement promises to make Mexico commercially one with its neighbors to the north, there is little scope for magnificent sorrow in the average citizen's life. In the smog-darkened center of Mexico City, or in its
monstrous, ticky-tacky suburban spokes, the average citizen on an average day is more concerned with beating the traffic, making the mortgage

payment, punching the clock. Progress has hit Mexico in the form of devastation, some of it ecological, much of it aesthetic. Life is rushed, the water may be poisoned, and the new industrial tortillas taste terrible. Favorite ornaments for the home include porcelain dogs and plastic roses, and for the two-thirds of the population which is confined to the cities, recreation usually takes the form of a couple of hours with the latest imported sitcom or the local *telenovelas*. Hardly anyone knows anymore what it is to live on a ranch or to die of passion, and yet, when it comes to the defining moments of *mexicanidad, ranchera* music, with its odes to love, idyllic landscapes, and death for the sake of honor, continue to reign supreme.

It is a hybrid music. Sung most often to the accompaniment of a *mariachi* ensemble, *rancheras* generate tension by setting the classic formality of the trumpets and violins against the howling quality of the vocals. The lyrics of many of the best known songs—*"Cielito Lindo,"* say—include verses that were inherited in colonial days from Spain. Many of the rhetorical flourishes—"lips like rose petals," "eyes like stars"—are Spanish also. But when *rancheras* turn, as they do obsessively, to the topics of death and destruction, alcohol and defeat, and the singer holds up his dying heart for all to see, or calls for stones in the field to shout at him, he is bleeding from a wound that is uniquely Mexican.

The spiritual home of *ranchera* music is in the heart of Mexico City—in a raucous plaza surrounded by ratty night clubs and forbidding ancient churches. The plaza, which is not far from where I grew up, is named after Giuseppe Garibaldi, the 19th-century Italian revolutionary, but the central statue is of Jose Alfredo Jimenez (1926-1973), who wrote more songs about weeping, alcohol, and women than any other *ranchera* composer. Jose Alfredo's statue is wearing

I n a world which is becoming homogenized with fearsome rapidity, Mexico is still a wonderful confusion and melding of disparate facts, eras, art, sociology, and mental climates. Mexico speaks innumerable Indian languages, including a strange vocabulary of whistling, and prides itself on its very careful Spanish. Some of its people are chic worldlings; many of their compatriots still move in the dark of superstition and witchcraft. The tropics dance, sing, catch fish and fruit as it drops off the trees, and sleep away the rainy season; an hour's ride upward into the hills enters an atmosphere of seriousness, hard work, and inwardness. The unyielding highlands are abandoned and their people join the squatter colonies on the edges of big cities. Much of Mexico is rural and little of it is bucolic; at one moment it is a garbage dump, at another moment it is the Garden of Eden.

—Kate Simon, *Mexico: Places and Pleasures*

mariachi costume, because that is what he wore when he sang, and because the plaza is home to dozens, if not hundreds, of men who are themselves *mariachis*, and who stroll the plaza at all hours of the day and night, singing Jose Alfredo's songs and those of other *ranchera* composers to anyone who pays to listen.

On three of the plaza's irregular sides are vast *cantinas* and a food market, where vats of highly seasoned soup are sold throughout the night to ward off or cure hangovers. At the plaza's dissonant center is a constantly moving swarm of blurry-eyed revellers and costumed *mariachis*. The people in mufti stroll, wail at the moon, stagger into each other's arms, or gather around a group of musicians and sing along with them, striking defiant poses as they belt out the words. The *mariachis* tag after potential customers and negotiate prices, play checkers with bottle tops, shiver in the midnight cold, and thirty or forty times an evening, play their hearts out for the revellers. Here and there, an electric shock vendor wanders through the crowd, offering a brightly painted box of programmable current to those who, for the equivalent of a couple of dollars, want to take hold of a pair of wires and test their endurance of electricity. A gaggle of tall, goofy-looking foreigners applauds and smiles at the *mariachis* who have just finished playing for them, and the *mariachis* smile, too, because tourists pay well. The people at Stand P-84, a whole-sale outlet for guavas and mangoes from the city's gigantic central pro-duce market, think the tourists are pretty funny.

Chuy Soto and his guava-selling colleagues arrived here around eight o'clock on this particular drizzly evening and now, five hours later, they have reached the euphoric, sputtering stage at which the spirit invariably moves a Mexican to reach for extravagant metaphors and sing the glories of his country. There is a little pile of plastic glasses and empty bottles to mark the site where Chuy's group has been standing all this time, and the singer for the *mariachi* ensemble that has been accom-panying them has just about lost his voice, but Chuy and his friends are full of vigor. "We come here to sing, and after a while emotions come out of us, and Mexicanness," Chuy says, blinking and pursing his lips as he struggles to focus. An adolescent tugs at my elbow, teary-eyed and anx-ious to share his own thoughts, but he can't get out a single coherent phrase, and he vanishes. One of Chuy's warehouse partners is trying to dance with a plump young woman whose acquaintance he has just made, but he's holding on too tight, and she pushes him away. The woman's friend is singing along with the *mariachi* (the name refers both to the group and to its individual members), for perhaps the fifth time, a song called *"Dos Almas"* ("Two Souls") but by now she can't get anyone to listen

The word in Spanish is *"lágrima."* A lovely, sad word. It is from the Latin, *lacrima*—related to our own *"lacrimal."* It also has to do with a sadder word of the Spanish language: *lástima. Lástima* incorporates the ultimate, the last, what Faulkner called "the final main." *¡Qué lástima!* they say. How sad! It has to do with grief and memories and tears. The tearing sadness, the lasting sadness not only of the young, but of all of us.

—Carlos Amantea, *The Blob That Ate Oaxaca & Other Travel Tales*

to her and she weaves off in a huff. The amiable Chuy is still explaining Mexicanness to my companion, who is Peruvian. "A Mexican's heart is always open and full of music," he stammers, but a buddy of his, who spouts profanity and has in general a sharper-edged vision of things, butts in. "A Mexican knows that life is worthless," he declares.

The *mariachi* singer Ismael Gutierrez and his group charge twenty-five new pesos, or about eight dollars, per song, but they offered Chuy and his friends the wholesale rate after serenading them with thirty *rancheras*. This meant that for a lucky evening of solid work each of the members of the *Mariachi Real del Potosí,* as the group Gutierrez belongs to is called, got about thirty dollars. The group is small, and not first rate. There's only one of each of the essential components of a *mariachi*: a violin; a guitar; a trumpet; a *guitarron,* or fat bass guitar; a *vihuela,* or small plinking guitar; and the singer—Gutierrez. Like many of his fellow-musicians who have land or a family trade in the provinces, Gutierrez comes to Mexico City every fortnight or so from his home state—San Luis Potosí, in his case—and puts up at one of the scarred buildings around the plaza, where, he says, the old-fashioned, high-ceilinged rooms are crowded with bunk beds stacked as many as five high. There, he makes sure he gets at least eight hours' sleep a day, to keep his voice going. That is also where he stores his costume, which is as essential to his occupation as any instrument.

In the old days, before the movies, *mariachis* used to dress like what they were: peasant musicians. But when the Mexican movie industry began producing musicals, back in the thirties, *mariachis* in Indian dress—big white shirts and trousers, and straw hats—came to seem too ordinary, and someone decided to outfit them in the elegant *mestizo* dress of the *charro,* or horseman. Its basic elements are a broad-brimmed felt hat, a short, fitted black jacket, and tight black trousers with double seams running down the outside of the leg. For show, *charros* decorated the seams with brass or silver fittings and with fancy embroidery. Mexico's Hollywood kept the ornaments and the embroidery and added color. The majority of Garibaldi's *mariachis* wear silver-trimmed black, but now they do this to signify that they are free-lancers, which means that if a customer approaches a *guitarron* player, say, requesting a song, the musician has to pull an ensemble together from the other blackclad free-lancers standing around. Ismael Gutierrez is a significant step up in the hierarchy: he belongs to a formally constituted group, and all the members of his *Mariachi Real* wear sober Prussian blue. Gutierrez—stout, cheerful, courtly, and equipped with a remarkable handlebar mustache— looks reassuring in his outfit, like a character out of an old-time movie.

Because Gutierrez belongs to an established *mariachi*, he has been able to weather a disaster that has affected Garibaldi—construction of a subway line which shut off the main access road to the plaza and cut down the number of potential customers so drastically that on any given Friday night the ratio of *mariachis* to revellers appears to be almost one to one. Gutierrez and his mates have discovered the advantages of business cards, and by handing them out (printed with a more prosperous relative's phone number) around local office buildings and to friendly customers, they have been able to make up for the loss of walk-by trade. Not so the free-lancer Jesus Rosas. Although he plays what his colleagues describe as "a very pretty trumpet," all he can do now is dream of joining a group or landing a permanent job with the *mariachis* who play inside one of the huge *cantinas*, such as the famous Tenampa, that face on the plaza. Rosas is only twenty-five, but he has been playing Garibaldi since he left home, more than a decade ago. He used to be in demand, because he plays well, knows a lot of songs, and has a particular affability, at once alert and courteous, friendly and firmly reserved, that is much prized by Mexicans. Now times are bad, but he is stubborn. While dozens of lesser *mariachis* are coping with the subway crises by heading for the Reforma, a few blocks away, to flag down cars and hustle for customers, Rosas, who finds such a procedure completely undignified, remains in Garibaldi. "The plaza is here," he says, but that means that by noon on most days he is already cruising it, his trumpet protectively cradled in a beat-up vinyl carrying case, trying to make up in long hours for the clients he has lost.

Mexico's subway is a tremendous achievement: it is now one of the longest urban railroads in the world; it allows millions of people to crisscross the sprawling city to get to work on time every day; it did not collapse, or even buckle, during the earthquake that shattered much of the city in 1985; it is clean; it runs smoothly. Its expansion has forced dozens of shop owners along the path of its construction into bankruptcy and brought the Garibaldi *mariachis* to the brink of despair, but if everything goes according to the official plan, once the station opens [in August, 1994] Garibaldi will be overrun by *ranchera* devotees, and *mariachi* income will soar. Gutierrez doesn't think this will happen, because people who can afford *mariachis* travel by car. Nevertheless, this is the kind of promise that Mexico's rulers are constantly making to their subjects these days: severe sacrifices are being asked, and times are hard, but the country is being modernized, and when modernity arrives it will bring great rewards.

"Modernity" is the buzzword, and, although hardly anyone knows how to define it, even the people in Garibaldi can recognize its presence in their lives. Modernity is what makes the *mariachi* Guadalupe Gonzalez—a man who boasts that he beats his woman regularly, out of a traditional sense of duty ("She misses it if I don't," he explains)—welcome the subway that Jesus Rosas dislikes. *"Hay que modernizarse,"* he admonishes Rosas, citing the contemporary imperative. Modernity is what makes Rosas look uncomfortable at the mention of wife-beating by his elders, and it is also what makes his young fellow-*mariachis* finish their *ranchera* practice and immediately tune in a rock station on the radio, to Rosas' distress. Modernity is the guiding impulse behind the latest gambit by the travel agencies, which consists of bringing tourists to Garibaldi by the busload to be serenaded by musicians permanently under agency contract, instead of letting the tourists wander about in time-honored fashion until they find a *mariachi* who strikes them as *simpatico*. It used to be, Guadalupe Gonzales says, the first-rate *mariachis* like him could deliver the traditional *ranchera* serenade outside the window of a house where a party was going on, and then prove their versatility by playing *boleros*, polkas, and even cha-cha-chas for the party-goers to dance to. Now, thanks to modernity, *mariachis* deliver their serenade and are waved away, and the party continues to the sound of a rock band, a *cumbia* group, or, worst of all, one of those tootling electronic organs with programmable rhythms and sound effects. Modernity, as it is understood here, means speed and high productivity and the kind of cost analysis that leads to one electronic organ rather than half a dozen friendly but expensively thirsty *mariachis*. Now that a North American Free Trade Agreement has been initialled by the trade ministers of Canada, the United States, and Mexico, the arrival of full-scale modernity is assumed to be imminent. The terms of the treaty state that fifteen years after its final approval all tariffs and barriers to trade between the three countries will disappear. In effect, this means that the continent will become a single, gigantic market, and government officials are already trumpeting the estimated benefits: great tonic shots of foreign investment that will make the economy roar. Less powerful people worry that they, like the *mariachis*, will lose their jobs to electronic substitutes. But a more common undercurrent of worry and doubt, in the endless private jokes, offhand conversational references, editorial cartoons, and television chat-show allusions to the free-trade treaty, is more abstract, and strikes deeper. What people want to know about the coming onslaught of modernity is: how Mexican is it to be modern? Or, rather, since everything modern comes from a large, powerful country to the north, how Mexican is it to be like the United States?

There is nothing new about such fears of cultural takeover, of course: Mexico has been under invasion from the United States in one form or another since the war in 1847 that cost the country half its territory, and since then the arrival of each new fad or technological improvement has been used by pessimists to herald the death of Mexican tradition. Rosas' worry that the *ranchera* is a dying form is hardly original, but it is not paranoid. Rock-music stations are increasingly numerous. *Mariachi* serenades are far less frequent. This doesn't mean that Rosas' rock-humming contemporaries are less Mexican than he is; it simply means that their culture is more fragmented. The remarkable psychic sturdiness shared by the inhabitants of a city that often looks like the morning after the apocalypse may or may not owe something to cultural coherence, but, as every Latino teenager in Los Angeles knows, the combination of fragmentation and social disadvantage can be poisonous. To the whiz kids from Harvard and the Sorbonne who run the Mexican government, though, the diversification of Mexican culture is also rich with promise. Nationalism and tradition are *retardatarios*, cosmopolitanism is creative, and what used to be called cultural imperialism is now known as "the inevitable future."

I went to see the postmodern *ranchera* singer Astrid Hadad's show a few days later, and as she worked her way to a tiny stage through the crowded bar where she was performing she peddled tacos from a basket. "What kind would you like?" she asked her customers. "Now that we have the free-trade treaty, I can offer you hamburger tacos, hot-dog

How to say "no" like a Mexican: Mexicans don't get followed for an entire block by the same bunch of kids trying to sell them something. And they don't have their windshields washed unless they want to. Nor do they say "no" 50 times to get the "Go away!" job done—each time a little louder in volume than the last. In fact, Mexicans don't say anything when they'd like to be left alone. They simply hold up one index finger and waggle it sideways, slowly. Everybody goes away. Remarkable. Astounding. And so easy even a blond *gringa* can pull it off and make it work every time.

—Paula McDonald, "Tantalizing Trivia"

tacos, chili-con-carne tacos...." For her presentations, Hadad likes to wear red lipstick with carnival glitter in it—on the eyelids—and a Jean Paul Gaultier-like cone-shaped bra, which she later rips off and replaces with a big, anatomically accurate foam-rubber heart. Her show, which has been attracting ever more loyal audiences over the last four years, relies heavily on the nostalgia value of *ranchera* music and on its inherent campiness, but it would not be so energetically appealing if her powerful voice were not a perfect vehicle for *rancheras* or if her understanding of a *ranchera* prototype—the brassy, hard drinking, love-wounded dame— were not intuitive. Hadad belted out, "As if I were a sock, you step on me all day," and her audience howled with laughter and the acid pleasure of recognition. When, in a frenzy of Mexican passion, she asked what would become of her heart—"this bleeding, burning, conquered, crunched, roasted, ground, blended, anguished heart"—a couple of people in the audience rose to give her a standing ovation. Hadad had come onstage with peasant style braids and wearing a typical *china poblana* embroidered skirt. Now she loosened the braids, tore off the skirt to reveal a slinky black dress underneath, removed the heart from the dress's strapless bodice, added long gloves, checked her image in any empty mirror frame, and retold the well-known myth of Quetzalcoatl, the god-king of Tula, and his rival Tezatlipoca, or Smoking Mirror. "Tezcatlipoca is jealous because Quetzalcoatl is blond, so he gives him some *pulque.* Quetzalcoatl gets drunk, screws his own sister, wakes up with a terrible hangover, and sees his image in Tezcatlipoca's mirror. He heads for the beach and sets sail, and as he leaves he promises to return. So he does, the blond, blue-eyed god, and that's how we discovered the joys of"—here Hadad licked her lips lasciviously—"cultural penetration."

Offstage, Hadad turned out to be a tiny woman with a sharp Lebanese profile (it is a curious fact of cultural life here that many of the most devoted *mexicanistas* are themselves—like Hadad and like Frida Kahlo—first- or second-generation Mexicans) and an intellectual manner. Not surprisingly, she declared that what first attracted her to *rancheras* was that they are so essentially Mexican. "I think it has to do with the attitude toward suffering that we inherited from the Aztecs," she said. "It's not that we have an extraordinary capacity for suffering— everyone does. It's the way we relish it. I think only Russians compare with us in that. And then there's the element of machismo. Again, it's not that men here beat their wives more, because I'm sure that Germans do it just as much; it's that here they boast about it. Obviously, I'm very critical of that, but what keeps me coming back to the music is the passion. Now that we're all becoming so rational and sensible, it's getting harder and harder to find passion in our lives; I think that's what we all seek in the *ranchera.*"

I flew from Mexico City to Tijuana, a scorching-hot border town that can be seen either as the hideous, seedy product of more than a century of cultural penetration or as the defiant, lively result of a hundred years of cultural resistance. Just a few miles south of San Diego, Tijuana reigns as the world capital of Spanglish, shantytowns, and revolting souvenirs, yet despite it all, remains completely Mexican. The United States may be just an imaginary line away, but on this side of the line driving becomes more creative, street life improves, bribes are taken, and hairdos are more astonishing. I thought Tijuana would be a good place to catch a show by Juan Gabriel, a singer and prolific composer who is the most unlikely heir to the mantle of *ranchera* greatness that could ever be imagined.

Juan Gabriel likes to perform at *palenques,* or cockfight arenas, which are a traditional element of state fairs. When I arrived at the Tijuana *palenque,* around midnight, several hundred people were watching the last fight, perched on chairs in a coliseum-like arrangement of concrete tiers surrounding a small circular arena. Those in the know say that hundreds of thousands of dollars' worth of bets are placed in the course of a fight, but all I saw was half a dozen men with little notebooks standing in the arena, catching mysterious silent signals from the audience and scribbling down figures, while the two fighting cocks were displayed by their handlers. After a few minutes, the men with notebooks left, and the cocks, outfitted with razorlike spurs, were set on the ground. The cocks flew at each other, spurs first, while the audience watched in tense, breathless silence. In a matter of minutes, one of the animals lay trembling on the ground, its guts spilling out, and the other was proclaimed the victor, to a brief, dull cheer. Instantly, Juan Gabriel's roadies moved in.

The instruments they set up—electric organ and piano, two sets of drums—are not the ones normally associated with *ranchera* music, but then Juan Gabriel is not what one would think of as a typical *mariachi* singer. For starters, he is from the border himself—from Ciudad Juarez, where he was born, and where he was raised in an orphanage. When he burst on the pop-music scene, in the early '70s, radio audiences often mistook his high-pitched voice for a woman's. His fey mannerisms became the subject of crude jokes. He has been press-shy ever since a scurrilous book by a purported confidant fed hungry speculations about his sexual preferences. Yet, in this nation of self-proclaimed machos, Juan

There had been a cockfight just that weekend, and down the street Juanito stopped where three or four other kids had gathered around a figure seated on the sidewalk. They were watching Pablo, who ran the town's best *cantina*. Pablo was bent over something in his lap.

"*Qué?*" Juanito asked his friend Chiquis.

"One of the roosters," said Chiquis. "He's sewing it up."

Sure enough, one of Pablo's hands was pulling a needle and thread from the direction of the rooster. The rooster had a deep gash in its stomach, where the razor strapped to the foot of its opponent had struck home. Usually such a rooster was simply sold as food, but Pablo had started a small side business through his surgical ability to resurrect fallen roosters: behind his house was a coop where several proud birds, each with a scar, strutted their stuff, awaiting the day they would go at it again. This rooster breathed heavily, blinking slowly, beak open.

"Think he'll make it?" asked one of the boys.

"This one, I don't know," said Pablo, shaking his head. "Big cut. But he put up a great fight. I think he'll make it." Using his teeth, he tied a knot down by the bird's oozy belly and applied ointment to the sutures.

—Ted Conover, *Coyotes: A Journey Through the Secret World of America's Illegal Aliens*

Gabriel has been able to perform before a standing-room-only crowd in the Palacio de Bellas Artes, Mexico's Carnegie Hall. He lives in Los Angeles, uses electronic backups and percussion, and writes songs that never mention drunkenness or two- or three-timing women, but when men in Garibaldi drink and fall into the confessional mode these days their musical inspiration invariable includes songs composed by Juan Gabriel.

As the first wailing *ranchera* chords tore through the din and Juan Gabriel emerged from the bullpen, there was a roar from the *palenque*, and in the roar there was a call for blood. The composition of the audience had changed: a majority of women, mostly middle-aged and in girls'-night-out groups, had filled the stands, along with a large minority of romantic couples and a dense sprinkling of men in groups. A lot of the men were wearing big *norteño* hats, and in the front row a group of couples and male buddies in big hats and heavy gold chains had set up beer cans and bottles of tequila along the concrete ledge that defined the arena space. The women in the audience were shouting their love for Juan Gabriel hysterically, but a couple of men behind me were shouting something quite different, and so were a lot of men in big hats. "*¡Marica!*" and "*¡Joton!*" they yelled, meaning "Fag!" or "Queer!" They yelled this over and over, and, because the cherub-faced Juan Gabriel in his graying middle age has put on something of a paunch, someone improvised an insult that was quickly copied: "You're pregnant, you faggot! Go home!" The men had paid between forty and sixty dollars a head to indulge in this pleasure, and Juan Gabriel, circling the arena slowly to acknowledge the majority's applause, also acknowledged this generosity with a small, graceful curtsy before he began to sing.

His music is proof of the fact that the *ranchera* has changed as much as Mexico has, and that in doing so it has survived. His backup singers at the *palenque* were two skinny, curvy black women in tight dresses: they chimed in on the chorus as required, but with distinctly *gringo* accents. Standing between them and his electronic band, Juan Gabriel sang and twirled to music from his pop repertoire, punctuating some of the jazzier songs with belly rolls and shimmies that drove the women and the machos wild in opposite ways. There was rather a lot of this cheerful music, and then he slowed down and began to sing a real *ranchera*, a song of bad love, loss, and pain, in which the composer makes abject offers to his departed love. In case the fugitive should ever decide to return, Juan Gabriel sang, "You'll find me here, in my usual spot, in the same city, with the same crowd, so you can find everything just as you left it." By the second verse, there was no need for him to sing at all, because the members of the audience were chanting the words for themselves with the rapt reverence accorded an anthem. "I just forgot again," the audience sang, "that you never loved me." I glanced at a couple of the big guys sitting in the front row, armed with their bottles of tequila, who had earlier folded their arms protectively across their chests and smirked whenever Juan Gabriel wiggled in their direction. Now they were singing.

A dozen fawn-colored *charro* hats wobbled at the entrance to the bullpen, and the audience, seeing the *mariachis* arrive, roared itself hoarse with welcome. Gold decorations along the musicians' trousers caught the light. The men lined up facing Juan Gabriel's band, adjusted their hats, took up their instruments, and filled the *palenque* with the ripe, aching, heart-torn sound of the *mariachi*. Juan Gabriel, singing this time about how hard it is to forget, was now not queening at all. The big guys sitting across from me leaned into each other, swaying companionably to the music, like everyone else in the audience. Behind me, the last heckler had finally shut up. Juan Gabriel sang a lilting *huapango* and a couple of songs, without pausing once for chatter. He segued from one song to the next or went through long medleys, the doo-wop girls bursting in occasionally with a trill or two. Then the girls left the stage, and so did the band. Juan Gabriel, alone with the *mariachis*, slowed down for the introductory chords of a song that begins, "*Podría volver*," and, recognizing these, the audience squealed in ecstatic pain. "I could return, but out of sheer pridefulness I won't," the lyrics say, in what is perhaps the most perfect of a hundred *ranchera* hymns to the unbending pride of the loser. "If you want me to come back, you should have thought of that before you left me." Here and there, his listeners yelped as if some very tasty salt had just been rubbed into their national wound. Life hurts. I hurt. The hell with you: I'll survive, Juan Gabriel sang. In the front row, the two big guys looked immensely happy, and just about ready to weep.

Alma Guillermoprieto writes about Latin America for the New Yorker. *A collection of her stories,* The Heart That Bleeds: Latin America Now, *was published by Alfred Knopf, Inc. Working as a stringer for the* Washington Post *in 1982, she broke the story—along with Raymond Bonner of the* New York Times—*of the El Mozote massacre of unarmed peasants in El Salvador's civil war.*

At the Parque Independencia in Mérida a dynamite twenty-three-piece band with five percussionists and piano poured out tropical music—mambos, sambas, and the lambada—into a green square. A dozen middle-aged couples executed the intricate steps with a superbly controlled sexuality, the women pulsating and turning with completely impassive faces behind sunglasses. My immediate favorite was a stocky woman who might have been sixty and who so evidently enjoyed herself, wiping her streaming face between numbers and smiling to her husband, then going back into the dance again, her features set, her feet in their high, black heels making the mincing mambo steps while her wide hips spoke to him under her beige knit dress. Equally arresting were the faces of some of the players. They looked as if the profiles from the Maya stelae had magically freed themselves of the stone surfaces and had come to life, and the juxtaposition of those classic features with European wind instruments made me gape.

And then, of course, there was the sound of the music. It seemed to me as I stood surrounded by it an informal, concise history of all that had gone into the making of this culture: the Spanish tinge, the African influence, and that greater influence of the tropics themselves—all that sun, for which so much in this land had been given; the hot blue of the skies; the sea; and the tough, heavy vegetation. So that the sound was playful and joyful, yes, but with a heat to it that sang of sadness and of danger. And beneath the melodies lay the rattling, chopping cross-rhythms of the percussionists, which I imagined now as the orchestration of that feverishly busy insect world that irrigated and fertilized the soil, and so made possible the rain forests of the peninsula.

—Frederick Turner, *A Border of Blue: Along the Gulf of Mexico from the Keys to the Yucatán*

JOEL SIMON

Crossing the Linguistic *Frontera*

A Yucatán bus trip becomes a window into Mexican life.

Of all the ways to study Spanish—books, tapes, classrooms—the best way to learn is by actually being in a place where the language permeates communication much as warm air permeates life in the tropics.

Take for example what one would expect to be a simple bus journey. You arrive at the terminal early in the morning after downing a piping hot cup of Nescafé. My wife, Kim, and I did exactly that. We were excited. We were leaving Chetumal, the ultimate whistle stop without a train. Mostly buses, trucks, and more buses and trucks stream endlessly through Chetumal going north into the Yucatán Peninsula, south to Belize, or west towards Mexico City. Now a free port, this border town has grown around the intersection of the sea and two main roads, perhaps ancient Mayan footpaths eventually paved over with commerce, transit, and time. Near the heart of the intersection, near the heart of the city itself, was our point of departure, the bus terminal (which has now been moved three kilometers out of town).

The place was packed. Not only with people, but nearly everything imaginable, and then some, including noise and fumes, in addition to buses. A nearly infinite line of buses, diagonally parked, under and beyond the short corrugated metal awning. The buses were all different, obviously different to those who spoke Spanish, yet looking frightfully the same to those of us who didn't. There were no signs. Well, not exactly—the buses themselves had small faded placards indicated a destination or part thereof. We were bound for the archaeological site of Palenque, perhaps the most beautiful of all Mayan ruins. It wasn't far, just a bus ride away, and well worth the journey, we were told.

We apparently looked as confused as we were, and a sympathetic gentleman approached, and speaking slowly and simply, offered his assistance. In my best attempt at Spanish I asked for the bus to Palenque.

"I'm sorry *señor*, there is no bus to Palenque," came the response.

I looked at Kim for a moment, then remembered my training watching "Jeopardy" as a child, and rephrased my inquiry: "How can we get to Palenque?"

"By bus is a good way," came the answer.

"Well then,...hum...(as I contemplated the apparent and sincere contradiction)...Which bus?" I asked.

The man looked at me kindly, not quite believing the question, but then, comprehension flashing in his bright dark eyes, answered: "Why the bus to Villahermosa of course...there you will find your bus to Palenque."

Ah-Ha! Now we were really getting somewhere... *Bueno*, then where can we find this bus to Villahermosa?"

"Which one?" the man kindly inquired. (I found out later, there were, in fact, several.)

I was determined not to yield to exasperation but my language skills and patience were beginning to wane. "The next one to leave here for Villahermosa," I answered, not even thinking to think over the question.

He flashed a broad smile filled with comprehension, gold-capped teeth and goodwill, pointed confidently down the nearly infinite line of buses, and said, "Down there, just ask for the bus to Villahermosa, the next one should be leaving pretty soon."

Kim looked at me and asked with a nebulous smile, "What did he say?" Summarizing as best I could, I repeated his gesture, and said he said: "This way." With our bags in tow, we slowly wound our way through the loading docks, densely packed with large families, larger bundles, bound and tethered animals, and quiet children, all patiently awaiting the imminent departure of the respective buses. I kept far enough ahead to ask, every now and then, "Villahermosa? Villahermosa?" and then repeating the answer and gesture (always the same) with assurance to Kim. By the time we finally arrived at the bus marked "Villahermosa" I experienced an unexpected sense of achievement, I was learning patience, practice, persistence, and Spanish, *and* we were going to Palenque. I asked the man selling tickets when the bus would be leaving.

"When it is full," he said simply. We happily purchased two tickets, wondering if these were the last two available.

When is a Mexican bus full? It depends on how well you speak Spanish. If you are a novice to this most beautiful of tongues, the bus was already full. Very FULL. Perhaps it was full even before you had your Nescafé. If you have some experience in the language, then you know the bus has only recently been filled. BUT, if you have mastered the nuances of the meaning of full in Spanish or, some would say, the full meaning, then you realize there is still *plenty* of room on the bus.

Full, for a Mexican bus, has nothing to do with the number of seats, or the amount of floor space available for chickens, or the number of babies draped across shoulders, or the square footage available on the roof for loads of bananas and everything else that can be passed up 14 feet, or the air pressure in the

> Leaving Monterrey, I see that the sixteen clocks of the bus station each tell a different time. Is that the Machine's independence from Man or a reflection of Mexico's legendary disrespect for the dictatorship of time?
>
> —Abbas, *Return to Mexico: Journeys Beyond the Mask*

tires—not to mention those clinging to exterior surface: side rails, back door, spare tire. True masters of Spanish understand that a Mexican bus is never full. Full is a function of tolerance, and Mexicans are very tolerant people.

So some lingual novices might have thought our bus, a reincarnated American schoolbus, was full, as we headed out across the base of the Yucatán peninsula from Chetumal towards Palenque. Indeed, it was full, crowned with humanity and recycled cardboard luggage bound with twine and faith. Like the buses of Mexico, cardboard luggage never dies, it just gets reinforced at roadside refueling stops and occasionally in-between. No one minded the squawk of a chicken or two as we settled into the torn and taped vinyl-covered narrow bench seats. Each seat held two and a half derrieres—the half that had no bottom support found stability by leaning against its counterpart from across the aisle. Everyone who spoke Spanish instinctively knew that the famous Mayan corbeled arch had nothing on us.

We rattled and we bounced and we shook and all seemed to be going along quite smoothly until a new noise joined the chorus resounding from the overburdened mechanical beast. At first the sound was barely discernible, a new clink joining numerous other clanks. But the repetitive hammering, feeling perhaps somewhat ignored amidst the other sounds, began to sing more plaintively, until it rang out, a solo voice against a veritable symphony—the brass section, the cast-iron section, the sheet metal section, the fan belt section, the radio static section. Was our vehicle noisy? Ah...no, noise is a function of functioning, a noise is only a noise when it impedes progress.

Even before the concert reached its crescendo, the driver's helper, riding side-saddle on the roof rack aloft and baseball cap to the wind, the one responsible for loading and unloading the multitude of parcels, began one-handed applause against the rear of the vehicle. Slap. Slap. Slap. The driver, seemingly oblivious to everything else, had his ears well-tuned for this sound. We began to decelerate and soon were over-taken by our own dust.

The slap, slap, slapping, slowed as we did. Only the churning dust maintained its former speed. Kim returned my inquiring glance, with equal unknowing. Oh good, a chance to learn Spanish! The driver climbed out his window, the roof helper rappelled off the rack, and they conferred, speaking with occasional kicks to the rear tires and tired frame. We held position inside. Few seemed curious about our unscheduled stop. No one was restless. The driver climbed back in, through the door, the helper ascended once again to his perch, and off we went...in a wide arc, turned around in a large flat place, and circled to an unmarked Mayan hut set back from the side of the road. And we stopped, engine still running. The bus now pointed back towards Chetumal.

No words were spoken, yet everyone somehow understood.

The problem of studied efforts to communicate is well illustrated by the experience of some friends. When they went to Mexico, the woman had a degree in Spanish from a large university and her boyfriend knew several obscenities and no grammar—good whorehouse Spanish. Within two weeks she felt her nerves straining every time she was forced to speak Spanish, caught between the rigid grammatical training of school and the sloppy everyday speech of the people. He was right in there, waving arms, laughing, gesticulating over this and that, throwing in an occasional inappropriate obscenity and generally making himself understood and liked.

—Carl Franz, *The People's Guide to Mexico*

What language was this? Decisions are a function of consensus.

Only the chickens stayed behind. Everyone slowly got off the bus. As though by unspoken command, "Women and children in the hut, men meet at the stern," I joined the men, who formed a casual semicircle at the back of the bus to contemplate our situation. With a loud creak and groan, punctuated by flourishes of undulating rusted metal, the driver lifted the hinged engine cover. There, gently pulsing, grunting, groaning, moaning, hissing, wheezing, and not seizing, packed in dust, dirt, grime, and oil of the ages, was the engine, apparently sounding fine and dandy. A murmur went round the crowd, hands speaking softly amidst punctuating voices and the occasional knowing laugh. The driver slipped the bus in gear, slowly letting out the clutch. Yes, the noise was there. More murmurs escaped from the gang.

A man emerged with a large wrench from the hut, and crawled under the bus. Only his scarred and torn tennis shoes remained visible. Bang, bang, and he called out in terse, rapid phrases. This elicited a few smiles and companion grunts of accord from the group. An even larger wrench came forth from the hut carried by a small boy further dwarfed by its size, and then a heavy rusted bar. More crawling around, bang, bang, bang, more murmurs amongst the team. Finally the man, the wrenches, and the bar, all sporting a fresh coat of ancient oil, dirt, and grime emerged. Our speculation: the size of the problem was a function of the size of the wrench.

Was the bus broken? A Mexican bus is never broken, no matter how broken a newcomer to the language might think it to be. Repair time is just a function of tolerance, both of passengers and of automotive parts. Anger serves no function. In Mexico one is never promised something by a contrived hour—it's never the laundry will be done by noon, it's more like laundry will be done later, when laundry is done. And when you travel, no one is encouraged to rely on arrival by a certain time. The tickets even try to tell you gently—you shall go from point X to point Y—but the time your journey will take is discreetly omitted. One of the great lessons of travel and its most profound joys to the initiated is that traveling takes as long as it takes—no more and no less.

The unmarked Mayan hut, it turned out, was the local mechanic's workshop. It was also his family's home, and impromptu restaurant/café. The interior echoed a sincere and basic lifestyle, cleanly swept dirt floor, wooden benches worn smooth over the years by countless posteriors, and an area reserved for tools (few) and spare parts (many). Miscellaneous used spare parts, everything from engine blocks, to alternators, from brake drums to extra cracked windshields, camshafts, transaxles, timing chains, exhaust manifolds, and even a few spare hubcaps were stacked, strewn, and generally piled in corners, both inside and out. Here was a collection of automotive prosthetics designed to fill even the most obscure improvisational need. Unfortunately, we were in a bus, not a car, and the issue of

Mexico is not always the easiest country to travel in even on the deep-grooved, somnambulist tourist routes. It is never indifferent, so you cannot be. It is vulnerable (though Nicaragua calls it the "Colossus to the North") and you find yourself vulnerable. Enchantment and exasperation are inseparable twins here and sometimes the whole stretch between El Paso and Las Casas seems to be a suburb of Behind the Looking-Glass. The degree of a traveler's pleasure in Mexico is a question of his own responses; here, as elsewhere, being a contented tourist requires some of the ingredients of a contented marriage—a willingness to be pleased and pleasing, sustained interest, openness, acceptance, and some self-knowledge.

—Kate Simon, *Mexico: Places and Pleasures*

scale could not be ignored. The wife was serving coffee, soft drinks, and rice to anyone wishing. Families had set up camp inside, and were sharing cookies, crackers, frijoles, in fact entire multi-course picnics intended for the journey. All were being set up on red checked, blue flowered, or cartooned plastic sheets and given graciously to anyone even remotely expressing an interest. We couldn't avoid the hospitality. We were immersed in it, and as a consequence were learning firsthand both culture and Spanish, its sounds, its flavors, and its generosity.

The mechanic sent his youngest son scampering down the dirt and dust lane. He returned standing astride the back of a pickup truck which he rode like a bronco bustin' cowboy, black hair pulled back by the wind, eyes glistening. By the time he arrived, the drive shaft, the differential, or some such part had been extricated from the bowels of the bus. It was hoisted onto the back of the pick-up truck with great care by its attendants, like a patient onto a gurney. To those who did not speak Spanish it resembled more a corpse on a slab. But WE knew, those of learning Spanish knew, that the pickup truck served as a flat-bed paramedic racing off to the operating room rather than a beaten, battered hearse on a one-way trip to the morgue.

In good time the truck returned and all hoped the patient had made a miraculous recovery. The part was soon re-installed with the benefit of much supervisory assistance. The moment of truth had come. The driver climbed back into the bus, inserted the *llave* into the ignition, and turned it. The engine sprang to life. Everyone listened. But above the engine noise, not a sound could be heard. The supervisory team heartily congratulated itself on a job well done. The mechanic then crawled from beneath the bus, brushing off his newest coat of ancient oil and grime. He cracked a quiet smile, and then a beer. Everyone was soon collected from the Mayan hut, all the picnics packed away, all the babies returned to shoulders, all the farewells and thank yous said and with all the bodies settling back into place, our bus rolled off into the night.

Did we get to Palenque on time? Time is a function of wisdom. The Mexican people are wise enough to know that one should not expect anything by a contrived hour..."on time" translates to "in time, "in due time." We arrived in Palenque and time was still with us, it was there to greet us. In fact, we had the time of our lives.

Joel Simon's photo assignments have taken him to all seven continents, including the North Pole, the Antarctic, and 95 countries in between. When not traveling, he's at home in Menlo Park, California, with his wife, Kim, cat, Ichiban, and an itinerant possum named Rover.

Who will someday sing the ballad of the Mexican bus driver? A great lover of *ranchera* music, which he ingenuously inflicts on all his passengers...A man who stops at noon, sometimes forgets to come back and has to be hunted down, who parks his bus at a crossroads, disappears, and then returns ten minutes later with three cases of Coca-Cola or a basket of tacos, who occasionally, after ten minutes of driving, makes all his passengers get out, refunds their money, and charges off in a different direction. In Mexico, you never know why the bus is stopping.

—Abbas, *Return to Mexico: Journeys Beyond the Mask*

DONALD D. SCHUELER

Temple of the Jaguar

Having lost his beloved to an early death, the author seeks solace in ruins,
wildlife, and desultory conversation with charming strangers.

Behind the Temple of the Inscriptions at Palenque, a trail climbs the
steep slope to the unreclaimed Temple of the Jaguar. If you follow it,
you can pretend you are entering a serious tropical jungle—the sort
of place where Tarzan or Rima the Bird Girl might swing by at any
moment. The air is green and dripping wet, and the trees appear to be
growing down instead of up. Their trunks flange out into swirled pleats
as they swoop earthward; and when they touch ground they divide and
subdivide into an elaborate network of exposed roots that forage hungri-
ly across the sunless forest floor. Everywhere, vines thick as a freighter's
mooring cables are busy tying things up. Without them, all this tangled
scenery would surely fall apart.

Señor Morales says it's falling apart anyway. He is partial to apocalyptic utterances, but in this case he is probably right. The jungle on this
little mountain is protected because it is part of the Palenque archaeological site, but it is only a measly fragment of the wilderness that covered
most of Chiapas a couple of decades ago. Now, if you overlook the
region from the air, you get an eyeful of other little mountains like this
one stretching back into the Chiapas hinterlands; and on the impossibly
steep slopes of almost all of them grow impossible crops of maize. Since
jungles do not do well as token bits and pieces of their former selves, the
long-term prospects for this small remnant are not promising.

For now, however, it not only looks like a proper jungle, it sounds
like one. Evening in the tropics comes on in a hurry—one of the few
things that does—and this is the favorite hour for black howler monkeys
to engage in group expression. The bunch that is sounding off near me is
higher up on the slope, on the other side of a ravine. Although the tree-
top foliage bends and sways under the considerable weight of its passage, they stay out of sight.

They are not called howler monkeys for nothing. On occasion their
stupendous bellowing has been known to send unforewarned tourists
running for their lives. Once one recognizes the source, however, all that

hullabaloo becomes the stuff of comedy. By now I have heard this bunch hooting and hollering so often that I have decided I even know what they are saying—things like "Stop hoggin' that damn branch," or "Have any of you made up your minds where we're gonna spend the night?" They are like a large, rowdy family in a tenement flat; they learn in their mothers' arms that if you wanna be heard you gotta speak up.

For a moment I find myself wishing I were up there in the treetops with them, yelling my head off. But quickly I suppress the thought. I have become self-conscious about this little quirk I have lately acquired, this tendency to wish I were almost anyone, anything, other than myself.

Compared to the excavated ruins on the palisade below, the Temple of the Jaguar is nothing to ooh and aah about. It is no larger than some of the rich folks' mausoleums in Metairie Cemetery back home in New Orleans. The jungle has overgrown the platform on which it rests and broken open the temple tomb itself. Graffiti of roots and vines deface the carvings and glyphs on the outer walls. Originally, the interior of the shrine could boast a fine tablet depicting the nobleman who was interred here sitting on a two-headed jaguar throne. Now, however, all that is left of the tablet is the bas-relief fragment of one of the jaguar's legs. The grave of the nobleman, in a small crypt beneath the temple, was plundered long ago.

None of this disturbs me. Indeed, the unrestored condition of the site is one of the reasons I keep coming back here. Each time, I feel I am the first person to set eyes on this place since the jungle reclaimed it. I rediscover it over and over again.

The other reason is that I like the name, the Temple of the Jaguar, even if it derives from nothing more evidential than that mutilated paw and foreleg on the inner wall. What matters to me is that there really was a Jaguar God, or at any rate the Jaguar aspect of a god. The fact that this little shrine was not dedicated to him in the days of the ancient Maya does not prevent me from dedicating it to him now.

Jaguars are the most splendid of the New World predators, and everything about them is of interest to me. Señor Morales, who enjoys playing Virgil to my Dante in the Purgatory that I have managed to make even of Palenque, says that the only jaguars that survive hereabouts are the ones the Maya carved in stone. He says the last real jaguar in the archaeological park was killed twenty years ago. I hate news like that. In better days, I would have been perfectly capable of feeling depressed for no other reason than that I was in a jungle where jaguars ought to have been but weren't. As matters stand, however, I am already so thoroughly dejected that the dearth of jaguars becomes, like the Jaguar God himself, a mere aspect of a more encompassing state of mind.

In recent years archaeologists have made considerable headway in decoding ancient Maya glyphs; but they still have only the fuzziest notions about the complexities of the Maya religious universe. Certainly the worship of ancestors and an extraordinary deification of all aspects of time were central tenets of Maya theology. But the exact nature and function of most of the numerous Maya gods remain elusive. The deities in the Maya pantheon came in every imaginable shape and size; apparently a great many of them represented—somewhat like Catholicism's Blessed Trinity— phases, attributes, or aspects of other gods whose nature was too complex or too schizoid to be contained in a single persona. The Jaguar God was evidently such an aspect. He is thought to have represented the Sun God during his arduous nightly journey through the Maya underworld, where his radiance was hidden from the eyes of men. That underworld was an inhospitable and menacing place, the abode of the dreadful death gods; so by the time the Sun-God-as-Jaguar completed his dark passage from west to east, he was

> Strange to say, cryptologists—those makers and breakers of codes from the world of espionage and counter-intelligence—have played little role in the great decipherments of ancient scripts. In fact, I remember the announcements in the American press that the famous husband-and-wife team of Col. William Friedman had received foundation support to decipher Maya hieroglyph writing. The Friedmans having achieved well-deserved fame by cracking the Japanese naval code on the eve of the war, it was a foregone conclusion that the ancient Maya were going to be a pushover for them. Nothing resulted from this doomed project, and they went to their graves without having deciphered a single Maya hieroglpyh.
>
> —Michael D. Coe, *Breaking the Maya Code*

utterly drained, the merest skeleton of himself, in dire need of a drink of human blood to restore his solar health.

I don't like to think about that gruesome thirst; but in other respects, the Sun God's nocturnal journey appeals deeply to my imagination. It seems exactly right that in the underworld he should assume a jaguar guise. I remember that somewhere in the Maya Books of Chilam Balam—a curiously stoned sounding collection of prophecies, folklore, and astrological references that comes down to us from colonial times— there is a pretty metaphor that compares the starry night to the pelt of *el tigre.* But if the ancient Maya had known of William Blake's famous image, I suspect they would have liked that one even more. They had, after all,

Mayan glyphs

anticipated it. How better to conceive of the fiercely beautiful Sun God passing through a world of death and darkness than as the Mesoamerican equivalent of a tiger burning bright in the forests of the night?

In much the same way, the jaguar passes through my thoughts now.

The howlers have shut up for a minute. As if waiting for that cue, the guards at the ruins start blowing their whistles. Closing time. Ready or not, it is time for me to make my way down to the human world below.

Señor Moisés Morales owns six hectares of land on the border of the archaeological park. His home is a sort of tree house, a small tin-roofed box on stilts set in a tropical glade. A spider monkey swings about on its belted leash. Nearby a swift clear stream hurries through a makeshift swimming pool that can be filled or emptied depending on whether the planks of a small weir are in place or not. Between house and road a larger stream serves as moat, obliging visitors, of whom Señor Morales has many, to approach his hideaway on foot. "I have this dream," he says, "to make this an ideal place. But with honest money, you understand, which means with hardly any money at all. I plan to die with 2,500 trees around me. I plant them all the time. I planted a tropical chestnut for each of my eleven children. I ask my friends who visit me to plant a tree so they will be with me in the form of that tree. There was a man who planted one and never came to visit it. I told him, 'I talk to your tree. It's doing its best, yet you never come to see it.' He was ashamed, and when he came, he saw that his tree was taller than he was."

Señor Morales holds forth like this whenever he gets the chance. He delights in being a sort of Mexican Thoreau, a man who has traveled widely in Palenque. He is a tourist guide at the park who knows more about local archaeology and ecology than some of the professors who come here. "They ask me where I got my degree," he beams. "I tell them, 'From the University of Hunger. The University of the Tortilla.' Which is the best degree of all!"

I am in a frame of mind to envy anyone who is not me. But even in better days, I think Señor Morales would rate an envious twinge or two.

His wife and many children have all gone their separate ways but he never seems lonely. He is a confirmed malcontent who is content to plant trees and talk and talk. He takes long views of the historical past and the cheerless future, and cheerfully anticipates the downfall of practically everything. He relishes his role as apocalyptic Jeremiah to a corrupt and decaying world, yet he enjoys to the hilt his everyday life in that selfsame world. I like him very much, but it doesn't seem quite fair that he should have it both ways.

He is enjoying himself tonight. His brother owns La Canada, the comfortable motel where I am staying, and all day long Señor Morales and other members of the family and staff have been helping to transform the place's dining room, a large, thatched *palapa*, into a setting appropriate for a big *fiesta*. Now, the flowers have been set out, streamers and *piñatas* hang from the rafters, and the band is belting out a sort of rumba-rock. This is a private affair: just relatives, friends of the family, assorted local dignitaries, a few hotel guests like myself. Everyone has the party spirit. I am reminded of the Cajun *fais-do-dos* I used to attend years ago. There are no generation gaps. Everybody dances, everybody makes the rounds of the tables, pounding backs, laughing, telling jokes, and where appropriate, kissing the rouged cheeks of pretty girls. Also, almost everybody becomes at least a little crocked on the nonstop supply of rum Cokes.

Señor Morales is on the dance floor much of the time, where he cuts a dashing, silver-haired figure. Conscious that I'm a stranger here, he checks up on me during the breaks; but for now, I am doing pretty well on my own. The man across the table has a thoroughly nice, mild face, with kind, patient eyes peering out at the world through steel-rimmed glasses. He is a *justicia*—a judge for the region. And he is a Maya. "Those two facts would have been a contradiction in terms not so long ago," he tells me. "To be an Indio—well, you were not expected to get ahead, you know? I have had to prove myself. I feel sometimes that I am the one on trial, you understand? But I am honest. I give fair judgments." He shakes his round head. "That's no easy thing in Chiapas. Or anywhere in Mexico."

We are just getting into the subject of local politics and prejudice when a fierce-looking person descends on the table. He has the look of a rather sinister hippie: deep-set dark eyes, long narrow chin, beaked nose, a thin clamped line of a mouth. His complexion is grayish brown. Straight black hair hangs down to the hem of his loose white shirt. He gives me a curt nod and then possesses the judge, hovering against his shoulder, talking softly but with an urgent intensity into his right ear.

The judge listens noncommittally, now and then nodding. From behind his steel-rimmed glasses, he gazes past my shoulder at the blank wall.

I am straining to catch the dark man's difficult accent when Señor Morales, having decided I need rescuing, comes to collect me. "There is someone I want you to meet," he says, hauling me from the table.

"Who was that man with the long hair?"

"Him? He is the son of the chief of the Lacandón Indians."

To judge from his tone, Señor Morales might be identifying the son of a local gangster. We pause at the edge of the dance floor while he fills me in: "His people own a great forest reserve to the south, 64,000 hectares. That sounds good, eh? But the sad thing is that they are the forest's worst enemy. In Mexico, we say that the law is made of rubber. Well, believe me, my friend, these Indians know how to stretch it! Because they are 'poor Indians,' nobody can be against them, you know? So they destroy everything. They have millions in the bank from the forests they sell to the lumber companies, who pay off the politicians, including our ex-governor, so they can cut everything down in this so-called reserve. And because they are 'poor Indians' they can slaughter the beautiful birds, just so they can put the feathers in the arrows they sell at the entrance to Palenque. Now they think they have political power! Not so long ago, they broke windows in the city hall because they wanted the governor to replace the mayor! They got their way, but violence is the way to chaos. We are supposed to be a government of law—"

> T'a k'in, the Lacandón word for money, literally means "the shit of God."
>
> —Peter Canby, *The Heart of The Sky: Travels Among the Maya*

He seems so well-launched on one of his commentaries on the Mexican condition that I am surprised when he abruptly breaks off, his expression suddenly softening. "Ah, over there. The person I want you to meet. She speaks excellent English. And she is a little lonely, like you."

Her name is Elizabeta. She is spectacularly handsome, with large, dark eyes and perfectly shaped full lips set in a neat, oval face. In the course of introducing us, Señor Morales had said she has a graduate degree in psychology, so naturally I assume she must be neurotic. Yet whether because of this or in spite of it, she radiates a vulnerability, a melting openness, that would make even the most cowardly and/or self-centered male want to protect her from lewd comments, Hunnish hordes, the chill night air. She is that rather rare thing in Mexico: a Jew. She is also dismayingly perceptive. Right off, she has a pretty good idea what is wrong with me. Which makes us instant soulmates. We head at once for the subject that concerns us. My own sad story is a simple one, quickly told. Hers is more complex, and she wants me to know everything.

Young as she is, intelligent as she is, she is working hard at screwing up her life. She has fallen ardently in love, this Mexican Jewess, with an Iranian refugee whom she met in Israel. He had been a journalist in Teheran who rubbed the Ayatollah Khomeini the wrong way, and now he is eking out a living as a cab driver in San Francisco. He and Elizabeta have not had much time together as yet, but in a few weeks Elizabeta plans to import him to Mexico. "We will live in Jalapa, I think. Far away from my family, who of course do not approve. A nice town, and not too big. Not too hot in summer. I can teach, perhaps. And he will learn Spanish. He can perhaps write. And he can cook." Pathetically she insists, "He loves to cook!"

Her beautiful eyes read the expression in mine. She places her fingertips lightly on my hand. "When two people truly love each other, that's all that matters. Nothing can put them apart, not even death. You know that. I know you do. Believe me, he is the great love of my life. He and I will manage somehow." She withdraws her fingertips, leans back, sighs. "Love is always enough."

Obviously, no one can protect this glamorous, uncontrollably romantic creature from herself. I agree with her that love is enough.

The party, however, is no longer enough. Not even Elizabeta is enough. With a couple of quarts of rum Coke sloshing around in the emptiness inside me, I bid her and Señor Morales goodnight and goodbye. I will be leaving early in the morning. "You'll see," Elizabeta calls tenderly from the table. "Someday, the memories of your love will comfort you."

Señor Morales insists on walking me to my cottage. "My friend," he says, "you should stay longer in Palenque. Because of the lovely ruins, it has become a crossroads of the world. Myself, I feel privileged to live here. Yucatán has important ruins, but nothing like so beautiful. And there is not the cosmopolitan atmosphere we have here. You'll see. Of course I can tell that something is bothering you. But for that very reason, you need to relax, try to enjoy yourself. Stay here a while, and maybe I will ask you to plant a tree."

Donald G. Schueler is an environmental activist and writer whose stories have appeared in magazines such as Audubon, Smithsonian, *and* Sierra. *He is the author of* Incident at Eagle Ranch, Adventuring Along the Gulf of Mexico, *and* The

Temple of the Jaguar: Travels in the Yucatán, *from which this is taken. He lives in New Orleans.*

We walked out toward the great green space where the ruins stand, with the powerful dark green jungle rising all around, we were quite overcome: it was marvelous.

Most striking, perhaps most beautiful, at first, are the colors: the black-gray-white of the ancient carved and weathered stones, and all the contrasting greens, the light green grass and dark trees, with every shade of green in-between, in bushes and vines and smaller trees. And then your eye returns to the ruins and you think again, How very beautiful, simply, the stones are.

—Alice Adams, *Mexico: Some Travels and Some Travelers There*

JEFF GREENWALD

Welcoming the Spirits on Janitzio Island

In caring for the memory of the dead, Mexicans show their appreciation for life and the living.

T he storm caught me by surprise. In less that a minute, the fine rain falling over the island had turned into a downpour. I ran for the nearest refuge as sheets of water waved through the streets, finally ducking into a crude cement construction site on a high overlook. All around Janitzio, bolts of lightning sizzled into the steel-gray surface of Lake Pátzcuaro—so close by that no delay separated the visual jolts from their apocalyptic report.

There was another man in the shelter—a laborer, I supposed. He wore an open leather jacket over a white t-shirt, and leaned against a thick plank supported by sawhorses. He watched the storm with satisfaction.

I hopped about in the cold, cursing piously as the rain turned to hail.

"*¿No le gusta a usted?*" he asked with a grin.

"Oh, it's terrific," I replied. "But my hotel's on the mainland, and I've got to catch the ferry before dark."

"There will be no ferries in this storm."

"I think there will be one more. But I may miss it. Is there a place to stay here on the island?"

"No," he said, still smiling. "And why do you visit Janitzio?"

"I've come for the *Día de los Muertos*, the Day of the Dead."

"*¡Muy bien!* Yes, that is very spectacular—as long as it doesn't rain!"

"Did it rain last year?"

"*Sí.*"

"Will it rain this year?"

"No."

"*Muy bien.*"

The storm had indeed subsided a bit, and I realized that it was now or never. A brief farewell and I was off, sloshing down the flooded steps.

31

The sky, opening to the low sun, had turned a flaming marigold orange, and the final launch was sputtering to life at the landing.

Early the next morning I sat aboard a ferry at the mainland dock, waiting for the boat to fill with passengers. It was the 31st of October. Bolts of sunlight and pockets of shadow played across the surface of Lake Pátzcuaro—a rough crescent of silver in the heart of Michoacán. Pátzcuaro is a lake capable of exhibiting many moods simultaneously, but all signs of the previous evening's rage had abated.

As we roared off I kept my eyes glued to the island. Janitzio is a deceptively small hump of land, dotted with white houses and crowned by an overlarge statue of the patriot-priest Morelos—progenitor of Mexico's constitution. About 1,500 Indians, descended from the fiercely independent Purepechas, live on the island. Long before the Spanish conquest, when the volcanic landscape of Michoacán was thick with jungle, the Purepechas settled Janitzio to escape the toll that jaguars and other wild animals were exacting from their ranks. Using rude dugout canoes and distinctive "butterfly" nets—both of which endure to this day—the Indians began farming the lake for its delicate *pescado blanco*, a small white fish in great demand on the mainland.

Many impolite accounts had been written about my destination; I'd read that it was "unsympathetic" on approach and "uninspiring" on arrival. Perhaps these reviews were not entirely unwarranted. Janitzio, after all, seems to have only reluctantly ended an age-old tradition of barring mainlanders from its shores. But like an old boxer who is somehow transformed at the ivories of a keyboard, so does Janitzio transform itself before the bones of *Día de los Muertos*, Mexico's ancient Day of the Dead.

Passage from the mainland to the island takes thirty minutes. I was accompanied on the short voyage by my guide, Señor Antonio Torres peered ruefully around the nearby waters, concentrating his gaze on the clumps of tall reeds by the receding shoreline.

"Mmmmm. Not so good," he said. "On this first morning there is usually a big duck hunt; maybe fifty or a hundred canoes. But I don't see any right now."

"Why might that be?" I asked.

> I f the Mexican ever risks revealing himself completely to a foreigner, showing the full range of his eclectic religiosity, his flint-hard resignation to the numerous defeats of his daily life, and his overpowering sadness even as flowers bloom, it is during the great national *fiesta*, the Day of the Dead, November 1 and 2.
>
> —Lee Foster, "Mexico: The Devil's Piñata"

He shrugged his shoulder. "We will have to ask about this on the island."

Día de los Muertos is one of the most unusual celebrations in the world. The pagan rituals of Aztec myth combine with somber Catholic dogma, producing a unique homage to death—not only to the spirits of departed family and friends, but to Death itself—the grinning skeleton that awaits us all with gleeful anticipation. The holidays are spread over two days and two nights, varying slightly but generally coinciding with our Halloween.

The celebration is a fascinating paradox, an occasion both pathetically mournful and outrageously festive.

Every town and village in Mexico observes *Día de los Muertos* a bit differently, but nowhere are the visiting spirits welcomed more passionately than on Janitzio. And since the island's famous celebration traditionally begins with a massive duck hunt, I was more than a bit alarmed by this year's mysterious cancellation.

We docked on Janitzio. Torres led me up a narrow street past rows of trinket stalls and restaurants. Everybody seemed to be cleaning up, repainting and preparing in general for the anticipated throngs—living as well as dead. We walked through the main plaza, past an overgrown bell tower and down a steep path toward the lanes where the fisherman live. Nets were hanging everywhere, weighted down by small stones. An old man came hobbling out of a doorway, slow of gait but otherwise quite fit. Torres accosted him at once.

"Don Luis Campos!" he cried. "Why is there no duck hunt today?"

"There is no duck hunt, Antonito, because there are no ducks."

It was sad, but true. For some reason the lake's waterfowl population had chosen this year to relocate; whether by accident or design, Don Luis could not say.

"He is sorry about the hunt," Torres informed me, "but insists you come back here this evening. Tomorrow morning, as you know, is the feast for the *angelitos*—the dead children—and tonight a special ceremony is performed in the homes. The godfather of the child visits the dead one's family, and blessing are made over the offerings. It is very beautiful. Will you come?"

I said I would. I had in fact found a modest lodge on Janitzio, so catching the ferry back to the mainland was no longer a concern.

Torres and I left Don Luis and walked along the well-maintained pathway that circles Janitzio. The island was a hive of activity. Entire families were engaged in preparing elaborate offerings for the spirits of the dead. Mothers and daughters sat in the kitchens, kneading dough for *pan de muertos*—the ceremonial "bread of the dead" that would be baked into fanciful shapes and placed steaming upon altars. Brothers wove brilliant yellow marigolds onto wooden trellises, punctuating the runs of flowers with an odd array of ornaments—animals, angels, and molded sugar skulls. A feast was being painstakingly prepared to assuage the hunger and thirst of the dead during their annual homecoming.

As we circled back toward the lodge a man in a leather jacket called out to me in greeting. I recognized him; he was the laborer I'd met during yesterday's storm. Now he was escorting a cadre of photographers, all laden with complicated gear; this was the crew from Michoacán State television, which would be filming the festival.

"That man seems to know you," Torres said, evidently surprised. "Have you met him?"

"Only briefly, while hiding from the rain. Does he work here?"

"You might say that!" Torres laughed, slapping me violently on the back. "That is Señor Alfonso Séptimo, the mayor of Janitzio!"

We'd had every intention of joining old Don Luis Campos for the godfathers' rite, but two things interfered. First, a heavy rain began to fall just after sunset. Then at eight—a power failure plunged the island into pitch blackness. I steeled myself for a long, dull evening—but it turned out otherwise.

As it happened, the proprietor of the lodge was himself a godfather, and his family invited us to join them as they brought their flowered offering to the home of the deceased godchild.

It was a journey I will not soon forget. Stumbling along blindly behind the procession, I literally clung to the shawls of the women before me as they navigated Janitzio's steep, rain-slicked paths. The word "path" is generous; I was sometimes scaling sheer rock. Rocket bombs exploded around me, lending a battlefield intensity to the sport. These, I later learned, were designed to guide the wandering spirits back home.

The souls of dead children are called *angelitos*; having committed no evil, they repair immediately to their reward in the heavens. As I staggered in from the storm, the scene inside the house seemed angelic indeed. Candles burned on the tables; the women, wrapped in dark shawls, were seated meditatively against a wall. A dozen or so children, eerily silent and well behaved, were also seated. Dominating the room was a wonderful offering, the labor of many loving hours. Bedecked with flowers and draped with fruits, *pan de muertos*, and sugar toys, it faced the mourners like a strangely overgrown easel, surrounded by incense and flame. Efforts to please the child's spirit had not ended there; a model of a souped-up Chevy van stood among the other offerings.

An enormous quantity of food was served, but almost none was eaten—after a ceremonial taste we passed our plates forward, heaping the beans, tortillas, and soup bowls before the altar. When the *charanda de caña*—a liquor distilled from the cane—was placed before us, I took a sip and regretfully pushed them along. My *faux pas* was instantly corrected by the godfather, who reminded me that children don't drink liquor.

The invocations that followed were mysterious and cathartic. The assembly waited patiently for the man who would lead the recitation of the rosary; he finally stumbled in from his rounds about the island, drunk but reverent. He transformed the family gathering into an uninhibited choir of grief and prayer, and the house began to swell with their lament. The mother of the *angelito* burst into tears. Rain drizzled in through the roof, soaking her offering and melting the little candy skulls.

I woke well before dawn on the first day of November. No alarm clock was necessary; rocket bombs had been bursting continuously since the first hint of daylight. The spirits could afford an early start—they had not been up till all hours drinking the deceptively mild *charanda de caña*.

This was *Día de los Niños*, the Day of the Children, and the cemetery was the place to be. The offerings, blessed the previous night would be placed on their respective graves, awaiting approval from the little souls. I scrambled into my clothes and climbed the long stairway leading toward the burial ground. In spite of the early hours there was much activity: a battalion of islanders soaped and scrubbed the plaza; women sat in doorways, pulling the heads off little white fish; shopkeepers arranged their displays. It was obvious that many visitors were expected for the famous nighttime celebration.

The sun that rose over Lake Pátzcuaro was blood red, a fair approximation of my own eye color as I leaned over a low cement wall and stared eastward. The dormant volcanoes that ring the lake rose through the lowland mist. Like the jungles and the Aztecs and the Spanish, their ancient threats had long been plowed under the soil of Michoacán. There is only one eternal enemy, I reflected; but on *Día de los Muertos*, even Death can be cultivated.

Shortly past dawn, the cemetery began to fill with people. Colorful offerings were placed on the appropriate graves, their golden-yellow marigolds electric in the early light. The color yellow has long been associated with death in Mexico, and these brilliant "flowers of 100

In approaching the Day of the Dead, be forewarned that you shouldn't trust your initial impressions. Looking at a candied skull with your name on it, bread shaped like human beings, and skeletons riding children's toys, you may exclaim: How grim! How macabre! But soon you'll begin to appreciate how the Day of the Dead expresses a sustaining humanity that enables Mexicans to cope with their precarious life in a subsistence culture.

—Lee Foster, "Mexico: The Devil's Piñata"

leaves" are universally acknowledged as the favorite flowers of the dead.

Tall candles burned fickly in the morning breeze. Little girls fondled the wax with their fingers. Some of the graves seemed almost lively—boys wrestled in the dirt while their mothers, wrapped in shawls, chatted softly. At others, a desolate silence prevailed. Every once in a while, the mood was shattered by a rocket bomb, but after a few explosions even the birds ceased to be alarmed by the blasts

Why do children die? I wanted to know the fate of Janitzio's *angelitos*, but it seemed inappropriate to conduct interviews in the cemetery. Later in the morning, as I strolled down toward the fishermen's launch, I met a woman who would speak to me about the children.

"Often they will die of bronchitis, or grippe," she explained. "And the whooping cough also takes many lives."

"Is there no clinic on Janitzio?"

"There is a small one," she said, "Which opened in 1983. But the doctor is not always on the island."

"But the town of Pátzcuaro has excellent facilities," I said. "Why aren't the children brought there?"

"They are. But since most of these illnesses occur during the winter, it is often the journey itself that kills them."

I left the tiny quay and walked back to the main ferry landing. Their morning vigil over, the Janitzians were well into an ecstasy of cleaning, baking, and decorating for the Night of the Dead. In the midst of the most frantic activity I often spied Mayor Séptimo darting from one scene to the next like a tireless master of ceremonies.

It was not yet noon, but many tourists were already combing the island in search of meals or souvenirs. Feeling a bit claustrophobic, I decided to return to the mainland for a lunch and a shower. Although the ferries were coming in fully loaded, nobody seemed to want to leave Janitzio; it was over an hour before I found myself ashore, hailing a cab to take me to Pátzcuaro.

Pátzcuaro is a fascinating place, bustling with street life and visibly proud of its historic importance. In the 1530s, the venerated Don Vasco de Quiroga opened the first schools in the Americas in this lakeside village. His success in organizing cooperative craft communes—based on ideas from Sir Thomas More's then-contemporary *Utopia*—brought the native Indians a prosperity that has lasted half a millennium.

I lunched in a quaint pizzeria, then wandered off to explore the town's two large plazas. Both were thronged with tourists and townfolk. The mainland was preparing for its own *Noche de los Muertos*, and the trappings of the holiday were visible everywhere: tables loaded with sugar skulls and toy coffins; stalls selling personalized *pan de muertos*; a modern drugstore hung with paper skeletons and imported plastic jack-o'-lanterns. I peered into a newsstand to read the *calaveras*—a word that literally means "skulls," but also refers to special verses published to satirize public figures through premature "obituaries."

Back at my hotel I was greeted by Señor Alvarez, the affable proprietor. He ushered me into the dining room, empty save for a distinguished-looking gentleman reading a magazine.

"I would like you to meet Señor Cámera," Alvarez chortled. "He is an architect, from Mexico City."

Cámera stood up and we shook hands. With his short gray hair and squarish jaw, he resembled a Mexican Norman Mailer.

Cámera had come to Michoacán to admire the buildings; the magazine he held was an out-of-print edition specifically about Pátzcuaro. He leafed through the journal with me, praising the ingenuity of the structures but bemoaning their present straits.

"Look at this photograph," he said. "This is the famous 'House of the Crooked Stairway,' one of the most unusual homes in the city. In its day it was an architectural marvel—do you know what it is now?"

The place looked oddly familiar; I flushed but held my peace.

"A pizza parlor!" Cámera snapped. "They've turned the place into a pizza joint!"

My brief encounter with Cámera stuck with me, because the fate of the "Crooked Stairway" house seemed an allegory for *Día de los Muertos*. In both cases a long-standing structure has been subtly altered, redesigned to suit the European invaders.

The Day of the Dead is rooted in ancient paganism and Aztec death rituals. These included the worship of Mictlantecuhtli, god of the underworld inferno—a sinister skeleton whose homage required living sacrifices. Over the centuries the rites changed. The Purepechas dismissed the bloody Aztec traditions. When the Dominicans arrived in the 1500s, they found observances not unlike the ones seen today. Souls of departed ancestors returned to their native villages, and were honored with food and flowers. Back then, the ceremonies took place in August. But as an attempt to fuse the Indian customs with Catholicism, a parallel was drawn between *Día de los Muertos* and the Church's All Soul's Day, November first. The syncretism was evidently successful, for today it is nearly impossible to determine where the aboriginal traditions end and Catholicism begins.

Like the House of the Crooked Stairway—and many other dwellings throughout Mexico—the Day of the Dead had been altered slightly to insure its survival in the modern age. My only hope, as I set off to return to Janitzio, was that the festival would have a more authentic flavor than did the pizza.

The Janitzio-bound ferry was jammed with passengers. Most of them were tourists from other parts of Mexico. There were even two mimes on the boat, hoping to extract a few pesos from the island's evening crowds.

Antonio Torres met me at the landing. He surveyed the crowded boat with alarm. "I'll tell you what," he said. "All of the tourists think the big ceremony happens at midnight. But that is the *worst* time to be in the cemetery."

"Well, what do you suggest I do?"

"Sleep until three or four in the morning," Torres advised, "and *then* go up there. By that time all the tourists will have decided there is nothing to see and will have gone home on the ferry." He lowered his voice. "But the late hours are the very best.... Oh, you wouldn't believe how beautiful it is!"

I considered his words as we docked. The island was already swarming, and more ferries were on the way. Three avenues led up and away from the dock; each one, I noted with amusement, had a sign reading *Subida Principal al Monumento*: Principal Ascent to the Monument.

Halfway to the island's crest I found a man I'd been looking for. Padre Rubén Ruíz sat beside a collection box on the side of the wide stairway. He was a droll-looking patriarch, dressed in black robes and holding a fat cigar between delicate fingers.

Padre Ruíz had served on Janitzio for 36 years, and I wanted to question him about that twilight zone between Indian ritual and Catholicism. But there were too many people; every few seconds an ascending tourist would appear and kiss the padre's hand, derailing his train of thought.

"How long," I asked, "have tourists been coming to see this celebration?"

"Hmmm. Well, the statue was finished in 1936," he said, "and many people began coming to see that. The Indians were kind of glad, because it brought a little extra income—before that there was nothing, and no one bothered to come here."

A group of attractive women mounted the steps toward us, and Ruíz automatically extended his hand. "Mostly, though, tourism for *Noche de los Muertos* began in 1948. A company from Mexico City came and made a film of it. I guess a lot of people saw that film, because every year there are more and more tourists."

"What do the Janitzians think of that?"

"In the beginning they resented it quite strongly, but now they're getting used to it. Now we don't mind. After a while one no longer cares."

"But how about the ceremony itself? Has the celebration changed?"

"The festival is the same," said Ruíz stiffly, and looked me in the eye. "The only difference is that now there are too many tourists. But I suppose you will see that for yourself."

By the time the sun set, Janitzio was crowded enough to pass for the French Quarter on Fat Tuesday. I hid in a corner of my favorite restaurant, dining on *pescado blanco* and *frijoles*. The scene outside was frantic. The television crew was running from place to place, turning the bright lights upon any sign of traditional activity. Up the hill on the basketball court, a Michoacán tourist board-sponsored dance and music show was underway; I could hear the bleating of trumpets. Not much for crowds, I finished my beer and returned to the lodge. Perhaps it would be possible to sleep for a while. But when to wake? Ignoring the warnings of the well-meaning Torres, I set the alarm for twelve.

I woke at midnight, wondering if I'd slept at all. It seemed as if nothing had changed. Through my window I could hear the ferries landing in rapid succession, each one solidly packed with obstreperous tourists. The restaurants were overflowing and the air crackled with the sound and smell of frying fish. Foot traffic up the main routes of town moved slowly, a cattle-like procession with its ironic end at the cemetery. Following the mob, I caught sight of an old Janitzian woman. She sat huddled in a doorway with her candles and flowers, clearly reluctant to continue onward.

The cemetery was very dark, a sea of anonymous figures milling about in confusion. As flashbulbs lit the darkness I caught strobed visuals of the tableau; people frozen in motion with cameras poised; wide-eyed children gripping their mothers' hands. The TV crew seemed to be filming something by the special coffin reserved for the symbolic Christ child, but getting close to it would have been like trying to reach the stage during a Grateful Dead concert.

Then I saw something that broke my heart. A pop of light illuminated a huge doughnut of people encircling the center of the graveyard. My height was an advantage, and I was able to see within. It was the woman I had spotted in the doorway. She crouched alone by a gravestone, surrounded by four tall candles and a tattered photograph of the man she had come to mourn. Flashbulbs exploded around her as she stared sorrowfully at the ground.

This was too much for me. I returned wearily to the lodge and flopped onto the bed, plagued by Malthusian nightmares until the alarm woke me again, at three.

Returning to the cemetery in the wee hours of the morning, my first thoughts were of Antonio Torres. The man had been absolutely right. I had never seen a more profound transformation. Nearly all the tourists were gone, and the graveyard had somehow become an otherworldly landscape of flickering candles—hundreds of them—and spectacularly flowered arches. Bells tolled mournfully from Janitzio's venerable tower while small groups of islanders sang the rosary before the graves of their ancestors. Magic and the smell of marigolds mingled in the air.

> In both cemeteries we visited, we were haunted and comforted by this cycle of remembrance. Each year, the living, from young to old, pay tribute to and remember those who are gone. And when one is gone, one knows that the family gathers to remember. Each human being moves through the circle remembering and being remembered.
>
> —Susan Hegger, "Day of the Dead, Night of the Living," *St. Louis Post-Dispatch*

I hiked up to a vantage point overlooking the entire scene. Viewed from above, the cemetery really did look like an elaborate, ghostly banquet—a banquet that only the most antisocial spirit could resist. Rows and rows of candles cast their glow onto the flowered trellises and cloth-covered trays of food. It was a breathtaking sight, more lovely and reverent than anything I had dared imagine earlier.

An odd thought struck me. Less than three days before, I had huddled in a nearby shelter with Mayor Séptimo as all hell broke loose around us. Had that first furious storm simply cleared the air for the arrival of more benign spirits? I remembered the curious look of satisfaction on the mayor's face as he watched the lightning, and I wondered how much I was willing to believe.

By 5 a.m. the graveyard was nearly silent, but as luminous as a vivid dream. I wandered among the offerings. Clusters of women, wrapped in shawls, sat nodding before the flames. Sleeping children lay curled in their laps. Once in a while a man came stumbling in from the drunken revelry outside, knocking over a candle or two before collapsing helplessly against a wall. I spirited myself away and kept my own vigil, mesmerized by the dancing lights, finally dozing off to the rhythms of a distant guitar.

Just before sunrise a velvet fog covered Janitzio. Dawn came very slowly, savoring the last mysterious flavors of the night. One by one, the families gathered their offerings and left the cemetery. They would later dine upon the leftovers, but with little enjoyment; the visiting dead, they knew, had already consumed the essence of the feast.

The second of November was blindingly sunny. Down at the landing, an odd assortment of tourists and villagers waited for the ferry. Everyone looked vaguely stupefied. The restaurants, which had been open for thirty hours, seemed befuddled by any order more complicated than a beer. A mixed group of *mariachis* wavered on the dock, blundering recklessly through a ballad. I bumped against them and was immediately engulfed by the crowd; a paper cup of *charanda*-on-the-rocks was pressed into my hand, and long arms were thrown around my shoulders.

But I wanted a last look at the cemetery before leaving Isla de Janitzio. Extricating myself from the musicians, I climbed up the wide, now empty, stairway.

The damp ground was covered with crushed marigolds, all that remained of the night-long trance. It was difficult to believe that, only hours before, the enigmas of Life and Death had sojourned here. An Aztec verse ran through my mind:

> We only come to sleep,
> We only come to dream;
> It is not true, it is not true
> That we come to live on earth...

I scooped up a few golden petals, and watched them blow away in the morning breeze.

Jeff Greenwald is the author of two books about his time in Nepal, Mr. Raja's Neighborhood *and* Shopping for Buddhas. *He's a contributing editor for* Wired *magazine, and his next book is about the still-huge size of the world, based on a trip around the globe without the benefit of aircraft.*

41

In Mexico, the expression *"Ya le tocaba,"* the equivalent of "his number was up" or "his turn finally arrived," often condenses the only possible reaction in the face of ineluctable doom.

In the Western conception, human life is a precious gift to be defended at all costs. The Aztecs viewed life as a prison, whose chief merit was its transitoriness. Each time human life seems wasted, Western civilization reacts with boundless indignation and angry outcry. The moral sense is in a dudgeon: the outrageous violation should not have happened, cannot be tolerated, must never happen again. Mexican fatalism replies with *"Ya le tocaba,"* his turn was foreordained, and it has come to pass.

—F. Gonzalez-Crussi, *The Day of the Dead and Other Mortal Reflections*

FREDERICK TURNER

A Routine Night in Veracruz

One man's cacophony is another man's music.

omewhere above Tampico I had crossed the Tropic of Cancer. Years
ago my wife and I had taken a train into the Barranca del Cobre
region, which is the heart of the Sierra Madre and about as inaccessi-
ble and Mexican as you can get. But now, south of the line, I felt for the
first time that I was in the heart of the country. The feeling was exciting,
yet I had to admit to myself that there was a true tinge of anxiety to it as
well. When I had checked into a hotel on the plaza of Veracruz's old
center, the first thing I did was to get out my large-scale map to see
where I was—which was really to see how I might escape from where I
was if I needed to. The evidence spread out before me produced the
same mingled sensation of excitement and fear I'd felt on arriving in the
city. I was certainly way down there. Yes, sir, way, way down. I was in
fact a lot closer to Guatemala than to anywhere in the U.S. I was somewhat reassured to see a drawing of a tiny ship on the map and a dotted
line indicating there was boat service between here and Key West. But
shortly I was a lot more reassured by the spectacle of Veracruz itself.
Walking out into the plaza was like walking into a movie set, with the
vital difference that this was real, intensely so.

On three of its sides the plaza was bordered by heavy, confectionary
buildings whose fronts formed an arcade, the arches lined with strips of
red and green neon tubing. At one corner sat the weathered pile of the
cathedral, its bell sounding as if a child were striking a tinny toy with a
stick. Balancing it was City Hall. In between, strings of small light bulbs
had been swung across the marble-flagged square, attached here and
there to palms and acacias. Clusters of globed lights like slightly tar-
nished moons stood atop white painted poles. In the very center a fountain flung its waters up through the lights toward the evening sky. There
must have been at least four marimba bands at work when I entered.
They were serenading the tables under the arcade, and at 6:30 on a
weekday evening those tables were full, some of them already showing a
serious collection of empty beer bottles and piles of shrimp peelings.
There were crowds of strollers here, too: white-suited sailors from the

naval base; young girls linked arm in arm; and a long succession of portly business types in short-sleeved shirts with briefcases in hand who frankly gave the girls the thrice-over.

I settled myself at a table outside the Hotel Prendes, ordered a beer and some ceviche, and turned to face the music, in this instance entirely a pleasurable choice since I found myself between two of the marimba bands, both playing furiously. And if you thought—as I did—of a "marimba band" as producing a soft, pellucid sound, you have the wrong idea of what was to be heard in Veracruz. Both bands had two marimba players, plus tenor sax and drums, and they produced one hell of a sound and beat. Here in the complex cross-rhythms over which danced the hollow sound of the marimba was in truth the African-Caribbean voice. Listening to it was like taking a bath in *salsa picante*. Some of the tables did appear to be listening to this phenomenon, but most took it for granted (as Americans do Muzak), even when they were seated right under the bell of the sax or touching the rims of the drums. Soon the lead band moved on, its percussionist passing his gourd scraper among the tables, and a trio of singers came on, backed by a mandolin, guitar, and harp. Looking farther down the arcade on my side, I saw a strolling guitarist with a colleague rolling along his big bass. It was like knowing what your next course was going to be.

White-jacketed waiters, vendors, beggars, and streetwalkers vied for what little space there was between the tables, the waiters balancing full trays on flattened palms while executing balletic avoidance maneuvers. Men and children sold necklaces, souvenir cane spears, nuts, dolls, candy, seashells, wallets and assorted leather goods, cigars, cigarettes, Chiclets, sunglasses, shawls, tablecloths, and bouquets of flowers. The streetwalkers were selling themselves, of course, but they seemed pretty

I ordered the specialty of the *fiesta, mole negro*, which must have been the blackened distilled quintessence of chili sauce. I began to eat an imprudently large spoonful.

The waiter, a university student named Pedro, asked me, "The sauce? It is *muy picante* for you, *Señor?*"

"Yes, very, very hot!" I replied, reaching for a glass of water, not allowing the leisure of an inquiry whether the water was purified or not.

"*Señor,*" he continued, "you must wonder how my people can each such hot foods."

"I do," I admitted, giving him a charred grin, careful not to set the tablecloth afire with my breath.

"We can eat this food," he confided, "because our ancestors came from hell!"

—Lee Foster, "Mexico: The Devil's Piñata"

good-natured about that, and when two of them came past my table and saw me scribbling in my notebook, they paused and asked, *"¿Qué haces?"* ("What are you doing?") *"Un hombre de letras,"* I replied, giving myself airs. They thought it was funny, too, giggled, and passed on. Even if this had been ridicule, I felt it conferred a sort of status on me, that I had been taken as a potential customer and so was a functional part of this scene. By the time I had followed my beer and ceviche with two margaritas and the famous local dish, *huachinango veracruzano* (red snapper in a spicy tomato sauce), I was feeling even more at ease here—if a little less functional.

By this time, too, the plaza was getting into full swing, the tables under the arcade now jammed, the spaces between clogged, and the benches in the square filled with spectators. Balloon men were out in force, and when they passed directly under the globed lights their high, floating wares were illuminated as from within. Up on the bandstand in front of City Hall a twenty-piece naval band in starched whites was hoisting its glinting instruments in preparation for entering the musical lists. When at last it crashed into heavy play the cacophony was magnificent. I asked my waiter in delight and astonishment whether all this went on every night, and he smiled, shrugged, and said, "Oh, yes." I had to wonder how long it would take before I, too, like those veterans of the ringside tables, simply took it for granted.

My hotel room unfortunately didn't overlook the plaza, otherwise I might have tried to stay awake to see how the whole set was at last dismantled as dawn came up. But when I opened my window I could distinctly hear the festivities coming up at me, and as I drifted into a happy sleep there was the naval band, charging with spirit high above the strings, percussion, and mallets of the musical competition.

Frederick Turner has written several books on a variety of subjects, from New Orleans jazz to a meditation on exploration. He has received awards from the National Endowment for the Arts and the Guggenheim Foundation. This story was excerpted from his book, A Border of Blue: Along the Gulf of Mexico from the Keys to the Yucatán.

"¡Hay Menudo!" Regulars recognize the weekend signs—often hand-scrawled—outside restaurants and street stalls all over Mexico, and frequently seen around border-area cities and states, too. *"¡Hay Menudo!"*—'There is *menudo*!'—announcing that a fresh batch of

Mexico's famous spicy tripe stew is at hand. But why is *menudo* usually served only on Saturday and Sunday mornings?

Normally, Mexico's mornings-after fall on weekends, and *menudo* is Mexico's official hangover cure. Thus, any party person knows that the more you indulged last night, the more you need *menudo* this morning to set your head straight again. True believers swear by their particular regional favorites (red or white like clam chowder), but nobody quibbles over the soup's curative powers. *"Desayuno de campeónes,"* as it's nicknamed everywhere in Mexico: "Breakfast of champions."

—Paula McDonald, "Tantalizing Trivia"

RON BERNTHAL

Bays of Huatulco

*The Mexican government develops a new megaresort, hoping to integrate
lessons learned from past projects.*

Five years ago, Robert Gutierrez and his family lived in a one-room
stick shack near the southern Mexican fishing village of Santa Cruz.
Every morning, before sunrise, Señor Gutierrez and the other men
from the village would take their boats two miles offshore and pull in a
few pounds of sea bass and cuttlefish, just enough to feed their families
until the next day.

During the hot afternoons the men would take long siestas, sleeping
in netted hammocks strung between two palm trees, while their kids
bathed in the nearby Copalita River, which was fresh and cool after
rushing down the steep sides of the Sierra Madre del Sur mountains.

Today, Roberto Gutierrez spends 72 hours a week in his air-conditioned Nissan Maxima, shuttling tourists from the new hotels on
Tangolunda Bay to the "new" village of Santa Cruz, where seaside restaurants and tourist facilities have replaced the stick shacks of the "old" village. Señora Gutierrez has a job at the new 346-room Sheraton Hotel,
cleaning rooms on the hotel's sixth floor, rooms whose balconies overlook the pool and Tangolunda Bay. The Gutierrez's teenage children
walk to the beach in front of the hotel, carrying photo albums with
scenic shots of the nearby bays. Asking sunbathers if they would like a
"bay tour by boat" for $60 (U.S. dollars), the Gutierrez kids often have
more customers than they can handle.

By any standards, but especially here in Mexico, the Gutierrez family
has gone from rags to riches. They have disposable income now, and can
afford medical care and life insurance. Their former living quarters in
Santa Cruz were bulldozed, but a free housing lot was provided in nearby La Crucecita, a town started from scratch just a few years ago. Their
new house, with two bedrooms, a garden, and indoor plumbing, is one of
the nicest on the street. The family even has electricity now, and a small
black and white television.

The impetus behind the sudden middle-class trappings of the
Gutierrez family, and thousands like them along Mexico's southern

Pacific coastline, is the National Fund for Tourism Development (FONATUR), the Mexican government organization responsible for tourism development in the country. Their newest adventure, the development of Bahías de Huatulco, the Bays of Huatulco, is a massive project, that, when completed in the 21st century, will transform nine pristine bays along Mexico's southern Pacific coastline into a well-planned, environmentally protected, hotel and marina megaresort.

The Mexican government has long been involved in tourism development, beginning in the late 1940s, when it turned the small fishing port of Acapulco into a jet-set resort. Since then, FONATUR has developed resorts at Ixtapa-Zihuatanejo, Los Cabos, Loreto, Cancún, and other places in Mexico.

It was the image of Cancún, however, Mexico's most visited tourist destination, that kept coming to my mind as the jet lifted us above the brown stagnant air of Mexico City and headed towards the Bays of Huatulco, only fifty minutes away. Cancún, a slender finger of sand off the Yucatán coast, was once surrounded by the cleanest water in the Caribbean, and inhabited by only 117 people.

> It is both remarkable and dismaying how little Spanish one needs to speak in resort areas these days. Our waiter yesterday was perfect—he encouraged our Spanish gently despite the fact that he spoke English well. This is a better way to go.
>
> —James O'Reilly, "I Was A Teenage Iguana"

Today, beachfront hotels are lined up like Monopoly pieces along the white sand beach, almost 20,000 rooms altogether. Cancún, a metaphor for "growth at any price," receives more than 1.5 million visitors a year, causing a myriad of problems with traffic congestion, noise and water pollution, and hurricane-evacuation plans.

A tour guide I know has been visiting Cancún every year, and each time she returns more depressed: "The more they fill it up, the emptier it gets," she says.

When I finally landed at the small thatched-hut Huatulco airport, I was expecting the worst, an ecological disaster that would make Cancún seem like a tranquil nature reserve. After all, the same people who brought us Cancún were now boasting that the Bays of Huatulco, all nine of them, would one day accommodate 345,000 residents, 30,000 hotel rooms, and receive two million visitors a year.

Santos Morales, a FONATUR representative, drives me from the airport to Tangolunda Bay, the first bay to be developed. "We have learned a great deal from Cancún," he says, sensing my apprehension as he navigates the Volkswagen Beetle through the beautiful S-turns which slice between the mountains and the sea. "Seventy-five percent of the area will be kept green, and we have constructed sewage treatment plants, an efficient fresh water network, and have protected the soil from erosion."

What Señor Morales was saying, I was to learn later, was all true. The reason that FONATUR is going to such lengths to protect the environment here is because it is the most scenic, underdeveloped area in all of Mexico.

It is said that when government planes were overflying the country in the late 1960s, scouting out potential tourist sites, the nine Bays of Huatulco were considered the most beautiful coastline in Mexico.

They also happened to be the least accessible, almost completely cut off from the rest of the state of Oaxaca. It was so underdeveloped, so isolated, and so empty, that FONATUR put the Huatulco project on hold for twenty years while other areas, perhaps not as beautiful, but more accessible, were developed for mass tourism.

Because of the trend toward ecotourism, and the environmental lessons learned from previous destination development, FONATUR is doing its best to protect the Huatulco site. They have constructed a new town, La Crucecita, away from the beaches, where schools, clinics, service industries, and employee housing is located. To make room for hotel construction, hundreds of families like the Gutierrezes were relocated from their primitive ocean-front dwelling to modern homes in town. Hotels are required to conform to a rigid set of architectural regulations, both in design and color scheme, enabling them to blend into the tropical environment.

Although a few small hotels have opened in Santa Cruz and La Crucecita, it is Tangolunda Bay that has been first affected by FONATUR's project. Club Med Huatulco, the largest Club Med in the western hemisphere, opened on the west side of the bay in 1988, followed shortly by the Sheraton and Royal Maeva Hotels, a Holiday Inn, and a deluxe Omni Resort.

Although the Club Med has five garishly painted smokestack-

> We encourage you to shop in markets and not to spurn the lowly street vendor. We've noticed a trend in Mexico toward increasing tourist-oriented galleries and stores and fewer and fewer market stands. Not only will you pay more in the fancy store but if you exclusively patronize the *ladino* (non-Indian Mexican) owned store, you are contributing to the elimination of the Indian merchant.
>
> —Steve Rogers and Tina Rosa,
> *Shopper's Guide to Mexico*

like pillars identifying its residential units, all three resorts use muted colors and foliage so as not to distract attention from the sea and mountains.

Chuck Ortega worked in Cancún for five years before moving to Tangolunda Bay last year with his American wife and their two children. The Ortegas feel that the Bays of Huatulco will be very different than Cancún, and are establishing themselves early as local guides, expecting the current trickle of visitors to grow as word spreads.

"It will take time," Mr. Ortega says, as we sit on his rooftop terrace and watch the sun drop like molten lava into the Pacific. "But everyone will want to experience Huatulco, which is good, because it gives the developers time to plan for the environment, and it gives the residents time to prepare for being good hosts."

But how long can the beaches remain unspoiled?

"Look," Ortega explains, "there are nine bays, and each is separated by hills, so you can't see one bay from another. And the growth of each beach is tightly regulated. Besides, when you see how much better the people are living now, it is difficult to say that this project is bad."

> Resort development is a tricky issue worldwide. While bringing some obvious economic benefit to local people, it also usurps local cultures and values, usually with predictable consequences.
>
> —JO'R and LH

How can one argue about giving people electricity, medical care, and a decent income? The state of Oaxaca is one of the poorest in Mexico and the government expects this tourism project to benefit the region enormously. Tourism is Mexico's third largest source of foreign exchange, after oil and the maquiladora industry (the labor-intensive factories set up along the U.S. border where Mexican workers assemble foreign products). In a country where more than half the people still don't have running water, the government has targeted tourism as a major growth industry.

Mexico's investment law now permits 100-percent foreign investment in tourism projects. This has allowed the big chains, like Marriott, Sheraton, and Holiday Inn, to increase their visibility here, and prompted by Hilton, which abandoned the country in 1973, to look into coastal properties for development.

The appropriation of land and water rights in Huatulco, however, which began after FONATUR obtained title to over 52,000 acres of land, has met with some local resistance from the campesinos. Families who had fished these bays for generations were not happy about being displaced to make room for the 18-hole golf course, or a Har-Tru tennis court. But without strong local support, and tempted by offers of cash and new homes in town, many residents have become loyal supporters of the multi-billion dollar government project.

Ironically, one of the barriers to Huatulco's success may be the very reason it is being developed—its splendid isolation. There are no large cities nearby, and it has only been in recent months that FONATUR has paved some roads, enabling motor traffic to reach three of the nine bays. The hills behind the beaches are not slated for development and the beaches themselves, deep crescents of soft white sand, discourage building more than two or three sites on any one bay.

The closest tourist town to the Bays of Huatulco is Puerto Angel, a fishing village forty miles to the west. Puerto Angel is a vintage Mexican dropout town. Claimed by Jack Kerouac and the "beats" in the 1950s, and frequented by hippies a decade later, Puerto Angel is what Mexican tourism was like before the megaresorts of FONATUR. If Cancún, as Mr. Ortega describes it, "is a computer printout gone crazy," then Puerto Angel is a dog-eared handwritten document.

Young people still flock here, and to the nearby seaside community of Zipolite, where beach hammocks rent for a dollar per night, and fresh lobster dinners are little more than that. At one local café, Shambhala, long-haired patrons sit smoking marijuana and listening to old Bob Dylan tapes, casually watching German and Dutch tourists swimming *au naturel* in the warm surf.

The contrast between scruffy Puerto Angel and the new development down the road at Huatulco is striking. The hotels and tourist facilities at Huatulco are clean and manicured, almost sterile, compared to the down-at-the-heels look of Puerto Angel.

But the Mexican government is planning its megaresort for a generation of tourists who are not interested in dust-blown Mexican fishing villages. At Huatulco, the water will be kept clean in the bays and purified in the bedrooms, and traffic will flow smoothly on tree-lined roadways. The hotels will scatter hibiscus petals on the bedspreads and employees will learn to say "thank you" in fourteen languages. In many respects, the Bays of Huatulco are being designed for a generation of environmentally conscious travelers who have not even been born yet.

FONATUR has invested heavily in this huge tourist project. Will it succeed? Or will outside factors divert the tourism traffic away from Mexico, leaving the government, and the new hotels, staring at empty beaches?

For now, the Bays of Huatulco are just perfect, with a few deluxe hotels and a whole string of undeveloped, gorgeous bays. And FONATUR, slowly and methodically, is committed to completing the project for, as the Mexicans say, *"Cuando el vino esta abierto debe ser bebido"* (when the wine is opened, it must be drunk).

Ron Bernthal is a columnist for the Sunday Record *in Middletown, New York, and an associate professor of environmental tourism at Sullivan County Community College. He lives in Hurleyville, New York.*

I sit alone at the wooden table on the patio of my cottage, my new home, the one with all the heat and flies and ants. A couple of burros are making rutting noises out back. The radio across the street is playing loudly. I am drinking cheap *tinto*, the local specialty, being strong and thin and wiry, like the people here. I'm eating the crunchy *pan bolillos* topped with a round of the bitter vinegar cheese that Nano buys for me at the public market. I think I must be one of the luckiest people around, here at the edge of the Pacific, the Pacific which, at night, if you listen carefully, thrums so mightily against the rocky cliffs, near the mouth of the bay—thrumming as it has for a million years or so: rising up out of the darkness of the great Oaxacan Trench that lies just outside the harbor. The waves pound with a force born out of that darkness, a darkness of the crevasses below and the mountains above—the dark of it all; the waves, *"las ondas;" "el fondo"*—the depths.

Down there in that rift, down there in one of the great cuts in the earth's sea floor, strange eye-lantern creatures and phosphorescent fish move about under a pressure equal to 200 atmospheres. These beasts move slowly, ferreting across a sparse and barren sea bottom. I am a mile and a half from them in the soundless dark, me in the warm air, with my wine, and cheese, the bread—Puerto Jesús and I—touched by this delicate veil, a sweet night breeze from the west. It is at this moment that I decide to return, briefly, to the north, to the world of clouds and cold and rain, the place where there's clear water that one dares to drink. To the north, the land of fear and too much money and too little time. I'll spend a week there—ten days at most—draw my life together, briefly, before I return to my beloved Puerto Jesús, my new home.

—Carlos Amantea, *The Blob That Ate Oaxaca & Other Travel Tales*

PETER CANBY

A Walking Witch

*Stranded in Chiapas, the author takes a long walk in the rain
and gets a lesson in superstition and generosity.*

W hen I tried to board the bus, I was told it was not going back to San
Cristóbal, but farther out into the mountains. It would return to
San Cristóbal the next morning at five-thirty. I waited for another
forty-five minutes until the bus that was supposed to return to San
Cristóbal that afternoon was long overdue. Even though everyone
assured me that it was coming, no one else seemed to be waiting. I began
to make inquiries.

"That bus didn't come up this morning," a reliable-looking storekeeper told me, "therefore it won't be going back tonight."

At first I choose to dismiss this observation. It wasn't what I wanted
to hear. But after further questioning, I was forced to conclude that it was
probably correct, since it was now four-thirty in the afternoon. It was
also at a point in the rainy season when the rain started in the late afternoon and was likely to continue all night. Storm clouds were gathering
around the mountain tops. Occasional trucks were still coming into town
from the direction of San Cristóbal, but for several hours, not a single
one had headed back. I knew, because I'd asked each one. I conferred
with the storekeeper. "That's it for the night," he told me, "although six
or seven kilometers away there's the junction with the road to Chenalhó
and you might catch something there."

I could hear thunder in the distance. It was about to pour. It would
soon be dark. I didn't have a sleeping bag. I had no evidence that the
road from Chenalhó, an even more remote Indian village, would produce
any more traffic than the San Andrés road. It was twenty-two miles
through the mountains to San Cristóbal. Logically, I should have swallowed my pride and walked the hundred yards up the hill to the weaver's
house, but I couldn't bring myself to. I set off walking.

At first I had the illusion I was outrunning the storm. While I followed the high road along the ridge, it seemed to slide along the valley
below me. I was going at a good clip. The mountain air filled my lungs
and I began to perspire lightly. But two kilometers and two steep climbs

later—too late, in my opinion, to turn back to San Andrés—I saw that the storm had outrun me. It had circled around in front of me and was waiting in ambush. I kept walking anyway. Over the third ridge, the rain began. I pulled out my bottom-of-the-line rain jacket. It was a curious jacket. Although it gave the illusion of keeping out the rain, the jacket's interior was always lined with moisture, whether through condensation or leaks I could never decide. I trudged on. No traffic had passed me in either direction and darkness was beginning to fall quickly.

Between San Andrés and San Cristóbal lies Chamula, the land of the Chamulas, the largest, poorest, and most belligerent of the Tzotzil groups. As I crossed the line into Chamula, I found four or five hopelessly drunk Chamulas lying outside a house in the rain. One of them held out his hand and asked me for a thousand pesos. Welcome to Chamula.

I had come into an Indian hamlet, a *paraje*, strung out along both sides of the road. I began to notice kids peering at me from behind rocks and bushes. I smiled and waved as if nothing were wrong. "Just another tourist out for a rainy night-time stroll!"

Instead of waving back, they ran—without smiling. A woman herding a flock of sheep in front of me quickened her pace and brandished her machete in the air as if fighting off invisible spirits. As I passed the school, two boys taunted me from a distance.

I began to realize that although it was easy enough to pass through this territory on a bus, it was another thing to be a stranger, walking in the rain, with night approaching. It didn't have so much to do with the imminent possibility of my getting lost, or freezing, or catching pneumonia. It had to do with the Maya conception of what kind of person would be out walking by himself in the mountains at night.

The Tzotzils believe that they live in the center of the world. They also believe that the edges of the world, near where Htotik, the sun, plunges daily into the underworld, is a dangerous place. It is filled with demons, wild animals, and strange human beings who are related to the Earthlord. Among such people are the foreigners, the *kashlan*. *Hrinkos*, *gringos*, are *kashlan*. Like the Earthlord himself, the *kashlan* can be a source of great wealth, but they're very powerful and extremely dangerous. Count one against me. I am *kashlan*.

Second, the Tzotzils divide the earth into the *naetik*, the parts of the world in which the gods have been placated and human activities are safe, and the *te'tik*, the wild, wooded areas that, like the edges of the world, are filled with dangerous animals and people. Only shamans or witches, who are capable of transforming themselves into other shapes, would walk alone in the *te'tik* at night. More witches than Indian communities care to talk about have been chopped up by machetes when they were caught wandering alone at night.

I may look like a *kashlan*, but perhaps I'm really a witch masquerading as one.

These things were on my mind when, after an hour or so of hard walking, my feet and trousers soaked, my upper body bathed in sweat, I finally saw the Chenalhó road in the distance. I also saw a man in the road ahead of me. I soon overtook him and stopped him to explain my plight. His name was Marcelino. He was a Chamula and a *chofer*, a driver, although he had apparently misplaced his vehicle. He pulled out his *chofer* card to show me. It had his picture on it. Marcelino, too, seemed to have been drinking, but at least he was cheerful. He told me he'd driven all over Mexico, from California to Quintana Roo. "California, Quintana Roo," he repeated, laughing hysterically as if it were some comic mantra.

I was tremendously relieved to encounter Marcelino. He

The Maya conceptions of soul are complicated and multifarious. Still, they sometimes find partial parallels in Western experience. For example, John Sosa's informants in the Yukatan culture conceive of two *pixom*, "souls"—one good and the other bad. The contrast of good and evil is familiar to us. While the concept of two souls is not, this idea points to a fundamental and distinctive duality of spirit inherent to Maya reality. Zinacanteco Maya also have two souls, as do many other Tzotzil-speaking peoples of highland Chiapas. For them, one of these souls is invisible, indestructible, and divided into thirteen parts. A scary accident, like a fall on a mountain path, can cause a person to lose a piece of this soul and become ill. Evil witches can also steal pieces of this soul and sell them to the Earth Lord. Shaman seers can find the missing piece with proper preparation, the cooperation of the subject, and supernatural help and restore the human soul. Zinacantecos call this kind of soul *ch'ulel*, which has the same root as *ch'ul* or *k'ul*, a word used by ancient Maya scribes to describe "holiness" and "divinity."

—David Freidel, Linda Schele, Joy Parker, *Maya Cosmos: Three Thousand Years on the Shaman's Path*

didn't know it, but his fate was now linked to mine. He was my guide, my interpreter, my friend, my ("Mexico, Quintana Roo! Ha, ha, ha!") Virgil.

I asked Marcelino where he was planning to spend the night. In Chamula, he told me—San Juan Chamula. This was reassuring because San Juan Chamula, the Chamulas' municipal center, was only a few miles from San Cristóbal.

"But how will you get there?"

Marcelino didn't answer. He just laughed as we wandered off into the gloom.

A little way beyond the road junction, we came upon a house by the side of the road. I followed Marcelino into a dirt-floored, dimly-lit room with bags of corn in one corner. Some young Indian men entered behind us. Everyone seemed to know Marcelino. Marcelino asked if I'd like a *refresco*, a soda. I accepted and reached for some bills to pay for it. He waved my gesture aside and said something in Tzotzil. One of the Indian men reached into the corner, picked up a rusted enamel coffee pot, filled a dirty glass with clear liquid, and presented it to me. It was moonshine, or *pox* ("posh"). Pretty hard to refuse in my situation. I downed the glass in two gulps. My stomach rebelled. My eyes misted over. The top of my head felt as if it were lifting off.

The man was pouring me a second glass, when suddenly, in the distance, I heard the grinding of a motor. It was the Chenalhó bus. We leapt out of the house and flagged it down. I got on first. Behind, Marcelino—forgetting all about me—picked up the bucket that the driver used to fill his leaky radiator (every bus in the region has a leaky radiator and every bus carries a bucket with which to refill it at roadside pools and streams), inverted it, sat down next to the driver, and began making loud jokes. I eased into a regular seat farther back. My seatmate was a tiny Indian man with a crew cut. The bus was an old schoolbus, as most of them are. It was warm and moist inside, and pitch black by now outside. The windows were fogged up. The motor made a comforting roar. We shifted into gear and headed for San Cristóbal. It was like heaven. The impression was furthered by a Virgin Mary surrounded by twinkling lights, mounted over the windshield. Below this little shrine, along the top of the windshield itself, was a fringe of braided material that looked like a Shetland pony's bangs. It was absurdly beautiful. I had an overwhelming sense of well-being.

I suddenly noticed that my seatmate was fingering my leaky rain jacket. How much did it cost, he wanted to know. I told him. He leaned back into what I assumed was a stunned silence. The sum I'd named was probably close to the gross national product of his hamlet. A few minutes later he nudged me. How much did I want for it? I thought for a moment, peeled it off, and handed it to him. Somehow he didn't seem surprised.

"*Dios te paga.* God will pay you," he said.

Peter Canby is a former staff writer for The New Yorker *and is the author of* The Heart of the Sky: Travels Among the Maya, *from which this story is taken.*

Leave time for the unexpected; and try to be as courteous, gentle, and tolerant with the Mexican as he will be with you. Even if he is wearing a cracked straw hat and torn pants, he is still the fruit of several sophisticated cultures—Indian and European—which did mighty deeds while we were crawling on all fours. Except when tequila overtakes him, he is humane, generous, resourceful, quick-witted, and to be respected as a citizen of the only country which, in spite of the Conquest and through bloody history, valiantly held on to its great Indian heritage and continues to. The only "reservations" in Mexico are a few ghettos of expatriate *norteamericanos*.

—Kate Simon, *Mexico: Places and Pleasures*

CARLOS FUENTES

Where Gods Abide

Eons of Mexican history, layer upon layer, live in Mexico City's main square.

W hen I was a young law student, I used to cross the *Zócalo*, the central square of my terrible and wonderful Mexico City, every day. At seven in the morning I would take the broken-down collective taxi near my home on the Paseo de la Reforma, the broad boulevard designed in the 1860s on the orders of Empress Carlota to resemble the Avenue Louise of her native Brussels. King Leopold's daughter lived in Mexico for only a short period, as short as the reign of her husband, the emperor Maximilian von Habsburg, imposed on Mexico by French arms.

In my youth, the Paseo de la Reforma was still lined by Second Empire *hôtels particuliers*, with mansard roofs waiting eternally for the snow to fall on Mexico City. The avenue had a very French look, but already many infant skyscrapers were elbowing out the aristocratic mansions. The avenue first looked like something designed by the Baron Haussmann. It now looked like a vision of Bauhausmann.

The taxi would turn into the Avenida Juárez—named after the patriot who defeated Maximilian and had him shot—at the point where the equestrian statue of Charles IV of Spain was beginning to be swallowed by traffic and fumes. Avenida Juárez went down one side of the broad Alameda park, and its white, somewhat erotic marble statues faced the few churches and monasteries surviving on the other side, blushing in red volcanic facades. They, too, were being surrounded and cracked, on the mushy lake bed of the city, by the new skyscrapers.

The thoroughfare would then narrow down to the canyon of Avenida Madero, renamed (from Plateros, street of the silversmiths) after the young lawyer and liberal landowner who started the Mexican Revolution. The former evocation of Mexico's mineral wealth was certified by the abundance of Baroque palaces and plateresque churches, alternating, once more with a sprinkling of modern buildings and a few reminders of the 19th-century, French-oriented past.

This ride was enough to give one a sense of the palimpsest that is Mexico City, comparable to Rome in its almost geological strata of superimposed civilizations. Yet my daily taxi ride was but a prelude to the truly fascinating vision I then had.

The taxi would stop at the corner of the Hotel Majestic and I would step out onto the immense square, the *Zócalo*, doubting every morning whether I could possibly render justice to its vastness, uniqueness, and beauty. As I was about to cross the square, I had to remind myself: once more I am on the Plaza de la Constitución. The citizen takes his city for granted too often. He forgets to marvel. The sense of awe wears out, whether he is crossing the Place de la Concorde, the Piazza San Marco, or the *Zócalo*. This I had to fight against each day in my otherwise uneventful way to the School of Law of the National University of Mexico on nearby San Ildefonso street.

Certainly I saw what was there. To the north, the great Baroque cathedral, Catedral Metropolitana, the largest in Latin America, with its sensation of bringing together the purest, most serene marble and the warmest lava rock, and blending them together in silvery brilliance. To the south, the twin buildings of the municipality. To the east, again, a potpourri of styles, from the colonial nobility of the National Pawnshop to the Art Nouveau gaudiness of a large department store. And to the east, the Palacio Nacional with its three-storied facade of red *tezontle* stone, the seat of presidential power in a traditionally authoritarian system.

I saw this, crossing the plaza every morning, trying not to lose my sense of place and my sense of marvel. When the Spanish conquistador Hernán Cortés took the city from the Aztecs in 1521, the ancient Indian capital was razed and the Spanish city built on top of it. But as I gazed at the structure of Spanish colonial domination, every day another vision arose before me.

Near the site of the present Catholic cathedral, I would see, in my mind, the vast *teocalli*, the

A t Cinco de Mayo and the western edge of the *Zócalo* stands the imposing Monte de Piedad, of restrained baroque. Reputedly this was the site of Moctezuma's palace. Later, in Colonial times, it was the palace of new god-kings, the Viceroys sent to rule by the Spanish Crown. Now the National Pawnshop, it displays carefully labeled typewriters, earrings, enamel kitchen tables, radios, watches, antiques, and "antiques" in its endless row of beehives. Visitors are lured by stories of mounds of viceregal jewels sold at the price of glass. In actual experience they may have been there yesterday or will be there tomorrow, but never today. Whether you find treasure or not, it is worth a visit, if only to see how big, variegated, open, busy, and democratic a government pawnshop can be, as opposed to the shame-faced stores which hide in our obscure neighborhoods.

—Kate Simon, *Mexico: Places and Pleasures*

central religious temple of the Aztec world. It was a complex of pyramids within pyramids, stairs, and passageways, and its base—110 by 88 yards—was a series of serpents, evoking the founding deity of the Indian universe: Quetzalcoatl, the Plumed Serpent, the god of creation and brotherhood. Lined by serpent's heads, the stairs led up to twin temples, one dedicated to Tlaloc (also known as Chac Mool, god of rain and agriculture) and the other to Huitzilopochtli (the Hummingbird Wizard, the god of war). Blue and white stripes graced the temple of Tlaloc, along with stylized sculptures of shells at the top. White skulls against red walls decorated the temple of war.

The twin temples were crowned by tall thatched roofs and were enlarged with terraces. Two terrible walls protected the ensemble: the wall of serpents, the *coatepantli*, and the wall of skulls, the *tzompantli*. Inside these pantheons, the Aztec deities stood (or lay, as in the case of the jacent Chac Mools, which inspired the work of Henry Moore) on turquoise pedestals.

Gods of war and prosperity, of wisdom and sacrifice, of want and satisfaction, dual divinities preached their estrangement from humanity, their monstrous difference from mere mortals. Gods of wind and fire, goddesses of fertility and drunkenness, ladies bearing both filth and purification, youths shedding their skins each springtime, all of them illuminated by the ruling rotation of the stars. Venus, first light to shine in the evening and last light to die out at dawn, was the star that guided the sacred world of the Aztecs. Its center was right here where I walked every morning.

On the site of the modern Palacio Nacional rose the palace of Moctezuma, where the emperor lived with his multitude of servants, guards, and councillors. Foremost among these was the

Aztec sacrifices do not appear to have been devised as torture, but as a means to produce copious hemorrhages. Surgeons today greatly fear the slightest accidental nick in the inferior vena cava. To suddenly rip this vein, and to tear at the same time the great vessels emerging from the heart, the aorta and the pulmonary artery and veins, would produce huge spurts of blood in seconds. This horrible fact inclines scholars to believe that the ritual was deliberately chosen by the Aztecs to secure the most dramatic and abundant of hemorrhages, in keeping with the need to spill the precious liquid that alone could ensure the fertility of the earth and abet the progress of the sun god's course. As his passage through the skies ended, he was believed to undertake a journey in the shadowy underworld, from which he would emerge daily—if properly assisted by his votaries—to inundate the world with light.

—F. Gonzalez-Crussi, *The Day of the Dead and Other Mortal Reflections*

Cihuacoatl, his majordomo and high priest, a man whose title meant "Woman Serpent" and whose feminine garb derived, perhaps, from the tradition of a recently deposed matriarchy.

There were houses for the dwarfs, the albinos, the beasts of the emperor. An aviary—with peacocks, hummingbirds, and pools—faced his palace, while behind it his pleasure gardens unfolded under the haze of the snow-capped volcanoes, Popocatepetl and Iztaccíhuatl. The emperor's title, the Tlatoani, meant "He of the Great Voice." His empire was built on conquest, sacrifice, exaction, legitimation through assimilation of the more ancient and respected culture of the Toltecs, and a profound sense of style, perpetually mixing horror and beauty.

The Spaniards did not recognize the aesthetic riches of the Indian world as much as its material ones. To the west of the square, the palace of Axayacatl held chambers entirely built of silver and gold. And to the south, canals opened onto this island city, an Indian Venice, on which canoes and barges bore the produce of the land to the market at Tlatelolco.

It was the oldest living city of the New World. The Aztecs founded it in 1325 at the end of their pilgrimage from the north. The site had been foreseen by their chief Tenoch: a lake with a rock in the middle, on the rock a cactus, and on the cactus an eagle devouring a serpent. They named the city Tenochtitlan after him. Actually the central square was not built until the 15th century, under the emperor Itzcoatl (1428-1440), making it an Indian urban ensemble coinciding with the European Gothic period.

This Indian world lived in fear. Its moral principles, inspired by Quetzalcoatl, taught the values of peace, concord, and education. Its state philosophy, dictated by Huitzilopochtli, demanded war, conquest, and human sacrifice. Quetzalcoatl had abandoned Mexico on a raft of serpents, sailing toward the east and saying that he would return one day to see how this land, created by the gods, had been attended to by men. Now the city, Tenochtitlan, was shaken by the winds of augury. The gods were about to return on a day forecast by the precise calendars of the Indians, who measured a cycle of 365 days before the Europeans did.

Like Quetzalcoatl, the gods would be white, blond, and bearded. They would also be mounted on four-legged beasts, they would fight with smoking arms, and they would wear armor of silver and stone. The exact coincidence of the arrival of the Spaniards with the prophecy of the return of Quetzalcoatl sealed the fate of Tenochtitlan. Led by Cortés, a band of a few hundred Spanish soldiers arrived in the imperial city in 1520. Moctezuma greeted Cortés as if he were a returning deity: "You have come back to your house. Now come and rest."

But the soldiers of Spain, in the name of their God, their King, and their own material appetites, refused the divinity offered to them. What they found, nevertheless, was enchantment. "What a marvelous place!" exclaims the chronicler of the conquest, Bernal Díaz del Castillo. "Never will a city such as this be discovered again." He rubs his eyes. The towers, the canals, the lake, the pyramids, the mountains, a square as large as Seville's: They resemble, writes Bernal Díaz, "the things of enchantment" told of in the

I can only imagine how the Indians felt when they were first confronted with the Spanish. Their first difficulty was deciding whether the Spanish were mortals or gods. In *The Conquest of America: The Question of the Other*, the French structuralist Tzvetan Todorov makes the interesting argument that this confusions varied in direct proportion to literacy. The Incas, who could not write at all, were convinced the Spanish were gods. The Aztecs, who had pictograms, initially thought that the Spanish were gods but soon changed their minds. The Maya, who could read and write, knew from the beginning that the Spanish were men. The Maya, therefore, were the most difficult to conquer.

—Peter Canby, *The Heart of The Sky: Travels Among the Maya*

medieval books of chivalry. He doubts whether all these things, "never seen before," can truly be told. They are told, beautifully. They are also destroyed, horribly. The marvels beheld by European eyes now are fallen, writes Bernal, "strewn, lifeless, destroyed forever." Enchantment went hand in hand with death. The symbols of colonial power—the new church, the new state, the cathedral, the crucifix, the Virgin, the viceroy's palace, the municipality, the moneylenders, the houses of the conquest—took over the sites of the Aztec city. Political legitimation demanded that the power of the conqueror be built on top of the defeated power of the conquered.

But the conquered, perhaps, were never truly defeated. A new Mexican society was born of the clash of the conquest. Catholicism became tinged with pagan rites. Baroque architecture was an open form into which the flora, fauna, and spirit of the Indian world crept. Vertical power under the Aztec emperors continued to be vertical power under the Spanish Habsburgs. But the horizontal life of food, dress, music, furniture, crafts, sexuality, song, perhaps even dream, was forever syncretic, mixed—part Indian, part Spanish.

So was the life of the square. A certain rhythm has marked its existence during both colonial and independent times: a tension between order and chaos. The latter is represented by the people, who constantly rush into the vast space of the *Zócalo* with toys, shawls, flowers, rockets, ceramics, refreshments, spicy foods. The former, by the authorities, who seek to clean the square up, restore its beauty and dignity. Time and again, the merchants, the peddlers, the singers, are expelled from what, after all, both the conquered and the conquerors see as a sacred ceremonial space—but also as the place of authority.

The cathedral takes a long time to be built. The first stone is laid in 1573; the twin towers are not completed until 1788. But children are born every day and seek the pleasure, the opportunity, the challenge of the city. The majesty of the architecture contrasts with the constant invasion of barracks, dogs, filth. The proliferating Third World city is constantly trying to overcome the stately see of power.

No one does more to bring order and symmetry to the *Zócalo* than Revillagigedo, Viceroy from 1789 to 1794. He expels the riffraff, sweeps away the garbage, paves the square, inaugurates the sewer system, covers up the foul-smelling canal left as the city dries up and loses its lakes. He tears down the gallows. But the fight goes on. The cathedral is surrounded by railings and chains. The palace looks like, and is, a fortress. The popular markets grow back. They are once more demolished. The square is twice named Plaza de la Constitución, first when the Mexicans swear allegiance to the Spanish charter of Cádiz in 1812 and once more after the revolution, in honor of the Mexican Constitution of 1917. But popularly it remains the *Zócalo*, "the foundation," the base for the monument to independence that was to be built there in 1840. It is never built; too many things happen. Independence is menaced, first by the United States, occupation of 1847; then by French invaders in 1862.

Balcony of our national history, the *Zócalo* also remained the witness to popular life. Musical kiosks were set up and torn away. Viceregal carriages gave way to mule-driven trams and then to automobiles. Typists wrote letters

Zócalo. One explanation for the derivation of the word is that in colonial Mexico, the period of Spanish rule, *zócalo* referred to the pedestal of a statue, and most statues, then, were of some conquering Spanish hero, a conquistador. All over Mexico, while these pedestals were waiting for their statues, appropriately placed on the main town square, the squares themselves became known as *zócalos*—as they are to this day.

—Alice Adams, *Mexico: Some Travels and Some Travelers There*

for the illiterate under the arcades.

All of this is part of the story of the oldest living square in the Americas. It has been leveled, consumed by fire, flooded. It has been the scene of throbbing popular manifestations, from the mutiny of 1692 protesting against food shortages, when the palace was set on fire, to the cannonades of the Ten Tragic Days of 1913 during the Mexican Revolution, to the demonstrations of students against a revolution grown complacent and institutionalized in 1968, to the celebrations of a new Mexican democracy being born in 1988. It all happened here, in the *Zócalo*.

> Mural painting is Mexico's greatest contribution to contemporary art. A cultural product of the Revolution, mural painting flourished in Mexico well into the 1950s. The work of Diego Rivera, David Alfaro Siqueiros and José Clemente Orozco astounded the world.
>
> Murals were painted in Mexico as far back as in pre-Columbian times, but the murals of the Revolution are something else again. They are explosive.
>
> —Kal Müller and Guillermo García-Oropeza, *Insight Guides Mexico*

Still, as I crossed it every morning as a young man in the 1950s, I thought that the marvelous Indian city that once existed here was lost forever. I believed that I walked over the ashes of a dead civilization. Then, in 1978, some municipal works uncovered the remains of the great *teocalli* under the square. There it all was. There they all were: the gods were only slumbering temporarily in their underground exile. The diggings uncovered the temples of Tlaloc and Huitzilopochtli. The red Chac Mools were there, gazing at us in their eternal Henry Moore poses. The burnt offerings of the last day of the empire were there: dried-up flowers in terra-cotta vases, skeletons of frogs. The wall of the serpents and the wall of skulls...there they were. There she was, the moon goddess, Coyolxauhqui, torn apart by her murderous brother Huitzilopochtli for demanding a second pregnancy for their mother, the Earth. The goddess—limbs ripped, breasts flayed, torso and head askew—is like a cubist vision of the divinity captured within the circle of a magnificent disk; a sculpture with a form comparable to that of the moon itself.

What I thought was dead had come back to life. I realized that while I had believed I was walking over the cemetery of a culture, the culture had been abiding under my feet. What I had trod upon was not the death but the mystery of a culture. I learned then that in Mexico nothing ever dies because nothing is ever condemned to death. The Mexican celebration of death is a manner of saying that all is life, including death.

Order and confusion, riches and poverty, power and freedom, gravity and joy, come together every year on the night of independence, September 15, when a million people pack the *Zócalo* to hear the president and wave the flag. I am now convinced that along with that multitude, on that evening, the gods are present, mocking our ceremonies, rubbing shoulders with the living, unrecognized because they, too, are a we, a plural embracing in the plaza, the meeting ground, the common place of Mexican history.

Carlos Fuentes is a novelist, analyst of contemporary Latin American politics, and one of Mexico's foremost authors. Among his many books are Where the Air is Clear, The Death of Artemio Cruz, A Change of Skin, *and* Distant Relations.

The Virgin of Guadalupe, to whose basilica in Mexico City thousands of pilgrims from all over the country walk and crawl at various times of the year, almost had to appear when she did. An Indian peasant boy, Juan Diego, saw her only a few years after the Conquest, at a time when Indians were submitting to conversion but scarcely in numbers large enough to constitute a mass movement toward Catholicism. The swarthy Virgin appeared to Juan at the place which reputedly held a temple to a local fertility goddess, and it was that spot on which a church was to be built. Juan was to tell the archbishop that she said so. The boy's report of the miracle and request was rejected several times; the friars wanted proof. Reporting back to the Virgin, he told her of his difficulties and she gave him miraculous proof: she caused masses of roses to bloom on the dry hill. He gathered them in his *serape* and dashed off to the monastery to show his miracle to the archbishop. On opening his cloak, they found, instead of the bouquet of roses, an image of the Virgin stamped on the coarse cloth. The story and the miracle of the dark-skinned Virgin induced more conversions, her church was soon built, and by papal decree in the 18th century, she became the guardian of all New Spain. The devotion to the Virgin of Guadalupe grew so great in time that Father Hidalgo used her image as his banner in the 1810 War of Independence and his troops called her name as a battle cry. Since then, and before, she has been called on to help in other battles, in plagues, in drought— whenever Indian-Mexican misery and fear needed a mother protectress.

—Kate Simon, *Mexico: Places and Pleasures*

PETER HELLER

Wild Baja

*The back roads and bays of Baja California are a paradise for
lovers of nature and solitude.*

We careen through the desert. The bus driver is reckless and the
desert is green. Between the giant cardon cacti the flinty ground is
covered with yellow flowers and thornbushes delicately flecked
with crimson. Guillermo Velasquez is amazed. He points out the window. "This orange flower, this is malva. She comes with all the rain."
Then he addresses the flowers themselves: "In thirteen years here I never
see you! Nice to meet you!"

We are on our way to go sea kayaking with whales in Magdalena
Bay. Guillermo is a professor of social science at the University of La
Paz, and a sometime trip leader for Baja Expeditions. He is a slight man
with a sparse beard who knows as well as anyone the ephemeral expressions of life, both past and present, of this dangling, eight hundred-mile
corridor of coasts, desert, and forested sierra. He has written scores of
papers on subjects ranging from the fishing techniques of Baja's now-vanished Guaicura people to the distribution of endemic mountain oak.

"Fifty thousand!" he says with passion. "This is how many Indians
were on the peninsula when Hernán Cortés arrived in 1535. How many
do you think exist now? None! In 1908 there were six old Pericu with no
descendants. Now there are none left. None."

We look out the window, out over the vast cactus plain and the
rugged mountains to the east brooding in haze—once the domain of the
Guaicura. The desert, it seems, has absorbed them, leaving only signs—
arrowheads and bones.

The descendants of Cortés have left signs too: in the bottom of a
deep gully rests a rusted automobile. By the road is a cross and a statue of
a semi truck, and a bouquet of plastic flowers.

The channel is silver and slick as mercury. One explosion, then two.
PPPAAUUOOWWHHH! The mist hangs over the water, refracting the
evening light into a band of amber, and the whale surfaces, her black
back humped and barnacled, her calf beside her, and then they are gone.
Farther out there is another blow.

Baja California is a fierce, sun-blasted land, a narrow strip of desert roughly 800 miles long that separated itself from the Mexican mainland in a slow tectonic slide about five million years ago. The Pacific Ocean rushed in to fill the void, forming the Gulf of California, the youngest of the world's deep-water gulfs. This vast arm of the Pacific, two miles deep at its mouth, was once known as the Vermilion Sea, and indeed, under a rising sun, the warm, tranquil water shimmers like pale blood.

The mountains are stark, ridged and crenellated and bare. The land supports a variety of obdurate and malicious flora: There are thistles underfoot and cardon cacti towering overhead. It is little given to agriculture or ranching. Every growing thing, or so it seems, sticks, stabs, or stinks. There are red-dirt roads branching off the paved road that bisects the peninsula and that was built to attract American tourists. The rutted secondary roads lead to dusty towns where generators provide electricity for two hours a day.

—Tim Cahill, "Good, Clean Fun in Baja," *Outside*

I had never seen a whale. Now they cruise so close to camp you could hit them with a pair of binoculars.

Our group, fourteen clients and six guide staff, is camped on a shore of endless sand, the protected inner side of one of the long barrier islands that form Magdalena Bay. The "bay" here is a narrow channel, no more than a mile across, which snakes for more than fifty miles between the stark dunes of the islands and the dense green mangrove of the coast. It is full of gray whales. In late January, they are just arriving in force, having swum 6,000 miles from the Bering Sea in only eight weeks. Once hunted to near-extinction (in the late 16th century there were 52 whaling ships operating in Magdalena Bay), they have prospered under several protective covenants, both national and international. Scientists believe that their population is back to pre-whaling levels of at least 20,000, and there is heated controversy over whether to relax their protection, which some fear could lead to renewed hunting.

The whales come south to breed. In the bay, the world's first whale refuge, they act distinctly at home. They nap on the surface like logjams. They mate, twenty tons of swirling passion, which roils the water and causes small waves to wash into the roots of the mangroves. They "spy-hop" suddenly, their wedge-shaped faces breaking ten feet into the air, presumably for a look around. Squadrons of pelicans glide single-file over their heads, sinking and rising in roller-coaster curves. Ibises and willets, stabbing the mud flats, ignore everyone. Dolphins loll in the shallows. It is a sea kayaker's paradise.

We get in our boats and paddle gingerly over the bay. On the first afternoon, Annie Coburn, a young mother and real estate agent, rests in her double kayak and looks apprehensively into the water.

"What's the matter?" I ask.

"Well," she says, "it's nothing. I just don't want to become a hood ornament."

Baja Expeditions, our hosts, do not want that either. They tell us that it is not polite to pursue a whale in a sea kayak. Whales can't hear you the way they can a small motor, and they can surface next to you and become disoriented and mad. So we use the kayaks to paddle to our next camp up the island, usually staying close to shore, and we do most of our whale watching from the motor skiffs that accompany our trip and carry all the gear and food.

For me, whale watching is an exhilarating and frustrating activity. A whale surfaces and blows, her twin jets making a cloud of mist the shape of a heart. She shows you a length of glossy back, which looks exactly like a slab of rock in a rainstorm. Maybe she lolls and reveals an edge of fin, a tip of fluke. Then she disappears. You circle on the water, blinking into your camera, trying to anticipate the next rise.

Even more frustrating is the desire to communicate. You know, you can feel it, that the whale is at least as intelligent as yourself. And she is much kinder: the last time an animal one-1,000th of your size buzzed around your head for a look, you swatted it flat. I wanted more than anything to jump in the water and swim with the whale,

Whales exhibit a number of behaviors to which humans, with their intense need to classify things, have attached quasi-scientific names. "Spyhopping" is when the whale, vertically aligned in the water, slowly extends her "nose" straight up, often six feet or more above the surface. "Bubble bursts" are underwater releases of air (or gas?). One of my favorites is "firkydoodeling," whale foreplay. In the intense winter tides that drain Magdalena Bay, the whales often play, diving and "breaching" (leaping clear of the water) with the help of the strong currents.

—Kent Madin, "Spyhopping and Firkydoodeling on Mag Bay," *Adventure West*

to talk in small musical bleeps about the meaning of everything. I wanted to apologize for people, and to tell her that despite our mistakes we were all brothers and sisters. Several years ago, Paul Winter and his Consort came to the bay and floated a huge transparent ball on the water. They got inside and played jazz to the whales. The whales did not seem to mind.

Ballena means whale in Spanish. It is also the name of Pacifico brand's liter-sized beer. There is a whale on the label, and an anchor. On our trip, if you wanted a Ballena you held your paddle vertically. The motor-boat promptly arrived. Miguel opened the bottle. It was ice cold and fit in your hand like a small whale.

As much as I am fascinated with the whales, I like our island just as much. Isla Magdalena. What a beautiful name. The island is made completely of sand. It humps in a chaotic sea of steep mounds, rippled by the wind, and over the mounds, and between them, are green mats of sand verbena, with succulent leaves and clusters of magenta flowers. In the deep troughs are clumps of a willow-like milkweed with creamy blossoms. There is a yellow flower I do not know, which looks like a mallow. The air has a smell of sweet flowers, very faint, mingling with the heavier scent of the sea.

On our second evening out, I run away from camp: there is only an hour of sky between the big sun and the furthest rim of dune, and I want to see the wide Pacific ocean, which I can hear, faintly, in pulses of wind. Also, our group has just started on a fresh-fruit rum punch, and Shelagh Doyle, an intensive-care nurse whose wit has been seared to the driest of ironies, is retelling a long, heavily accented French Canadian joke I told the night before, punctuating each beat with "Then you say that five or six times."

Barefoot, I thread the mounds and pass over the tops for a jump. The blond sand is covered with tracks. Coyote prints, smaller than the ones at home, run together, and make dark trammelings that contour and dip along the easiest routes. Rabbit tracks testify to dashes between bushes. A flurry of infinitesimal foot impressions and leaf fragments are the signs of a mouse chewing on an ice plant. A straight, mechanical line, stuttered like the track of a tiny tank, was left by a beetle. A snake, probably the island's endemic rattleless rattler, has slipped out of the verbena. Judging by the signs, nighttime must be a circus.

Somewhere in the middle of the island I drop into a hollow, and it is filled with seashells and the scattered bones of a deer.

I am beginning to get this sense about Baja: a lot of life here is beneath the surface. Now and then it peeks up and leaves a sign: an orange flower, an arrowhead; tracks, shell and bone; and then, like the whales, it vanishes.

The mounds are becoming steeper, more chaotic. They look like a Dr. Seuss landscape. Only their tops are fringed with vegetation, like a hundred crew cuts. The rush of surf is constant. The sun, molten orange, is very low. Suddenly, between two dunes, I see the Pacific.

Tier after tier of angry irregular surf breaks and piles in overlapping sheets of foam. The wide beach, scoured by the sea, stretches north and south in a haze of spray. The sand reverberates. The dark husk of a tree is the only distinct shape in all that immensity. It's sheer, inhuman wildness. Riveted, I stand at the edge of the beach. The wind comes flat off the waves. I feel like yelling with glee. I step across a band of pebbles scattered with shells and sand dollars, onto the wet sand of low tide, into the water. Down the beach is a single small coyote, moving away, insubstantial in the haze. He must be very thin: he stops to look back and he seems to be barely holding himself against the wind.

A week later, back on the Gulf of Mexico, in La Paz, about 150 miles southeast of Isla Magdalena, it rains so hard that the runoff gouges a five-foot-deep gully in the dirt street beside our favorite restaurant. There is very little organic soil here. Mostly it is sand, minerals, fine gravel, laid over a substratum of rock. When it rains, the water percolates quickly and runs into the sea. Consequently, Baja has had trouble supporting a large amount of successful agriculture, which is one reason the peninsula remains mostly primitive and the human population relatively sparse.

John Steinbeck, in his classic narrative *The Log From the Sea of Cortez*, describes a collecting trip he took in the Gulf of Mexico with his great friend the biologist Ed Ricketts in 1940. They went up and down the gulf in an old sardine boat, gathering and recording the life they found. Steinbeck describes how unbelievably rich in life the gulf is. Contributing to this biological clamor is a curious overlapping of tropical or "Panamic" fauna with species characteristic of the more northern coast.

What Steinbeck barely speaks of is the abundance of marine mammals. There are sea lions, and over twenty species of whales and dolphins have been seen in the Bay of La Paz alone. The gulf is the only place on Earth outside of St. Lawrence, Canada, where blue whales can be seen close to shore. One early morning, under a sky of breaking cloud banks, we cruise north out of the Bay of La Paz aboard the

> What was the shape and size and color and tone of this little expedition? We slipped into a new frame and grew to be a part of it, related in some subtle way to the reefs and beaches, related to the little animals, to the stirring waters and the warm brackish lagoons. This trip had dimension and tone. It was a thing whose boundaries seeped through itself and beyond into some time and space that was more than all the Gulf and more than all our lives. Our fingers turned over the stones and we saw life that was like our life.
>
> —John Steinbeck, *The Log From the Sea of Cortez*

dive boat Rio Rita, heading for a sea lion rookery on a rocky island. Tim Means is with us. He is the founder of Baja Expeditions, and one of Baja's most active and informed environmentalists. As we pass the burnt cliffs and green inlets of Espiritú Santo Island, Means speaks about his fears and hopes for the gulf. He is so concerned about the indiscriminate destruction caused by drift netting, he is using his own funds to buy up drift nets from fishers. Means is not a talkative person; it is often difficult to get him to say hello. But when he talks about the gulf, he loses his shyness. He says bluntly: "They're going to have outlaw drift netting, unless they want this to become the next Dead Sea."

Means sees the gulf as an extraordinary, unique opportunity for Mexico and the world. He'd like to see the entire Sea of Cortés become a sanctuary:

"That's the beauty about the whole Sea of Cortés. There are very few problems here compared to other areas, and the problems are very resolvable. There's not a lot of people around the seashore.... There's a real good chance something could happen here."

The scope of his concept is staggering—to take one of the richest seas in the world, a place with distinct land borders that has not yet been greatly affected by pollution, and manage it as a reserve. Means says, "The idea is to have a management plan that everyone agrees on, and that the local people can be proud of and support. A plan that people have a vested interest in. That's the only way it will work."

He points to the sagging fishing industry, which is becoming less and less profitable as species such as shrimp are fished out. He says many of the large shrimping boats could be replaced with small boats using special nets specific to shrimp, which wouldn't have other side-catch. This would take less toll on marine life and inject more money into the local economy, because large boats often run by big fishing cooperatives whose directors don't live in the area.

That afternoon, beneath a rock islet white with guano, I snorkel with a sea lion. My friend Billy and I are in the water a long time, beginning to shiver with cold, watching the animals soar by like F-15s. Suddenly I feel a tugging on my flipper. A small female sea lion has it in her mouth. Watching me with large dark eyes, she begins to shake it. Gingerly, not quite sure if this is real, I twist around and squeeze her tail. We circle slowly. Then we brake, and I reach out, and she takes my hand in her sharp teeth and gently mouths it.

I am no longer cold. I look over at Billy, and there is a pup playing with him. For a long time, for what seems like a day, the four of us turn somersaults, tug and brush, hold flippers, tails, hands. I forget to breathe and come up gasping. It is the first time in my life I forget I am a person.

A day later my professor friend Guillermo takes me to a small beach within the La Paz city limits. Some fifty yards from a construction site, he squats beside the water and nods. "Here he is. Come."

I look. Four inches under the lifting tide is the outline of a small human skeleton. It is a pre-Pericu Indian, beginning to calcify after 2,000 years.

We can hear the traffic in the street. Small yachts bob in the harbor.

I thought again about signs, about life glimpsed, vanished or vanishing. The same tide would be lifting in Magdalena Bay, where the fog would just be clearing, and the blows of the whales could be heard for half a mile. It would be creeping up the beach where I saw the coyote. In an hour, this skeleton would be barely noticeable under another few inches of water.

We would leave signs too. Right then, looking past Guillermo to a line of hotels by the water, I wished the signs we left might be so quiet: a shell, a stirring of water, bone.

Peter Heller is an avid kayaker and a professional river guide who has been on whitewater expeditions throughout the world. His writing about rivers occasionally crops up in magazines such as Outside *and* Paddler, *and he is the author of* Set Free in China: Sojourns on the Edge, *a book of stories about his rambles. He lives in Paonia, Colorado.*

My friend was getting married and I was in charge of the champagne. The altar was a patch of sand verbena at the base of a sand dune. The reception centered around a large fire complete with spitted goat. The dunes, the moonlight, the festivity, and the champagne all conspired to lead me to the water's edge, where, weaving pleasantly, I observed our skiff leaving, unattended, on the night tide.

I took pains to remove my sandals and cap, neglecting my wallet in my pocket, and took the plunge. On arriving at the skiff's bowline, I was immediately distracted by the fascinating patterns of bioluminescence that trailed off the rope, my hands, my whole body. Floating in the warm water, glowing like a firefly, I could hear around me the explosive exhalations and the sonorous inhalations of hundreds of whales as they dreamt leviathan dreams. Some produced an organ-like tone that would have made the Phantom of the Opera proud. Others were more breathy, some had a "hitch," and one seemed to produce two notes at once, a talent formerly only within the realm of Tibetan monks. Upon realizing I could no longer see the glow of the matrimonial campfire, but was beginning to pick up the sound of crashing surf, I scrambled aboard and started the outboard.

When the moon is full in Magdalena Bay, there is no horizon. The edge of the water blends seamlessly with the dunes and mangroves that define the shore. Racing back to the wedding, I could identify constellations from their reflections, so still was the bay's mirror surface. It was a singular moment; the moonlight, the warm air, the sensation of floating across a bottomless sky. With hardly a ripple, a tall, black wall arose from the watery stars in front of me. With no time to react, I watched dumbfounded, snapping my head around as I passed. At its base, a single huge eye, reflecting the moonlight, watched me skim past.

—Kent Madin, "Spyhopping and Firkydoodeling on Mag Bay," *Adventure West*

SHEPARD BARBASH

Machete Dream Carvers

The author delves into the lives and imaginations of woodcarvers in Oaxaca Valley.

M anuel Jimenez is every bit the difficult artist. He is by his own account one of the greatest geniuses the world has ever seen. A master woodcarver, he commands prices four times that of his most expensive competitors. A reformed alcoholic, he lives behind a wall topped with shards of glass that overwhelms the adobe huts and open dirt patios of his neighbors. He is a self-proclaimed faith healer and prophet, and is convinced the world will end with the end of the century.

"No one endured what I endured," Jimenez often says, "I suffered, but I robbed my destiny." Deprived of an education, he taught himself how to read. Deprived of land by his father, who beat him as a boy, he became the largest landowner in his village. Addicted for years to alcohol, two of his brothers already dead from drink, he stopped drinking entirely.

"Mine is a sacred history," he says. "I am not just anybody, I am a real tiger. I was born intelligent. Everyone here is living off my initiative. If I hadn't started carving, no one would be doing anything. I invented a whole tradition. They should make a statue of me in the plaza with an arrow pointing to the house and rename this street 'Jimenez Street.' For Jimenez will never die. I am like the sun in the sky. Oaxaca without Jimenez would not be Oaxaca."

To a point he is right. Jimenez has pioneered a renaissance of folk-art carving in the Oaxaca Valley in southern Mexico. Even he is surprised when he is told there are now two hundred families of carvers (including five Jimenez grandsons) and dozens of stores in Oaxaca that carry their work. The boom has converted poor villages of subsistence farmers and itinerant laborers into prosperous communities of artisans. It has brought isolated peasants into daily contact with tourists, merchants, and gallery owners from around the world. Above all, in the space of just a few years, Oaxaca woodcarving has become legitimized as an art form worthy of critical attention and exhibition.

"What you have in the carvings is an exuberance of form and color and detail that is simply irrepressible," says Maria Teresa Pomar, former director of the Museo Nacional de Artes e Industrias Populares in Mexico City and an authority on Mexican folk art.

Handmade with the crudest of tools, the carvings are at once bewitching and guileless. "You sense the person behind the object," says Marsha Bol, former curator of Latin American folk art for the Museum of International Folk Art in Santa Fe. "I don't want to use the words 'charming' and 'delightful' because that's what people always say about folk art and it misses what's going on; the work is very much based in the religious and everyday life of the people who make it. It's mysterious. At the same time, it's just so friendly and approachable."

The carvers' range of expression is enormous, their subject matter limitless, their technique often masterful. They carve cactus and kings, mermaids and devils, virgins and oxcarts, musicians and churches, Christ figures and skeletons. They make every animal known to Man and then some. They capture the immediate world of village life and the universal world of dreams. Naked, bird-headed women mingle with monsters, psychedelic cats, and San Isidro, patron saint of the peasantry. Fierce purple lions tower over dancing chickens. Many insist the carvers must eat hallucinogenic mushrooms. They don't—they just have active internal lives and fearless palettes.

Stretching out from the capital, the Oaxaca Valley nurtures an encyclopedic diversity of crafts, some of whose origins date back more than a thousand years. There is black pottery, serape weaving, basket weaving, tin,

M exican Market Goodies:

Cajeta: a liquid caramel with a burnt-sugar flavoring that is probably the most popular sweet eaten in Mexico. Popular as an ice cream, a sauce over ice cream, or just eaten directly from small wooden boxes found in candy stores and mercados everywhere.

Tamarindo: a sour snack eaten raw in pod form, or used to make a very popular sour candy and ice tea-type drink, which is the most popular non-alcoholic beverage in Mexico.

Pirulis: amazing candy umbrellas with a clear, mysterious consistency like glass. Three intense flavors in each. Eat slowly. Don't chew. When sucked slowly, the piruli will begin to pull and grow long—kind of like blowing glass.

Panocha: the Mexican equivalent of brown sugar with a sweet molasses taste, the panocha look like wierd little volcano-shaped lumps. Gnaw on it, as is, for a sugar buzz (don't break your teeth) or use it for cooking.

—Paula McDonald, "Tantalizing Trivia"

jewelry, and puppet making. For the Night of the Radishes, in December, Oaxacans carve elaborate scenes out of radishes. For funerals, they paint with sand. Few places offer a richer, more complicated variety of cultures. Vast and mountainous, the state of Oaxaca is home to sixteen linguistically distinct Indian tribes, who continue to survive within the country's dominant culture of Spanish-speaking *mestizos*.

History lives everywhere. The great Zapotec ruins of Monte Albán not only survive above the capital city, but grow, as pyramids are continually being unearthed and excavated. Archaeological surveys piece together ancient settlements throughout the state. One carver dug up a pre-Hispanic funerary urn in his backyard and now uses the hole as a barbecue pit. *Pelota mixteca*, a ball game ten times older than baseball, ranks behind only soccer and basketball in popularity among team sports. Hundreds of active Catholic churches—many of them more than 300 years old—stand as reminders that the Spaniards came, conquered, and, even after Mexico's independence, stayed on.

Most of the artisans now carving began within the past twelve years. Lacking the constraints of a long artistic tradition, they have been free to mine the region's creative heritage—its jumbled culture of Indian and Spanish, religious and commercial, foreign and local. Motifs seem to change monthly, driven by competition.

As with most folk art, quality varies as widely as the subject matter, from carver to carver, and within the cumulative work of an individual. The magic is often serendipitous. Artisans—they almost never refer to themselves as artists—are the first to admit that they don't always know why a piece is deemed good. If it sells, they say, it's good.

On the other hand, buyers who try to turn their suppliers into cheap, high-volume jobbers are often disappointed. Consistent, dependable, repetitious, these people are not. One jewelry-store owner from Vancouver, British Columbia, brought down five samples of Northwest Coast Indian art—sacred symbols from a distant world—and asked a carver to knock off one hundred of each. The jeweler even flew down an Indian artist to show him how. It didn't work. The carver got bored less than halfway through and began changing each piece just a little. He finally abandoned the order.

Buyers with more noble intentions are quick to discover that buying and selling Third World folk art is no easy business. Competition among dealers is intense, top-quality work is scarce, and shipping costs from *pueblo* to gallery are high. Retailers in the United States must generally charge four to five times what the carvers are paid just to stay in the black. The market for carvings also is confused and fragmented. They have sold at fancy galleries for up to $3,500 and at department stores for a lot less. They have been direct-mailed out of a catalog and sawed in half and marketed as napkin holders. They can be found in art museums and tacky border-town markets.

The emergence of this art form is easy to chart. Oaxacans have carved toys for children and masks for *fiestas* for 500 years. The style that dominates today, however, can be traced back to the irascible 71-year-old Manuel Jimenez from the tiny village of Arrazola. It was Jimenez who first used the wood that all the carvers now use, copal, after experimenting with a dozen others. It was Jimenez who took the tradition of miniature-toy making and gave his carvings a grander scale and finer execution, and who tackled more ambitious subject matter. It was Jimenez who, through his tremendous commercial success, established the international market.

It wasn't easy. For 35 years, Jimenez was among the poorest peasants in a very poor village. Settled tightly at the base of Monte Albán, Arrazola is a former sugar hacienda only now recovering from a century of serfdom. Jimenez herded goats as a boy, making models of his flock in clay. For twenty years he moved from one job to another—canecutter, mason, bandleader, barber. He carved masks to sell at Monte Albán. Finally, in 1957 he was discovered by an American living in Oaxaca, Arthur Train, who launched his career.

"I've never seen another like him," Train, who has since retired, says now. "The individuality of Jimenez is unique. You say 'Three Kings' and he can visualize them, and in his own way. In all the years I was here I ran into very few people whose work really expressed something of themselves as individuals. For Jimenez that was always true."

Ninety percent of the carvers live in three villages near Oaxaca—Arrazola, San Martin Tilcajete, and La Union Tejalapan. Since 1986 when sales first soared, these villages have been transformed. One in three families devotes some time to carving. Buoyed by their export art, dozens of carvers have built new houses, replacing adobe or bamboo with brick. Curiously, they choose not to leave their villages; their ties to their families and communities are too strong. The most successful have bought cars. Many more have bought farmland. A few have been flown to the United States to give demonstrations as honored guests of art galleries and museums.

In the rural areas of a country like Mexico, such success is phenomenal. Squeezed by inflation and recession, the average Mexican is poorer now than he was ten years ago. These carvers are at least twice as rich. A good one can earn several hundred new pesos (more than $100) per week—more than an elementary school teacher, and as much as some masons earn in a month. In a successful carver's family no one is idle; fathers and older sons carve, mothers and older daughters paint, young children and elders sand.

Eleven years ago, Epifanio Fuentes was an illegal alien. Five times he crossed the border into California and was jailed each time. On the sixth try he made it for the orange harvest, working for less than the minimum wage, just as his father had done before him. "There were people who hated us," Fuentes recalls. "It was best to be invisible, do your work and go home."

Fuentes, 43, a proud, intelligent man, has since become the most successful carver in San Martin. Father of seven, he is part of an extended family of ten carvers, including his father, a brother, an uncle and two sons. Last year, Fuentes and his wife, Laurencia, who paints his figures, were invited to the Heard Museum in Phoenix as distinguished visiting artists. This time, Fuentes was anything but invisible. After being introduced to the

museum's gala dinner crowd, he threw his arms up in the air like a prizefighter who had just won the heavyweight championship and then strutted around the stage like a cock. The crowd applauded.

To understand Fuentes' carving, it is important to go back to his village. Of the three carving villages, San Martin is by far the oldest, largest, and richest in communal tradition. Carvers proudly tell of their ancestors who paid tributes of corn and beans to build Monte Albán

---

Strict national laws prevent the exportation of genuine artifacts, pre-Columbian, from Mexico—laws that came much too late, after scandalous wholesale plundering of tombs; still, in the bushes surrounding Mount Albán there lurk rather scruffy-looking hawkers, with shards of pottery extended toward *gringos* (or Germans, or Mexican tourists, probably), along with loud whispered assurances that these are genuine, true artifacts from the ruins here at Monte Albán. Or from the tombs at Mitla.

We stayed there for quite a while, standing about and marveling, trying and failing to stretch our imaginations back to that ancient civilization, quite possibly three thousand years back, this piece of land that had been occupied by at least three groups, or tribes.

Each of these groups contributed many skillful and some inspired artisans of gold and ceramic objects, most of which were carted off, in one way or another. I myself remember as a child, sometime during the thirties, hearing about newspaper reports of fabulous discoverings of buried gold in Mexico.

Also, in theory, there are around ninety-two thousand ruins in and around Oaxaca that still remain unexplored.

—Alice Adams, *Mexico: Some Travels and Some Travelers There*

2,500 years before. Pottery shards dating from the 6th century B.C. have been found on the treeless hills outside of town, on land now abandoned by all but the ghosts of local legend. An 18th-century church rises six stories into the pure desert sky, visible from every home.

Mass is well attended; 99 percent of San Martin's 2,500 people are Catholic. Families are huge and intertwined. People born here usually marry, have families and die here. There are no celebrities, not even Fuentes. This is a united town. In the last statewide election there were 317 votes for Mexico's governing Institutional Revolutionary Party, zero for the opposition. No one protested.

A rich tradition of religious *fiestas* inspires and shapes a carver's sensibilities. *Fiestas* are the fullest expression of a Oaxacan's belief in the promise of magic, of fable, of something beyond death. Every *fiesta* is accompanied by the village band (Fuentes plays the trumpet), so carvers make musicians. Liquor is plentiful—alcoholism is rampant in the *pueblos*—so carvers make drunks. Every town celebrates its own manifestation of the Virgin Mary, so carvers make Marys. Ancestors come back on the Day of the Dead; carvers make skeletons.

Fuentes is renowned for his serene, robed angels, and his inspiration is not far away. Last year his 7-year-old daughter was chosen as the *madrina angel* (an intercessor), to parade on a float carrying a floral offering to the church. She had undergone surgery shortly after birth, which corrected—miraculously, according to her father—a crippling spinal defect. In gratitude he had put her name on the list to be a *madrina*; her name is—what else?—Angelica.

In San Martin, no one carves musicians better than the Xuana family, and no one carves better drunks, or drinks harder himself, than Adrian Xuana. Indeed Xuana's neighbors describe his exquisite drinking skeletons as self-portraits. At age 30, bored with his life in the village, he drinks and sings in the *cantinas* of Oaxaca, where he studies the musicians closely. Xuana's carved musicians are exuberant, hard-drinking, and comical. "People don't buy my work because it's good; they buy it because it's funny," he says.

Like the rest of rural Mexico, Oaxaca is a land rich in superstition. Goats are the devil, black dogs are good luck, snakebite cures rabies, mescal stops diarrhea, and skunk meat clears up acne. Witches and other temptresses inhabit the hills outside all three villages; there's a rock in San Martin that turns into a woman at noon. And if you don't think Adrian Xuana's grandfather could really fly, try telling that to Xuana. Fanciful carving comes not from mushrooms or mescal but from the carvers' simple willingness to imagine with extraordinary fecundity—a world less exhausting, dreary, and filled with death than their own.

"See these? These are people," says carver Ventura Fabian, who perhaps best fits the image of an eccentric folk artist. He holds up a pair of dancing chickens.

"They are not chickens, they are Nahuals," he says, ordinary peasants who can turn themselves into animals under a full moon. In Fabian's peculiarly private world, reality mixes with something less immediately verifiable. He lowers his voice as he cautions visitors that his niece who lives next door

A ny contact with the Mexican people, however brief, reveals that the ancient beliefs and customs are still in existence beneath Western forms. These still-living remains testify to the vitality of the pre-Cortesian cultures. And after the discoveries of archaeologists and historians it is no longer possible to refer to those societies as savage or primitive tribes. Over and above the fascination or horror they inspire in us, we must admit that when the Spaniards arrived in Mexico they found complete and refined civilizations.

—Octavio Paz, *The Labyrinth of Solitude and Other Writings*

is a witch. His figures are the weirdest, most crudely expressive of all. Alongside a thriving crafts industry, routine life in the *pueblos* of Oaxaca is dominated by the most elementary, physically demanding chores of survival. The three carving villages combined have no paved roads, no stoplights or road signs, no movie theater, no restaurant, no high school, no garbage pickup or sewage system. They have two telephones, a tiny agricultural surplus, and more farm animals than people.

La Union is a collection of adobe and bamboo huts spread thinly across a series of bare hills. Named in recognition of its inhabitants' knack for working together, La Union is the smallest, poorest, prettiest, and most remote of the three carving villages. Getting there entails crossing the same river three times, twice without benefit of a bridge.

There is only one full-time carver in the village, Jaime Santiago; the others divide the daylight hours between carving and farming on the scattered half-acre patches of corn, beans, squash, and alfalfa. The small landholdings are treasured because job opportunities away from the farm are scarce. The plows are pulled by bulls.

Santiago, 31, one of the most talented, versatile carvers in the valley, lives on a hillside overlooking the village. His house has no plumbing; he must carry water by bucket from a brackish stream. His wife, Reina, spends several hours a day cooking tortillas indoors over an acrid wood fire. The couple and their three children have no latrine. Their house, made of cement, was financed by the proceeds of his carving.

Santiago can afford to pay someone else to work his land, so he is considered something of a miracle worker by his fellow villagers. "I have always trusted in my good luck," he says, flashing a gold-toothed smile. He also works hard and efficiently—eight hours a day, six days a week, turning out 100 small, consistently good figures a month. A typical order from a client might include 20 lions, 30 tigers and 60 rabbits. For a less talented carver such quantities could spell disaster; but Santiago has the ability to give them all slightly different poses and expressions. His rabbits, bucktoothed, wide-eyed, poised to hop or hopping, are true cartoon personalities. Santiago's pieces are painted with water-based aniline dyes. Many carvers began with aniline—another Jimenez contribution—but switched to acrylic house paints after sales picked up and clients complained that the dyes faded. "They fade, but they don't hide the grain of the wood," Santiago responds. "Many of my buyers think aniline is more authentic."

Authenticity. Indigenousness. These are perplexing concepts when applied to Oaxaca woodcarving. Does it matter where the carvers get their ideas, or for whom they work? Is their talent diminished by the fact that it has always been practiced for foreign consumption, or that their craft is barely two generations old? Questions like these engage buyers, folklorists, and art historians. Happily, the artisans don't seem to care.

Miguel Santiago, 25, is one of Arrazola's finest carvers. He studies farm animals for hours. He watches dogs urinate and bay at the moon, or throws rocks at their feet to see how they move. But then he retreats to his studio-library to leaf through a ten-volume encyclopedia of the world's fauna. Some of his most graceful, realistic animals—the wild Saharan dog, for example—he has never seen, but he considers them no less "authentic" than the burros that bray outside his door. "I'm on my own, no one is teaching me, so I get my ideas from wherever I can," Santiago explains.

There are no restrictions on where the artisans can find inspiration. Three years ago Jesus Sosa of San Martin came down with a stubborn case of typhoid fever. For months he was too weak to work his regular job as an electrician, so he started carving. While waiting for his doctor's appointment he flipped through an illustrated brochure and opened to a page on amoebic dysentery; the pictures astonished him.

"I went home and started painting amoebas on my animals," Sosa recalls—and later, perhaps more appropriately, on his skeletons. The splotches have become smaller, finer, and more complicated since, but the basic motif remains the same, and it is vibrant. What's more, it sells. Thanks in large part to a pest that infects half the population of southern Mexico, Sosa is building his new two-story house.

Next door to Sosa, Coindo Melchor hit upon his best-seller, the mysterious, bird-headed women, in a paperback book on mythical figures. His son, Inocente, takes ideas from calendars, with beautiful results; another son, Jesus, gets his cows from live models kept ten yards from his bed. When Coindo is asked about the myth behind the bird women he makes, he doesn't know. He can barely read. Stolen or inspired, "an idea is simply an idea, and anyone can have one," Jaime Santiago says. "It is the artisan who must use talent to give it life, and that's the hard part."

The tools of the woodcarver are as simple as the inspiration is eclectic. Most of the work is done with machetes, and kitchen and pocket knives. The wood comes from the copal tree, hardwood that once grew in abundance on the hills around the Oaxaca Valley. "It was a fourth-class wood," good for nothing until carving came along, Epifanio Fuentes says.

Carvers cope with all kinds of hazards. When the copal is green it is soft and readily worked. It does not split easily and it sands to a smooth finish. Still, carving it is difficult. Adrian Xuana's brother, Abad, once sliced into his wrist and narrowly missed a vein, which popped up out of his arm. He pushed it back in, bandaged the wrist and resumed carving the next day. He was a novice at the time, he explains. Knives are filed daily, sometimes twice a day. The sharper the knife, the less likely the carver is to cut himself. Two liquids are recommended to staunch the bleeding in a nasty cut. One is gasoline (in Mexico it's usually leaded). The other is urine.

Once carved, a piece is adorned with the simplest of materials. Ventura Fabian cuts the hair off his 9-year old son to make his paintbrushes. He glues goat hair from his own herd down the backs of his wooden goats and pigs, and snaps off cactus spines for their teeth. Gabino Reyes of La Union uses pig hair for the tiny whiskers on his armadillos.

"Carving is in a peasant's blood," explains Alejandrino Fuentes, Epifanio's brother, a trained engineer who left his profession to carve. "A peasant carries his machete like a friend; it's indispensable. We use it to cut roots when we plow and clear paths when we need to. There's always a chance that you'll run into a snake. Or for that matter a Nahual or a witch, against whom a machete is considered the best defense.

The final ingredient in any crafts renaissance is a willing buyer. Natural talent notwithstanding, this boom has always been dealer-driven. Wholesalers have scoured the villages, bartering Reeboks and VCRs and cassette players for carved wooden figures, bringing in high-quality tools.

How long will it last, this serendipitous interplay of market forces and creative spirit. Some carvers, their sales declining, have already gone off to work illegally in the United States. Plenty remain successful, of course, and seem to have established enough of a following to insulate them from the market's inevitable ups and downs—some because they are especially talented, others because they sell cheap.

Still, the carvers are wary. The better ones have become more worldly in recent years, and they are working like there is no tomorrow. The Coindo Melchor family sometimes works all night, painting by candlelight after the electricity goes out, as it often does in the *pueblos*. Next door, Jesus Sosa frequently pulls all-nighters to finish his orders on schedule.

Like so many poorer Mexicans, Sosa has bounced through a long string of jobs, each one ending for reasons beyond his control. Since 1981 he has been an electrician, has worked on two government jobs, and has raised, slaughtered, and cooked pigs. He keeps bees. He was unemployed or underemployed for three years, until carving came along. Sosa is 33. "This work has been a blessing from God," he says, "but who knows how long it will last? That's why we have to work night and day. Frankly, I don't take a day of rest. We never stop working. While I sleep, my wife paints. I'm trying to finish my house. When the good times pass, when the buyers stop coming, I want to at least have the house."

Shepard Barbash is an author and former bureau chief in Mexico City for the Houston Chronicle. *His first book,* Oaxacan Woodcarving: The Magic in the Trees, *was published by Chronicle Books. His work has also appeared in* Smithsonian, *the* New York Times *and other publications. He currently covers real estate as a stringer for the* New York Times *in Atlanta.*

The majestic Tehuanas are now in Oaxaca's museum. Having spotted an American couple, they move toward them. Displacing the man with their bulk and might, they greet the woman and proceed to examine her. They feel the cloth of her dress, touch her hair, and discuss among them whether its color is natural or dyed; differ about the seemliness of so much lipstick, and as if she were a doll, turn her for a better look at the cut of her dress and hair style. After a leisured survey, suspecting that she might possibly be human and sentient, the eldest and largest asks here where she is from. She answers, "New York." Unimpressed, the Tehuana answers, "We're from Juchitán. We'll be in the market on Sunday. Come. Don't forget. Good-bye." They move off like ships in full sail.

—Kate Simon, *Mexico: Places and Pleasures*

DAVID FREIDEL

Rainmaker

*An archaeologist worries that his digging in ancient temples has upset a
community's spiritual balance, but his mind is eased by a shaman's ritual.*

T
he plains of Yaxuna in northern Yukatan are usually covered with a
green sea of waving maize plants and waist-high grasses in the
month of July. The temple-mountains of stone rubble rise skyward
like the gray, forested islands of a landlocked archipelago, but in the
summer of 1989, the sea had become a desert. Red dust jumped in small
puffs as I stumbled, heat-stupid, through the stunted weeds and stillborn
cornstalks from the June planting—the second failed planting of that
year. Stripped of its life-sustaining greenery, the plain was a maze of low
rock patterns, the homes and household lots of the ancient community's
farmers, warriors, craftsmen, and merchants. The earth, torn up by bur-
rowing iguanas, was littered with
the broken pottery trash from
two thousand years of habitation.
The shards glittered in the
relentless glare of midmorning. I
climbed the steep broken stairway of a temple pyramid and saw
two Maya farmers sweating over
thirty-pound chunks of quarried
stone at the bottom of the shallow square hole on the summit.
Torn from the earth two thousand years ago by their ancestors,
who bore them by tumpline from
nearby quarries and piled them
into platforms to raise the eyes and voices of kings and shamans to the
horizon above the tangled forest, the stones were being moved once
again by the muscle and will of Maya men, who were heaving them into
neat piles by the side of the pit. At the bottom of the pit, the men had
cleared away the rubble to reveal the summit of an earlier temple—a
mountain inside a mountain. Its stairway of brown-plastered masonry

Yucatán is where the Spanish first
encountered the Maya, and the very
name is a monument to the gulf that
existed between the two cultures. The Maya
called the peninsula *u luum ceh yetel ctuz*, "the
land of the deer and the currasow"; but
when the Spanish asked where they had
landed, the Maya are said to have responded, *"Ma c'ubuh than,"* "We don't understand
your language"—which became "Yucatán."

—Peter Canby, *The Heart of The Sky:
Travels Among the Maya*

disappeared under the rubble of the temple built on top of it. I jumped down and carefully brushed clean the surface of the floor so that I could stand on the ceremonial platform. Maya rulers had last stood there when the Maya civilization was new, centuries before the birth of Christ in an alien world far away. This was one of the first temple-mountains raised by the Maya in this northern country.

My exhilaration of discovery was tempered by worry as I struggled out of the pit and scanned the eastern horizon for the blue-black shadows of rain-yielding thunderheads. The cloud-borne *Chakob* were riding the wind, but they weren't coming our way. They were headed south toward the village of Santa Maria. No one around me had spoken of rain for some time; it had been days since the last sprinkle on the lands of Yaxuna.

"They held a *Ch'a-Chak* at Santa Maria yesterday. The shaman from K'ankabtz'onot came and they killed two deer for it," said a young villager.

Sometimes shamans perform *Ch'a-Chak* ceremonies for the tourists who throng to Yukatan to admire the temples. These rituals are supposed to call upon the ancient gods to bring rain. Here in Yaxuna, however, *Ch'a-Chakob* were a deadly serious business, a plea for relief from the drought that threatened the lives and well-being of my friends.

Drought was perfect working weather for my project, but it was catastrophe for the villagers who lived along the western edge of the ancient city around the ancient well of Yaxuna. Drought is a time when old tensions surface and chronic afflictions feel worse. It is a time to redress the balance between the people and their place in the world through communion with the unseen beings of the Otherworld. In the old days, said some of our workers, people could seek out wild honey in the high forest in times of drought and live on honey mixed with water to still the grumbling in their bellies and stretch their dwindling supplies of corn. Now the high forest is gone, cut down for lumber, cleared for farmland, and replaced by tangled young growth. Wild honey is hard to find.

The archaeologists working on the ancient site of Yaxuna were a part of that tension. We brought desperately needed wage work. Now that the stocks of seed corn were depleted, we brought money to buy new seed corn and money to buy corn to eat. We had divided up the work among as many families within the village as possible, scheduling the men in awkward three-day shifts during a field season when it would have been better for us to have the same men working longer stretches of days. We had brought the village some financial relief, but we had also dug into the temple-mountains, the dwellings of the old gods. Perhaps by upsetting them, we were bringing misfortune along with opportunity. We had a camp of thatched-roof native houses at the edge of the village where the ruins began, on land that belonged to everyone, lent to us by every family in Yaxuna. Because of all of these things, we were of the community—and we were part of its crisis.

Next door to us lived Don Pablo, the village h-men or "doer." He was joining in the common effort of the shamans from villages throughout the neighboring region by preparing a Ch'a-Chak ceremony to bring the rain gods to Yaxuna. Several nights earlier, he had come over to our household after dinner with Don Leocario, the mayor, to visit and to discuss the coming ceremony. But he had said nothing to us directly about this sacred work. I reminded him that we had

The trail was steep and slippery—a slick red clay over polished knobs of limestone. Along the sides of the trail you could see that even in the flat spots there was only an inch or two of topsoil over the clay. Nevertheless, halfway up the valley wall we came upon a *milpa*—one of the tiny fields in which from time immemorial, Maya farmers have grown the trinity of squash, beans, and corn.

For the Maya, *milpas* are more than simply their place of work. Among the Tzotzils *milpa* land is referred to as *hamalaltik* and represents a third category of space after *naetik* and *te'tik*. *Milpa* land is land reclaimed from nature, after the gods have been appeased and represents the collaboration between man and the gods that is the basis of life for the Maya. *Milpas* are scrupulously tended, kept clean. Even Maya who, for whatever reason, don't need corn, still make a *milpa*. It's considered an act of piety, something to honor the ancestors, something close to the Maya conception of self.

—Peter Canby, *The Heart of The Sky: Travels Among the Maya*

offered to help and asked what we could contribute. Since Don Pablo lives and works with people of modest means, his request that night, out of courtesy, was for small quantities of inexpensive things—two bottles of the cheapest rum, ten candles, ten bags of incense. I suggested that we might supply chickens as well, and he agreed that we could bring two live chickens for the ceremony.

Since Ch'a-Chak ceremonies are a community effort, the work and the materials were all contributed voluntarily. Don Pablo brought his knowledge, his prayers, and his sacred stones. The other men built the altar and dug the nearby fire pit where the sacred breads would be cooked. Their altar looked simple and improvised, a shaky table of poles held together with vines. During the ceremony, however, it would become the center of the cosmos. All the participants brought the dough

Maís (corn) has been cultivated in Mexico for about 4,000 years. It was worshipped as a sacred plant by the Aztecs and had various deities repesenting it. Reverence for corn can still be observed today: road-workers clearing brush from the shoulders of the highway will rarely whack down stalks of volunteer corn. The same is true of groundskeepers at public parks; it is not at all unusual to see corn growing in a downtown plaza or in the middle of a construction site.

—Carl Franz, *The People's to Guide to Mexico*

made with corn ground by their womenfolk for the sacred breads that are layered, like heaven and the underworld, on the altar, as well as the cooked meats, and the "wine" made from honey and "virgin water" from a deep natural well.

That day, while I was studying the ancient cityscape and presiding over our excavation in the temple-mountain, the ceremony was well underway in the woods at the far side of the village. Don Pablo and his helpers had set aside three days for the prayers and preparations. The following day, all the villagers and archaeologists together attended the climax of the *Ch'a-Chak* ritual and witnessed the legacy of thousands of years of Maya devotion and ritual knowledge. This is the *Ch'a-Chak*, the "Bring-Rain," ceremony.

Once we were assembled, Don Pablo began. With quiet dignity, he crouched down beside the altar and picked up a tin can nailed to a stick. Holding the handle of this homemade brazier, he rummaged in his pocket, pulled out a little bag of white powder—*pom*, dried fragrant tree sap— and sprinkled it on the coals that were burning inside the can. As the sweet smoke rose in billows, he raised his voice in prayer and began moving counterclockwise around the leafy green arbor of bound saplings and baby corn plants. The incense cloud undulated back and forth in the hot air.

Pitching his voice into a higher octave to show the proper respect, Don Pablo spoke softly to the *Chak* Lords, the rain gods. He circled around the tall, thin cross made of sticks that stood behind the altar and the four young men stationed at its four corners. These men were making the roaring sounds of thunder, *ruum-ruum-ruum*. They were clapping small wooden sabers and pistols together, and sprinkling fresh, clean water from little gourds onto the boys who crouched at their feet beside the corn plants of the arbor. The men embodied the *Chakob*, the boys were the frogs of the rainstorm. The boys chirped and croaked, "whoa-whoa" imitating the many night sounds that are heard when the land and the crops are sated with the rain they were trying to bring with this ritual.

As Don Pablo passed in front of the altar, he paused to pray more loudly, shaking the arching branches of the arbor the way the thunder shakes the roof of a house. He pulled on one of the six vines that radiated outward from the center of the arbor. Entranced, his eyes half closed, he raised his face heavenward and summoned the gods to save the crops of the farmers who stood anxiously around the altar observing him. The late-afternoon air hung heavy, still, and expectant over the fallow corn-field with its tangled thicket of new-growth trees. Clouds passed by above the treetops and suddenly everyone heard a distant rumble of thunder. Perhaps it would not come that day, but soon, they knew, the *Chakob* would bring back the rain. They had heard the *h-men's* prayers.

Every one of us, the men and boys of the village and the motley crew of American and Mexican archaeologists working nearby, was caught up in that moment. That hopeful rumble of thunder broke the tension caused by our hesitant, sympathetic attempt to believe and the mild embarrassment of the villagers caught between their faith in ancient knowledge and their aspirations to become "modern" people. Being present at this ceremony was like something glimpsed from the corner of your eye, something you're not really sure you've seen. For a brief time Don Pablo had gone a little beyond our view, into a place represented by an altar set with cooked breads, gourd cups of corn gruel, and magical stones. He talked to god in that place and god listened to him. Don Pablo is an *h-men*, a "doer," the shaman of his town.

Shamans are specialists in ecstasy, a state of grace that allows them to move freely beyond the ordinary world—beyond death itself—to deal directly with gods, demons, ancestors, and other unseen but potent beings. Shamanic ecstasy can last moments, hours, or even days, but the amount of time spent in trance is less important than the knowledge of its existence. As the spell broke and the villagers began joking, passing around drinks of honey wine, and doling out the feast of breads and chicken stew that had been sitting on the altar—we, the archaeologists, believed that we have at least tried to help our friends. By our presence, our goodwill, and our heartfelt desire to suspend our own belief, we had aided Don Pablo on his journey to ease the suffering of his village from the drought that burned their land.

On the surface Don Pablo appears an ordinary man, a farmer, robust and enormously energetic, with dark, intelligent eyes and a quick smile. Although he heard the calling rather late in life, he has walked the shaman's path for some years. Yet his journey did not begin with the dreams that called him to help his people. It began thousands of years ago, when human beings first conceived of a place beyond death inhabited by ancestors, spirits, and gods—the place between the worlds. To journey to that place in ecstasy and return alive is a very special talent, and shamanism is a special institution we humans have invented to harness that particular talent.

The idea we are asking you to entertain as you read is that this place, which the ancient Maya called Xibalba, the "place of awe," is real and palpable. It is real because millions of people over the millennia have believed it to be real, and have shaped their material environment to accommodate that reality. The Maya world we are entering is a world of living magic. There we will see the earth and the heavens through the eyes of educated Maya whose ceremonies reaffirm age-old ideas about how things work—ideas that have endured through a hundred generations to the present day. We come in search of the buried power and ruined knowledge of Don Pablo's predecessors, the sages and holy lords who ruled, divined, and taught in Don Pablo's world eons before the discovery of the Americas by Europeans.

Once we have discovered the rationales of the Maya—through the words and actions of the Maya themselves—it is our heartfelt belief that we will also discover a central truth: that Don Pablo's rickety altar of saplings erected in the parched woods, the ruined temples of Yaxuna built at the dawn of the Maya civilization, and the Castillo of Chich'en Itza raised in its final glory are essentially forms of the same thing. They are all symbols of the Creation of the cosmos. They are all instruments for accessing spiritual power from the creative act, and that power continues as a fundamentally human experience and responsibility. In this common purpose, they are signposts on the Maya road to reality stretching across the landscape of history.

> We drive south down the highway that leads eventually to Bacalar, Chetumal, and the frontier of Belize. Yellow butterflies, warming themselves on the hot tarmac, lift at our approach and blow like confetti around the truck.
>
> "I hate to see the little bodies crushed on the windscreen, but there's nothin' you can do about it. The Maya believe butterflies are the souls of the dead, you know. You can't convince them otherwise."
>
> —Ronald Wright, *Time Among the Maya: Travels in Belize, Guatemala and Mexico*

Maya kings and lords of old were shamans, but contemporary Maya shamans are not kings. Maya society has changed profoundly over the last three thousand years, especially since the arrival of Columbus and those who followed him. The Spanish conquerors and their descendants worked hard to destroy all vestiges of indigenous government, and they tried even harder to warp Maya belief to fit their own expectations. Under this pressure, the cultural reality of the Maya changed and adapted—but it endured. Just how much that reality has changed is a matter of intense interest to many anthropologists working with contemporary Maya, and historians working with archival records from the last five hundred years. The nature of these changes is even more important to a small but growing number of educated Maya, striving to understand their own historical roots.

Some scholars have presumed that the trauma of the Conquest destroyed most of indigenous Maya culture. From their point of view the rituals performed and the beliefs held by Don Pablo and his people are products of the colonial experience of Maya peasant farmers during the five centuries since the Conquest. We prefer the view of other scholars who perceive the Maya as adaptable and capable of absorbing and synthesizing new ideas into their vision of the cosmos. We recognize, of course, that Maya culture and cosmology have changed over the centuries. The world around them has surely changed. The Maya have experienced alterations in their physical environment with the introduction of new domesticated animals, new crops, and new ways of growing them. They have also experienced modifications in the material conditions of their lives through the appropriation of their lands, slavery, the bondage of the haciendas, the exploitation of wage labor, and the maintenance of rural poverty. Nevertheless, we believe that changes in the world of their actual experience caused by the arrival of the Spanish have been accommodated by their capacity to transform their models of the cosmos without destroying the basic structures of the models themselves.

Perhaps the most dramatic example of this kind of transformation is embodied in the Maya's adaptation of the Cross of Christ, the central symbol of European domination. The Maya promptly appropriated and reinterpreted the most Christian of all symbols by merging it with the World Tree of the Center, the *yax che'il kab*, as the Conquest period Yukatek Maya called it. The Christian cross became, quite literally, the pivot and pillar of their cosmos, just as the World Tree had been before. Anthropologist Evon Vogt often recalls with irony and amusement his discovery that the ostensible Christian piety that the present day Zinacanteco Maya of Chiapas display toward their wooden crosses is, in fact, a declaration of cultural autonomy from their oppressors. This, we believe, is how the Maya vision of the cosmos works. It is a dynamic model combining historical knowledge, myth, and the practical experience that is perpetually being recreated through ritual performance.

A significant number of pre-Columbian Maya ideas from the deep past have survived up into the present time. Maya cultures evince continuity particularly in their core ideas about the essential order of the cosmos, its patterns and purposes, and the place of human beings in it. Maya shamanism as a social institution has survived the last two and a half millennia because the shamans help their neighbors in their communities to recreate this view of reality over and over again—when they heal a sick child, or bless a new home, or renew the nurturing bonds between the inhabitants of this world and those of the Otherworld. Through participation in these rituals, the Maya, both exalted and ordinary, reaffirm their culture's deepest truths. It is no wonder, then, that when the Spanish arrived, the principal god of the Yukatek cosmos was Itzamna, the greatest shaman of all and the patron of his human counterparts.

Modern Maya live in a metaphysical, philosophical, and religious tradition bridging the ages, from the time of the Classic kings to the shamans and ritual leaders of today; from sovereign states of old with their huge royal capitals embracing tens of thousands to the villages and small towns that now encompass the lives of most Maya. The very persistence of these traditions implies that the Maya of antiquity were unified in their view of the world regardless of their station in life. A vision that embraces and accommodates social differences and inequalities has to be informed by a limited number of central ideas that everyone can comprehend. These ideas must be universal enough that all who adhere to the tradition conceive of themselves as belonging to one substance and nation through their shared understanding of the nature of reality. The great cultural and religious traditions of our contemporary world, among them Christianity, Judaism, Islam, Buddhism, Hinduism, and Confucianism, work in exactly this way. The pre-Columbian world of Middle America gave birth to a great universalizing tradition just as successful as that of the European Old World, and the Maya cultivated one of the most eloquent of its variants.

David Freidel is an archaeologist and author who wrote A Forest of Kings *with Linda Schele. They collaborated with Joy Parker to write* Maya Cosmos: Three Thousand Years on the Shaman's Path, *from which this piece is excerpted.*

Many people view the contemporary Maya as being in the process of absorption by the outside world. They see Maya villages as isolated outposts of pre-Columbian life gradually succumbing to modernity. The problem with this essentially gloomy perspective is that it assumes that the Maya are losing an isolation that they actually never had. Most colonial historians now agree that throughout their post-Conquest history, the Maya have been firmly in thrall to the outside economy and that village institutions that on the surface appear pre-Columbian owe at least their formal structures to the influence of the non-Maya world.

This distinction is important. In what might be referred to as the "dying-folk-culture" point of view, the Maya are an endangered species whose every small accommodation to the modern world is to be regretted. By contrast, if one looks at the Maya as a colonized people who have retained their institutions to meet the demands of the outside world, their culture can be regarded as a vital and even expanding one.

—Peter Canby, *The Heart of The Sky: Travels Among the Maya*

Para Servirle

The author explores a small but important part of the linguistic labyrinth.

T he language of public life essentially mirrors the language used by Mexicans in their day-to-day relationships. It is a language of formality in which endless subtleties can be hidden. Some ornate phrasing is used unconsciously. A child is taught to introduce himself by giving his name and adding *para servirle*, or "ready to serve you." A Mexican will refer to himself in the third person as *su servidor*, or "your servant." He will describe his own home as *su casa*, or "your house," to which a mumbled *gracias* is expected. But among close firends, the language is enormously flexible. There are words for all seasons, and talking—wittily and cynically—is what counts. (The *mitotero*—someone who literally creates myths or stories to inflate his own importance—is particularly mocked if he can be exposed.) Meaning is tucked between lines, in pauses, emphasis or intonation, even in odd sounds or gestures. Jokes are usually self-mocking or derogatory about Mexico in general, while close friends will constantly verbally joust with each other. Many words from *nahuatl*—the language of the Aztecs—have been assimilated into Spanish and carry special significance, while *jeux de mots*, biting sarcasms and sexual double entendres are scattered through conversation, with some highly charged words used in a dozen different ways.

One word in particular, *chingar*, dominates the vernacular of curses and serves almost as a pivot of the conversation of lower-class urban men. Meaning literally "to rape," its weighty significance has been traced to the Spanish conquistador's taking of the Indian woman who became the original *chingada*. The traditional Spanish expletive *hijo de puta*, or "son of a whore," therefore became in Mexico *hijo de la chingada*, or "son of a raped woman." Endless variations on the concept have since emerged. The climactic insult of *chinga tu madre*, or "rape your mother," is invariably a prelude to violence, while *vete a la chingada* is the local variant of "go to hell." A *chingadazo* is a heavy physical blow and a *chingadera* is a dirty trick. A Mexican can warn, jokingly or threateningly, *no chingues*, meaning "don't annoy me," and if he loses out in some way, he will admit that *me chingaron*. It is high praise to describe someone as *chingón*—that is, he is clever enough to *chingar* others—although an irritating person is *chingaquedito*.

Many words are juggled with a similar spectrum of meanings, although few more than *madre*, or mother, rich in pyschosexual and religious connotations. *Nuestra madre* refers to the Virgin Mary, yet puzzlingly, the word is usually used negatively. The insult of *chinga tu madre* can be reduced to *tu madre* with little loss of intensity, while *una madre* can mean something is unimportant and *un desmadre* converts a situation into chaos. A *madrazo* is a heavy blow, a *madreador* is a bouncer or hired thug and *partir la madre*—to "divide" the mother—means to shatter someone or something. A person with *poca madre*—"little mother"—is without shame, *a toda madre* is equivalent to a superlative and *me vale madre*—literally, "it is worth mother to me"—means "I don't give a damn." A son will use the diminutive form *madrecita* to address his own mother, *mamacita* is a vulgar sreet comment to a passing girl or a term of endearment for a mistress. In contrast, the father figure—*el padre*—plays a lesser linguistic role. A *padrote*, or "big father," is a pimp, while something that is excellent is *muy padre*. Perplexingly, a mother will call her young boy *papito*, "little father," and her husband *mi hijo*, "my son." In these endless linguistic contortions, the Mexican's fascination with detail and obsession with nuance are constantly satisfied.

Alan Riding was born in Brazil and educated in England. In 1971 he began his career as a correspondent in Latin America—based chiefly in Mexico City—for publications including the Financial Times *and the* Economist. *He was the Mexico bureau chief for the* New York Times *from 1984-1989, and is currently based in Paris.*

Mexico was memory—not mine. Mexico was mysteriously both he and she, like this, like my parents' bed. And over my parents' bed floated the Virgin of Guadalupe in a dime-store frame. In its most potent guise, Mexico was a mother like this queen. Her lips curved like a little boat. *Tú. Tú.* The suspirate vowel. *Tú.* The ruby pendant. The lemon tree. The song of the dove. Breathed through the nose, perched on the lips.

—Richard Rodriguez, *Days of Obligation: An Argument with My Mexican Father*

Jim Conrad

Pig in the Rain

A pig can teach you a thing or two about yourself.

With the road above El Madroño washed out after five days and nights of hard rain, and the whole town without electricity because of a fallen pine, I stand at the door of the half-finished store watching the rain come down. Today I'm heading farther up the road, rain or no rain. The temperature has dropped to fifty-five so surely that signals the approach of cool, dry weather. Before strapping on my backpack, I notice a pig standing beside the highway in front of the store.

The pig has been rooting in the grass, but right now it's just standing with its legs straddled, looking up into the sky, sniffing. A large mat of red dirt and uprooted grass lie on tip of its snout, so that it must see the sky through a blurred network of disorganized grass stems and leaves. The pig's inch-long, reddish brown hair, looking like filthy bristles of a hairbrush used for a very long time without being cleaned, is matted with gummy dirt and miscellaneous dark debris; silvery globes of water hang suspended among the bristles. Maybe I have never seen a creature so thoroughly enmeshed in what it's doing.

Even I smell the morning's mud, hot tortillas, beans and coffee, human and chicken and pig manures, wet sawdust from the mill up the road, lingering diesel fumes from the last bus that passed by, and a certain sweet-mint odor that always I smell in high mountains, whether in the Alps, the Andes, or the Rockies. What must that pig smell, there in the rain?

The toilets here are built so that wandering pigs may easily pass beneath the seat-holes and eat what's been deposited there by humans. Seeing this, and then later eating those same pigs, El Madroño's children must early acquire a certain profound and practical insight into such fundamental elements of ecology as nutrient cycling, energy flow through the ecosystem, and predator-prey relationships. Who knows how the pig's sense of reality is affected by its daily perspective there beneath those holes?

Today I feel like a pig—a pig that roots superficially into whatever comes along, digests what it can, then moves along. For the truth is that today I am leaving El Madroño not because I really sense that the rain is about to end—it's already intensified since dawn—but because something about the friendliness, generosity, and loveliness of this town's people unnerves me.

Since establishing myself in this unfinished store beside the highway I have received an unending train of invitations to coffee, and hardly ever have I been without someone to talk to. Perhaps because of their poverty and life of struggle, everyone I meet, even the children, has a sharply developed personality, with all the good and bad aspects and every emotion out where it can be seen. We *gringos* are bland and homogeneous by comparison.

I should be writing about this wide-spreading bouquet of people, but instead I write about a pig; I should be human enough that now I would need to stay longer, but, instead, I leave now, like the pig in the rain, who—when he sees me watching him—abruptly ambles away.

Jim Conrad, a native of Kentucky, is a naturalist and author who meditates in Mexico whenever possible. This selection was excerpted from his book, On the Road to Tetlama: Mexican Adventures of a Wandering Naturalist. *He is also the author of* The Maya Road: Mexico, Belize, Guatemala, *from Bradt Publications.*

At dawn the next morning I decided to spend the day in the mountains. I figured that Aldous Huxley, one of my boyhood heroes, who used to hang out at the Rancho La Puerta health spa in Tecate, would have done the same thing. I took my binoculars, an orange, a hard-boiled egg, and a one-ounce bottle of Tabasco for the egg.

Four hours into the mountains I ate the egg and the orange. I was seated downwind from a bobcat cave, hoping for a sighting but knowing it was doubtful until just before dark. The cave had a dank, overpowering feline odor similar, I imagined, to that of the basement of a thousand-year-old Chinese whorehouse (the visionary propensities of hunger!).

Then out of the chaparral appeared a tough, ragged-looking Mexican who asked me if I had anything to eat. I said no, wishing I had saved the orange. He smiled, bowed, and continued scampering up Mt. Cuchama, presumably toward the United States and the pursuit of happiness, including something to eat. He had chosen the most difficult route imaginable, and I followed his progress with the binoculars, deciding that not one of the Rancho's fitness buffs, including the instructors, could have managed the mountain at that speed.

I didn't feel the couch liberal's guilt over not having saved the orange for him, just plain Midwestern Christian guilt. In my deranged state I thought that maybe the guy was Jesus, and I had denied him the orange!

—Jim Harrison, "Hunger Real and Unreal," *Just Before Dark: Collected Nonfiction*

CHARLES BOWDEN

The Wedding and the Land

The meaning of life waits to be rediscovered, out there in the Mexican campo.

T he town is ready for the night. The dress has come from Tijuana and costs six hundred dollars. The band has been hired, the cattlemen's hall rented. Vendors of *tacos, elotes, exquisitos,* and *chicharrones* line the street in front of the building. There are fifteen sons and daughters and very little money. The old man works for twenty-two dollars a week, his son shovels cement and makes ten dollars a day, and so forth. But this is different, this is the wedding, the youngest daughter is being married, and a celebration is in order.

The family rises to the occasion. The old man with fifteen sons and daughters cries at the ceremony. He is wearing new bedroom slippers instead of his usual *huaraches.* And then the event shifts into another gear. Hundreds stream into the reception, the bride enters with her maids, and the band strikes up a number that sounds like the bump and grind of a burlesque hall. The maid of honor wears a black dress with a plunging neckline, a large black hat, and dark eyes that say yes, yes, yes. She never smiles, she hardly can. After all, she is a goddess tonight. One glance from her could break a man's heart, grind up his bones to dust, destroy his dreams, and leave him a spent shell empty of blood. The men are dressed in their very best jeans, their best belts, their cleanest shirts, and all wear polished boots. The young women are shimmering clouds of satin, their faces masks. It will take hours and hours. By the early morning, the drinking will have taken hold and there will be a few fights. The dancing, well, the dancing will say what is on everyone's mind. Everyone will want to touch someone else, to be held, to hold, to taste, dream, believe. We will all be as helpless as insects before a blooming flower, drawn in further and further. Don't tell me about the senseless waste of money on this *fiesta.* Shut up about demographics, overpopulation, infant mortality, malnutrition, death, dying, doom. No one here, thank God, will listen. See those lips, hear that beat. The breast swells, the child hungers for the milk, the night wraps around like velvet.

No one is poor tonight. No one at midnight fears the morning. No one doubts anything. Perhaps, no one thinks. Can we truly be that

> Our poverty can be measured by the frequency and luxuriousness of our holidays.
>
> —Octavio Paz, *The Labyrinth of Solitude and Other Writings*

lucky? At times it is impossible to grasp fully the poverty of the people of the forest. And at times it is impossible to believe in the poverty of the people of the forest. Of course, nothing that is happening tonight is new. I am grateful for that fact. This is now, tomorrow, the day after. It is in the blood. But we often forget that fact, forget the blood. We forget the deeper promptings that make us what we truly are. And that is when we are truly poor.

The *metate* lies by my foot, a dark, rock slab busted in half. There are pieces of pottery, worked edges of stone—over there is a *mano*. All around me is scattered the debris of an earlier people, the stamp of an earlier time. I am with a friend down by the Río Cuchujaqui and this is his land, his *rancho*. For an hour we have hopped on boulders across streams, waded under giant *sabinos*, watched butterflies flutter past our eyes. In town, he is a reserved man, a serious man given to business. In town, he always speaks very carefully, as befits a man of his position. He is in his forties, his town house is splendid, and often he sits there watching the Los Angeles Dodgers play, the image sucked down from the heavens by his satellite dish. But out here, he bounds about like a child, with *huaraches* on his feet, and every time I touch a plant he instantly supplies a name, tells of a use. It is almost like he is introducing me to old friends.

He asks if I want the *metate*. Ah, the taking, the collecting, that demon deep within me, within us all. We must take to prove we have been there. We loot to assure ourselves it has all happened, to show others where we have gone and who we have been. I am tempted, but I say no. On my patio, the *metate* will be a stone. In time, I will forget exactly where I found it. And then in more time, I will forget that I even have it. Here it still whispers of a world.

I am learning, slowly to be sure, but I am learning. My friend is part of what many consider the problem. His land by the river, it is not what we call natural. There is very little understory because his cattle eat it. They devour the homes of insects, the sanctuaries of birds. They befoul the waters that shelter endangered species of fish. They live off his land. And these steers are so damn tame. They come up to us out of the forest like dogs, pushing their heads toward us. He smiles, and explains that they want salt, that usually he carries salt for them and they eat it from his hand. They also munch down all those plants he keeps telling me about, those plants that make a dye, or cure a bad stomach, or fight a cold. He points and plucks up what looks to me like an undistinguished weed. This plant, he says, is excellent for clearing the sinuses, but only the young growing tips, he laughs. Take too much, he warns, and it can make you very ill, it can kill you. How did he learn the proper amount for a cure, I ask. Oh, he says, from his mother.

Besides this constant feeding by his cattle on the forest, he cuts large swathes of the trees down for planting the buffel grass, that South African import. The grass lingers, he says, for about ten years and then its energy is spent, the land must be butchered again, and new seed cast. From this effort comes calves and they are shipped to the United States and go to feedlots. There they eat grain for a short while, and then they go to the slaughter house and onto my table.

Against these simple economic facts, there are the butterflies. Yesterday some friends of mine who are experts in these matters identified fifty-six species in one February day. When they told me this, I felt like a blind man. I could at most notice a half dozen, some white ones, some yellow ones, a black one, some orange ones. But fifty-six? Obviously, I do not know what is going on around me. The butterfly experts told me that in the summer after the rains, they probably could find ninety species in a day.

As I look down at the *metate* with my friend, a zebra butterfly floats by, its big wings black and yellow. They tend to fly in groups in a kind of single file, each one following the leader. Two things about them are unknown. No one has figured out if the leadership of the flight changes. And no one knows why they follow each other. Well, I can feel some sympathy for them. I am barging about the forest, following a whole bunch of leaders, and I'm not sure why and I'm not sure who exactly gets to be the leader. My first impulse in this place is to save it. I am stuffed with phrases like endangered species, ecosystems, balance of nature, carrying capacity, and the like. And I've got facts and figures to back up all this babble. When I fly over this forest, I see impending ruin. Big chunks are missing. Peasants on the *ejidos* slaughter everything. Ranchers like my friend consult experts, and then take huge patches. Up higher in the sierra, international banks finance a lumber industry that obliterates ancient forests. This is like every other place on a planet of about six billion human beings.

I say none of this to my friend. I doubt it would be news to him. We walk on, cross a small river, cut under a big fig tree, and climb up a hill. I ask him, as we stumble on, if those younger than himself, if the genera-

And so, more or less as middle-class Mexicans do, we each gave small amounts (or secret large ones) to most of the beggars we passed.

I had a most curious encounter, in that way: I was bending down to hand a painfully twisted woman some money (she was so dark and infinitely wrinkled, although she could have been about my age) when I slipped on something, and I would have fallen to the sidewalk, except that a strong, firm hand was extended to me, restoring my balance. Her hand. I thanked her and dropped the money onto her lap, and then she thanked me, and then back and forth we thanked each other for several minutes. It was almost funny. Almost.

—Alice Adams, *Mexico: Some Travels and Some Travelers There*

tion growing up, will know the plants as he does, know the uses and methods of the forest like he does. "No," he says, with no apparent problem, "they will learn other things. Perhaps, better things."

Then we reach the bench above the river. Here he has built a *jacal*, a thatched-roof *ramada* without walls. He tells me that he comes out here to think. He pauses and says, "If I lose everything, I could still come out here to this land and I could survive." I know he means it. When he was a child, he used to walk 37 miles into town. His village was against the sierra and Tarahumara Indians would come down to trade. I have been to his native village and it is still a place a couple of centuries away from his satellite dish and house in town. I sit under his *jacal* and drink a cold beer. I hear his voice saying that here he could survive. I believe him and I know that left to the same ground I would die, my stomach growling from its exquisite diet of ecological truisms.

I have no answers and for that I am grateful. The answers, I know, belong to the past. They are very tired answers about leaving nothing but my footprints, about not making fires, never leaving litter, never straying from marked trails, and carefully burying my feces. Answers that say pack everything out, and stay in designated camping areas. They are answers of pure mind and tell me nothing in this forest of the flesh. The future, if there is to be one, must find new answers. Maybe the beer helps. As we sit there and listen to the flies buzz, I ask him if he sees many deer. While we were walking, I saw some fresh tracks in the sand by the river. He slowly smiles and tells me that a couple of Indians look after his ranch and they shoot everything they see. And then he says, I can come out anytime I want and camp here. I thank him. Because I would rather be here than in a national park. When I listen closely, I can hear past the flies buzzing and what I catch is a faint cry of the future. A place where if there is to be a forest, we will be in it. All we get to decide is if our presence is for better or worse.

Of course, there are other days. Sometimes I climb high into the sierra and go up canyons where the cows cannot follow. The way will be blocked by huge boulders, cliffs, hard scrambles where I fear falling. I find pristine waterfalls splashing into deep, clear pools, orchids clinging to rocks within easy reach of my hand. On the cliff above, amapas bloom and rare cacti obstinately make a home. I climb up on a huge boulder and find *Ectinocereus gentyi,* a species Howard Scott Gentry first discovered in the '30s and one I have never found growing in the wild before. I become wildly excited and then I look over and see other specimens growing on a cliff, strands of it two- or three-feet long hanging down like spaghetti as thick as my fingers. A hummingbird roars past my head, magpie jays cry out and watch me from a tree, and God, I want nothing here ever to change, not a leaf or a pebble. I want the place declared an international treasure and after I leave it today, I will blow up the mouth of the canyon, hiding it forever the way the early Jesuit fathers are rumored to have hidden their precious (and mythical) gold and silver mines. I will keep this place safe from, from...from what?

From my mouth, from my teeth, from my alimentary canal? From all the others just like me who would like to be here? From the six billion of my own species? From the guy I know in town who collects odd plants and sells them to Americans? From the scientists who will insist on collecting something or the other? From the fireplace where I like to sit with a glass of wine in the evening and watch the flames lick the wood of the forest? From the photographers who will follow my footsteps and spend hundreds of dollars on film and on chemical processing in order to capture these precious moments of that thing we call wilderness? From the all but extinct wolf that is no longer at my door?

A while back I was having a drink on the roof of a restaurant in a small town further south in this same forest. It is a town almost no one goes to, a colonial town that time and tourism has forgotten. In the narrow cobblestone street below, a funeral procession filed past with a couple of hundred people dressed in black and on foot following the coffin to the *campo santo* on the edge of town. Another American suddenly came out onto the roof—ah, no place is far enough!—and we drank and talked. He said he was from California and one day he read a book and it changed his life. The book said that if one were willing to live on fifty to seventy-five dollars a day, one could live anywhere in the Third World. So he was looking, and had just driven into this isolated town. I swallowed my glass of wine, and did a quick computation in my head, and thought, my God, he's trying to pare his life down to between eighteen and twenty-seven thousand dollars a year. Most of the people I know in the forest make, if they are lucky, five bucks a day and the truly lucky ones make say ten dollars a day. From this they fabricate a world, complete with love, failure, birth, and death. There is a good deal of music also. And they eat everything they can find.

I mean eat it. Once a friend of mine was driving in the forest and found a man walking with a dead *coati mundi* (a raccoon-like animal) dangling from one hand. My friend stopped and asked the man what he was going to do with it. He said the meat was very good for *tacos*. So I listened to the American describe his new frugal future with a good deal of scorn, the cheap kind of scorn we all gleefully indulge in. But I was no different than he was. It takes a king's ransom just to keep me rolling in the manner to which I have become accustomed. When I am sitting in my secret canyon with the rare cacti and the orchids and the pure pools under the waterfalls, I look at birds through binoculars that cost three hundred dollars. I pull them from my two hundred-dollar backpack. And so forth. I can't say that I feel guilty about spending this kind of money. Like everybody I know, I figure I am just getting by, walking lightly, and barely making it. And I am not likely to change of my own volition any more than the people I know in the forest are going to change of their own volition.

We need new answers and our old answers only get in the way. They are like those Sabbath values 19th-century writers like Mark Twain always made fun of—pieties we tell others but that we make sure do not confine our own lives and habits. We've got a pantry full of junked words like progress, development, capitalism, communism, industrialism, and environmentalism, and, if we really get desperate, we haul out that old favorite, lifestyle. We prefer this rhetoric to facing a rather simple problem: in a world where almost everyone is poor, our species takes things faster than they are replaced. And whether one heads into the forest with a machete or a two-hundred-dollar backpack, this simple fact does not change.

Always, I leave my secret canyon and descend back into my comforts. I come down the mountain on a trail carved deep into the rock by centuries of burros going to and fro. I walk under huge trees, carefully skirt giant cacti, catch now and then the flash of orioles in the canopy of green, and once in a while see a trogon. The sound of rushing water always makes my heart light, and when I get lower I take pleasure in the small corn fields and stone walls that chew small bits of the forest. I look at them and smell fresh tortillas hot off the *comal*. I go past the shrine to the Virgin, negotiate with cows coming up the trail, and finally cross a stream and come out at a small public park on the edge of town. It is usually by then afternoon and the heat is on.

One day I find a couple camping in a van. They hail me, and offer a cold beer. They have been in town, they say, for two days and not yet left this small patch against the mountain, have not yet even ventured the half mile or so to the plaza. The man is in his sixties, the woman younger. They came in during the night, they say, and are looking for a place to live in Mexico. As they drove up the rutted dirt road to the park in the night, they tell me, suddenly a Mexican man dressed in a white sheet stood before their headlights with a huge flagon of beer. He invited them to his house for a drink and then took them to the campsite. They had brought clams from the coast and they gave them to him. As I drain my beer and listen, their story begins to leap and bound and lose the annoying logic that we so depend upon. The next morning, they continue, they met a man who lives in a small house near the park. He had just had six teeth extracted and invited them to park at his place. Then he consulted with his daughters, and offered them free a small hut down the road as a home for a few weeks while they looked for a permanent house. They went to inspect it and as they stood in the back yard the man they had met that first night came to the patio wall of the adjoining house, and handed over a platter of *paella*, a rice dish he had made from their clams. A feeling of magic to be sure. They were moving in that afternoon.

The Mexican man who has had six teeth just extracted comes over with one of his daughters and we exchange greetings. I am very tired from my hike. My head is full of rare cacti, plump orchids, a platter of food handed over the wall, the clatter of first worlds, second worlds, third worlds. The heat is on and the cold beer tastes very good.

Later I realize I have missed what is right before my eyes. The man who finds the American couple a free house, he owns no house. He is in his fort and he

The endurance of Mexico may be attributed to the realm of *tú*, wherein the family, the village, is held in immutable suspension; whereby the city—the government—is held in contempt.

Mexicans will remember this century as the century of loss. The land of Mexico will not sustain Mexicans. For generations, from Mexico City, came promises of land reform. *The land will be yours.*

What more seductive promise could there be to a nation haunted by the memory of dispossession?

The city broke most of its promises.

—Richard Rodriguez, *Days of Obligation: An Argument With My Mexican Father*

has never for a single instant owned a square foot of this earth. I learn this fact in a rather simple way: one morning I get up, and just down the road find that two hundred of the desperately poor families in town have seized and occupied twenty idle acres that happen to be owned by a Mexican friend of mine. The man with the six extracted teeth is one of the soldiers in this invasion. Then I learn that my neighbor two doors down, a schoolteacher, is one of the leaders of this land seizure—he too has never owned house or a patch of dirt. The families that move onto the land throw up a few *jacales* made of sticks and plastic garbage bags, wield machetes, and seemingly overnight clear the ground of brush. Then they divide it all up into lots, each twenty-five meters by fifteen meters. The government hesitates, then agrees to buy the land from my friend and sell it with long-term mortgages to the families. Such an expropriation by the poor has never happened in the town before, at least not since the bloody revolution between 1910 and 1920.

I go with my schoolteacher neighbor to the land for the big day, the day the lots are assigned by a drawing. There are 153 lots and these are not enough for all the poor who want a home. They stand under a *ramada* on the cleared land around a battered kitchen table with a huge hole in it. A glass gallon jar with folded pieces of paper rests on the table top. It is 11 a.m. and the heat and stillness of the day have fallen with weight on everyone's shoulders. People press in closely, the men hiding their nervousness behind their passive faces, the women willing to be more openly anxious, some even smoking in public. Many of the people are short and dark. A name is called and a man steps forward, reaches into the jar, pulls a slip, hands it to a clerk, and his lot is recorded. Sometimes the new owner can sign his name, sometimes he cannot. One old woman can make no sense of the slip she pulls out of the jar because she has never learned how to read numbers. As each person draws his lot, there is a light flutter of applause and smiles here and there. I follow the new owners out into the field as they search for their future homes in the maze of little plots. The men, when they find their lots, instantly check the boundary stakes. The women tend to stand in the center of their lots and smile. Some skip and dance. I see the man who befriended the American couple on the very day he had six teeth pulled. He looks over at me, gives a quick smile and a thumbs up, and strides on with his son to find his lot. I talk with another man who is twenty-six years old and has a wife and two children. He has never had his own home before. His work? Ah, he does a little of this and that he says. He pauses and explains that he also hunts deer in the sierra. And then he starts checking the boundary markers of his new, tiny domain.

I have never seen such a ferocity for a patch of earth in my life. Nor have I ever witnessed such pleasure as the people displayed that day. It was quiet pleasure, one made up of very slow movements and soft almost velvet-like gestures. We can never save the forest if we ignore that hunger. Nor can we ever save the forest for ourselves if we let our hungers consume everything and justify everything.

What we want, always and everywhere it seems, is a program, a list of absolute and clear rules, a manual of procedures. And what we get are contradictions, forces, feelings pouring from deep wells we cannot even admit to very often. This time no engineers will be able to help with cold plans of dams, aqueducts, and tables of figures. The engineers have already had their fun with us and their clear simple blueprints have not solved the problem. The work, I suspect, will be done on the ground, in the forest, with machetes, computers, weddings, burials, steers, butterflies, and now and then a backpack. It will be a faltering kind of work, a groping without good light. We will try this, we will try that, we will hesitate, and then plunge on ahead. Often, we will make up things as we go along. It will not be a bad experience but it will be an experience that lacks the sense of certainty that has comforted us in the past and blinded us in the past. At times, we will sit under a *kapok* tree, and watch the fluff from its pods blow away in the wind. A small green frog will boom out its lust with the first rains and by our feet a trail of *mochomos* will march past carrying loot stripped from a tree overnight. The shadow of a hawk will cross our faces and we will not fear.

Charles Bowden is the author of several books, including Blue Desert, Killing the Hidden Waters, *and* The Secret Forest, *from which this piece is excerpted. He lives in Tucson, Arizona.*

I went to a village in the state of Michoacán, on the far side of Lake Chapala.

A dusty road leads past eucalyptus, past the cemetery, to the village. For most of the year the village is empty—nearly. There are a few old people, quite a few hungry dogs. The sun comes up; the sun goes down. Most of the villagers have left Mexico for the United States. January 23 is the feast day of the patron saint of the village, when the saint is accustomed to being rocked upon his hillock of velvet through the streets. On that day, the villagers—and lately the children of the villagers—return. They come in caravans. Most come from Austin, Texas, from Hollister, California, and from Stockton, California. For a week every year, the village comes alive, a Mexican Brigadoon. Doors are unlocked. Shutters are opened. Floors are swept. Music is played. Beer is drunk.

Expressed fragments of memory flow outward like cigarette smoke to tumble the dust of the dead.

Every night is carnival. Men who work at canneries and factories in California parade down the village street in black suits. Women who are waitresses in California put on high heels and evening gowns. The promenade under the Mexican stars becomes a celebration of American desire.

At the end of the week, the tabernacle of memory is dismantled, distributed among the villagers in their vans, and carried out of Mexico.

—Richard Rodriguez, *Days of Obligation: An Argument with My Mexican Father*

PART II

Some Things To Do

Rob Schultheis

Into Copper Canyon

The author explores a land of wild ravines and forested highlands,
home of the hardy Tarahumara.

A train on the Chihuahua al Pacífico line rumbles out of Chihuahua City at seven o'clock on a chilly November morning. At the other end of the line is the Mexican town of Los Mochis, 405 miles and 13 hours away on the Gulf of California, but most of us are on board for the journey itself, the country along the way.

Up ahead, on the crest of the Sierra Madre Occidental, the railroad skirts the mysterious, convoluted territory referred to as the Barranca del Cobre, or Copper Canyon. There, great rivers have carved a 10,000 square-mile maze of magnificent gorges into the stony, forested highlands. At least four stretches of canyon are even deeper than our own Grand Canyon of the Colorado. Some 70,000 Tarahumara Indians inhabit the area, insulated from the modern world by the isolation and intractability of the landscape. Other venerable entities survive in the *barrancas*: 17th-century Jesuit missions and silver mining towns. Also jaguars, mountain lions, and wolves. Some say the last few Mexican grizzly bears, *Ursus horribilis mexicanos*, live on in the northern reaches of the region. We are riding the rails into another realm, another time.

It's a jolly trip from the outset. There are a couple of dozen foreign tourists on board—*Norteamericanos*, Europeans, Australians—and everyone chats and exclaims at the scenery as we roll along. A few of the conductors who speak English join in. We climb into the eastern foothills of the Sierra Madre, across rolling blond grasslands, along the rims of wild ravines. Here and there, in clearings and meadows in the forest, are the farmsteads of Tarahumara and Mexican settlers: plank and split-shake cabins, log corrals, winter fields of dry, silvery cornstalks.

Around noon we cross the Continental Divide. Behind us, the Conchos River system flows east and north to the Rio Grande and the Gulf of Mexico; before us, the streams and torrents of the *barrancas* travel west, toward the Gulf of California. A short while later we grind to a halt in the dusty, rough-edged little town of Creel. Creel is the main jumping-off point for travel into the canyons, and this is where I get off. I say goodbye to my new friends on the *ferrocarril*, grab my backpack and suitcase, and clamber down to the platform.

After checking into one of the local hotels, I set out to explore the town. Despite its incipient tourist industry, Creel retains a raw, Wild West charm: the local lawmen in the plaza pack six-guns, *vaqueros* on horseback trot the streets, and from doorsteps and curbs, Tarahumara women in long cotton skirts and blazing kerchiefs hawk pottery and baskets. A giant concrete statue of Christ watches benevolently from the cliffs north of town. The Jesuits have been proselytizing among the Tarahumara since back in 1607, and Creel is one of their centers. In the sky above, buzzards and bald eagles cut high, lazy circles. Like everything else in Creel, the café where I eat dinner is cheerfully primitive: a raw lumber room with eccentrically tilted booths, decorated with a variety of gaudy religious prints, antlers, a stuffed and mounted river otter. The food is simple but good: a tough, tasty little range beefsteak, potatoes, refried beans, tortillas, and a marvelous fiery green salsa.

One of the most disheartening facts we discovered was that the canyon and the surrounding forests are virtually empty of wildlife—the tragic result of the unregulated hunting and timber practices that gave no thought to replenishment or conservation. No wild bird songs greeted us at dawn, not even chipmunks scurried away from us. Yet, old timers say that forty years ago the forest still teemed with animals including bears and wolves. In the 1890's, explorer Carl Lumholtz described the woods as "quite lively with birds. Everywhere I saw bluejays.... Never have I been at any place where deer were so plentiful... there were also wild turkeys." The forest and canyon are now sadly far different from those descriptions. An American forester, James E. Lotan, whom I met in Creel, bluntly stated, "I have never seen a forest so devoid of wildlife."

—Flías Castillo, "Mexico's Copper Canyon," *Great Expeditions*

The next day, after the sun burns away a morning fog, I catch a ride out to the Copper Canyon Lodge, near the Tarahumara hamlet of Cusárare— "Place of the Eagles"—some 13 miles south of Creel.

There are hotels that are merely places to stay, and then (rarely) there are Hotels with a capital "H" that seem to embody the very essence of where they are. This turns out to be one of the latter. Most of the employees are Tarahumara, and their lives twine through the hotel. Indian farms extend right up to the dusty parking area, and bright-eyed children shout and play on the long veranda. The rooms are log and plaster, heated by wood stove, lit by kerosene lamp; there is no electricity. Meals are served at big communal tables in a dining room with a stone fireplace in one corner. The hotel chef is a merry little Tarahumara woman who cooks like an angel. The place is a veritable Hotel Paradiso.

I have brought a couple of reference books on the Tarahumara with me, and I spend the midday hours studying up on these fascinating people. They live on corn, beans, and squash; cattle, sheep, and pigs; apples and peaches raised on their hard-scrabble farms. They are also master hunters and gatherers, scraping an incredible array of edibles from the austere landscape: catfish, eels; the flesh of deer, opossums, wolves; insects, worms and grubs; snakes, toads, and lizards; berries, fungi, cactuses, 13 kinds of roots, and 39 varieties of weeds. To the Tarahumara, their world is a gigantic delicatessen, a salad bar as big as the state of Vermont.

They are also undoubtedly the greatest natural runners on earth; they call themselves Rarámuri, "The Runners" or "The Running People," and there are many tales of their prowess on foot. Men and women alike regularly compete in ultra-marathon races called *rarajípari*, which can last several days and nights and cover hundreds of miles of rugged country. In competitions, they dribble carved wooden balls around circular courses. Tarahumara deer-hunting technique is simple: they chase an animal until it collapses and then finish it off with poisoned arrows or stones.

One of the other hotel guests is a stocky, mustachioed Californian named Candelario Ramos. Like me, he is an enthusiastic hiker and outdoorsman; unlike me, he speaks fluent Spanish. A perfect traveling companion. We decide to team up for a couple of treks into the backcountry.

We talk with Liliana Carosso, the charming young Argentinian woman who manages the hotel, and she advises us to start out with the easy hour-and-a-half round-trip down Cusárare Creek to Cusárare Falls. It is a nice warm-up stroll, she says, and tomorrow we can do something more ambitious. Fine—off we go. The trail heads west from the hotel, crosses a wooden footbridge over deep green pools, and follows the creek from there, along gravel bars and sandy beaches where Tarahumara women scrub laundry. Some of them have arranged displays of clay pots and pine-needle baskets, wooden dolls, and bright woolen bags, an impromptu trailside bazaar. I buy a sublimely graceful little basket from a girl so shy she doesn't look at me once during the whole transaction, just smiles off to one side, blushing furiously.

Liliana has told us to keep our eyes peeled for both bald eagles and eared trogons—small, iridescent, orange-plumed birds renowned for their beauty. We don't see either today, but Candelario glimpses a ringtail, cousin of the raccoon, leaping away across the boulders beyond the stream, and we find the tracks of ringtail, coyote, and deer on the banks.

The view of the falls themselves, at dusk, is breathtaking: thin tresses of white water plunge a hundred feet to a seething cauldron below. Beyond, Cusárare Canyon winds away between cliffs and timbered crags. We are hovering at the edge of Terra Incognita...the Void of the Canyons.

The next morning we set out on a much more ambitious tramp, to the Recohuata hot springs at the bottom of Tararécua Canyon. Liliana warns us that we will never find our way there without a guide, so we hire one, a broadfaced young Tarahumara named Antonio. The hotel kitchen supplies us with three lunches of fried chicken, ham-and-cheese sandwiches, hard-boiled eggs, bananas, and bottled sodas. By 9:30 we are out on the trail, accompanied by one of the hotel's resident dogs, a spry little dust-colored creature who obviously has designs on our larder.

We begin by retracing yesterday's route along Cusárare Creek, and then Antonio leads us on a steep side trail up over the ridgeline to the north. It is Sunday, and the trail back down to Cusárare is busy with Tarahumara couples and families on their way to Mass. Antonio stops to chat with them in Tarahumara, a quicksilver tongue that delights the ear, but after a while the trail empties, and our guide goes into high gear, scooting along as if he has electric motors in his calves and wheels in the soles of his feet. By Tarahumara standards he is just ambling along, but for Candelario and me the pace is exhausting. We zoom over one mountaintop, and another, and another. Every twenty minutes or so we beg for mercy and flop to the ground, gasping for breath, while Antonio regards us with bemusement.

After a couple of hours, during one of our halts, Candelario engages Antonio in conversation in Spanish, and then bursts into laughter.

"*Qué pasa?*"

"I told him we were tired," Candelario replies. "And he said he was a little tired, too. He told me he spent the last three days and nights tracking stray cattle through the *barrancas*; he hasn't slept since Wednesday night. He got home early this morning and was going to rest up, but then Liliana told him there were two *turistas* who needed a guide into Tararécua Canyon. He decided it might be fun, and he could use the money."

I look at Antonio, at the wry grin hovering around the edges of his mouth, and then I can't help it, I start laughing too. So much for trying to match a Rarámuri on the trail.

We trudge on. The views are astonishing, cloud's-eye vistas of wooded mountains and coiling stony gorges. Finally, after a good four hours, we reach the rim of Tararécua Canyon and start down. The thousand-foot descent takes another forty-five minutes, skipping and sliding down sharp switchbacks, over loose rubble and dust, past cliffs and parapets of lichen-spattered volcanic duff. We reach the bottom, follow the headwaters of the Río Tararécua a few hundred yards along the boulder-strewn canyon floor, and then, at last, there they are: the crystalline geothermal waters of Recohuata, gushing from the north wall of the gorge.

This is heaven on—or in—the earth. Someone has hauled pipe and concrete down here and built a primeval open-air bathhouse on the mountainside. Candelario and I strip down to our hiking shorts and jump into the lower tank; Antonio hops into the one above. The water is blood warm, with the faintest scent of plutonian sulphur, subterranean salts, and ores. We float there, drinking sodas, gazing up at the looming canyon walls. Hawks curve and soar above the rimrock. Below, the green torrent of the Río Tararécua boils through water-polished blocks of stone. Butterflies with glimmering wings flash by on a warm breeze.

Too soon, it is time to go; the shadows are lengthening across the canyon, and we don't want to be benighted on the trail. We lunch, feed the scraps to the dog, and we're off. Antonio sets an even faster pace than he did this morning, and we follow as best we can. Our route across the rolling highlands is different, more direct, than the one we took this morning; Antonio wants to get us home before dark. A good idea, as Candelario and I are wet, and the temperature last night at Cusárare dipped to 25° F. No guide wants to freeze-dry his clients.

Sunset catches us on the last big summit before the valley of the Río Cusárare. The air turns icy; the twilight fades. We hike the last mile along the creek in near-darkness, arriving at the hotel just in time for dinner. Perfect timing. The cook has outdone herself: we feast on corn soup, sweet-cured pork chops, French fries, *refritos*, tortillas and butter, and sliced bananas drowned in condensed milk—washed down, in my case, with two stiff margaritas and three bottles of soda. Well, it *was* a long hike. When I'm ready to turn in, Candelario is still sitting at the table, regaling the other hotel guests with tales of our great trek. More power to him; I am fast asleep the moment my head hits the pillow.

The next day I wake up and decide to do practically nothing. I see Candelario off at the station in Creel—he is heading on to Los Mochis, with more excursions into the *barrancas* along the way—and then I mosey on back to the hotel and settle in on one of the benches on the porch. I get out my maps and guidebooks and start looking for new destinations, and I find a village called Batopilas, at the dead end of the road a little over 80 miles southwest of Creel, in the depths of the Río Batopilas gorge. You just can't go any farther. It sounds intriguing; I have to go. Liliana helps me hire a guide, a man named Jésus Manuel Olivas, otherwise known as Chunel. The next morning he and I head out for Batopilas in his battered old Ford pickup.

A word or two about this Chunel. He spent his childhood roaming the *barrancas* with his father, who was a trader with the Tarahumara, and by now, in his 61st year, he knows the country better than any other living man. He is a legend, and he looks it: lanky, weathered, hawk-faced, with fierce, kindly eyes, and extravagant grizzled sideburns. The old cowboy hat sits on his head as though it has been there forever. He limps slightly, from a broken leg suffered a couple of years back, but he is still fit. According to Liliana, he regularly out-hikes people half his age on multiday treks through the canyons. A classic character.

The journey to Batopilas exceeds all expectations. We cross canyon after canyon, past Tarahumara and Mexican villages, orchards, and farms; through dense forests of pine, fir, hemlock, and oak; by eerie stone formations shaped like toadstools, parasols, pagodas. The Basíhuare and Urique rivers boil away into lost chasms. As we travel farther south, we enter the territory of ever more traditional Tarahumara, the ones the Mexicans call Cimmarones, "The Wild Ones." Many of the Indian men we see along the road are in aboriginal garb: bare feet, white muslin kilts, loose shirts, and scarlet headbands. It adds immensely to their aura of dignity, of strength. These people have chosen to eschew material wealth. They lead a harsh, austere life, but in a sense they are also aristocrats, noblemen of the Neolithic. No one else could have survived here as they have.

Up until now I haven't really seen the big canyons; I have been exploring around the edges. All that changes just after we pass through the sprawling, ramshackle town of Quírare, on a sky-scraped saddle. We wind through more forest and crags, and then, suddenly, the earth falls away and we are on the rim of Batopilas Canyon.

Chunel pulls over, and we get out. Below us, the road snakes away in dizzy zigzags and heart-stopping hairpins, crossing steep slopes of scrub jungle and hanging deserts studded with monster cactuses, winding between massive stone buttresses. At the bottom, more than a vertical

> Unless a serious reforestation campaign is soon started, this magnificent area could be forever ruined. On the canyon slopes, goats, donkeys, and cows brought in by Mexicans and Tarahumara Indians are devastating the plant life and compacting the earth with their hooves so that nothing can grow to keep the sod from washing away. The Tarahumara's need for firewood is also taking its toll on the slopes.
>
> —Elías Castillo, "Mexico's Copper Canyon,"
> *Great Expeditions*

mile below, the river batters its way down a bed of alluvial debris. Miles away, on the opposite canyon wall, more forests and cliffs soar to the sky. Here and there are the tiny patches of Tarahumara fields scratched into the ridgelines, with lonely cabins trailing blue plumes of woodsmoke.

The ride down is, well, call it an adventure. Chunel is having trouble with his aged truck. It keeps dying, and he restarts it by coasting until we pick up enough speed to jump the motor in second gear. This definitely adds to the inherent excitement of descending 5,500 vertical feet of rough dirt road. There are many places so exposed that if we went over the edge, we wouldn't stop falling until we landed in the Río Batopilas. In addition, Chunel continues his guide duties as we ricochet down the *barranca* wall. "See, over there, the Tarahumara man climbing the cliff? See the big cactus? It is called the *pitahaya*," says Chunel, pointing with one hand, holding the wheel with the other, and turning to smile enthusiastically at me as we slew around a curve six inches from the gulf of thin air. I'm sure it's actually safe—Chunel has driven this road hundreds of times and he knows what he is doing—but it also is definitely exciting.

We finally reach the river and continue on toward Batopilas. The road roller coasters along the southern side of the canyon, high above the river. We pass by abandoned mines, tiny hamlets of one or two or three shacks and shanties, through surreal forests of ten-foot-tall upside-down candelabra cactuses, wiry trees with leaves like smoke, wrought-iron thornbush. There is a well-trodden trail on the opposite riverbank, all the way down the gorge. Chunel tells me it is called the Camino Real, and that up until fifteen years ago, when the final leg of the road was completed, it was the only way to reach Batopilas. Today it is still used regularly by Indians, gold and silver prospectors, and the like. Signs of Tarahumara are everywhere. Chunel points out trails carved in impossible slopes, cabins perched on airy pinnacles, fields clinging to mountainsides. I see a Tarahumara fish trap in the river, an ingenious rock-walled chute leading downstream to a manmade pool, a design thousands of years old. A few miles farther down

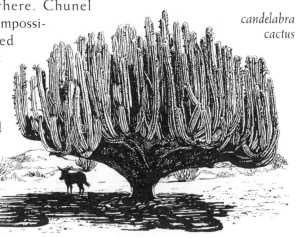

candelabra cactus

the road, we pass two Tarahumara men trotting along with enormous peeled logs the size of telephone poles on their backs. They are bound for Batopilas, Chunel says, where they will sell them for roof beams; they still have ten or fifteen miles to go. I ask if we can stop and offer them and their cargo a ride. "They wouldn't accept," Chunel tells me. "They always carry the logs like that; that is what they do."

And then, at last, we come to Batopilas. Imagine Tahiti, Treasure Island, hidden in the bottom of the Grand Canyon. We pass the majestic bougainvillea-covered ruins of Hacienda de San Miguel, built by turn-of-the-century expatriate silver-mining tycoon Alexander "Boss" Shepherd, and then we recross the Río Batopilas on a high bridge into the outskirts of town. Batopilas is much bigger than I had expected, strung out for over a mile along the river. We bump down the narrow cobblestone street, past gardens bursting with tropical flowers, mangos, bananas, papayas, lemons, and oranges. Palm trees sway in the sky. The air is languid, lazy, at least thirty degrees warmer than on the canyon rim.

The wealth around Batopilas was first discovered in the late 16th century. Mines were built and passed from company to company. The town boomed during the gold and silver rush of the 1800s, and most of the beautiful buildings in Batopilas today were built between 1880 and 1910. Now, according to rumors and tales going around the *barrancas*, the local economy is at least partially based on contraband and smuggling. There are stories of marijuana and poppy fields hidden away in the Sinforosa, the next great valley to the south, of mule trains loaded with secret cargo crossing the mountains on back trails to the seacoast, of armed *federales* manning roadblocks, looking for smugglers. Who knows? When I ask Chunel, he just shrugs, winks, and laughs. Whatever they do for a living, the people of Batopilas are definitely friendly: everyone we meet seems to know Chunel, and we are greeted with smiles, cries of "*Buenas tardes*," and the soft, formal handshakes of old-fashioned Mexico.

We check into the Hotel Mari, across from the town church, and then head out for an afternoon walk. We visit the old Shepherd estate, and then we explore one of the silver-mine tunnels west of town. Luckily, I have brought my headlamp with me; the torch Chunel improvises out of a length of dead cactus refuses to keep burning no matter how many times he lights it. The maze of shafts seems to extend forever; Chunel tells me that the mine reaches all the way to the far end of Batopilas, close to two miles away, and that there are more levels below us. In its day this was a hectic, bustling place, with thousands of miners, riotous *cantinas*, hustles, and fortune hunters from everywhere; the Shepherd family hauled in a grand piano over the Camino Réal for their

fetes and soirees. Now the wildness of the *barrancas* has returned, recon-
quered. The fever and the glory are gone.

We make our way back out into the waning daylight and amble back
into town. Birds twitter in the jade green trees. A horseman canters
across the plaza, leading a string of pack burros. A Tarahumara man and
his young son sit in quiet companionship on the steps of the church,
watching the world go by. The bell tolls for evening Mass.

We end up at Michaela's for dinner. This, it turns out, isn't exactly a
restaurant; it is Michaela's front porch, and the menu is whatever the
smiling, middle-aged proprietress happens to have cooked for her family.
Tonight that means tuna-noodle casserole, bean, tortillas, and salad. A
couple of other foreigners are dining at the next table, and I get to talking with them. One is Canadian, the other American; there are six or
seven other tourists in town, they tell me, including a couple of
Australians, a Frenchman, and a German. They themselves have been in
Batopilas for a week and a half, and they are finding it hard to leave. The
bus to Creel leaves three times a week, at 4 a.m., and they just can't bring
themselves to get on it. I can definitely understand. I have been here for
no more than a few hours, and I am already fantasizing about staying on:
a room at the Mari, riding a horse up the gulches and draws above town,
coffee at Michaela's while the warm spring rains fall outside, a thousand
and one dazzling sunsets on the walls of the gorge...yes, it would be
beautiful, indeed.

But it is almost time to go. The next morning we drive the last five
miles down-canyon to the abandoned mission church at Satevo. No one
knows who built this pale dusty red edifice, with its lofty, airy dome and
belfry—or when. Some say the Jesuits back in the early 17th century
used Tarahumara to do the labor, but by the time the church was completed, the Indians were so disgusted with working for free that they
refused to worship there. Or so they say. Like so much, it is a mystery.

We park in the dusty desert out in front and go inside. The interior
of the church embodies the historical layers and human subtleties of the
barrancas: on the altar are the gaudily painted, life-size religious statues so
popular in Mexico; the whitewashed walls are stained with purple berry
juice, representing the blood of Christ. There are a pair of crypts set in
the brick floor; I lean down and read the inscription on one: "Martina V.
de Ontiveros, Abril 24, de 1881." I find an inscription, dated 1630, on
the big black iron bell in the belfry. Who knows what it all means?

Every corner and niche contains a talisman: a poker-faced wooden
Tarahumara mask, a rough-hewn cross, a wreath of thorns, an ancient
iron baptismal font, a painting of a bleeding, tormented Christ. Satevo is

a shrine to fierce, tangled faiths, to dark, knotted histories no one will ever unravel or truly understand. Like the canyons, it seems beyond our knowing. Outside, the dust blows in the wind, the Río Batipolas rolls away from us, down its measureless gorge, into the unknown.

One last bit of adventure. We are driving east from Batopilas, a few miles beyond town. We round a corner, and there, blocking our way, is a pickup across the road, with three big men standing next to it. The three big men are armed to the teeth. Among them, they have an M-16 assault rifle, a snub-nosed submachine gun, and three pistols. "Federales," Chunel says to me. "They look for the smugglers." I should be nervous, I guess, but somehow it just seems part and parcel of life in the Barranca del Cobre. We stop and explain ourselves, and after a few uncertain moments they tell us we can go. As we drive off, a pickup full of men from Batopilas is pulling up at the roadblock. The *federales* are glaring intimidatingly, but the Batopilas crew doesn't seem impressed; they are laughing together, joking and wisecracking, as they get out of their vehicle. Well, people are tough in the canyon country.

It takes until nightfall to reach Cusárare. The next day I board the train at Creel, heading west to the Gulf of California.

This last leg down the western slope of the Sierra Madre is by far the most exciting part of the entire train trip. From Divisadero, 7,800 feet up on the rimrock, we gaze back down into the enormous gulf of the Río Urique drainage, with the river winding through green scrub jungle nearly a mile and a half below. Slowly we descend on snaky switchbacks, across trestles, through tunnels bored into the mountainsides; the way down is so precipitous, so twisting, that the train feels as if it is going to snap in two. At one point, the place called El Lazo, "The Loop," we double back so tightly in our descent that the train actually crosses under itself! No wonder it took till 1961 for the railroad to be completed from Creel down to the coast.

Evening falls as the pines and oaks give way to warm forests of madroña, sycamores, palms, colossal cactuses. We ramble down the dank canyon of the Río Sepentrión. I can smell fruit trees on the night air. We must be nearing sea level. The *barrancas* are behind us now, back there in the cold and darkness of the mountains, hidden again by landscape and time.

Rob Schultheis has lived in several Asian countries. He is the author of The Hidden West, Bone Games, Night Letters: Inside Wartime Afghanistan, *and a screen adaptation of Heinrich Harrar's classic book,* Seven Years in Tibet. *He currently divides his time between the San Juan Mountains of Colorado, Los Angeles, and Central Asia.*

At first, the drums sounded distant and sporadic. But a few days later, they rumbled close, constant and loud. They made a droning noise, a thump followed by a long buzz, from a bead strung against the drumhead.

These droning drumbeats were echoing through the canyons of the Sierra Madre Occidental in northwestern Mexico. It was Holy Week, *Semana Santa*. That's when the Tarahumara Indians stage an elaborate ritual combining indigenous religion with Christianity. The centerpriece is a mock battle that climaxes with the burning of Judas in effigy the day before Easter.

At the climax to the Tarahumara's *Semana Santa*, the clergy were nowhere in sight. I felt witness to a revolt, albeit a symbolic one, and at the same time witness to something intimate; an uninhibited collective expression of liberation, and a direct communication with a source of renewal.

The Pharisees ran to a nearby field, chased by the soldiers. The soldiers grabbed at the Judases ever more aggressively. They tore away the clothing. One man grabbed a hat, another a shirt. Other men pulled at the straw stuffing within, others at the arms and legs. One man yanked out a phallus. Everyone cheered.

Both armies carried the dismembered Judases to the far side of the field and burned them under a pine tree. The fire blazed in the shadows; thick gray smoke billowed into the crystal-blue air.

Two boys grabbed each other by their loincloth sashes and began to wrestle—a Tarahumara custom and a traditional end to the Easter proceedings—but no one else was much interested in wrestling. People were already dispersing back into the canyons, where several days of *tesguinadas* (marathon parties named after *tesquino*, their home-made corn beer) awaited them, and then planting, and then the hope that *Tata Diosi*, the Great Father, would grant them a good crop.

—Marshall Krantz, "Droning Drums and Burning Judases: A Tarahumara Easter"

Lynn Ferrin

I've Still Got Mexico

Traveling alone on public buses and colectivos, *the author observes the oddities of bird and human behavior.*

A t day's end a few visitors have climbed to the top of the observatory, that odd square tower rising over the labyrinthine palace of Palenque. We sit in silence, looking across the forest canopy toward the hazy plains, thinking about the people who built this place, whose civilization thrived here—and disappeared—long before the Spanish came. All around, in the late afternoon light, the ruins have taken on a pale yellow glow against the jungle wall. Across the way stands the Temple of the Inscriptions, where the Lord Pacal lies buried in his exquisite tomb. Nervous tourists cling to its formidable stairway like barnacles on a piling. From far away comes the baritone wheezing of howler monkeys.

For years I'd felt the pull of Palenque. Other travelers had told me it was the loveliest, most magical, most aesthetic, of all the great Mayan ruins. Images passed through my musings on Mexico: vines dripping over intricately carved stones, swirling vapors, wondrous birds.

But Palenque is a bit off the main archaeology-tour routes of the Yucatán. It lies at the western edges of the Mayan realm, in the state of Chiapas, where the jungles of the highlands dip down to the flatlands fronting the Gulf of Mexico.

So it seemed that Palenque should be a destination in itself. I would fly to Villahermosa, capital of the state of Tabasco, explore that city and its environs, then journey the 85 miles or so to the ruins. I'd follow my favorite mode of travel in Mexico: alone, making do with my meager Spanish, lodging in good hotels, but getting around on public buses and *colectivos* (those marvelous Latin American taxis that follow regular routes—urban and rural—filling with passengers as they go).

Villahermosa is a prosperous, modern city on the banks of the Río Grijalva, in the green lowlands of southern Mexico. Its riches came from petroleum, not tourism, and its people are proud, hardworking, and somewhat standoffish. My hotel was bustling with Mexican businessmen and well-to-do locals.

If the town has a spiritual or historical heart, I couldn't find it—but as it turned out, I was surprised to find so much of interest for a visitor.

To bone up on local archaeology, I spent my first afternoon at the elegant Carlos Pellicer Museum, endowed by a local anthropologist, with antiquities carefully selected for their aesthetic value—like a case of those marvelously expressive ceramic "smiling faces" from the Vera Cruz classic era, 200 to 900 A.D. (The English translation labeled them "smile infaces.") The early Vera Cruzans must have been a jovial lot—there's another exhibit of their laughing, dancing, tail-wagging ceramic dogs.

Later, in the twilight, I walked along the river on a path paved with a mosaic of red pebbles. A long black snake came swimming alongside the shore, and a heron rode by on a floating log, like a proud captain. Snowy egrets sailed in to roost in the trees; young men stood along the banks, fishing. I reached the *malecón*, lined with white wrought iron benches. Every few blocks there was a ferry dock, and little blue boats carrying townspeople back and forth across the river. To an outsider's eye, anyway, it all seemed a picture of people perfectly content with where and how they live.

That night, back at the hotel, I dined on *pejelagarto*, the delicious fish of the Río Grijalva. It was served cold, with limes and chili peppers, its fierce alligator head and teeth still attached, and it managed to bite me even though it had been dead since morning.

Armadillo, venison, fish and other less identifiable animals are also sold pre-cooked, most commonly in markets and small towns with a strong Indian influence.

In southern Mexico you may be offered *tepescuintle*. It is a delicious meat, even if it is from the *agouti*, a racoon-sized rodent. I've yet to meet a hungry carnivore who didn't love it.

—Carl Franz, *The People's Guide To Mexico*

When tourists need a reason to venture to Villahermosa, it's usually to see the "big heads." These are the colossal stone human heads carved by the Olmecs, whose culture expanded here from 800 to 200 B.C. and are often called the "Mother Culture of Mesoamerica." The heads—and other ceremonial monuments—were found in coastal swamps by oilmen and moved into Villahermosa, where they are exhibited in an outdoor museum, Parque La Venta.

Early in the morning, slathered with insect repellent, English-language guide-map in hand, I ambled a couple of blocks from the hotel to the gates of La Venta. Inside, pathways wind past nature exhibits, carvings and the famous heads.

It was all very pleasant; for one thing I had the place to myself. Lit by sunbeams filtering through the mini-jungle, the Olmec heads were full-lipped, round-cheeked, sensual. At each exhibit benches were arranged for lingering to contemplate the objects. There were several stone altars, with human figures emerging from niches, some of them holding struggling children. What do they mean? For now, it's all surmise and guesswork. There's an unusual sculpture of a whale—or is it a dolphin or manatee? In a large enclosure two jaguars prowled, their golden eyes following my every move. There were wild animals, too—coatimundis feeding behind a stela, and an agouti sniffing among the trees. A parade of industrious leaf-cutter ants, as always, kept me entertained for a stupidly long time.

A Mayan ruin I'd never heard of, Comalcalco, lay an hour's drive north of Villahermosa, toward the Gulf. Comalcalco is unusual among pre-Columbian ruins—indeed among all great ancient monuments—because it was built of kilned brick. To get there, I joined a local tour. The roads took us through neat and pretty towns. The latest harvest of cacao beans—the Maya used them as currency, which certainly fits my value system—were spread to dry in the sun. In the marshes, women filled baskets with freshwater shrimp to use as bait for river fishing.

At Copilco, we stopped to see the "folk art" church—a precious wedding-cake affair, its exterior blinding white under the tropical sun. Inside, circus colors: red pews, blue arches, yellow columns—and lots of polychrome carvings of cherubs and saints.

An owl called as we walked along an avenue of trees into Comalcalco: egrets picked through the deep green grass. The temples here are in surprisingly good condition, considering they are brickwork which has survived more than a millennium in the warm rain. Followed by two giggling boys, we spent a couple of hours among the ruins, examining the stone and stucco sculptures—such as a crocodile carrying three people, and a stone skull that's scary even at noon. In the site museum there are other artworks found here—including some fine bricks decorated with deer, monkeys, armadillos.

On another day, I braved the second class bus system to visit some limestone

Olmec head

127

caves near the railroad town of Teapa. Although my guidebook ridiculed La Grutas de Cocona, I found them quite extensive and amazing. An energetic little boy was my guide on the half-mile trail among the stalagmites and stalactites, past underground ponds, and tiny waterfalls. A taciturn gentleman walked ahead, turning on the lights. The boy spoke no English, so he'd act out the fantastic formations. Squawk, squawk! Chicken? ¡Si! Flapping of arms, baring of incisors. Bat? ¡Si! and so on, with wolf, whale, tortoise, eagle.

My return to Villahermosa was fast, in a *colectivo* driven by a traffic terrorist and crammed with people flashing a great many gold teeth.

That evening, I strolled at dusk along the Lake of the Illusions, amid the din of parrots and melodious blackbirds gathering in their appointed trees for the night. Next morning, to Palenque!

Several comfortable first-class buses leave Villahermosa each day for Palenque—if you buy your ticket early you'll have a better chance for an up-front window seat. A few other solo travelers from the north shared my journey: a man vagabonding from Seattle to Cozumel, a woman headed for a remote church mission. For three hours we rolled through the moist, verdant countryside, past miles and miles of banana plantations, toward blue hills. The driver played the radio loudly, singing along and gesturing with gusto.

When we crossed from Tabasco into Chiapas, the roads turned horrible. The bus stopped in modern Palenque town, about five miles from the ruins. Its shops were full of poorly made souvenirs and synthetic clothing. Backpacking youths hung around on corners, waiting for the minivans to Agua Azul, the travertine terraces and turquoise pools farther along the Chiapas jungle road.

Visitors to Palenque these days are a diverse bunch: glaze-eyed hippies cross-dressed in indigenous textiles, scholarly types with archaeology texts, mammoth bus-loads of French and German tourists, who are nuts about pre-Hispanic Mesoamerica. There are lodgings of every style to house them.

I settled into the pricey Chan-Kah, halfway to the ruins, with cottages on terraces stepping down to the river and a large rock-lined swimming pool. Also staying there was a birding expedition from the States, seeking the aplomado falcon and other winged wonders of this region. At night they played their tapes of the vermiculated screech owl to the indifferent Mexican night.

Most visitors seem content to spend two or three hours at Palenque ruins; for me there was enough to occupy the better part of three days. I struggled up and down the temple stairways, cooled my toes in the river's tumbling waters, tried to read the meanings of the amazing murals and calendar glyphs.

The Maya were obsessed by time. They tracked it backwards and forwards, even over millions of years—keeping count of events, mythology, prophecies, dynasties. Their calendars were probably the most accurate ever developed, certainly more than ours and a thousand years older. Today, in remote areas of Mesoamerica, there are still those who keep the Mayan calendars.

Twice I descended the dank stairway deep into the Temple of the Inscriptions to look at the famed carving on the tomb of Pacal the Great, who ruled here from 615 to 683 A.D. The elaborate carving shows Pacal descending into the jaws of the earth, and the world tree, or Mayan "foliated cross," which has misled some people to conclude that the Maya had some early contact with Christianity. Others, even loonier, have fantasized that Pacal's tomb carving shows an ancient astronaut taking off in a spaceship.

Palenque's heyday was from 600 to 800 A.D., during the Classic Period of the Maya, and

What we feel when confronted by a relief at Palenque is not what a Maya experienced. That is true. But it is also true that our feelings and thoughts on seeing the work before us are quite real. Our understanding is not an illusion: it is ambiguous. This ambiguity is present in all our views of works from other civilizations and even when we contemplate works from our own past. We are not Greeks, Chinese, or Arabs; yet neither can we say that we fully comprehend Romanesque or Byzantine sculpture. We are condemned to translate, and each of these translations, whether it be of Gothic or Egyptian art, is a metaphor, a transmutation of the original.

—Octavio Paz, *Essays on Mexican Art*

is particularly renowned for its artworks and glyphs. Only in the last decade or so have epigraphers, archaeologists, and linguists begun to decipher the Mayan hieroglyphics, which tell the stories of the rulers and their ways and rituals, accomplishments, and lineages. In the museum, there's a beautiful tablet of 96 glyphs, carved by the ruler Kan-Xul.

For a while I hung out with the birding group, a single-minded bunch. One morning, for example, they rose at 5 a.m., breakfasted, birded in the fields, and arrived at the gates to Palenque at 7:45 a.m. With not so much as a glance within, they played a tape of the slaty-tailed trogon to the treetops. By early afternoon they were still outside the ruins, adding to their life lists. But their persistence, and the help of their superb ornithologist/leader Rick Bowers, paid off. In one small flowering tree, within a quarter hour, they spotted a collared aracari, olive-backed euphonia, blackheaded saltator, grey catbird, yellow-winged tanager, emerald toucanet. And the lovely cotinga, a singular and seldom seen creature of shimmering blue and purple.

Finally, inside the ruins, as their learned archaeology guide Alfonso Escobedo expounded on the palace murals, they all ran off to peer at a pair of white hawks.

That evening, I joined them for a van ride into the Usumacinta marshes, where we found not one aplomado falcon, but a pair, mating. We drove down lonesome roads paved with mist, silvered by a slender boat of new moon sailing through the Mexican heavens.

On my last morning I discovered the horses. There they stood, a mile or so below the ruins: a dozen of them, all saddled and ready to ride, tied to a fence beneath the shade trees. So why was I having so much trouble renting one?

At first there was no one around; then I found an old man in a near-by shack who said, yes, it was possible, perhaps I could find someone else to help me. But it wasn't clear whom. Back to the horses, who eyed me suspiciously. Some young men appeared and stood at the crossroads, talking. I was roundly hooted when I posited, *"¿Se rentan caballos?"*

After a while they untied a few of the horses, mounted, and rode away.

Only then did I get it: this was no stable of tourist horses. It was a hitching post for locals from the hills, who parked their quadruped transportation here while they rode the bus into town for business.

Shamed by my tourist arrogance, I tried to slink away.

But wait! Here was a man who said yes, he'd rent me his horse.

I urged the reluctant beast up the dirt road, passing a field where a few *gringo* longhairs foraged for magic mushrooms. (I'd heard that, at night, the nearby campground was raucous with hallucinating youths.) Some Mexicans, on enviably peppy steeds, trotted by, surprised to see me. Butterflies flickered in the sunshine. To the north, I could see out across the coastal plains toward the Gulf. This was lovely country, green and rich.

The track rolled up and down and around, like the road to Oz. The breeze was warm, the morning dreamy. I thought I could ride forever, here in the hills of Chiapas, with their grand ruins and blue rivers and toucans calling.

After an hour or so, my right stirrup broke out of the rotten leather. It was an awkward ride back, holding one steel stirrup in my lap, the horse now trotting with enthusiasm.

But as the first leg of the journey home, it had appealing variety. Next, the *colectivo* to Palenque town, the big bus to Villahermosa, the night flight to Mexico City.

There's this country western song with the cowboy's lament of betrayed love: "He's got you, I've got Mexico."

I know what he means: years ago I went south to ruminate over a thorny romance, and ended up loving Mexico better than I loved the man. And I've still got Mexico.

Lynn Ferrin has traveled throughout the world—on horseback as much as possible—in her thirty-year career at Motorland *magazine, where she is the editor.*

In the hills of the state of Guerrero a city man returns a horse he had hired for the day. The house of the farmer is a shack made of bits and pieces over an earthen floor, the bottom of poverty. The rider asks, tactfully, where the owner bought such a fine horse. "Oh, our son won it in a lottery and gave it to us to sell. We haven't enough land to use it here." The city man asks how much for the day's hire. "Nothing. It was a pleasure to have you enjoy my horse." "May I offer you a drink then?" "No, thank you. When I am a guest in your *tierra* then you may buy me a drink. Here you are my guest and for that reason I cannot accept a drink from you. I should like to have drink and food to offer you, but all I have is the horse. Should you come back this way and the horse still be here, please know that he is yours to ride."

—Kate Simon, *Mexico: Places and Pleasures*

RICHARD A. COLE

Sometimes a Shave

...can be too close.

My college roommate once told me the highlight of his vacation to Rome was having an Italian barber give him an old-style shave. The thought stuck in my head as I drove through the small Mexican village near Mérida, and eyed a tiny barber stall tucked between a tortilla stand and a tire repair shop. Inside a bewhiskered barber busily lathered a customer serenely settled into a barber chair so old the red leather had faded to pink. My hand unconsciously scratched a few day's growth, and my mind wandered to dreams of hot lather and a velvety smooth chin.

It was a big mistake. I should have been warned by his sign advertising a "special" that was the equivalent of a dollar and "guaranteed for one year," but, like any good traveler, I was an opportunist eager for a bargain.

"Sit down," he commanded in Spanish as he sharpened the straight-edged pearl-handled razor against a leather strap. At that moment I realized that I was about to close my eyes and expose my throat to a man I did not know, I could barely communicate with, and who held a dangerous weapon. Suddenly, I noticed the wrist and ankle straps on the chair. Now I have met potential employers and girlfriends whom I wanted to like me, but I really wanted this guy to like me.

"Ummm, nice day," I tried.

"Sit down," he commanded again. I leaned my head back, noticing a crucifix overhead. I wondered if it had been put there by a customer. Now that I thought about it, Jesus probably wore a beard for a reason.

"Are you Catholic?" I squeaked. "I'm Catholic," I lied. "I love Mexico...the people are so friendly.... We should increase foreign aid...," I babbled on.

At one point I leaned forward enough in my chair to notice the back of his sign that offered the dollar special. This side advertised my barber's expertise as a dentist. "All teeth fixed or broken immediately—Cheap." I wondered if the customer had a choice. Talk about one stop shopping, this guy was ready for health care reform and NAFTA.

I closed my eyes and began my biofeedback-based self-hypnotic calming meditation as he lathered my face, pausing only momentarily when he lathered my nose. Actually this could not be all that bad I thought. After all, I had seen Clint Eastwood get shaved like this in the movies without moving his cigar.

Now understand that I consider myself a tough guy. None of this '90s sensitive new man stuff for me. I can take pain. I broke my ribs once playing football and finished the game. I've had emergency stitches without anesthesia. I even walked away from a motorcycle wreck that busted my ankle. If Clint can take it, I can take it.

At this first swipe of the razor I leapt out of the chair as if he had tapped my spine with a cattle prod. By the second stroke I was flopping around like a hooked fish in the bottom of a boat. This wasn't a shave, it was dermabrasion.

"Good?" the barber asked.

"No!" I screamed. He stropped the razor in reply.

The next thirty minutes were terror. Three times I tried to get up. Three times he pushed me back down. I pleaded for a last cigarette or at least a blindfold. It was the most thorough shave ever given. I felt like he was using a hand trowel on my face, and wondered if my nose, ears, and lips would survive. I was certain the mole on my cheek was gone forever.

When at last he finished, I hung limply onto the barber chair. He leaned into my ear and asked, "*Alcol? Alcol?*"

"*Alcol?*" I murmured.

"Ah." He beamed and turned his back. I tried to slink from the chair, but he caught me and slapped alcohol on my face. Maybe it was to revive me. Frantically, I paid him and gave him a generous tip—not because he had done a good job, but because I had survived. Clutching my belongings, I backed through the crowd and headed for a mirror. I was amazed that everything was still there—nose, ears, lips, even the mole. There was no blood anywhere.

But it has been three days now, and I have noticed something. None of the hair on my face has grown back. I think it's afraid to.

Richard A. Cole has lived, traveled, and studied in over seventy countries; worked as a commercial fisherman, bodyguard, foreign correspondent, and lawyer; eaten things he cannot describe; and is currently working on his book, Mr. Motorcycle Man, *detailing the year he spent motorcycling from the U.S. to the tip of South America. He lives in Seattle, Washington.*

I sat on a wave-enameled log, drying my feet with my socks, and feeling the Gulf waft me into a meditative mood I knew was inappropriate: I had a good many miles to make before twilight intensified the dangers of the Mexican road. But helplessly I felt myself going into a kind of nod and recalling dreamily the opening to *Moby Dick* where Melville says that all footpaths inevitably lead down to whatever water is available, and that there at the water's edge—even if it was only a humble pond—you would find people staring off into the depths. Water and meditation, he claimed, are forever wedded. I had followed no footpath to this shore, but I had surely felt the lure of the Gulf and had followed the two truckers down here. Maybe they, too, had been lured by the simple, grand presence of the Gulf and had sat wordless on the sand thinking of time and transience.

But if I believed myself alone with these thoughts, I now realized that I was about to have company, for along the slant of the beach there came a lone horseman. It was futile to think of running for my clothes: they were well out of reach of the wavelets, and when I spied him at last the horseman was much too close. There was nothing to do then but sit there and wonder what this bearded man would make of the person he saw sitting on a log wearing nothing but a 1929 St. Louis Browns cap. He came on, his eyes wide but his bearing completely graceful. When he was abreast of me, he glanced casually, his eyes died down, and a small smile came across his lips. He pointed up at the high sun and said simply, "*Caliente*," and then he was past, his bright chestnut horse nimbly picking its way along the strand just out of reach of the lapping tide.

—Frederick Turner, *A Border of Blue: Along the Gulf of Mexico from the Keys to the Yucatán*

ANTHONY DePALMA

In Nahuatl It Means Butterfly

Mexico City tries to help itself by helping its children.

As one of the biggest, unruliest, most dangerously contaminated places on Earth, this is one tough city to live in, especially for kids. Some children in Mexico City are trained to tell the toxicity of the air by the red or black flags that fly over their schools. They are drilled on how to handle an earthquake. They can't avoid the thousands of street children who sell gum or beg for handouts at car windows they aren't even tall enough to see into.

Oh, Mexico City is a tough city, but lately, there's been an attempt to tame this monstrous place and make it a little more civilized for the 16 million people who live here. To truly become a first-class city and a world-class economic capital, Mexico City must also address the quality of life, starting with the very smallest lives.

So the city opened a spectacular new children's museum featuring a five-story maze, a musical staircase designed by the same man who did the tap dance piano in the move "Big," and a Rube Goldberg-type motion machine that uses bowling balls and at one point runs for six hundred feet.

It is already considered one of the largest and most technologically sophisticated touch-and-do museums in the world, the result of intense research, dedicated work, and, perhaps more than anything else, a willingness to try to make Mexico City a better place to live.

"We're trying to make Mexico City a more cosmopolitan city," said Juan Enriquez, head of the city's Department of Metropolitan Services, which oversees the museum project. "What this place is about is opening up a world-class children's museum and saying children here are important."

The formal name of the children's museum is Papalote. In Spanish it means kite, but in the native Indian language of

> Chiclets were invented in Mexico. The name comes from the word *chicle* which means chewing gum. The right price for Chiclets, Mexican to Mexican, is 10 little packets for a peso or about 30 cents. Don't pay more no matter how cute the seller is.
>
> —Paula McDonald, "Tantalizing Trivia"

Nahuatl, it is the word for butterfly. Thus, in either of the two main sources of Mexican culture—European or Indian—Papalote represents the museum's central theme: to raise the children of Mexico, and Mexico itself.

While a new museum fits into the city's scheme for reinventing itself, the political push for the complicated and expensive project came from Cecilia Occelli de Salinas, the wife of former President Carlos Salinas de Gortari. She was especially interested in finding alternative ways to teach young people in a country where most children don't go past the sixth grade.

The museum was built on the site of a former glass factory on the edge of Mexico City's central park, almost directly across from Los Piños, the Mexican White House.

The seed money came from the Salinas administration, but most of the $15 million it cost has been raised through donations and corporate contributions.

The architect was Ricardo Legoretta, who designed several Camino Real hotels in Mexico. The 33,000-square-foot complex is covered in traditional blue tiles, making it one of the first tile buildings built in Mexico in one hundred years.

The sculptor Sebastian donated a huge mobile that—depending on how it's viewed—looks like either a kite or a butterfly.

Located on the city's busy ring road, the Periferico, and in Chapultepec Park, the most visited place in Mexico City (more that 100,000 people use the park on the weekend), the museum's joyous exterior already has become a landmark. What's inside is likely to make it even more so.

Twenty years ago, there were just a handful of children's museums, in Brooklyn, Boston, Indianapolis, and a few other cities in the United States. Now there are hundreds all over the world. But few are located inside custom-designed buildings or come near the 250 exhibits in the new Mexico museum.

"They did a super job of doing their homework," said Nikki A. Black, the program director for the Children's Museum of Indianapolis, one of the largest and oldest children's museums in the world. Black said Papalote has "a world-class building," and some ingenious exhibits, like the rain forest tree. "They've made an excellent start," she said.

The Mexican museum's creative team visited dozens of exhibits around the world, picking the best ideas from each and then applying their own imagination. About 70 percent of the exhibits were designed and built here, but have not been patented, making them available for museums around the world.

Perhaps the single most spectacular exhibit, and the one that kept my three experimenters, DePalma children all, from sleeping the night after a recent visit, is the fantasy maze and light show inside a five-story-tall green-tile sphere.

Museums in Boston and Charlotte have similar mazes designed by the same man, Tom Luckey. Spencer Luckey, his son and assistant in Mexico, said insurance regulations and the lack of space in the United States—where most museums are built in existing structures—have always kept their designs modest. In Mexico, he said, they were able to give free reign to their ideas.

Anthony DePalma has been a reporter for the New York Times *since 1986, and is currently a correspondent in the Mexico City Bureau. He won a National Education Writers Association award in 1993, and lives in Mexico City with his wife and three children.*

Back on the street, the sound of children singing lures me to the crest of a bleak hill. There, the state secondary school is opening for the evening session. Maybe a hundred youngsters are mustered in the quadrangle, boys in spotless khaki, girls in gleaming white blouses and blue skirts. The broad-beamed principal and his matronly teaching staff are leading them through the not-very-stirring stanzas of Mexico's national anthem. Afterward, an honor guard of high-stepping girls parades the flag. Everyone stands at attention and gives the arm-across-the-chest salute. The children, with their shiny black hair, large dark eyes, and lively expressions are a very appealing lot. By U.S. standards, most are underprivileged. But they are cheerful-looking and beautifully behaved. Remembering the near chaos I've observed at some public school assemblies in my own country, I wish the educational system in Samula would export whatever it is that it is doing right.

—Donald G. Schueler, *The Temple of the Jaguar: Travels in the Yucatán*

RONALD D. GOBEN

The Flamingos of Celestún

Flamingos, and other things, thrive in an unlikely tourist spot.

There's really only one reason to go to Celestún: to see the flamingos. That's all the tourists hear about and it's likely that without flamingos no non-natives would ever visit Celestún.

Well, they're worth the trip. The sight of thousands and thousands of gorgeous birds floating on the estuary or taking off in a pink cloud is a sight that can be matched at few places in the world.

But Celestún has some surprises. There are miles of sandy beaches inhabited almost exclusively by small clusters of Mexican fishermen, children, and dogs. The thousands of sun-baked tourists who crowd the shores of Cancún on the opposite side of the Yucatán Peninsula are nowhere to be seen—although the beaches are definitely of the same quality.

Celestún is a small, primitive fishing village on the Gulf of Mexico, about 60 miles west of Mérida, the capital of Yucatán. Tourists use Mérida as a base for exploring the Mayan ruins of the Yucatán. A few—a very few—may take a side trip to Celestún.

Most of those who go take tour buses. But we had been assured that the best time to see the flamingos is shortly after daybreak. To do that, you must stay in Celestún overnight. And to stay in Celestún overnight, you must have a car.

Therefore, we left Mérida one afternoon in an ancient rented Volkswagen and headed due west over a virtually unmarked road that had no curves and

A left turn signal isn't always the same. On a highway, it means you're giving the guy behind you permission to pass. If you want to turn left off a highway, pull over to the right, let traffic pass, then cross the highway. There are often *retornos* (turn-around) that will make it even safer. The left turn procedure is changing due to urbanization, so you can't always depend on it. Just don't YOU put on your left blinker when somebody's behind you on a two-lane road and you'll do okay. On freeways, a left turn signal is a left turn signal.

—"Mexico" Mike Nelson,
Mexico from the Driver's Seat:
Tales of the Road from Baja to the Yucatán

almost no signs of life except for two tiny towns and a few grass shacks along the way.

The center of Celestún is one block from the beach. We drove that block and turned down the dusty path that served as a beachfront road. Gasping with thirst (the dominant feature of existence for an American tourist in the steamy Yucatán), we stopped in a little store for a soft drink.

"Hotel?" I said to the boy behind the counter. He pointed across the street and delivered a few words in Spanish.

It turned out indeed to be a hotel, one of three in Celestún and the newest of the three. In fact, it was so new it wasn't even finished. We discovered eventually that our room had no towels, a light that didn't work, and even lacked a toilet seat.

But it was clean, it was right on a magnificent sandy beach, and it had an eager proprietor who eventually provided all of the missing items except the toilet seat. And the price was right.

When we rented rooms, we asked about flamingos. The owner arranged a trip for us the next morning at 6 a.m. Since he spoke almost no English and we had only high school Spanish to help us, the transaction was accomplished largely through gestures—arm-flapping to indicate birds—drawings of a boat and written figures to indicate cost.

Once settled in our lodgings, we set out to explore Celestún. It didn't take long. There were a couple of small stores selling food and drinks; four or five restaurants, all featuring much activity centered around beer-drinking males (it was 4 p.m.); a fishing pier, at which the chief attraction for us was a woman carefully bathing her pet burro; and an astonishingly well-stocked boutique selling women's clothing and accessories, operating out of one of the small cottages lining the main street.

During our stroll, we were approached—almost attacked—by a teenaged boy on a bicycle, who went through the wing-flapping pantomime indicating flamingos. We tried to indicate

The coastal environment at Celestún was quite different from the coastal scrub along the north and east edges of the peninsula. Lagoon marshes and swamps occur along a narrow coastal strip, just inland of which is thorn forest habitat that is quite savannah-like in character.

The picture-memory I have of downtown Celestún is of the balcony of a store across the street from the hotel where two young boys held up a huge boa constrictor to show us. The snake must have been twelve feet long, and they could barely hold it up high enough to show it off. They wanted to sell that dead snake to us.

—Roland H. Wauer, *A Naturalist's Mexico*

that we had already booked a trip, but he seemed unconvinced, leaving us only when we returned to the hotel.

At about seven in the evening, we ventured out to eat, guessing that the late-afternoon drinkers would be gone from the restaurants.

They were gone all right—and so was everyone else. We walked past two, three, and finally half a dozen restaurants. All were shuttered. Nobody was eating dinner in Celestún at 7 p.m., and it was apparent that our timing wasn't the typical misstep of tourists getting out too early for the local eating times. No one would be eating in Celestún restaurants that night.

Ah, but we did. A dim light coming from the back of one open-air but vacant restaurant prompted us to follow it to its source: the kitchen. There we found a small older man, a young woman with a baby, and a black Labrador dog of uncertain age. The old man was clearly the proprietor and cook, and when he ascertained that we wanted to eat, he produced a menu.

We ordered fish. That we could tell from the menu. But we weren't at all sure how it would be prepared or what it would come with. Then we opened a couple of cold beers and waited.

I have no idea what kind of fish it was, but it was clearly fresh—probably hoisted from the sea three or four hours earlier. It was fried in some sort of garlic oil, and it was superb. It was accompanied by equally delicious fried potatoes.

We ate alone in the vast patio designed for approximately 200 people, visited from time to time by the family members who would say something to us in Spanish that we only dimly understood. The dog, Negra, sat at our side, resting her head on our laps and occasionally climbing part way into our laps. Nobody chased her away or even reprimanded her. Many dogs in Mexico are mistreated and ill-fed but Negra was as pampered as one of Queen Elizabeth's Corgis.

The next morning we were awakened at 5:30 by shouting outside our door. It was time to go flamingo watching. When we got down to the first floor, the hotel owner pointed to our guide: the teenaged boy on the bicycle from the afternoon before. We never did understand how he got the job, but he hopped on his bicycle and led us and our Volkswagen through the dust to a house where we were joined by a rotund, smiling young man in a t-shirt that said "Ruthless S.O.B."

Ruthless also spoke almost no English and probably had no idea of the meaning of his t-shirt. He got into our car and directed us by pointing to the lagoon and his boat. It was a launch with a canopy top to protect us from the sun and it could have easily seated twenty people. Again, we were the only passengers.

And out on the estuary we were almost the only boat, certainly the only passenger boat. It was a glorious morning, and the water was glassy smooth.

About three miles up the estuary, we saw a thin band of orange in the distance. It was our first sight of the flamingos. Soon we were drifting close to the sandbars on which they rested. Thousands of flamingos were resting in various spots along the open estuary. Every once in a while, a flock would take off, first three or four birds, then the whole flock in an enormous burst of flapping wings.

We drifted near several different flocks for about 45 minutes, then Ruthless turned toward shore. But instead of landing, we followed a narrow inlet back into a twisting mass of mangroves while Ruthless signaled us to be quiet. This was lagniappe to the flamingo tour—a private enclave that was home to dozens of varieties of birds. Eventually, we got out of the boat and walked around, stepping on tree roots that jutted up out of the water, listening to bird cries, and watching them dart back and forth in the trees. We couldn't talk it over with Ruthless because of the language barrier, but we had the impression this was his own secret place, and it was a place he loved.

Ronald D. Goben has worked for news organizations in Tokyo, Honolulu, Chicago, Denver, San Francisco, and Palo Alto. Currently he is a free-lance writer living with his wife, Lorrie, in the Sierra Nevada foothills town of Camino, California.

The next and last morning of my stay at the station [in Sian Ka'an Biosphere Reserve], I take a final drive down to the Glorieta Rojo Gómez. Beyond an imposing stretch of *selva alta*—tall jungle—the road eases itself onto a narrow causeway. The mangroves take over. A few minutes later I am at the end of the line, surrounded by blue sky, blue bay.

And birds. Hundreds of birds. Great blue, little blue, green-baked, tricolored, yellow-crowned, and tiger herons; snowy, great, and reddish egrets; roseate spoonbills, white ibis, pelicans, cormorants, frigate birds; and scores of gulls, terns, shorebirds. In short, all the birds that were supposed to be at Laguna de Muyil when I was there and weren't, because they were all here.

—Donald G. Schueler, *The Temple of the Jaguar: Travels in the Yucatán*

FREDERICK TURNER

Road Warrior

Driving in Mexico can be a true test of nerves.

Mexico, as everyone knows who has driven in it, is emphatically not a country in which you should be determined to "make time" on the roads. By the same token, there is a fair amount that may be learned about the country while crawling along a road system that is by the standards of the developed world primitive. If you choose to travel along Mexico's Gulf coast road, there is plenty of time for that kind of learning with the numerous delays where car ferries take you across bays and lagoons. Inland from the coast the roads are more heavily used, in rougher shape, and your opportunities for learning severely circumscribed by dangers. On these roads if you see an *Aviso* (Warning) to slow down, you had better heed it: the sign is likely telling you that the pavement utterly disappears around the next *curva peligrosa* (dangerous curve).

It isn't just the road system that is in bad repair, of course. Because of the pervasive poverty many of the vehicles you meet with are in alarmingly poor condition, but because of the ethos of the road they are driven as if they were prime. By far the best-maintained vehicles you meet are the company trucks. The petrol tankers and beer company rigs I saw were huge and spotlessly shiny, many of them bearing nicknames or slogans emblazoned on their front bumpers, and their drivers were true paladins of the highway. Inevitably, I traveled in company with these men and found myself awed by their nerve and élan. To be chased into one of those *curvas peligrosas* by a trucker and then to try to force yourself to accelerate through it while all your instincts screamed (like your tires) at you to brake—this was the daily duel of the Mexican road. And when your nerve failed and you did brake, you saw every glowing inch of your tail light reflected in the chromium grille behind you. Yet, to be sure, the trucker wasn't trying to

> Mexico's Green Angels patrol every major tourist road twice a day to help stranded tourists. Their help is free and good.
>
> —"Mexico" Mike Nelson,
> *Mexico from the Driver's Seat:*
> *Tales of the Road from Baja to the Yucatán*

kill you; he was merely trying to make time under difficult conditions. You either had to run with him and his fellows, or cede the road, and to run with them hour after hour took a stamina and a steadiness of will I found hard to maintain.

Mexican law only recognizes Mexican car insurance (*seguro*), so your insurance from any other country will not help you in Mexico.

Though not actually required by law, it is foolish to travel without Mexican liability insurance because if there is an accident and you cannot show a valid insurance policy, you will be arrested and forbidden to leave the immediate area until all claims are settled, which could take weeks or months. Mexico's legal system is modelled on the Napoleonic Code, under which all persons involved in an incident are assumed to be guilty until proven innocent; trial is by a court of three judges, not by a jury. Your embassy can do little to help you in such a situation, except to tell you how stupid you were to drive without local insurance.

—Tom Brosnahan, et al.,
Mexico – a travel survival kit

There were other hazards, as well, almost all of them symbols of a culture that exists in some apparently perpetual limbo between ancient ways and the modern industrial state. In agricultural areas at all hours but especially toward sundown you routinely encountered herders moving stock along the highway or its margins. Slow-moving horse- or ox-drawn carts, perhaps heaped in this season with stacked cane, lumbered along two-lane stretches, backing up motorized traffic for miles, but nobody honked in exasperation. At least, I thought as I waited out one of these processions, I wasn't in danger here of being shot by a motorist crazed by delays on roads where he assumed a right to travel full throttle. Always there were the pedestrians, either in the road itself or just off it. In the long, sobering reaches of Tabasco and Campeche there were solitary *campesinos* walking the roads with machetes slung at their hips, their faces like carved wood under battered straw hats. Outside Escárcega in Campeche I saw a peasant woman walking the sizzling asphalt barefoot. When cars blew past her with inches to spare the wind flattened the folds of her bright dress against her, but her expression never changed, and her eyes seemed set on some long horizon.

Dead dogs were everywhere—tossed up on medians where they withered to the consistency of wood; flung aside by impact to lie for who knew how long, stiff-legged and belly-up; newly smashed and right in the flow, their innards smeared wider with each successive hit, tails grotesquely wagging again and again, as if they hoped still for some token of human friendship.

At dusk dangers clustered. In broad daylight the burning of the fields, the pollution from oil refineries and sulfur plants, and diesel emissions combined to create a mist over the land. At dusk, though, the air thickened, and you felt you were driving through an endless veil of dark gauze. Even so, few drivers did so much as turn on their parking lights, and when I cravenly turned on my headlights, approaching truckers would flash theirs at me to ask what the hell was the matter. Even at the very edge of full dark many drove lightless. And at that hour, too, we were all hurrying toward our destinations and taking the kinds of risks we thought were worth it. So we hurtled, braked, stopped, waited, started, and hurtled on again in the not-light, a herd of vehicles thundering toward Villahermosa or Champotón or Campeche, hazed by the truckers who, perhaps alone, truly knew what they were doing.

Frederick Turner also contributed "A Routine Night in Veracruz" to Part I.

> **W**ho has the right of way at *glorietas*, those crazy Mexican traffic circles? The cars already going around, not those waiting to get in.
>
> —Paula McDonald, *"Tantalizing Trivia"*

Mark and I do a road count on Highway 200 between Puerto Vallarta and Puerto Escondido. This is what we see:

Eight dead dogs, with flies and vultures attached;

One mama pig, with nine little piggies, with nine little piggy tails;

One donkey, upside-down, feet in air, R.I.P.;

One truck with the phrase written on the back bumper *Un mundo de ilusiones* ("A world of illusions");

17 civil guards with guns, who ask, each time they stop us, where we're going, and who help themselves to the pens, bank bags, and whatever else they find in the glove compartment;

One lovely electric-blue lizard, reported at twelve feet (me) and six inches (Mark);

6,573,510 schoolchildren, various ages;

503 taco vendors;

15 flat, flatter, or flattest birds;

912 Tres Estrella buses going between 60 and 95 miles an hour;

Two amazingly velveteen, roseate sunsets;

One sunrise: gentle green-blue-orange, sweet;

27 men with bent frames (Lord Buckley's phrase);

35 women ditto;

One Old Crone of beady eyes and moustache, vigorously attempting to wave down *gringo* VW bus, thinking it a public bus;

811 trucks belching great black gaseous diesel fumes, racheting through hill and dale;

73 Brahmin cows, moving at between two and three miles per hour, firmly in the middle of Highway 200, between Jamiltepec and Pinotepa National, despite all buses, trucks, and *gringo* VWs.

—Carlos Amantea, *The Blob That Ate Oaxaca & Other Travel Tales*

JENNY LENORE ROSENBAUM

The Hills of Guanajuato

A brief whirl through Guanajuato nearly seduces the author into staying.

A disconcerting theme in some writers' reflections about Guanajuato is its cloak of lassitude, its sense of being broken by the burden of its past—oppressive political struggles and ruinous floods. Alice Adams, for one, calls it a city with "a brooding, dark sense of ruin, battered by time and a too-violent history."

True, during the War of Independence, the blood of revolutionaries gushed through the streets in a wild slaughter of innocents. For ten years the royalists hung the heads of insurgent heroes in cages at the Alhóndiga where independence forces had staged their first major military victory of the war.

But to my mind, it was a place stunningly devoid of melancholy: laughing children hawking flowers at twilight in what must be the coziest *zócalo* in all of Mexico; snaking *callejones* (alleyways) and arched bridges that give the magical Venetian labyrinths a run for their money; the Callejon del Beso (Alley of the Kiss) so narrow that sweethearts can (and do) embrace across it from facing balconies; colonial architecture that any fantasist would die for.

There is only one road south from Zacatecas to Guanajuato. You start out with scenery that looks like the backdrop for an old-fashioned western: the plain is arid, the cactus are scrubby, and mesas dominate the horizon like immobile ocean liners. But as you drive on, things begin to change: the cactus give way to maize, the valleys become green, the hills forested, until you climb up through the mountains and then dip down into Guanajuato. Zacatecas looks in upon itself—there are few outdoor cafés, and the bullring and the monastery of San Francisco both offer the exterior world the more severe side of their character—but Guanajuato is the opposite. Some two hundred miles to the south, the climate is gentler, the land more fertile, and its spirit is almost Mediterranean. The town meanders around, its streets following the serpentine contours of the hills it is built upon, with glimpses of green countryside visible at the far end of narrow alleyways.

—Guy Trebay, "Treasures of the Sierra Madre," *Condé Nast Traveler*

Its essence is that of an orchid: dramatic, intimate, exuberant, unfolding in exquisite ways.

The first morning, a casual stroll into the heart of the town revealed more astonishing echoes of Tuscan hill towns, Andalusia, Provençal, France, and even Greece's Aegean islands, than I ever thought could be found on the American continent. While lounging in the mist of a fountain, an aristocratic Spanish couple told us they had to come because they'd heard that Guanajuato surpasses Toledo (to which it is often compared) in splendor.

I knew of no two nations anywhere on the planet, with touching borders, as culturally dissimilar as the U.S. and Mexico. And here, in this one tiny valley, was not just another world, but worlds.

A bewildering profusion of styles—Moorish, French rococo, Italian baroque, Doric, and the extraordinary Spanish Churrigueresque—rubbed shoulders with uncanny grace. All this had arisen in the most improbable and inhospitable of settings: a narrow ravine straddled by the 6,700-foot sierras of central Mexico.

No trade route ever wove through this terrain. The *raison d'etre* for its emergence from relative obscurity was gold and silver—incredible quantities of it—unearthed in the 16th century. The now legendary San Bernabe mother lode, and later, the Veta de Rayas vein had transformed the town (among Mexico's oldest, founded soon after the conquest) into one of the wealthiest cities on earth, a place of unrivaled opulence in all of Latin America, the richest mining town in the world, and the third largest metropolis in the empire after Mexico City and Havana.

The urge (was it erotic or spiritual or both?) to merge with the town took over. Guanajuato, I sensed, could only be deeply known by becoming lost in it. In this regard, it is like Venice, and, indeed, the town shares with the Serenissima qualities that transcend their mutual fondness for labyrinths.

My companion Daniel and I, in a burst of gaiety, abandoned our guidebooks and maps at the hotel and stepped into the maze: passageways that, Escher-like, metamorphosed into hidden

P art of Guanajuato's magic is the rabbit warren of tunnels beneath the city where the bulk of traffic goes, leaving many streets above free for pedestrians. The original tunnel was blasted early this century to divert the river for flood control. Later the city made use of the local mining technology to blast tunnels to ease traffic congestions.

Guanajuato is famous for its annual Cervantes festival, and it is also a Mexican national monument, and a UNESCO World Heritage Zone.

—JO'R and LH

150

staircases; staircases that spilled into tiny plazas (fifteen in all) that offered the most satisfying balance of *sol y sombra*, sun and shade. At the far corner of one was a huge Day of the Dead mural depicting grimacing skeletons striding, with the determined glare of dinosaurs, across the town's landmarks. And everywhere were colonial facades beaming infinite shades of mint green, terra cotta, and mauve.

Extravagantly punctuating the city were churches which, as a local legend has it, were built of mortar mixed with silver powder and then moistened by choice Spanish wines. When I mentioned this to an irreverent nomad staying at our inn, he commented that this was clearly an attempt to buy off the Supreme Deity and, at the same time, get Him drunk. I, in turn, betraying my infatuation with the place, couldn't resist interjecting that perhaps the wine-soaked mortar was why the city had aged so intoxicatingly.

For a few breathless moments, we ducked into the neoclassical *tour de force*, the Teatro Juarez, where Placido Domingo sometimes gave impromptu performances owing to his affection for the town. It was straight out of *The Arabian Nights*—a pleasure palace draped in crimson. I implored Daniel, restless as always, to wait outside while I luxuriated in my own fantasies, triggered by eavesdropping on a local guide. She told of how operatic luminaries of past eras would bypass Mexico City as too provincial and instead go directly to Guanajuato.

I edged closer to her proud narration: "In its heyday, viceroys, presidents, and assorted voluptuaries, from Mexico and abroad, journeyed to this exact spot and to the baronial mansions surrounding it." Their purpose I already knew—to pay homage to the place that had allowed the Spaniards, and some *criollos* as well, to literally wallow in wealth.

Once outside, we got caught up in the student fervor of the neighborhood and were swept along towards the lofty flight of stairs leading to the University of Guanajuato. There, we stumbled upon, of all things, a postmodernist dance troupe of young Guanajuatans, rehearsing to a hypnotic Philip Glass score. For a moment, we thought we were back in Manhattan's East Village, and we left a bit dazed.

The lengthening shadows of late afternoon were suffusing the tiny plazas with a haunting rapture. Years ago in Burano, that dazzling island in the Venetian lagoon with rainbow-colored houses, I remember relishing a similar quality of light. But here it was different, perhaps more sublime.

It was a radiance explainable, I was convinced, by a phenomenon of physics only occurring in this town's plazas: the facades were so saturat-

"B ut," Octavio finally concluded, "There is really only one reason to go to Guanajuato, and that is to see my aunt." It turned out that Octavio's aunt had lived there (in a manner of speaking) for many years. For so many, in fact, that he couldn't tell me the precise number. When I looked puzzled, he delivered his punch line with glee: *Tía* Dolores was one of the famous mummies of Guanajuato. These macabre creatures, whose bodies had been preserved by the minerals in the earth, have been unceremoniously exhumed from the local cemetery and are now propped up in glass cases in the Museo de las Momias, earning valuable *turista pesos*. Octavio took both hands off the Dodg'em's steering wheel, clenched his cigarette between his teeth, contorted his arms in a hideous illustration of his long-dead aunt's body, and said, "You will promise to visit her?" Once again I was too amazed to say no.

—Gully Wells, "Cities of Silver,"
Condé Nast Traveler,

ed in roseate and creamy hues that they emitted a light wave all their own. And their frequency was actually intensified by the beams' entrapment within the circumscribed space.

Daniel, whose scientific frame of mind permitted little playfulness with the rigors of physics, looked at me like an escapee from the cuckoo's nest as I explained this to him. But I couldn't have cared less.

Nourished by some guava nectar but only partially reconciled, we threaded our way up to the *Carretera Panoramica*, the scenic highway encircling the town at its upper rim. Few tourists were out prowling. Still, our solitude was disrupted by recurring presences staring at us from shop windows—bizarre representations of Christ as black, bald, and starving. Had Guanajuato's centuries of isolation bred some arcane form of Christianity?

I never uncovered the real scoop. One wizened shopkeeper, however, wryly speculated that this image's popularity in the region might have its source in the fact that it reminds the people of a middle-aged, exhausted miner. Empathy with Christ's suffering always was, I recalled, an ingredient in Mexican Catholicism.

By the time we reached the summit, we ourselves felt like such a miner. But the panorama of the city, spread out below us, dissolved our fatigue.

Above us, tucked away amidst eerie boulders and the creviced, mined-out hills, was the town hospital. As Daniel is a surgeon, he was pleased by the discovery. Utterly unsterile in atmosphere, it was surely the most beautiful hospital I'd ever seen. The interior was total luminosity. Picture windows everywhere—culminating every corridor and in every room—afforded luscious views of the cityscape spreading over the stark mountains. We fantasized, for nearly an hour, about his working there and our living in the town.

The drama of early dusk had begun. To the east, an indigo mist was sifting, stealthily, across the plains of the Bajio. The complex tiers of the city were being claimed by shadows, then assuaged by a violet-lavender hush.

That night, in the silence of the Plaza de la Paz, I grappled to understand the city's magnetism. Perhaps it was its existence as a startling microcosm of the Old World cultures which have infused my spirit over the years. In this way, it was an odyssey unto itself. But I suspect it had more to do with oddities like unfathomable shades of coral and ochre, and the ancient precipices to which they clung. This was no ordinary city, living in the thrall of time, but a timeless mandala as elusive as the way home.

Our final days there flowed together like the river of gold which had carved it. I could barely distinguish one trembling dawn from another. The town came to feel like an inscrutable lover, alternately wanton and discrete, tender and aloof. My tryst with the siren called Guanajuato had almost seduced me into abandoning my fickle, wandering ways—almost.

Jenny Rosenbaum is a writer who feels she escaped Manhattan just in time. She now lives in San Francisco but feels more at home in Japan, Italy, Greece, or Mexico.

I will always remember that dark and windy winter's eve in Guanajuato when a constant knocking at the door of my 17th-century home obliged me to release my stranglehold on a bottle of Mexican beer, turn down the TV, put a smile on my face, and open to inclement weather. Before my eyes stood a figure in dark robes of the last century, about 80 years of age, sincerity written all over his weathered face.

"I have come to thank you for what your countrymen did for Mexico in '47."

My neurons raced around in an unforgiving brain. I thought, Christ, what happened in '47? Second World War had finished, Korea hadn't started, Vietnam was in a time machine, and anyway, "Paddy" wasn't exactly overtly involved in those shenanigans. He stood there expectant of some kind of acknowledgment. Play for time, I thought. "Oh yes, of course," I replied. It was an interesting moment. "Probably a long time before we see the likes of it again."

"Yes," he said. "A noble gesture against the invading North American forces."

Gotcha, I thought. He's on about the Saint Patrick's Brigade, who fought with the invading forces, switched sides at intermission, fought with the Mexicans, refused to surrender for obvious reasons when the tide turned against them, and had achieved undeniable glory amongst Mexican historians. (I suspect their U.S. counterparts do not share the same viewpoint.) He then presented me with a romantic novel about the Paddy's Brigade by one Patricia Cox.

Without further ado he bade his farewell and left me numbified. Here was a gentleman of humble origin with carefully kept clothes of an era long past, who had reserved a few pesos to buy me a novel in gratitude of an event which occurred in 1847. Tears welled in my eyes. Some months later Mustafa died.

With this newly acquired information I now felt I had an historical right to be here, considering the heroic acts of my forefathers, not blood relations but close enough to make no difference.

—Desmond O'Shaughnessy Doyle, "An Irishman in Guanajuato"

CAROL PUCCI

Riding the Rails in Sonora

When travel plans go awry, opportunity arises.

It was 5:30 a.m. as the sun broke out of the clouds. But instead of throwing open the door of our hotel room to bask in the warmth of another Sonoran sunrise, we were camped at the train station, surrounded by hobos who had spent the night on the floor huddled under blankets. Aeromexico had just declared bankruptcy and we found ourselves stranded in the seaside city of Guaymas, Sonora, about 350 miles south of Tucson. We were looking for a way back home.

One-way rental cars were hard to come by and very expensive, and we'd been told there was a three-day wait for a bus. But the 6 a.m. train to the Nogales border crossing would let us connect with a Greyhound bus to Tucson, where we would catch our plane to Seattle. As it turned out, the $5 train fare not only bought us transportation, but an eight-hour adventure that certainly wasn't written into our itinerary for a relaxing Mexican vacation.

The small, dirty station with several broken windows, a large clock missing one of its hands, and a shuttered ticket window contrasted with places in Mexico that American tourists usually frequent. We seemed the only ones there with luggage bigger than a bedroll. As a freight train pulled into the yard we learned why. The men wrapped in blankets hopped aboard. We were left to try and find out when the next passenger train was due.

A young man staggered up to us. He had no information about trains but offered Tom, my husband, a swig of beer. The only other people nearby were a man selling Chiclets and an old woman in sandals sweeping the stone walk outside.

We sat down on wooden benches and waited. Gradually, the station started filling up with families, grandmothers, and businessmen. The ticket window opened at 7 a.m. "First class?" I asked. "*No más,*" the ticket seller said. We learned later that the first class section had been turned into a dining car. The train to Nogales arrived at 8 a.m. Mexican military men, armed with machine guns, patrolled the platform as we searched for a car that wasn't full. We squeezed into the vestibule above the couplings between the final two cars. It was standing room only. It would be for the rest of the trip.

"*Mucha gente,*" a friendly young man laughed as he hopped aboard. "Many people."

He sat down on a giant burlap sack of clams he was bringing to friends in Mexicali. We made ourselves comfortable on our suitcases. Digging into his duffle bag, he passed around some Spanish comic books and a few of his wedding pictures.

"Mexicali?" he asked.

"No, Nogales," I answered. It was then we learned that the train would split soon, and this car would be going to Mexicali.

We jumped off at the next stop with a "*Muchas gracias*" for our friend and ran to squeeze into a car bound for Nogales. We stood in the vestibule next to three Mexican teenagers who wanted to know why we didn't take the bus.

"The bus is much better," said one of the fellows.

"Why didn't you?" we asked.

"All full," he laughed.

> The train system is not as extensive nor as punctual as the bus system. Even when they are on time, trains can take twice as long as buses to reach their destination. Riding the rails is best for lesiurely travel in very picturesque areas. (The 12-hr. sleeper from Guadalajara to Mexico City is reputed to be pure joy.)
>
> —Harvard Student Agencies, *Let's Go: Mexico*

The food vendors made their way through the cars—a man with a big plastic bucket of shrimp with a bottle of hot sauce hooked on the side, women selling homemade chicken tostadas, another with a single ceramic plate of tamales, tacos, and fruit. We were tempted to throw caution to the wind and indulge, but thought again, and decided to make do with a carton of juice and two chocolate chip cookies we had brought along with us.

Soon we were serenaded by an older man who boarded the train with his guitar and a tape deck tied to his neck with a red bandanna. "*Permiso,*" said a well-dressed woman, stepping out on the vestibule for some air, and to throw her baby's disposable diaper out the window. She went back to her seat in the car, and returned a few minutes later, politely excusing herself again, as she dumped a half-quart of orange juice out of the train.

For the next several hours, we soaked up the sights, the smells, the sounds, the dust—and we welcomed the word "Nogales" when the train finally pulled into the station two miles from the U.S. border. Did we wish we had rented a car after all? Not a chance. Funny how an experience like this can change your perspective about traveling styles. The more you pay, the less you often see, let alone taste, smell, and experience. Besides, by this time our idea of luxury was a seat on that Greyhound bus bound for Tucson.

Carol Pucci is the Business Editor for The Seattle Times *and a free-lance journalist. She has traveled extensively in Mexico, Europe, and Asia.*

En route for Chihuahua...across a bare desert landscape, its dust, like that of the vast Asian plateaus, suddenly enveloping everything on the road...and that wind, the desert flute playing through the panes.... I love those stretches where the eyes are not under constant siege, where they can get lost in the immensity of the earth joining the sky, where dreams become possible. To travel in a bus, see the landscape roll by like a silent movie, and I absent, lost in my thoughts, sometimes feeling a total emptiness inside myself, gazing through the window unconcerned about nature, people, or things, absorbing only the motion.

—Abbas, *Return to Mexico: Journeys Beyond the Mask*

Diving with Hammerheads

Hammerhead sharks do not eat people, or so the author hopes.

In his book *The Fishes of New York,* Samuel Latham Mitchell tells us that during the month of September, 1805, Joshua Turry of Riverhead, Long Island, N.Y., netted three hammerhead sharks.

"The largest," Mitchell wrote, "was eleven feet long. On opening him, many detached parts of a man were found in his belly: these were collected and buried; there was also found a striped cotton shirt, patched on the sides and sleeves with bright-colored pieces."

The disjointed somebody who was mentioned by Mitchell may well have been dead before his rendezvous with the shark. In fact, like most sharks, hammerheads pose little threat to people. But the thought that a hammerhead *could* complement its usual diet of stingrays with a human being is something held in common by all divers hoping to see one.

At least that's the case with the divers who seek out hammerhead sharks at El Bajo, literally "the Deep Place," a wide swatch of Sea of Cortez near La Paz, circled by sugary beaches and cacti standing on tan hills that enjoy less than an inch of rain every hundred years.

The same sun that broils the hills heats much of the sea to a glorious 80 degrees by late summer, luring more than 750 species of fish from the chilly Pacific. In so doing, it puts the Sea of Cortez in the same league as the Caribbean, the Red Sea, and Micronesia as among the world's best dive spots.

Although hammerhead sharks can be seen at El Bajo year-round, the underwater visibility is best from July through September. That's also the best time for snorkelers to visit, as the water is warm and filled with more fish than in the colder months. Summer air temperatures often exceed 100 degrees, but it's a very dry heat.

scalloped hammerhead shark

Amid the plethora of marine life at El Bajo are scalloped hammerheads, one of eight known hammerhead species, which can grow to at least twelve feet and have been seen in groups of several hundred. Within El Bajo, the place to find scalloped hammerheads (so named because of the scallop-resembling grooves in their heads) is the worn tip of a submerged extinct volcano known locally as the Sea Mount.

From boatside, the water above the Sea Mount is dark turquoise, and on a good day one can see the beige-sand top of the undersea mountain eighty feet below. Entering the water, a scuba diver sees schools of small fish, possibly a barracuda or two, and a sandy ocean bottom that now appears to be stitched together with patches.

As the diver descends to thirty or forty feet, the "patches" are exposed for what they are: dark mounds of rock and coral typically rising some ten feet off the ocean floor. And seen gracefully weaving between the piles—if the diver is lucky—are hammerheads apparently on the prowl for stingrays nestled beneath the sand.

The thing is, the hammerhead is an expert at ferreting out buried rays. Its head has evolved into a flat hydrofoil resembling a stubby airplane wing, permitting the shark to cruise almost effortlessly just above the ocean floor. The fish's eyes are at the front of its head, and the whole structure is speckled with tiny sensors that detect through electrical reception. Divers have reported seeing a hammerhead scoop out a stingray completely buried in the sand.

According to researchers at the Scripps Institution of Oceanography in La Jolla, California, there are no records of a scalloped hammerhead ever tracking a *person*—in the Sea of Cortez, at least. But that fact is quickly forgotten when a few hammerheads sweep past.

Although over 60 species of sharks are found in Baja waters, some are rather rare while most stay clear of humans. The more common species are found offshore to inshore from Magdalena to the Midriff, including the smooth hammerhead, common thresher, bonito, sand, blue, black-tip, and the world's largest fish (reaching up to 18 meters and 3,600 kilograms), the whale shark.

Rays are quite common in warmer offshore to inshore waters throughout Baja. Many varieties have barbed tail-spines that can inflict a painful wound when the ray feels threatened. (Contrary to myth the barb is not actually venomous, although a ray "sting" easily becomes infected.) Experienced beachgoers know to perform the "stingray shuffle" when walking on sandy bottoms. If you bump into a ray resting on the bottom it will usually swim away; if you step on one, it's likely to give you a flick of the barb.

—Joe Cummings, *Baja Handbook*

On a gorgeous day in September, I found myself in just that position.

I was diving with a buddy, Rick Traversi of Sacramento. We'd made arrangements to make four dives with a La Paz-based company that I'd hired the year before for a sea lion-watching expedition. As planned, a boat picked us up at the beach behind our hotel, and 45 minutes later we were dropping anchor above the Sea Mount. On the first dive, we saw several long barracudas, a couple of hideously ugly green moray eels, and a wide variety of brightly colored fish, and we even swam within 30 feet of a large marlin (a rare sight these days), but, alas, no hammerheads. Although hammerhead sharks can be found in the vicinity of the Sea Mount year-round, it wasn't until our last dive of the trip that we actually came across one.

Rick and I were out front of a group of five divers, swimming against a slight current that carried bits of grayish-brown crud kicked up by a recent storm, reducing our visibility to 50 feet. The sea floor appeared and disappeared as clouds of crud passed, and I was beginning to give up hope of seeing a hammerhead shark on this trip when Rick pointed at something down and ahead.

There, gliding without apparent effort between masses of coral, was an eight-foot-long shark with an unmistakable T-head that jutted out front of a thick, gray body. In a moment it slipped out of sight, disappearing into a murky wall that we were quickly approaching. But just a beat after it vanished, a pair of even larger hammerheads emerged from the same cloudy mass below and in front of us—and just as suddenly disappeared again.

We were running low on air at this point when three more hammerheads appeared out of the grayness about 75 feet below and in front of us. The trio was moving toward us. At about 60 feet, two of the sharks moved to the right and vanished. The third, however, an animal we later estimated to measure about 12 feet, kept coming. And it was moving its head from side to side—the way sharks do when they're tracking prey.

Several divers had told me that hammerheads are very skittish around scuba divers; the fish apparently are turned off by all the bubbling the tanks produce, they said. By the time the hammerhead was within 15 feet of me, its big head undoubtedly picking up *lots* of electrical impulses from my pounding heart, I took to frantically waving my arms and making as many bubbles as I could. To my extreme relief, the giant fear-inspiring beast glided past, its predatory dead eye and rows of gnarly teeth practically in reach, but its appetite apparently unwhetted by this obviously spastic creature in a body-hugging rubber suit.

In the days that followed, Rick and I snorkeled with sea lions, raced a school of fun-seeking dolphins in a rented boat, and partied with other travelers on one of the area's many secluded beaches. But what we'll remember most were those hammerheads, especially the one that came so close before turning and skipping back into the grayness of a stormy sea.

Scott Doggett reported on wars in Afghanistan and El Salvador before joining the Los Angeles Times *as an editor in 1989. He has visited more than 50 countries and is writing his first book on the history of the Ho Chi Minh trail.*

We cling to the anchor line, human dive flags flapping in the Sea of Cortez's underwater breeze. Safety stop. Dive over. A shadow as wide as a cruise ship drifts by. I look up and my mask plate is filled with white spots and blue skin. A whale shark is swimming through us like we're laundry on *his* line.

Behind a goatee of remoras I can see his long grin. Is it a mockery? A friendly greeting? The sweet contentment of knowing you're the biggest fish in what has been called the world's richest sea? He lumbers past us like a mile-long freight train, disappearing into the vague blue distance.

Mental note: In the Sea of Cortez, Señor Big favors you with a visit when you least expect it.

They say you're not supposed to come down here looking for the big stuff—manta rays with 20-foot wingspans and clearance to land at O'Hare, whale sharks, schooling hammerheads, marlins taller than Manute Bol. They say overfishing has made encounters with Señor Big too unpredictable. Content yourself with the 250 species of reef fish and 750 species of other fish—more fish of different sizes, shapes, and colors than just about anywhere else on the planet.

—Jim Sommers, "In Search of Señor Big," *Scuba Diving* magazine

Golden Guadalajara

The author passes on a family heirloom: Mexico's most Mexican city.

N o wonder some children got lost. Through the archway I could see the street, with its jumble of noise and color: the reds of bougainvillea blossoms, the plumes and sequins of dancers, the smoke from kiosks where tacos were cooking—and a jostling crowd of two million people witnessing the annual six-mile pilgrimage from the Cathedral of Guadalajara to the Basilica of Zapopan.

Here in the patio of the city hall, I counted nineteen lost children. But none were crying. Pretty, dark-eyed volunteers were entertaining the youngsters with toys, games, videos, and enough junk food to spoil their appetites through junior high.

The only person who seemed upset was a distraught mother who'd just arrived. "Maria Elena!" she cried. "You're here, thanks to God! Come, we must go home."

But Maria Elena was of another mind. "Please, Mama," she begged, "I want to stay."

I could sympathize. When I'm enjoying the glamorous city and environs of Guadalajara, I certainly don't want to go home. And, in fact, I have stayed here for many a month, and in many a year. Why do I keep returning?

Well, Guadalajara is delicious. This city is to Mexico what Seville is to Spain—the voluptuous, sun-ripened essence of the whole country, a romantic anthology of all the national clichés. It's Mexico's most Mexican city.

Here is the home of the musical *mariachis* and the land of the dashing horsemen called *charros*, those same suave gallants who lend their broad-brimmed *sombreros jaranos* to their famously beautiful ladies for the Mexican hat dance, which also originated here.

Guadalajara, the nation's second city in population, sits in a high valley some 300 miles northwest of Mexico City and presides as the capital of Jalisco, the prosperous state that leads Mexico in producing corn for tortillas. And if you want to toast Jalisco success, you must reach for the national drink, tequila—also a local invention.

But it's more than that. "If I knew of a better place, I'd go there," says Marshall Wright, an American expatriate. The Guadalajara area encompasses one of the largest colonies of retired Americans and Canadians living abroad—between 18,000 and 30,000, depending on the season and who's counting. And since the area has an estimated five million people, the English-speaking residents blend right into the flower-garnished landscape.

I can't quarrel with their choice. At an altitude of 5,200 feet and comfortably tucked into the Tropic of Cancer, the city enjoys mild temperatures all year: never ice, rarely sweat, orchids and palms outdoors, blankets on the bed.

Decades ago, on the advice of my parents, I chose this spot for a half-year residence to write a book. My wife and I brought our months-old firstborn son, Kelly. All of us thrived. Naturally, we regard Guadalajara as a family heirloom.

When I returned to Guadalajara recently for the Zapopan pilgrimage, I again took with me that firstborn son, Kelly. He is now himself a father graying at the temples, but he remembers other visits from his boyhood. This time Kelly and I found Guadalajara two different cities. The center of town is a stroller's city, with narrow streets and intimate plazas separating old buildings of weathered beige sandstone. This is the old city we remembered from long ago. But farther out, we needed a car; streets are wide, distances wider, buildings new and taller. Traffic moves like the grand prix. But both these concentric cities have the same flavor, poinciana and lemon trees, roses and fountains everywhere. (Officially, the city counts 146 public fountains, but I bet there are more.)

Kelly calls Guadalajara "time travel." So it is, if you start at the elegant center of town, the Plaza Tapatía. Since the completion of its restoration in 1982, the seven-block plaza has become the city trademark—what Rockefeller Center is to New York and St. Mark's Square to Venice.

Actually, this is not one plaza, but a whole chain of plazas architecturally anchored at one end by the 16th-century cathedral. This cathedral looks like no other in Mexico, for it's a summary of styles from three centuries of construction and alteration. Its twin towers resemble steeples sheathed in glossy yellow and blue tile. Inside, while choirs send musical echoes through three cavernous naves, the faithful light candles and pray before a dozen altars, a balsam-wood statue of Our Lady of Roses, and a 17th-century painting of the Virgin of Murillo. Outdoors, the tropical glare seems fierce, and visitors are glad to find a shady bench in the open spaces of the Plaza Tapatía. These subplazas are interrupted and defined by other landmarks built through the centuries. At the neoclassical Degollado Theater, which bears a likeness to Milan's La Scala, visitors can take in ballets, symphony concerts, or plays.

Farther along, strollers pass flower beds, statues, shops, fountains, reflecting ponds—and, at last, the Cabañas Cultural Institute. This building, with its crested rotunda and 23 patios, was built in 1801 as an orphanage—perhaps the most spectacular orphanage in the New World. Indeed, four hundred orphans lived here until 1980, when the youngsters got a modern home outside town. Now the Cabañas has been turned into a multipurpose civic center, with art shows, poetry readings, and musicales. Almost any day you can find art students here, arguing seriously about their work, studying, flirting, and arguing more seriously about their fun.

Behind the Degollado Theater, a fountain-sprayed bronze sculpture depicts conquistadores and their retinue as they founded the city. Court intrigues and Indian unrest made the early capital a restless thing; it moved three times before builders started work near this plaza on February 14, 1542.

Founded on Valentines' Day, how could Guadalajara escape a romantic reputation?

"What do you think of our women?" a young man in the plaza asked me. He pointed out some passing beauties, and I agreed they were lovely. "Not just that," he said. "The *best!*" His civic pride had hormones.

Although we had become fond of the series of squares behind the Degollado Theater, known as the Plaza Tapatía (people from Guadalajara are called *tapatías*, from an Indian phrase that means "three times worthy," a proud and boastful nickname), and we had admired the imposing façade of the building known as the Orphanage, the Hospicio Cabañas, it was not until almost our last day in Guadalajara that we managed to get there at a time when the place was open (strange, unpublicized hours of opening and closing can be a problem in Mexico). No longer an orphanage, it is now a cultural center, housing some of Orozco's most magnificent murals—a ceiling of murals, in fact, that is quite overwhelming: four gigantic male figures, supposedly representing Earth, Wind, Water, and Fire. Orozco always refused to elaborate any further.

Also magnificent are the stone fireplaces, huge and very plain; one imagines pigs on spits, at the very least.

It is hard indeed to imagine orphans in this place. How awestruck they must have been, poor mites.

—Alice Adams, *Mexico: Some Travels and Some Travelers There*

Romantic. On wrought-iron park benches, lovers fondly braid themselves together—even at high noon. And at night, when the moon is full and the air scented with orange blossoms, when *mariachis* sing plaintively of unrequited love, then even a newcomer can see why Jalisco produces poets.

And dashing horsemen. That's another thing about this big city: it's still a rural town. In the Corona Market, near the cathedral, you see big-hatted ranchers buying bridles and chicken troughs and big-roweled spurs. Boot makers display their flashing reptile-skin products in shop windows along Avenida Juárez. But don't expect to buy boots here if your shoe size is as large as a 10; Jalisco cowboys have small feet. I wear a size 10 1/2, and boot salesmen thought I had a pituitary problem.

The nearness of the countryside makes possible the *charro* tradition. In Mexican folkways the *charro* is somewhere between a cowboy and knight errant. His arts—like those of the American cowboy—began in the workaday skills of cattle ranching.

Every Sunday at noon, Guadalajarans go out to the *charreada* ring on the edge of Agua Azul Park to cheer for these skills of man and beast. Men don't just rope bulls. They do rope tricks, "Flowering the lasso," as they describe it, stepping through the loop stylishly before dropping it over an animal's head.

I have rarely seen tourists at these exhibitions, and I don't understand why. *Charreadas* are colorful fun, even if you don't understand all the rules. Whole families turn out. *Mariachis* play rousing tunes. There's tension when hoofs thunder out of the chute, a collective gasp when a man gets thrown by a bronc, and a taut silence when the *charro* performs the "pass of death," leaping from one bareback horse to the back of another—all at breakneck speed. And when a contestant shows special skill, the roaring crowd hurls hats into the dust of the ring. (The *charro* gallantly tosses each hat back to its owner or someone nearby.)

Visitors turn out in greater numbers, of course, for bullfights. And Guadalajarans manage to get some of the world's best matadors, especially on big holidays. One Sunday afternoon, Kelly and I saw an impressive young *rejoneador*—a bullfighter on horse back—named Rodrigo Santos. Controlling his horse only with his legs, Santos placed barbed *banderillas* into the bull's neck and wheeled away just ahead of the horns. For killing the bull, Santos risked only his own skin and wielded the sword afoot. But the great moments were those with man and horse moving in perfect coordination. Watching such a performance, Kelly and I could understand why the Aztecs thought that a horse and its rider were all one beast.

The Monday after that bullfight, I checked local sports pages. The newspaper convinced me: bullfights don't bring the crowds that other sports do now. The city boasts four professional soccer teams and easily hundreds of amateur teams—plus baseball, tennis, and swimming. The metropolitan area lists four 18-hole golf courses and one with 9 holes. Add to that squash and racquetball and handball.

There's even boating—on Lake Chapala, the country's largest body of fresh water, 25 miles southeast of the city. It is a beautiful lake, rimmed by steep hills, dotted with verdant islands, framed by mango trees on the shore. Depending on the light and time of day, Lake Chapala can resemble a shadowless Japanese print or a gaudy postcard from the Riviera.

As ever, my son and I made the touristic rounds: churches, parks, arcades. Guadalajara's museums have their own flair. The regional museum, for example, is housed in a thick-walled baroque colonial building that was once a seminary; the setting is perhaps the best exhibit of all. The handicrafts museum displays the enormous range of folk arts here—and offers most of them for sale, with only a slight markup. I am partial to the Orozco Museum, the well-preserved home and studio of that giant of painting, José Clemente Orozco, a loyal local son who died in 1949. Some of his finest—and largest—paintings can be found in Guadalajara, including one of his vast last works, a violent fusillade of paint, "Hidalgo and the Liberation of Mexico," in the Palace of Government.

Visitors who choose to come to Guadalajara in October get one of the great shows in the New World, the annual October Fair. A calendar of events fills a catalog. Pavilions sprout in the plazas. Outdoor stages, spotlights, and sound systems bring lianas of electronic wiring. And you can take your pick of *mariachi* bands from all over the republic, dance groups, poets reading their works, and singers both good and awful. (Mexicans will politely applaud the flattest of vocalists; a bad bullfighter, though, gets pelted with scorn and beer bottles.)

Besides the fair, the great pilgrimage of the Virgin of Zapopan takes place each October 12. The center of attention is a tiny corn-

In Mexico, don't ever be shy about sampling. You can ask for a taste here—of anything. The national pastime is nibbling. And sniffing. And trying before buying. So feel free to ask for a freebie. A little piece of this, a pinch of that. Simply smile and ask, "*¿Puedo probar?*" ("May I taste?") The answer will aways be, "*¡Sí!*" and suddenly a whole, wonderful world awaits you.

—Paula McDonald, "Tantalizing Trivia"

cob figure. This humble likeness of the Virgin was brought into a desperate battle in 1541, when the Spanish were losing to rebellious Indians. The tide turned, the Spaniards won, and the little Virgin has been venerated ever since.

The early morning pilgrimage itself is best watched while breakfasting on a high balcony along the parade route. And parade it largely is: in addition to the pious with their banners and sincerity, the parade includes mounted cowboys, marching bands, police cars with ear-wrenching sirens, troupes from a score of church parishes doing their versions of Indian dances, people masked for Halloween, red devils, and enough gold lamé to make you snow blind—200,000 marchers and ten times that number watching. Silence falls over the crowd when the carriage of the Virgin moves by, for here fun is not foreign to piety.

My cheeriest pastime in Mexico is people watching. And in Guadalajara the best place is the Plaza Tapatía by evening, and especially on a weekend: squealing toddlers and tottering grandmas, flirtatious girls swaying on high heels, guys whispering appreciation for a lady's too-tight skirt, peddlers offering candy or painted plates or caged canaries twittering past their bedtime. A blind beggar holds a cup of coins while singing an earnest hymn; passersby drop change in the cup—unbidden: this is still a land of personal charity.

Some nights musicians fill the park bandstand for an evening concert; strollers stop, music starts, and old men keep time with their walking sticks.

Nostalgically, I am transported around town—and across some decades—by a horse-drawn carriage called a *calandria*. I can remember when these buggies, with their uncertain convertible tops, were the cheap transportation of the poor. Now both the horses and the fares are fatter; *calandrias* carry tourists. Bright paint has made them quaint, and they await their clients beside the Church of San Juan de Dios, two blocks from the Plaza Tapatía.

Up a few steps, a plaque identifies the Plazuela de los Mariachis, a deformed little plaza now under repair. It was here that party givers would come to audition *mariachi* bands and bargain for the price. This was the very cradle of *mariachis* in the last century. When the French came here under Napoleon III, they naturally fell in love with beautiful *tapatías*—and hired musicians for wedding parties. And so, it is said, the French word *mariage* was adapted.

I think back to my dear mother's memories of this city, when she and my father chose restaurants that guidebooks described not as "three star" but simply as "clean." And now, more than 40 years later, with dozens of famous restaurants and 10,000 inviting hotel rooms, Guadalajara gives the visitor easier access to its traditional past. This city in the sun, this heirloom, seems older, newer, and better all the time.

Bart McDowell is a retired National Geographic *editor who has worked in 65 countries, including Mexico. He has written numerous articles and five books for* National Geographic, *and now lives in Maryland and Texas.*

My mother remembered Mexico as a girl. She remembered the taste of Mexican ice cream, creamier than here. She remembered walking with her sisters round the plaza at night, the warm Guadalajara nights. She remembered a house—an address—tall shadows against a golden wall. In Mexico her mother made laces to sell, seeming to pluck the patterns out of the air with her fingers—laces fallen, like snowflakes, through time. My mother kept a cellophane bag full of lace in a drawer in the kitchen. She brought the bag out to show us, unfolding the laces tenderly as cobweb. Mexican women are real women, my mother said, caressing the antimacassar spread open upon the table. But the beauty of the lace troubled her. She admitted she never wanted to learn it.

Oh, but my mother's brother Juanito was tall as a tree, strong as a tree, with shade in his eyes. And people threw coins when my mother danced on a table in high-button shoes, tossing her head like a pony at the call of her nickname, Toyita. Toyita, she remembered the lyrics of a song. Ah, there are no love songs like the love songs of Mexico. This country is so dry, like toast, my mother said. Nothing like Mexico, my mother said, lapping the blue milk of the memory of Mexico.

—Richard Rodriguez, *Days of Obligation: An Argument with My Mexican Father*

ALICE ADAMS

Finding Frida Kahlo

*In a San Francisco gallery, the author discovers a love for the work of painter
Frida Kahlo. This leads her, naturally, into Mexico.*

When I thought of a return trip to Mexico City, with some friends
who had never been there before, I remembered the Camino Real,
which would be as far out of the fumes and the general turmoil as
one could get, I thought—with advertisements featuring three swimming
pools.

And this trip's true object, twenty years after my first contact with
her, was Frida Kahlo: I wanted to make a pilgrimage to her house, and I
had talked two friends into coming with me—Gloria, a writer, and Mary,
an art critic.

All of this more or less began in the spring of '87, when there was an
extraordinary exhibit of Kahlo's work at the Galeria de la Raza, in San
Francisco. So many painters' work is weakened by its mass presentation
in a show, but this was not so with Kahlo's work: the overall effect was
cumulative, brilliantly powerful, almost overwhelming. Her sheer
painterly skill is often overlooked in violent reactions, one way or another, to her subject matter, but only consummate skill could have produced
such meticulous images of pain, and love, and loneliness.

I began to sense then, in San
Francisco, a sort of ground swell
of interest in both her work and
in her life—and the two are inex-
tricable. Kahlo painted what she
felt as the central facts of her life:
her badly maimed but still beautiful body, and her violent love for

> One of the pleasures of traveling in
> Mexico is finding amazing art every-
> where, such as the murals in civic
> buildings throughout the country.
>
> —JO'R and LH

Diego [Rivera]. In fact, these days Frida has become a heroine of several
groups; she is a heroine as an artist; as a Third World woman; and also as
a handicapped woman. And then there is still another group popularly
referred to as "women who love too much," the "too much" referring
especially to men perceived as bad, as unfaithful, and not loving enough
in return.

171

I began to read all I could about Frida Kahlo.

The accident that maimed her occurred when she was eighteen: a streetcar rammed into the trolley in which she was riding, and her spine was broken in seventeen places—it is astonishing that she should have survived. Her pelvis was penetrated by a shaft of metal (a "rape" of which Frida made much), her reproductive organs were gravely injured.

Considerable controversy continues over the precise facts about her injuries. Medical records are lost, or missing. It is now impossible to determine whether she actually did, as she claimed, have seventeen corrective operations; Frida did tend to exaggerate, to mythologize herself, but even a dozen such operations would be quite a lot. It is also uncertain whether she could or could not bear children, or whether she really wanted to. Certainly she was pregnant a number of times and suffered both therapeutic abortions and miscarriages. It would seem to me that she was extremely ambivalent, to say the least, about having children.

She was not ambivalent about Diego; she adored him, she loved him too much.

In the course, then, of reading about Frida, of looking at what paintings I could (even in reproduction they are, to me, both intensely beautiful and powerfully moving), and of talking to a few Kahlo scholars, one of the first things that I learned about her was that, in addition to her extraordinary and absolutely original talent, Frida had a capacity of inspiring feelings of an exceptional intensity in almost

Among the famous muralists to have worked in the formative years of the Revolution, Diego Rivera has achieved the most renown. His murals at the Detroit Institute of Arts and the Rockefeller Center in New York City exposed his political themes—land reform and Marxism—to a wide audience and embroiled him in international controversy. The two other prominent muralists of the 1920s and 1930s, David Alfaro Siqueiros and José Clemente Orozco, also had disciples outside Mexico. The formally innovative Siqueiros could not resist a curved surface. Orozco focused on the violence and brutality of the Revolution, but was less explicitly political than his colleagues. In his work, the mythic dimension of human history and existence prevails.

The therapeutic role of art receives its moist eloquent testimony, however, in the life and work of Frida Kahlo (1907-54). Partially paralyzed in a traumatic bus accident at the age of 18, Kahlo married Diego Rivera and was welcomed by André Breton into the Surrealist fold of the 1930s. Her paintings and self-portraits are icons of pain: red smudges on the frame of *A Few Small Nips* project the bed-ridden, writhing body from the canvas out into the world. The Museo Frida Kahlo is in her childhood home, Coyoacán, a part of Mexico City.

—Harvard Student Agencies, *Let's Go: Mexico*

anyone who encountered her. And she would seem to continue to do so, even in death. (I should here admit my own enthrallment, with which I seem to have infected my friends, Gloria and Mary.) Thus, a trip to the Frida Kahlo Museum, which was formerly her home, the blue house out in Coyoacán, is apt to have the character of a pilgrimage to a shrine. We went there to pay homage as well as out of curiosity. And we had, I am sure, like all passionate pilgrims, a burden of expectations, or preconceptions, some quite possibly unconscious.

In any case, the museum contained some vast surprises: considerable beauty, much sadness, and several disturbing questions.

The first surprise for me was quite simply the intensity of the color of those high outer walls; to a Californian (I suppose I am one), the phrase "blue house" implies a pastel, surely not the violent, vibrant blue of Frida's house, which is like certain Mexican skies. Its size, too, was unexpected: it covers a small town block. High walls, then, and a gate guarded by two papier-mâché Judas figures—and by a small, somewhat shabby real guard, who assures visitors that their entrance is free and warns them that they may not take pictures.

To the right, just as one passes between the Judas giants, there is a small room with a glassed-in counter and some shelves, obviously designed as a bookstore-postcard display area—and now quite bare. Empty, that is, except for one rather gaudy pamphlet, entitled "Altar in the First Centenary of Diego Rivera," and in which there are many references to, and an introduction by, Dolores Olmeda, the "Life Director of the Diego Rivera and Frida Kahlo Museums." Frida is mentioned only once, as Diego's third wife. No books on Frida, no posters or postcards. (*Why?*)

The garden area that one next sees is rich and wonderful, however: a barely tamed green jungle, a perfect habitat for Frida's pet monkeys, for birds. (Cats would love it there, I thought, not seeing any.) At the time of my visit a large bed of pink lilies blossomed, the kind called Naked Ladies. And great tall trees. And a tangled profusion of vines.

On a wall near the entrance to Frida's house an inscription informed us that Frida and Diego had lived in this house from 1929 to 1954—a touching announcement and quite untrue (and who put it there, I wonder?). For although Frida was born in that house, which was built by her father, Diego's residences were both multiple and brief; he came and went very much as he chose, neither remaining at home nor staying away for long (one knows the type). The abode most lengthily shared by Frida and Diego is the two joined houses in San Angel, now the Diego Rivera Museum.

The first room of the blue house is rather low and small, as are all the rooms in this semicolonial sprawl. One can imagine the house as warm and wonderful, hospitable first to the large Kahlo group (her father, by two wives, had six daughters), and then to Frida and Diego and their enormous circle of friends: Trotsky, Siqueiros, et cetera. But it takes considerable imagining, so little household furniture is left (and whatever happened to it? Where are all the ordinary tables and chairs that were used by Frida?).

Frida's paintings line this entrance room, and while interesting and highly original, as is all her work, they are simply not her best; in no sense is this a major Kahlo exhibition—a great pity, since her work is extremely hard to find. Most of her paintings are in private collections, including all the paintings that she willed to Rivera and that he in turn willed to a trust for the people of Mexico, along with her house. She is barely represented in museums in Mexico City.

The most striking of that small collection is the bright still life of watermelons, *Viva la Vida*, thus titled and signed by Frida very shortly before her death. But this painting's appeal seems emotional and historic, rather than intrinsic.

The kitchen is cozily furnished indeed, with bright painted chairs, red and yellow, new-looking (too new to have been there when Frida was), the sort that one might find in any Mexican open market. And glazed plates and pottery, cooking implements. Tiny jars affixed to the back wall, high up, spell out Frida y Diego in large letters. This seemed an unlikely note of kitsch, and indeed I was later told that these names were a later addition, put up some years after the deaths of Diego and Frida.

Other rooms house an extensive collection of pre-Columbian figures, and paintings, mostly by Rivera, some by friends, both Mexican and European. And there is Diego's bedroom, with his surprisingly small bed for such a huge man, and his rough, enormous boots. Then, going upstairs, within the broad, dark stairwell is the vast collection of *retablos*, small Mexican votive paintings, said to have profoundly influenced the art of Frida.

And then one comes to Frida's tiny, narrow, poignant bedroom, the room in which, at forty-seven, she died and was laid out. And photographed, lying there.

Since she was so very, very often photographed in life (more often than Marilyn Monroe, it has been said)—the daughter of a photographer, she must have been early habituated to what seems to many people an intrusion—it is not surprising that she was also photographed in death, on this same narrow white bed, with its florally embroidered sheets. One of the terrible plaster casts that she finally had to wear (and that she decorated with painted flowers) lies on the coverlet. Still, this sense of her death makes visiting this area both macabre and embarrassing: I felt that I should not have been there.

It seems more permissible to enter the studio, built for her by Diego, in 1946, and wonderfully open to views of her wild green garden. It is a cheering, open room, and one can forgive Diego a great deal for having built this space for Frida's work.

Which leads us to a question that often seems to trouble Frida's partisans: why did Frida remain in such a state of adoration for a man who was continuously, compulsively unfaithful to her, and who was for long periods of time conspicuously off and away with other, often famous, women? It seems to me that there are two explanations, insofar as one can "explain" a major passion—one rational, one not. The rational explanation would be that Diego entirely supported Frida's work; he often spoke of her as one of the greatest living painters, he cited the intensely female, anguished complexity of her work. He even compared his own painting unfavorably to hers (quite correctly, in my own view).

And, more darkly, irrationally, Frida was absolutely addicted to Diego; she could be said to have been impaled on her mania for Diego, as she had been literally impaled in the horrifying streetcar accident that, when she was eighteen, so painfully, horribly transformed her life. She herself referred to the "two accidents" in her life, the streetcar crash and Diego.

Rivera was deeply Mexican in his love of color and soft shapes and in his strong identification with the Mexican Indian. An excellent draftsman and watercolor artist, he created an image of a sweet, primitive Mexico, inhabited by brown, tender-loving girls and dreamy children carrying huge bouquets of flowers. Naturally, there was sentimentality in all of this.

—Kal Müller and Guillermo García-Oropeza, *Insight Guides Mexico*

In the course of reading and thinking intensively about Frida Kahlo, one night I watched a TV special on Billie Holiday, and I sensed, I thought, a connection between the two women, whose life spans overlapped: they surely shared extremes of talent, as well as of personal beauty (Frida in photographs is much more beautiful than the self she painted) and addictiveness.

But Frida's studio seems a lively, heartening place. Even the wheelchair placed before her easel seems emblematic of great courage, rather than of debility and pain.

The Diego Rivera Museum, in San Angel—it is almost adjacent to the very posh, very beautiful San Angel Inn—is quite another matter. Crowded with collections—pre-Columbian figures, folk art, paintings (none, significantly, by Frida Kahlo)—and with furniture, it is meticulously kept up. Frida's house, adjoining, linked to Diego's by a high crosswalk that she sometimes closed off—Frida's house in San Angel is closed, roped off, forbidden. There is even a curious eroticism present in this homage to Diego, this shrine: in one room a chair that is obviously Diego's, with his boots on the floor, a coat flung over the back—this Diego chair faces a large portrait of a sexily semiundressed young woman, whose transported eyes stare raptly at the Maestro.

The basement bookstore is richly filled with postcards and posters and books, representing both Diego and Frida. There are even copies of the marvelously gotten-out biography of Frida by the Mexican printer-publisher and Kahlo scholar, Martha Zamora, *Frida Kahlo: The Brush of Anguish.*

Two words often used in connection with Kahlo are narcissism ("All those self-portraits") and masochism ("All that blood"). Both seem to me quite wrongly applied. I rather believe that Kahlo painted herself and her images of personal pain in an effort to stave off madness and death, a desperate enterprise in which she was hardly alone and in which she was not entirely successful—as who can ever be, for good?

I have recently read that there are no longer any Frida Kahlo paintings in her house—and I do not plan to go there again, it is simply too sad.

But this fall, the fall of 1990, it is rumored that Dolores Olmeda will open her house, La Feria, in the Xochimilco district of Mexico City (not far from Coyoacán) as a museum, featuring 137 works by Diego and 25 by Frida. As one report has described it: "Sequestered in a tiny courtyard room removed from the main galleries, they (the Kahlos) seem reduced to a mere supporting role. Passing between the two areas is like going from Charles Dickens to Emily Dickinson." (*Connoisseur*, October 1990)

I can only say that were I forced to make such an odd literary choice, I would inevitably choose Ms. Dickinson.

Dolores Olmeda's acquisition of the Kahlos and her subsequent removal of them from the blue house has a somewhat odd history: she got several Kahlos from the widow of the Mexican ambassador, Eduardo Morillo Safa, because the Bank of Mexico, which was supposed to get them, had defaulted on the sale. And Olmeda did this because, she said, Diego, in tears, had begged her to do so. The problem is that at the time of this sale Diego was already dead; also, Olmeda is known to have intimate and extensive connections with the Bank of Mexico. It is all very murky and very (unhappily) Mexican.

In the same article that so vividly describes the placement of the Kahlos in the new museum, Olmeda is quoted as saying, "I didn't like Frida. We were different. She was a lesbian, you know, and I didn't like that. I don't like her paintings. They are very trashy. I admire her very much, but I was never a friend of hers." (Perhaps it was just as well for Frida not to have had such a friend?)

But I plan to visit that museum and to see all those Kahlos—soon.

Alice Adams is the author of several books, including Caroline's Daughters, Superior Women, *and* Mexico: Some Travels and Some Travelers There, *from which this story is excerpted.*

The paintings, carvings, and sculptures by Kahlo express the anguish and hopes of her existence: one called *Marxism Will Give Health to the Sick* shows her casting away her own crutches. Trotsky lived only a few streets away, and Rivera and Kahlo were part of a high-powered but far from harmonious leftist artistic-intellectual circle. Stalin appears as a hero in some of Kahlo's paintings, done after Rivera and Trotsky had fallen out.

—Tom Brosnahan, et al., *Mexico — a travel survival kit*

JOYCE GREGORY

Se Habla Español

In language learning, contact is everything.

"**S**iete, por favor."

The operator punched the button for the seventh floor. Then he turned to me with a radiant smile. "You espeak Espanish berry well."

I resisted the urge to throw my arms around the young man. Never mind that he had delivered his good-natured flattery in English—my first attempt at communicating in Spanish had been a success! Even before I stepped off the elevator to my hotel room, I resolved that I would one day master this language that brought such immediate rewards.

In quest of my goal, I did the obvious: sat through snail's-pace adult evening classes; bought language tapes that promised native-like fluency in thirty days; and traveled to Spanish-speaking countries whenever I could. But after languishing for some years in an intermediate-level limbo, I took the plunge. I enrolled in a Spanish immersion course at the Center for Bilingual Multicultural Studies in Cuernavaca, Mexico.

I knew I had made a good choice when I walked onto campus for the first day's orientation. *El Centro Bilingüe* presents a nondescript face to the street, but, like Cuernavaca itself, inside the gate it's all flowering trees and fountains and flagstone paths leading past bougainvillea-draped walls. Instructors striding by toss out welcoming smiles along with a *"Buenos días"* or *"¡Hola!"* Students sip coffee at outside tables or stretch out on chaise longues around the pool. There's scarcely a furrowed brow to be seen.

You may think this bespeaks a lax attitude toward learning. *Al contrario.* El Centro's relaxed, friendly atmosphere is part of an approach to language learning that's both current and effective. Unwittingly, I had stumbled onto the campus of the most highly-regarded language center in a city that makes language learning its business. With more than twenty schools dispensing Spanish lessons, Cuernavaca is to language learning what Hollywood is to filmmaking.

In language learning as in life, motivation is everything. Experts have determined that those verb conjugations I used to struggle with are useful mainly for passing grammar tests; memorized dialogues work best if you converse with someone who knows the other half of the dialogue. A smarter tactic, say linguists, is simply to focus on real communication in a nonthreatening environment. Sometimes the best language learning takes place when you don't even know you're learning. At the Centro Bilingüe, they've taken the application of this theory to new heights.

> Anywhere in Mexico, "*Solo mirando*," accompanied by a smile, will let a store-owner or sidewalk vendor know that you're "Just looking" and not ready to buy or begin the bargaining game. Use it alone or make a "V" sign with two fingers pointed towards your eyes and you'll be left alone to browse.
>
> —Paula McDonald, "Tantalizing Trivia"

For three hours each morning, instructor María Luisa managed to keep things moving as she nudged upward the language level of each of her four students: a prison administrator from New York State, two young women from Germany, and me, a linguistic dilettante from California. Grammar exercises segued into discussions of social issues or cultural idiosyncrasies or personal passions.

Isa, a pretty blond *Fräulein* with a serious bent, often continued the discussion into recess. Sometimes Isa and I carried on our Spanish conversations over dinner at one of Cuernavaca's *al fresco* restaurants. At Casa de Campo, looking out over the lush gardens where Mexican generals once plotted military strategy, Isa and I debated women's issues.

Alvaro, a charismatic soccer player, served as my afternoon tutor. With Alvaro, I learned how to argue politics and how to embroider my basic Spanish with subtler nuances. "Don't you think that sounds a little abrupt?" he asked one day, after reading an essay that I had polished until I thought it was devoid of errors. I revised the piece until it earned his praise.

Beyond the daily classes—and this is its strength—El Centro offers a dizzying array of conferences and *mini-cursos* and activities and excursions, all, *por supuesto*, conducted in Spanish. With offerings in history, archeology, dance, cooking, sports, sing-alongs, it would be unthinkable not to find something that interests you. The ostensible goal of these lectures and demonstrations is to teach students something about Mexican culture. But there's more than meets the eye—or the ear—to all this activity. The talented instructors use history or dance or whatever as a vehicle to develop listening comprehension, that essential but elusive skill that gets short shrift in traditional courses.

At the end of the school day, I went home to more Spanish practice with my "Mexican Mama." María Elena welcomed me into her elegantly appointed home in a gated complex, complete with swimming pool and two German Shepherds. I occupied the room belonging to one of her college-age sons. Since the house lay beyond walking distance to the school, María Elena drove me each way. *"Sea lista a las siete y media* **en punto,**" she directed me the first evening. Watching María Elena jockey for position on Cuernavaca's narrow, car-choked streets the next morning, I could see why she was anxious to leave the house at 7:30 *on the dot.* So much for stereotypes of Mexican time.

María Elena, a sophisticated, fortyish divorcée, introduced me to the cosmopolitan side of Cuernavaca. The city has been a favorite vacation spot for Mexico City's elite since the days of the Aztec emperors. Now the grand mansions belong to modern industrialists and government officials who forsake their smoggy capital on weekends for "The City of Eternal Spring." The wealth concentrated in Cuernavaca supports a fine selection of galleries, boutiques, and restaurants. María Elena and I sampled French cuisine at Ma Maison, and Japanese delicacies at Sumiya, the Japanese showplace that heiress Barbara Hutton imported from Japan. We also dined at the ex-Hacienda de Cortés, a marvel of ancient stone interspliced with tree trunks and branches.

Whenever I could break away from school activities, I explored other reminders of Cuernavaca's legacy—the cathedral begun by Cortés in 1525, or the complex built by Taxco silver baron José de la Borda, or Emperor Maximilian's House, now restored as a small museum. No one should miss the grander museum at Cortés Palace, where Diego Rivera's bold 1932 murals depict in chilling detail the destruction of local Indian civilizations by their Spanish conquerors.

With the signing of the North American Free Trade Agreement, a large contingent of North American business men and women enrolled at El Centro. Among them were "Ricardo," a telephone company executive from St. Louis, "Carlos," who managed a *maquiladora* on the Texas border, and "Laura," a computer salesperson from the midwest. (VIPs, like everyone else, had Spanish names conferred on them.) If anyone appeared stressed out, it was these executives, who endured nine hours per day of intensive instruction. I couldn't help reflect that the college kids frequenting the town's bars and discos were probably acquiring more Spanish. They were certainly having more fun.

One evening I accompanied the business executives to Las Mañanitas, the legendary restaurant-hotel where a couple of signature margaritas and a gourmet dinner do wonders for flagging spirits. We watched peacocks strutting across a broad expanse of lawn ringed by poinciana trees and birds of paradise. Strolling violinists serenaded couples dining under green umbrellas. I hate to tell tales outside of school, but the execs dropped their Spanish at the gate when they finished their classes for the day.

Not so Claudia, a UNICEF employee from Austria who was learning Spanish in order to work in South America. This was her first trip to Mexico, and she was making the most of it. I had met Claudia in Professor Morayta's intriguing (really!) Economics class. Claudia and I marveled at Mexican "magic realism" in the phenomenally popular movie, *Como Agua para Chocolate* (Like Water for Chocolate). We also took one of the school excursions to Taxco, the silver mining town that defies visitors to leave without purchasing at least one silver *recuerdo*. But our best discovery was the resort at Cocoyoc, a 16th-century *hacienda* that combines dark colonial aqueducts with turquoise pools for a stunning visual effect. Its grounds served as the setting for "Butch Cassidy and the Sundance Kid," one of many movies filmed in the reliably sunny weather of this region.

One thing puzzled me. I seldom saw anyone making use of the school's language lab, that '60s-era high tech contribution to language learning. "It's available for anyone who wants to use it," explained Javier, the school's director, "but in Cuernavaca, who needs it? The whole city is a language laboratory."

He was right. Waiters and taxi drivers seemed to bend over backwards to accommodate fledgling Spanish speakers in their attempts to communicate. The real proof came when I dropped off my laundry at "Hall's Super Clean," the laundry service nearest the school. A handout on the counter provided a bilingual list of phrases, from "What's the price per load?" (*¿Cuanto cuesta una carga de ropa?*) to "What time will my clothes be ready?" (*¿A qué hora recojo la ropa?*) Talk about motivation! This was functional Spanish at its best—the right phrase at the right time directed to the right person.

At first, I wondered about the instructors' universal use of the familiar (*tú*) form to address students of all ages, and about their encouraging students to address them likewise. Javier set me straight again. "Most of our students have been exposed to the formal (*Usted*) form of address in previous Spanish courses, but they haven't had an opportunity to practice the familiar form, so we make a point of giving them practice in the *tú* form here at the Center."

By now, that overused term, "immersion," held new meaning for me. If my previous Spanish courses could be compared to wading in a toddler's pool, this immersion experience was akin to jumping off an ocean pier. ("The fire-hose approach," one of my fellow students called it.)

All too soon, the day of my scheduled departure arrived. Victor, a young *taxista* whose mother worked as secretary at the school, came to drive me to the Mexico City airport. Instead of the modern *cuota* highway, we took the old two-lane road that winds up into the mountains, through surprisingly rural vistas that separate the capital from its favorite weekend retreat. Victor pointed out the striking view of the snow-covered volcanoes, Popocatepetl and Ixtaccihuatl, afforded by the seldom-used route. When he inquired about my stay at the Centro Bilingüe, I related my experiences with enthusiasm.

I'll never know if it was part of the overall program, but as we descended fragrant pine-covered hills for the sprawling capital, Victor studied me in the rear view mirror. Then, with disarming sincerity, he proclaimed, "*Usted habla Español muy bien.*"

"*Gracias,*" I murmured.

> **W**hereas the architecture of Mexico is the hardened shell of a Spanish distinction.
>
> Treeless, open plazas abate at walls; walls yield to refreshment, to interior courtyards, to shuttered afternoons.
>
> At the heart there is *tú*—the intimate voice—the familiar room in a world full of rooms. *Tú* is the condition, not so much of knowing, as of being known; of being recognized. *Tú* belongs within the family. *Tú* is spoken to children and dogs, to priests; among lovers and drunken friends; to servants; to statues; to the high court of heaven; to God Himself.
>
> The shaded arcade yields once more to the plaza, to traffic and the light of day. *Usted*, the formal, the bloodless, the ornamental you, is spoken to the eyes of strangers. By servants to masters. *Usted* shows deference to propriety, to authority, to history. *Usted* is open to interpretation; therefore it is subject to corruption, a province of politicians. *Usted* is the language outside Eden.
>
> —Richard Rodriguez, *Days of Obligation: An Argument With My Mexican Father*

Joyce Gregory is a former educator who writes about travel for Alaska Airlines' inflight magazine and other publications. She touts language learning as the key to instant rapport in foreign lands—and more satisfying eavesdropping.

Keeping up with a language once you've come home is a real challenge. One helpful publication is *Perspectiva—World News Monthly in Intermediate Spanish for Language Learning.* For more information, write: *Perspectiva,* Educational News Service, P.O. Box 60478, Florence, MA 01060-0478, USA.

—JO'R and LH

PETE HAMILL

A Healing Place

The "best location in the history of movies" is a place where scars are healed
and ghosts come to rest.

I t was dusk in Puerto Vallarta, and we were in a restaurant called El
Panorama, dining with a Mexican woman we'd met that afternoon.
The restaurant was on the top floor of the Hotel La Siesta, rising
seven precarious stories above the ground on a hill overlooking the
town. For once the name of a restaurant was accurate. From our table,
while the *mariachis* played the aching old songs of love and betrayal, we
could see a panorama of cobblestoned streets glistening after a frail afternoon rain. We saw the terra-cotta patterns of a thousand tiled rooftops,
along with church steeples and flagpoles, palm trees and small green
yards, and little girls eating ice-cream cones. The aroma of the Mexican
evening rose around us: charcoal fires, frying beans, fish baking in stone
ovens. Over to the left in the distance was the dense green thicket where
the Río Cuale tumbled down from the fierce mountains of the interior.
And beyond all of this, stretching away to the hard blue line of the horizon, there was the sea, the vast and placid Pacific.

"It's so beautiful," the Mexican woman said, gesturing toward the sea.
My wife followed her gesture to gaze at the rioting sky, which was all
purple and carmine and tinged with orange from the dying sun. The
woman's face trembled as she talked about her husband and her son.
They had died within six months of each other, the husband of a heart
attack after many years in the Uruguayan foreign service, the son in a
senseless shooting at a party in Mexico City.

"When those things happened," the Mexican woman said, "I couldn't
live anymore. I didn't want to. I sat at home in the dark." She sipped her
drink. "My daughter was the one who told me to come to Vallarta. She
said I had to heal myself. I had to go away and get well. And she was
right. Beauty heals. Don't ever forget that. Beauty heals. I hurt still. But I
am healed."

Not all the stories we heard in Puerto Vallarta contained such elements of melodrama and redemption. But there were other tales of healing—the woman from Minnesota, broken by a difficult divorce, who

185

wandered south with a vague hope for escape. Now the gray years were erased by the sun and sea and the sound of children laughing in the still hours of the siesta; she worked in a clothing store and was catching up on two decades of lost laughter. There was a man broken by the culture of greed during the American '80s; back in Boston he had left a bankrupt company, a ruined marriage, a defaulted mortgage; now in the mornings he took a boat out on the blue water to fish for shark. Another man had lost a much-loved son to drugs; another had lost a career to whiskey; a third had postponed an old dream of becoming a painter. All had come to Puerto Vallarta to live a little longer or, perhaps, for the first time.

Generations ago, when Puerto Vallarta was a small, isolated town, there was only one beach, Playa Los Muertos, the strand of yellow sand that stretches for a mile south of the Cuale River. Old-timers still remember the Sundays and holidays when it seemed as if half of the families in Puerto Vallarta had come south of the Río Cuale, to Los Muertos Beach especially, to play in the surf and sand.

This is still largely true, although now droves of winter-season North American vacationers and residents have joined them. Fortunately, Playa Los Muertos is much cleaner than during the polluted 1980s. The fish are coming back, as evidenced by the flocks of diving pelicans and the crowd of folks who drop lines every day from the New Pier.

—Bruce Whipperman, *Pacific Mexico Handbook*

For centuries it was a fishing village, a few huts thatched with palm dozing along the shore of the great natural harbor called the Bahía de Banderas, which is 25 miles wide. The town was built around the Río Cuale, one of the four streams that now traverse the city. It never became a major port because the merchants of Mexico preferred to greet their Manila galleons in Acapulco, 800 miles to the south and a much shorter journey to the capital, Mexico City. For years no roads connected the tiny village to the large cities of the interior; mule trains labored for weeks to travel the 220 miles due east to Guadalajara. And Mexico City, 550 mountainous miles to the southeast, was beyond reach.

In 1851 a man named Guadalupe Sanchez settled his family on the edge of the Río Cuale, which divides the present Vallarta into north and south, and he is usually credited with transforming the cluster of fishing shacks into a town. But it did not prosper, and the locals apparently preferred it that way. They lived out their lives in its quiet cobblestoned streets to the familiar rhythms of day and night, rainy summers and balmy winters.

Then, in 1963, everything changed. That year John Huston arrived with a crew of 130 to direct the movie version of Tennessee Williams's *The Night of the Iguana*. This produced one of the most amusing scenes in movie history and the true beginning of modern Puerto Vallarta. The star of the movie was Richard Burton, out of Wales and Shakespeare. His female costars were Ava Gardner, Deborah Kerr, and Sue Lyon. Miss Gardner had abandoned Hollywood for Europe after disastrous marriages to Mickey Rooney, Artie Shaw, and Frank Sinatra. She arrived with a personal entourage and her Ferrari and soon became interested in a beachboy named Tony. Miss Kerr was married to Peter Viertel, who had written a scathing novel about Huston and was once involved with Ava. The 17-year-old Miss Lyon, who had become a star as the nymphet in *Lolita*, was there with her boyfriend, while the boyfriend's wife shared quarters with Miss Lyon's mother. The cinematographer was the splendid Gabriel Figueroa, who burst into operatic song while drinking, and Huston was supported in his work by the Mexican director Indio Fernandez, who had shot his last producer. And Tennessee Williams was there with his lover and his dog.

The movie set leaped into fantasy with the early arrival of Elizabeth Taylor. She and Burton had begun their great love affair on the set of *Cleopatra* the year before, and when she showed up, presumably to protect Burton from his female costars, media pandemonium ensued. Taylor was a gigantic star in the Hollywood solar system, and her presence was a monument to the old style. She brought with her dozens of trunks and suitcases, an ex-fighter to serve as bodyguard, her own secretary and one for Burton, a British cook, a chauffeur, and three children by two ex-husbands. One of these ex-husbands, Michael Wilding, was also on hand, reduced to working as an assistant to Burton's agent, and back in the States her current husband, the singer Eddie Fisher, was pouting and working on a divorce. The film's producer, Ray Stark, loved it (a few years ago he told me, "It was the greatest single movie location in the history of movies"). And Huston had grand fun. At one point he gave each of the players—Burton, Taylor, Gardner, Kerr, Lyon, plus Stark—a gold-plated derringer, laid in a velvet-lined box. Each box contained five golden bullets, engraved with the names of each of the others. He left his own name off the bullets.

Within weeks reporters and photographers from all over the world made their way to the sleepy little town of Puerto Vallarta. This was not easy; only one small plane a day flew in. Until then, few people had ever heard of the place. "They're giving us ten million dollars' worth of free publicity," the exultant Stark said. "We've got more reporters up here than iguanas." The Mexican tourist board was equally excited.

Although Williams had set his play in Acapulco, Huston thought that the port city was now too modernized, too sleek; he chose Vallarta. Huston knew the country; he'd been coming to Mexico since the 1920s and set one of his greatest films there, *The Treasure of the Sierra Madre*. The set for *Iguana*—a run-down hotel—was built by a team of almost 300 Mexican workers in the jungle above Mismaloya Beach, seven miles south of town, and some of the ruins can be seen today. But much of the action was around the bar of the Oceano Hotel, still at the corner of Paseo Diaz Ordaz and Calle Galeana. The bar is gone now, but the ghosts of Burton and Taylor remain.

"Burton was the greatest single drinker I ever saw," said a man named Jeffrey Smith, who claimed to have been here during the shooting. "He could drink anything and never get drunk."

Burton and Taylor took a house called the Casa Kimberley, up the side of the hill beside the Rio Cuale, and by all accounts they fell in love with Puerto Vallarta with only slightly less passion than they felt for each other. The movie company eventually finished its work and moved on, with no casualties from Huston's derringers. But Taylor and Burton bought the Casa Kimberley and added a house across the narrow street and built a bridge to connect them. It would be nice to say that they lived happily ever after. Almost nobody does, least of all movie stars.

Still, they had good years in Puerto Vallarta. They came down with great crowds of children and staff, spent holidays there, too often recuperated there from the bruising life of celebrity. The Mexicans loved them. They created scholarships for local children. They were an attraction that validated the town, and its population exploded (it is now about 250,000). By 1970, even Richard Nixon had come to Puerto Vallarta, for a state visit

On February 14th, *El Diá del los Enamorados* or the Day of the Ones in Love, every restaurant will have special romantic music, a special menu, and create an extra-special atmosphere of romance. Hey, remember...this is the land where lovers stop to kiss on the street, daytime, any old Tuesday. And where bouquets of roses are sold on every street corner *every* night. Imagine what it's like on a day dedicated completely to love.

In Mexico, February 14th is also *El Diá de la Amistad*, Friendship Day, a day when good friends get together and celebrate each other. Restaurants are not just filled with lovers but with groups of women having long, leisurely lunches or dinners together, too.

—Paula McDonald, "Tantalizing Trivia"

with the Mexican president. The Burtons had various celebrities as guests, but often they were alone. From the testimony of Burton's diaries (quoted by his biographer Melvyn Bragg), Puerto Vallarta also helped him heal. Sometimes Burton hid out in the top floor of one of the houses, reading and writing. He read eclectically, Octavio Paz, W. H. Auden, Ian Fleming, Philip Roth; he came back again and again to the work of his Welsh compatriot Dylan Thomas. Burton was an excellent writer, a self-punishing diarist, and a good, sly, open-eyed observer.

"Elizabeth is now looking ravishingly sun-tanned," he wrote in 1969, "though the lazy little bugger ought to lose a few pounds or so to look her absolute best."

In the late 1970s John Huston was to come back to Puerto Vallarta too, hauling his aging bones from the drizzly disappointments of a long sojourn in Ireland. He built a house in the jungle near Las Caletas, thirty miles from the town's center. It could be reached only from the sea. He didn't see much of Burton and Taylor. When the Burtons divorced, Taylor got the houses. For a while Burton lived in another house with a new wife. Her name was Susan. The house was called, after half of each, Casa Bursus. Today nobody can tell you its location.

But the old houses, with their connecting bridges, are still there. They've been sold and converted into a bed-and-breakfast. One afternoon my wife and I went to visit. A long flight of steps begins at a now dry and sour fountain, where we saw a Domino's Pizza carton darkening in the sun. At the top of the steps you can see in the distance the bridge, painted the color of strawberry ice cream. We rang the bell of a wooden door at 445 Calle Zaragoza, and a lean, tanned man named Jacques gave us a tour. He said he had worked in many places, from St. Barts to Polynesia, but was entranced with Puerto Vallarta.

"The people are very pure," he said, "and the town is very romantic. It has everything you don't find in the United States now. Puerto Vallarta is 1938. You can regenerate yourself here. It's very charming and not damaged."

Stairs lead to an open, white-tiled floor with a bar and couches and a cool breeze off the ocean. There are photographs of Taylor and Burton, posters for *Butterfield 8* and *Becket*, other reminders of lives once lived here. Off to the side (and in the house across the little bridge, beside the small swimming pool) we saw rooms named for various Burton-Taylor movies: the VIPs Room and the Comedians Room, the Sandpiper Room and the Night of the Iguana Room, the Taming of the Shrew Room and the Who's Afraid of Virginia Woolf? Room. Some were excellent movies; others were among the worst ever made. I found a bookcase against a wall, and among the weathered books was a copy of *Sanctuary V*, by my friend Budd Schulberg, dedicated to Burton and Taylor and dated December 17, 1969—a remnant of some lost Christmas. The place is clean and bright and pleasant. It also made me very sad.

A vagrant feeling of waste and loss followed me to the top floor, where a bedroom is now called the Cleopatra Room. According to the Bragg biography, this is where Burton came to do his writing, where he tried to make sense of his life, to find some center among the swirling currents of celebrity and alcohol. He never found it. He knew that once he had been a serious actor but had become a cartoon figure, part of a team called Dick'n'Liz. Here, where there are now tasteful wicker chairs and fresh-cut flowers, he could walk onto the balcony and look out over the town to the sea. Too often he saw only the waste of his own talent and his life. We looked around, feeling oddly like intruders at the scene of some private tragedy, and then we fled.

The town that Huston, Burton, and Taylor saw in 1963 has been enveloped by the much larger Puerto Vallarta that is here now. It has the usual transcultural clutter that you see in places designed to give pleasure to strangers from *El Norte*: Denny's and McDonald's and a lot of boutiques. But it's still a good town for walking. In the mornings we strolled along the beaches, often pausing on the one called Los Muertos (The Dead), named for a group of silver miners who were murdered here by pirates a long time ago. The sea is clear and translucent; the city fathers have worked hard to avoid the calamity that ruined Acapulco. On most days the leaves of the palm trees drooped in the heat. We saw a lean brown horse tethered to a lone palm tree on a spit of shore, waiting for riders. Mexican men contentedly sold blankets and hats.

"I have the best job in the world," said a brown-skinned man named Marcos Villasenor, who was 44. "I come on my horse in the morning from there, up by Nayarit. I give people rides. They pay me. Then I go home." He smiled broadly. "And all day while I am working I am in a beautiful place."

His feelings were clearly shared by others. On each day of our stay the beach was crowded with a mixture of tourists and Mexican families. The Americans looked pink and awkward and lonely. The Mexicans were friendly, even sweet, but they were more concerned with children than with visitors. Here, as everywhere in Puerto Vallarta, a visitor sensed a relaxed manner among the Mexicans. Among workers and visitors, no one felt the seething hostility that poisons so many resorts, particularly in the Caribbean.

Not much of the Mexican past remained here. The cathedral dates only from the turn of the century, and in a land where brilliant artisans once worked with brick, it is made of concrete. No pyramids rise here, no ruins of the cultures that existed in Mexico before the arrival of the Europeans.

But Puerto Vallarta does have a vibrant gallery scene. The sculptor Sergio Bustamente has his own gallery. There are a number of other galleries, several antiques shops, and stores selling Mexican folk art. We spent some time at the superb Galeria Uno, on Calle Morelos, run by an American woman named Jan Lavender, who has been in Vallarta for more than twenty years. She features many of the best new Mexican painters, but for many American residents her gallery also served as hangout and communications center, a place for hearing gossip, making business contacts, and buying gifts for friends in the States. While we were there Lavender was excited about a new discovery, a young Mexican artist named Rogelio Diaz, whose brilliantly colored paintings combined power and draftsmanship in a style that could be called Mexpressionist. "This is the finest artist I've seen in years," she said. "He is something else." She produced cold drinks, smoked a cigarette, and talked a while about Puerto Vallarta.

"First of all, it's a street town," she said. "Everybody is out in the streets. You see your friends there. You meet new people in the streets. The town is not social; it's certainly not formal. It doesn't have all those obligations. You can wear whatever you want to wear here, go as you want to go. It's not like Acapulco. My friends come down from New York or Los Angeles and say, 'Where are the parties?' And I say, 'There aren't any.' And there aren't. God knows, they have a good time, but it isn't a scene."

Running an art gallery has made her even more aware of the uniqueness of Vallarta and of Mexico. "You can't really capture Mexico in photographs or paintings, because they leave out two essentials, smell and

I am reminded of the quote by André Breton, the father of French Surrealism, who said after visiting Puerto Vallarta, "There is no need for our art movement in this country. Surrealism is a way of life here."

Puerto Vallarta, for all its popular images of mass tourism—"Love Boat" port excursions, modern, boxy hotels and condominiums, a multitude of tacky souvenir shops—is really a sophisticated and beautiful Mexican city. Local primitive painters, like Ada Colorina, and well-established American artists contribute to its reputation as one of Mexico's foremost art colonies.

—Ron Bernthal, "Artists Find a Home in Puerto Vallarta"

sound. Here we're used to air moving. We live open. In the States the windows are always closed and the air is imported and smells like cement." She laughed. "Here the weather is always great. I go to New York, and it's cold outside and sweltering inside. I go to Phoenix, and it's blistering outside and freezing inside. But here the windows are always open."

We never felt menaced while in Puerto Vallarta. There were no obvious hoodlums, no street gangs, no dope peddlers. We never saw the kind of homeless people who now collect on the streets of American cities like piles of human wreckage. Even after great expansion this remains a Mexican town built upon the hard foundation of the Mexican family. We did see poor people across the river in the area named after the Mexican revolutionary hero Emiliano Zapata. They live in dark, crudely built single-wall housing. You walk by and smell the rank odor of poverty. On the street called Francisco Madero we also passed a deep, wide, evil-looking, high-ceilinged pool room, the sort of place in which young men always find trouble in Mexican movies.

But the poor are not typical of the town. In the evenings you can walk along the seawall called the Malecón and see young men flirting with young women as they do in the evening in a thousand Mexican towns. The ritual is all eyes, glances, whispers, the private codes of the young. You can hear the growl of the sea. You can dine in the many restaurants, annoyed only by the garrulous flatulence of the public buses, throwing the fumes of burnt gasoline upon all who come near. One evening we sat at a window table in the second floor Japanese restaurant called Tsunami. The food was good, but strolling Mexicans kept stopping on the Malecón and staring up at us: groups of men, fathers with children, old women with disapproving faces. Or so we thought. When dinner was over we crossed the street and finally saw the true objects of their scrutiny. On the floor above the restaurant was an aquarium, the tank filled with the gaily colored denizens of the deep; above that a disco; and in the window we could see dark-skinned girls in tight bright dresses, the gaily colored denizens of the Mexican night.

That is Puerto Vallarta to me. You can wander down to Le Bistro, on the island in the river, and hear good recorded jazz. You can pause in the restaurant's garden beside the statue of Huston, which quotes from the director's eulogy to his friend Humphrey Bogart: "We have no reason to feel any sorrow for him—only for ourselves for having lost him. He is irreplaceable." Or you can have a good laugh at the restaurant called La Fuente de la Puente (The Fountain on the Bridge), where a statue of Burton, Taylor, and an iguana stands, carved from what seems to be Ivory soap but which turns out to be some kind of plastic. I wish Burton could have cast his caustic eye upon this masterpiece.

You can see these things or just watch a carpenter laboring with an artist's intensity in a small, crowded shop or kids pedaling tricycles down the steep hills or country people in sandals and straw hats gazing at the wonders of the metropolis. I carried all of them home from Puerto Vallarta, along with the sound of the rooster at dawn and the healing benevolence of the sun and the salt of the sea.

Pete Hamill began his professional writing career in 1960 when he became a general assignment reporter for the New York Post. *He has published six novels, a collection of short stories, a collection of essays, and has written many movie and TV scripts. His most recent book is* A Drinking Life: A Memoir. *He is the father of two daughters and is married to writer Fukiko Aoki. They live in New York City.*

Mexico was an unplanned, unexpected addition to our honeymoon. The day before our marriage in Miami, and three days before a required attendance at a business convention in Los Angeles, a number of airlines went on strike. The only way we could get to the West Coast was via Mexico City.

What a wedding gift it turned out to be. Everything Mexican appealed to us: the climate, the architecture, the gardens, the food, the music and dance, the history, and certainly the shopping. We were average Americans, unaware that Mexico City at the time of Cortez surpassed in glory any European city of its time. We had no idea of the surprises that the advanced Olmec-Toltec-Mayan-Aztec cultures combined with three hundred years of Spanish empire could present to us.

Our fascination with Mexico has never palled. We vacationed here year after year. Driving, flying, or busing about. Having a grand time. Eight years ago we determined this was the place where we wanted to retire. After thirty years in the travel industry, we had seen most of the world. Yet, deciding that Mexico was the place where we would stop going to the office was never a question. In our case it was Puerto Vallarta.

Culture, in a broad sense, is a real inducement for selecting Mexico for retirement. The Mexican way of life usually makes a good deal more sense to a retiree than the pace of life on, or off, the American freeway. Family values still exist, simple pleasures take on new meaning or, better yet, old meanings.

—Martin Pray, "No One Retires to Mexico—One Simply Begins a New Adventure in Living"

RICHARD BLOOM

The Underground World of the Yucatán

The author searches for Xibalba, the netherworld of the ancients.

Our guide, Leonardo, points to a well worn grindstone, a *metate*. "From the number of *metates* found in these caves," he tells us, "archeologists have estimated that 500 people lived here at one time." He gestures to the ceiling above us which is covered with the soot of ancient fires. We are standing in a communal kitchen which may be thousands of years old.

Evidence of ancient inhabitants are everywhere in Las Grutas de Loltun, the caves of Loltun. A face carved into a rock is perhaps the oldest relic, dating, Leonardo tells us, to 5000 B.C., before the Maya civilization began. Archeologists are certain that people moved into the Yucatán Peninsula about eleven thousand years ago.

Caves and *cenotes*, sinkholes with trapped water, have played a profound role in the history of the Yucatán. Only a single sizeable river exists on the entire peninsula, the Río Hondo, which cuts a natural boundary between Belize and Quintana Roo. But rainwater seeps through the limestone crust with ease. The underlying rock traps the water where lakes and rivers have formed. Without these storage areas, human life would not have been possible. It is easy to imagine a river running through the caves at Loltun, and Leonardo points to massive boulders that could only have settled where they did if the chamber had been filled with water, an event which occurred long before humans inhabited this area.

There are miles of caves here. Chambers vary widely. One is grand, like a domed stadium. In another we wander through a forest of stalactites and stalagmites. Some have merged into large columns, joined floor to ceiling, and Leonardo thumps his fist against one. Its deep, resonant sound fills the room.

Leonardo Pacheco Cohuich is an electrician by trade. He tells us with pride that he worked with an archeologist, Edward Wells, on a

When the ancient Maya let blood, they were feeding the gods their *ch'ulel* and giving of their souls. The modern Maya do not practice bloodletting to the same degree but use mainly intermediary offerings—chickens, deer, earth-oven breads, candles, and incense. They view these direct exchanges with the supernaturals as dark and dangerous adventures: they may commune with the Mundo or the K'oxol in the cave under the mountain fortress of Utatlan. The search for supernatural power can be rewarded with earthly treasure, but it can also result in the loss of soul and body and accusations of witchcraft. Surely the stakes were just as high in antiquity, but we know that the ancients did not let fear stop them.

—David Freidel, Linda Schele, Joy Parker,
Maya Cosmos: Three Thousand Years on the Shaman's Path

small dig many years ago. It is apparent that Leonardo volunteers at these caves for more than the occasional tip he receives. His enthusiasm for the history of his people is real. Even his name reflects that history. Pacheco, his father's name, is Spanish. Cohuich, his mother's, is Maya. It was less than 150 years ago that the local Maya fled to these caves and barricaded themselves against the onslaught of troops during the Caste War, a Maya rebellion that almost succeeded in ousting the *criollos*, the European-descended rulers.

The walls of the cave are adorned with paintings, and there are negative impressions of hands, much as you would get if you had spray-painted around your fingers. A spiral, an ancient symbol of energy, is found on one rock. A phallus, a symbol brought from Vera Cruz by the Toltecs, is carved into another.

Elsewhere on the peninsula cenotes dot the landscape. These sinkholes are formed when the roof of the cave has collapsed. The huge circular one at Chichén Itzá is famous. Myths persist about maidens who were sacrificed there. Weighted down by breastplates and heavy jewelry, the tales go, they were hurled into the hundred-foot pit to drown. Recent findings have proven these stories unlikely.

About forty kilometers east of Chichén Itzá is the underground cenote of Dzitnup. Its high-domed ceiling has a single small opening through which a bar of sunlight illuminates the clear aqua water below, surely one of the more beautiful natural sights on the peninsula. Dramatic clusters of stalactites hang from the roof of the grotto and glow in the yellow spotlights. A swim in the crystal clear water is refreshing.

The Maya treated many of these sites as sacred. It is easy to understand their practical significance as a source of water. But cave entrances were considered the doorway to the dark waters of the Underworld,

Xibalba, a parallel world where ancients and ancestors resided and to which kings and shamans could pass in ecstatic trance. The doorways of temples and other sacred buildings mimic these entrances, and everywhere on the peninsula we found ourselves crossing thresholds through the mouth of Chac, the rain god.

In 1959 an amateur speleologist and part-time guide, Jose Humberto Gomez, was exploring the small, rather ordinary chambers of the caves of Balankanche when he discovered a passageway that was tightly sealed with stones. He broke open the wall and squeezed through the narrow chamber which he followed until it opened out into a large grotto. In the center was a massive stalactite/stalagmite pillar surrounded by pottery, incense burners, miniature *metates*, and numerous other offerings. He had stumbled into an ancient sacred *adoratorio*, a chapel dedicated to the rain god. Local legend knew of the existence of this grotto, but it had been sealed for centuries, and no one had been able to locate it.

Archeologists were intrigued. Many of the offerings did not bear the characteristic marking of the Maya rain god Chac, but of Tlaloc, the rain god of the Toltec, who lived north of the Yucatán and whose influence is prominent in Chichén Itzá.

A native priest soon appeared. He requested permission to conduct a special religious ceremony to propitiate the guardians of the cave and protect the community. He returned the next day with thirteen assistants. For the ceremony and feast they had gathered thirteen hens, thirteen black candles, two bottles of anise, thirteen jars of honey, one turkey, copal incense, tobacco, corn, cloves, cumin, and other spices. The high priest arranged to be paid fifty-two pesos for his services and his priest assistants would receive thirteen pesos each. The numbers thirteen and fifty-two are sacred and appear in the various cycles of the Maya calendar.

For twenty-four hours the priests sat and chanted in the innermost chamber around the huge pillar, a symbol of the Wakah-Chan, the World Tree. Its roots plunge into the watery underworld; its branches soar to the highest layer of heaven. In between is the human plane. The model for this tree is the ceiba, which even today is the national tree of Guatemala where the highest concentration of Maya live.

The priests must have been relieved to have emerged to the grand feast that awaited them, for the caves are hot, humid, and airless. I, too, emerged sweat-soaked, the tropical air feeling cool and dry by comparison with the inner chamber. But the beauty and fascination of the cave remain.

To visit Las Grutas de Loltun, Dzitnup, and Las Grutas de Balankanche is to glimpse the world of the Maya and to share their wonder of forces greater than our own.

Richard Bloom took his first train ride when he was six months old, and the family vacations of his childhood were views from the back seat of a 1932 Plymouth. A psychotherapist in Santa Rosa, California, he writes about travel whenever he can get away.

Nowadays it is bad form for Westerners to be judgmental about past and present cultures—other than their own that is. But at the risk of getting poison pen letters from archaeologists and anthropologists with politically correct views, I'm bound to say that a great deal of what we call ancient Mesoamerican culture, including Maya culture, gives me the creeps. That doesn't mean I'm not impressed—as one is meant to be impressed— by the incredible feats of architectural engineering, the brilliant artistry, the elaborate calendars, the complex social structure, all that—especially since it was produced by a Stone Age civilization. But—I'm sorry—whenever I visit the really big ceremonial sites where a lot of restoration has been done, I am more than a little bit repelled by all those daunting pyramids, those skull-engraved altars, those monstrous faces of bloodthirsty gods. I especially feel this way at Uxmal and Chichén Itzá and Kabah, probably because of their overlay of Toltec-Itzá influences. But at almost any large site in Maya domains, I can't shake the thought that, to an extent probably unmatched by any other civilization (except other Mesoamerican ones), the *Zeitgeist* behind all that architectural grandeur was necromantic in its spiritual conception, totalitarian in its intention, dehumanizing in its execution, and, in the most literal sense, bloodthirsty in its religious function. Some sites, notably Palenque and Tikal, manage to be more beautiful than oppressive because the jungle setting (which wasn't there when those places were at their zenith) softens everything and at the same time serves as the Central American equivalent of Shelley's lone and level sands, reminding us of the transience of megalomaniacal ambitions in particular and worldly glory in general. But it's still there: a soullessness, an indifference to everything that is humane and individualistic in the life of our species.

—Donald G. Schueler, *The Temple of the Jaguar: Travels in the Yucatán*

198

PART III

Going Your Own Way

JEFF GREENWALD

Getting Wired in Oaxaca

The author, seeking electronic links in this Mexican city, ends up wondering instead about historical and evolutionary links.

I made my final phone calls from American soil, bought a roll of toilet paper and a package of pocket Wet Ones and kissed my life, as I knew it, goodbye. What had begun as a dare to myself sixteen months ago was about to become my living, breathing reality, starting with the infamous Mexican highway system. *Prepare su cuota.*

What followed was a five day purgatory of fried food, spleen-jostling roads, and a December 31st that leant new meaning to the Prime Directive of holiday merry-making: never eat dinner in a disco. Especially not in Guaymas; and especially not on the top floor of the Hotel Mirador, where you are likely to usher in the new year watching a couple of hyperactive Mexican five-year-olds mop the empty wooden dance floor with each other as your waiter brings too many beers and a celebratory scoop of shamrock-green rice. At midnight Sally and I stood on the roof of the Motel del Puerto, watching fireworks scream into the air as howling cats ran for their lives down the littered lanes.

But that was a lifetime ago. Everything's different now that we've arrived in Oaxaca. The warmth of this community radiates from the grills of the hot cake vendors, from the sun-baked walls of brilliantly painted buildings peeling and flaking in the Mexican sun, from the big-hearted strangers who leap from pick-up trucks to direct us to the *zócalo*. And it is the *zócalo* itself, the central community open-air plaza, that is the physical heart of this magical city. Every Oaxaqueno, it seems, passes through the *zócalo* at least once a day—to read the paper, chat with friends, have a shoe shine—before spiraling back out toward work or home via the maze of immaculately swept avenues. The rejuvenating effect is obvious, even to a foreigner. Arriving from the arterial streets like depleted red blood corpuscles, Oaxaca's citizenry relies on the *zócalo* for daily refueling: a vivifying dose of warmth and humanity. How do Americans manage without a *zócalo*? How do we survive the suffocating stresses of metropolitan life without a refreshing pool of community to dip back into? We don't.

Oaxaca would always be a warm city, but that's true this week even more than usual. Today, January 6th, is the twelfth day of Christmas: *Los Reyes*. The holiday commemorates the night when the three wise kings (i.e., *reyes*) arrived at the infant Jesus's manger bearing their elaborate gifts. Children place their shoes outside their bedroom doors, stuffed with notes—much like letters to Santa—telling the *reyes* what specific presents to bring (Jesus himself never had it so good). The toy stores stay open until 2 a.m. to accommodate these demands, and the narrow streets are filled with desperate shoppers.

It's a fantastic time to be in Oaxaca, as colored lights blink in front of the ancient stone cathedral and the smells of baking bread, frying tortillas, and exquisite hot dogs commingle with ozone and perfume. The broad plazas surrounding the *zócalo* are filled with an all-day carnival featuring Teenage Mutant Ninja Turtle balloons, local handicrafts, all manner of deep-fried foods, sweet stands swarming with drunken bees, and hand-lettered stalls where squinting *mestizos* armed with hypodermic needles will engrave your name on a grain of rice—a feat of nano-engineering just as miraculous, at least to this beholder, as IBM spelling its corporate symbol out in magnetized atoms. Street musicians and beggars wander between tables at the open-air cafés facing the *zócalo*, palms out but not pushy, relying on the generosity of the season. They are seldom disappointed.

And you will usually find me at those cafés myself, doling out those pesos while wrestling with my own double-edged Christmas gift. Last summer, Globe-Pequot Press in Connecticut commissioned me to travel around the world, writing a book about my experiences as I go. The trip, which I'd proposed last winter, is what I can only call (at this point) a sort of reluctant spiritual pilgrimage in honor and terror of my upcoming 40th birthday. The single condition—self-imposed in my proposal—is that I must circumambulate the globe (from Oakland, California to Oakland, California) without taking a single airplane. The point is to rediscover what got me into travel writing in the first place, and what I've lost my sense of after twelve years of same: namely, The Size of the World.

The great irony of this journey, which was not part of the original plan, is the writing you see before you now. Thanks to two powerful allies—Hewlett-Packard (who loaned me an OmniBook 300) and O'Reilly & Associates (who developed the Global Network Navigator, an online magazine, on the worldwide Internet), I now have the privilege—and burden—of being forever tethered to my electronic igloo back home. Once, hiking through the mountains of Tibet, my trekking partner, Rick, and I sat down with a scrap of paper and calculated that, no matter where you are, you're never more than five days from Chicago. That may be unsettling; but the implications of this correspondence, if it works out as planned, is even scarier.

One part of Global Network Navigator, a.k.a. GNN, is the Travelers' Center, a remarkable convergence of travel writing and electronic travel resources. To find out more, contact travinfo@gnn.com.

—JO'R and LH

Traveling around the Earth without using air transport is bound to remind me of how enormous this home planet of ours is but—thanks to the nifty telecoupler provided by O'Reilly & Associates—my brotherhood of Internetted cyber-tuna will never be further away than the nearest telephone receiver.

In theory.

In practice, it's already a different story. Right now I'm in the tourist office's astonishingly well-equipped computer room, just half a block from the *zócalo*. Carnival rides are spinning outside the window, couples are smooching beneath the eaves of the Cathedral and Sally, my irrepressible Australian traveling partner, is out drinking cold *cervezas* and watching folkloric dances as I hunt-and-peck my way through the electronic gate of this odd assignment. I've been coming back here—to this office—for the past two days in a continuing and so far futile attempt to connect with CompuServe from Mexico City; I know there are at least half a dozen numbers, my "go phone" commands told me so when I tested the system back home, but I idiotically didn't write the numbers down when I had the chance and now local information couldn't provide a single one for me. The computer center director, Juan Pablo Prudencio, promised to find the number for me by six this evening. It is now half-past eight, and he has yet to appear. Phoning directly to CompuServe in the Bay Area is not a viable option, as the Mexican government enjoys a monopoly on telephone service and a 15-minute link-up would run me the price of a small Chevrolet (calls within Oaxaca cost the equivalent of 35 cents a minute). So I wait for Señor Prudencio, write, wait, write, wait. With the sinking feeling that this unnerving pattern is bound to be repeated in Guatemala, Senegal, Turkey, Iran, Nepal, China.... But ah! Here is Juan now, and he brings news.

The news was not good. I won't bore you with details, but suffice it to say that, despite efforts bordering on the heroic (or insane, if you want to be realistic), there will be no link with my electronic web tonight. Which just goes to show: the world isn't quite as small (yet) as I was afraid it might turn out to be after all. Listening to the unrequited gargle of the Mexico City CompuServe telecom link failing to connect with my computer's modem, I enjoyed a sense of informational isolation and electro-existential solitude rare in this hard-wired age. Years of development, thousands of dollars, and I can't even check my e-mail. We still haven't got the bugs ironed out of this global village business. I could stick around and try to figure out what's going haywire, but I may have to start renting by the week....

But if there's one thing I've learned from this series of frustrations, it's that information—recent intelligence to the contrary notwithstanding—operates by its own rules. Take Oaxaca, for example. Twenty-five hundred years ago, this region was the site of the thriving Zapotec capital called Monte Albán: a spectacular city set on a manmade mesa overlooking the entire valley. During its inconceivably long history—from about 500 B.C. to the 15th century—Monte Albán was the birthplace of Mexican writing and a highly complex calendar developed still further by the Mayans. The Zapotecs excelled in astronomy and ceramics, had a sophisticated ritual and political structure, and must have presumed (not unreasonably, after the first awkward centuries) that they, or at least a cogent record of their achievements, would be around forever.

The future, however, had other plans. Yesterday afternoon Sally and I explored the broad hilltop, now a mammoth ruin heavy with naked stone stairways, round columns supporting the dusty sky, vast plazas overgrown with dry grass. Much of the architecture is beautifully preserved: an observatory oriented, apparently, toward magnetic south, friezes of captured (and evidently castrated) enemy rulers; empty ball courts where copper-skinned athletes once competed, some say, for their lives.

But despite the evidence of these effortfully displaced stones, the culture that built Monte Albán, and all record of it, has all but disappeared. It is an almost total enigma. Elaborate hieroglyphs appear in dark stone alleyways, but no one can decipher them. Archeologists can only speculate on what occurred in the plazas, and why. The broadest details of life on Monte Albán—how the city was governed, what the inhabitants believed in, how they entertained themselves—is anybody's guess.

Beholding the ruins of this eternal Zapotecan civilization, I couldn't help but think about the vagaries of information. What lasts, and why? Our bold and cunning computer age is less than 25 years old (beginning with the invention of the integrated circuit), but we are already proud and audacious enough to imagine that, if we back up our files often enough, the megabytes we are so steadily generating will last forever, providing future archeologists (God help them) with a nearly seamless record.

I doubt it. The naked truth is that nothing lasts. After the Oakland, California fire, in 1991, I helped my friends Patrick and Sheila sift through the ash of their incinerated home. Among the loose steel screws and bits of broken saucer we found a clear, oblong marble laying beside a bare twisted U of some unrecognizable material. These two mysterious elemental artifacts—fused glass and silica—were all that remained of their Macintosh computer.

> We arrived at a large parking area and walked up and through a very unprepossessing museum—and out to the incredible space that is Monte Albán. Not "use of space," in the current sense, but space itself, offered up to the sky, to whatever lurking gods might be around. Even when you are standing there, looking down at the very broad, flat field, with pyramids on either side and one in the middle, you know that you are looking at a larger area than you can imaginatively grasp.
>
> —Alice Adams, *Mexico: Some Travels and Some Travelers There*

The record of the Zapotecs, an amazing race who reigned supreme in the Oaxaca Valley for over fifty generations, was carved in stone. It is gone. What hope, I wonder, for those weightless electronic pulses, beeping through the ether?

Jeff Greenwald also contributed "Welcoming the Spirits on Janitzio Island" to Part I.

Pop a salted, dried shrimp from that bin into your mouth and you'll know why Mexican families eat them as snacks while watching TV instead of popcorn. Roll a foot-long, fresh cinnamon stick between your hands to crumble it and then smell your fingers.

You can do that in Mexico. Life isn't hermetically sealed, or glassed and bottled off from touch and taste. So go ahead. Stick your face right down in those big baskets of spices and take some mighty sniffs. You can hardly smell anything in the U.S. anymore, but the knack for rolling a sensational scent around in your nose and savoring it does come back to you—kind of like riding a bike.

—Paula McDonald, "Tantalizing Trivia"

REED GLENN

Up the Volcano

A climb up an active volcano presents unexpected challenges.

With white knuckles, I clung to the saddle waiting for Zapechita, my
Mexican horse, to crash to the ground, crushing me beneath her as
she tumbled down the steep trail. Though I was only five minutes
into what would be a six-hour horseback ride, I was convinced I'd made a
terrible mistake.

I never liked horses or riding them—which I hadn't done since high
school—and was astounded at my foolhardiness for undertaking this
expedition on a treacherous trail in a remote area of Mexico alone with
an Indian guide.

Jagged rocks poked through the trail's deep, eroded gullies, reminding me that if I fell, I'd probably hit my head on one and be knocked out
(or killed) before Zapechita rolled on me. As the horse slipped and fal-
tered, I could only shut my eyes and trust in her mountain-pony instincts
as Francisco, my Tarascan Indian guide, pulled us down the trail by a
rope. I had no desire whatsoever to take the reins of this unpredictable,
non-English-speaking beast in a foreign land on tricky terrain.

So why was I undertaking this perilous journey? I had only to glance
up at the gaping crater of Paricutín, looming ominously against the green
landscape like a black hole, seeming to swallow up the very daylight. I
wanted to climb this dark, primordial creature, this voracious volcano
that had swallowed two local villages since it sputtered into existence
only forty-some years ago.

As the story goes, a farmer was plowing his corn field one day and
noticed a strange hole in the ground spitting rocks and cinders. He tried
to cover it up, but by the next day the hole had become a mound. The
mound steadily grew into a large hill that soon threatened the farmer's
house and the whole town.

By the time Paricutín—named for one of the towns it eventually
buried—finally stopped to take a breath nine years later, it had risen to
over 9,000 feet. Though the great, black cone grew entirely from the ash
and rock cinders spit from two different mouths, other vents around the
mountain released a flood of molten lava that engulfed 40 square kilome-

Paricutín is the youngest of Mexico's volcanoes. She was born on February 7, 1943 in a cornfield in Michoacán. Imagine how Dionisio Pulido felt. He saw her emerge from the ground in a tiny sputter. When awestruck Pulido returned with his *compadres* the next day (can you blame them for being skeptical?), she was a cone six meters, or about 20 feet high. Then the goddess of the volcano went to work in earnest. Paricutín exploded, hurling great chunks of molten rock a hundred meters up and putting on a fiery-orange lava display. Paricutín continued to be active until 1952 and by that time she had poured out a billion tons of lava.

—Kal Müller and Guillermo García-Oropeza, *Insight Guides Mexico*

ters of the countryside. Fortunately, Paricutín's slow growth gave local residents plenty of time to evacuate, and no lives were lost. The only thing remaining of the two towns formerly at the site is a half-buried church—its steeple jutting defiantly out of the lava field.

Climbing Paricutín is relatively easy—getting to it is the hard part, mainly because it's a long way from the village. I had planned to walk to Paricutín and then climb it—in all, a 14-mile round trip. But I hadn't counted on almost an hour's wait for the bus in Uruapan to the village of Angahuán, the starting point for the hike. Angahuán is also an hour's bus ride from Uruapan, where my hotel was. Then, once in Angahuán I took photos of the pretty village church and famous wooden door with the story of the volcano carved into it. Then there was shopping for some fruit and snacks for the long hike, followed by a futile search for a bathroom in the village. And then two false starts down the wrong roads before I finally found the right one to the volcano, escorted by one of the many local guides pestering me to rent their horses and services: *"Señorita, es muy lejos,"* ("Lady, it's very far").

By this time it was past 11 a.m. and my Colorado hiker's resolve to walk (and spartan budget) was overcome by my common sense, which told me to take the most expedient way to the volcano—a horse—so I'd get back before dark.

So I hired a horse—another time-consuming process. Hiring a horse is easy—choosing which one and then negotiating the price is the hard part. In fact, the second I stepped off the bus in Angahuán I was surrounded by at least a half-dozen prospective guides and horses who followed me around the village despite my repeated, *"No, gracias, voy a caminar,"* ("No, thanks, I'm going to walk").

Angahuán is a rustically charming *pueblo típico*—a typical Tarascan village with no paved roads and a population of colorfully clothed indigenous people, many of whom don't even speak Spanish, only the native Tarascan tongue.

Besides weaving and woodcarving, renting horses and guiding people to the volcano is the town's main cottage industry. One well worth supporting, I later realized.

If you make it out of the village without a horse—as I did—you can still change your mind at a small lodge on the path to Paricutín past Angahuán. There, at the last roundup, dozens of guides, with horses spar with each other to win your business—each shouting a better deal than the last. Then you must choose from guides ranging from young boys to old men with steeds of all ages and conditions as well—and what you see is not necessarily what you get. You may hire a sage-looking guide, only to be told afterward that it's actually his little brother who will be taking you.

But for me, what was to be a long, free walk, was now looking like an expensive ride. First, they tell you how much it costs to rent one horse (forty new pesos), then they inform you that you actually have to rent two horses—yours and your guide's (another forty new pesos). Somehow I ended up with Francisco, a trustworthy-looking man about my age, and Zapechita, a small, calm-looking, white horse. And I felt good about the final price I bargained for: sixty new pesos, or about $20.

After a mile or so into the ride, the initial steep descent flattened out into a wide trail of fine black sand weaving gently through avocado orchards, corn fields, and pink-blossomed fruit trees. By now, my white knuckles had turned pink and my fear had turned to worry—oh the pain I would suffer later—my tender legs already complaining and chaffing against the rough, primitive saddle. But the verdant, lovely landscape, dramatically juxtaposed against the black volcanic netherworld ahead, distracted me. Giant gray-green maguey cacti, with their succulent, sabre-like leaves lined the roadside. All around the area other tree-covered cones bespoke the early violent history of this now-pastoral land.

It was about this time that Francisco—soft-spoken and sad-eyed—informed me that he would make no money at all from the day's trip unless I gave him a *propina* (tip), and could I give him twenty new pesos? I groaned at this hidden, added cost and agreed to give him fifteen new—maybe more. Of course he had a family and kids and there was no work in the village—the truth. He also told me to call him "Pancho" for short.

As we drew closer to the lava field, I could see white plumes of smoke rising against Paricutín's black slopes and huge lava ridges that engulfed the countryside. The plumes came from fumaroles, the smoke-stacks venting the mountain's great, steaming factory of fire below.

We rode perhaps another hour or more around and alongside the towering lava field—too jagged and hot to ride or walk over—which is why it's a long way to the foot of the volcano, weaving, as you must, through this maze. During our ride, Pancho and I discussed children, work, religion, birth control, the Pope, and other weighty topics challenging my inadequate Spanish. He said he had only two children and had purposely tried to avoid having more because there was no work in the village. Slowly, the thirsty horses climbed the sandy hills, steeper and steeper toward the base of the volcano. They had no water on the trip except the leaves they occasionally nibbled along the way.

Finally, we reached the volcano's base, where a few other horses were tethered to shrubs. A handful of other climbers appeared as dots on the black slopes. Pancho took me up a ridge and around the side to view some fumaroles. A white precipitate covered the rocks and extremely hot, odorless air streamed out of an opening like a boiling tea kettle. Pancho told me to bend closer toward the opening and listen. Sounds of seething fury came from beneath the earth. "The people here worshipped these," he told me, "They believed they were alive." Without Pancho, I would have missed these off-the-trail sights—and commentary.

Pancho was a full-blooded Tarascan, a descendant of the strong and prosperous civilization that was nearly always victorious over the better-known Aztecs in their numerous battles. In that bold spirit, he clambered over the sharp rocks wearing only nylon woven sandals with his toes sticking out. He insisted on accompanying me to the top of the mountain, a steep, but short climb of about forty minutes up a trail of very loose, baseball-sized, volcanic rocks. Atop the cone, we gazed at the gorgeous countryside and the 360-degree view of the huge lava field,punctuated with many steaming vents. Looking down into the cone, Pancho pointed out the two "mouths" where the action began. Currently, the cone itself is dormant, and only the steaming fumaroles around the crater attest to the continuing turmoil beneath it. Two white metal crosses on the crater rim commemorate the two buried villages, according to Pancho.

After we circumnavigated the rim, Pancho gallantly spread his poncho on the ground, and offered me a seat to hear the formal telling of Paricutín's history—part of the tour package—and only about a third of which I understood, with my less-than-fluent Spanish. Fortunately, I knew the basic story but Pancho added some parts I hadn't heard: "First, the farmer covered the rock-spitting hole with his sombrero," he said. I also hadn't known that the volcano buried two villages: San Salvador Paricutín and San Juan Parangaricutiro, site of the half-buried church.

We descended quickly down a sand slide. Chivalrous, once again, Pancho held my arm so I wouldn't fall (I didn't have the heart—or Spanish—to tell him I did this all the time back in Colorado) as we took giant steps in unison down the steep slope.

After we reached the bottom, Pancho once again gallantly spread his poncho on the ground, but this time it was another story—and not one about the volcano. It took me a moment to figure out what was going on, and when I did I grabbed Zapechita and clambered aboard. "Ack!" I thought. *"Tengo un novio en Uruapan,"* I blurted out ("I have a boyfriend back in Uruapan,")—which was actually the truth. I had met Samuel, a Mexican journalist, in my travels and because of a back injury he decided not to climb the volcano with me. As I sat astride my steed, Pancho gently massaged my thigh, urging me to change my mind. After I convinced him that I would not and we rode away, I later wondered what, indeed, it would have been like to make love with a full-blooded Tarascan from a tiny, dusty village—our lives so different. I liked and respected Pancho, but not that way.

Transformed by the wonders of the volcano and having built up some trust of my horse—I decided to take Zapechita's reins myself on the way back. I began timidly, but soon realized that Zapechita knew exactly where to go, had no desire to gallop, and may as well have been ridden by a corpse. My knees were getting really sore from the saddle and Pancho generously tucked his own pancho under my saddle for more cushioning—always the gentleman and seeming to bear no ill will after my rejection. He decided to pick up the pace so we could get to the half-buried church before sunset and instructed me in the art of galloping—which, to my surprise, I really enjoyed and felt like a real *vaquero* (buckaroo).

I was often looked at with curiosity by the Mexicans I met, though I was never treated rudely. *"Pobrecita,"* (poor little thing) the older women would say when I told them I was on a solo journey through their country. After too many *"pobrecitas,"* I started telling people that I was a student on holiday from my studies in Mexico City. To them that seemed more legitimate than being simply a traveler and quite frankly it got very depressing always having people feel sorry for me...There were times, however, when it was very lonely being in a culture that put so much emphasis on a woman always being with her family, or at the very least with an escort. As a result I found myself accepting invitations from men that could have been dangerous.

—Miranda Davies, et al.,
Women Travel, A Rough Guide Special

We reached the church just as the late-afternoon light glowed amber—perfect for photos. Pancho was a wizard of timing. The church's ivory bell tower jutted boldly out of its jagged lava prison against black, brooding storm clouds gathering over Paricutín. Like a Rembrandt *chiaroscuro*, golden rays of the setting sun danced across the dark lava field, seeming to illuminate the lovely ruined church against an ominous sky. "This could happen again!" the weather and volcano seemed to warn. The others we had seen earlier on the volcano now clambered around on the lava fields nearby looking like colorful ants.

As we rode back in the fading light, we overtook a group that we had been tailing all day. They were riding along, singing and laughing. We chatted and exchanged names, origins, and occupations. They were from Mexico City, off on a little vacation. Within earshot, one of the male riders remarked in Spanish to Pancho, *"Las periodistas, tienen mucho valor,"* ("Those journalists have guts"). *Mucho valor*, indeed—yes, I thought, I like the sound of that.

As the sun set and moon rose over the peaceful green forest canopy we sang *"Cielito Lindo"* (Beautiful Heavens). Alert as ever, Pancho had remembered that these people had arrived by car and were probably driving back to Uruapan where I was staying. He quietly suggested I ask them for a ride back rather than catch the local bus, as I had planned.

By this time I had decided that the fifteen new peso *propina* I had promised Pancho—and even the twenty he had requested—wasn't enough. This man had spent an entire day with me, climbed a volcano in sandals, shown me the off-trail sights, given me an oral history, taught me how to ride, lent me his own pancho for comfort—well, yes, had tried to seduce me, but gracefully took rejection in stride—had been a good companion and even found me a free, safe ride home in the dark. He also had a family to support.

When it was time to settle up for the ride and guide I gladly gave Pancho thirty new pesos extra (still only about $10, but at least more than he had requested). Earlier, he had said he hoped I'd write about my trip and good guide so others would visit Paricutín. And I have.

Reed Glenn is a volcano aficionado who, perhaps because she is a fire sign, would like to climb all of the somewhat active volcanoes of the world. She has written for Outside, Runner's World, *and several Mexico guidebooks. She lives in Boulder, Colorado.*

Northern Mexico is less congenial to women travelers than anywhere else in Mexico; Oaxaca, Chiapas, and the Yucatán are the most congenial. If you are traveling with a male friend, it may help to pose as a couple. This will assuage any misgivings hotel proprietors have about letting you share rooms and may serve to chill the blood of your Mexican admirer.

Remember, too, that as often as foreign women are stereotyped by Mexican men, Mexican men are stereotyped by foreigners. A man who offers to give you a lift or show you the sights may be acting innocently, but if you feel uncomfortable, politely refuse.

—Harvard Student Agencies, *Let's Go Mexico*

TED CONOVER

In the Land of Avocados

In his book Coyotes, *the author chronicles his life with migrant farm workers in the U.S. Here, in a remote town in Mexico, he traces the origins of some of his friends.*

T
he White Arrow pitched wildly around a hairpin turn on its descent into Ahuacatlán. The road was a ledge, chiseled into the steep mountainside; a deep valley, a vast volume of air, separated us from the other valley wall, more than a mile away. It was easier to look at those far mountains, golden green in the afternoon sun, than at our own; everything nearby seemed either way above us, up unscalable heights, or far below. Instead of guard rails around the hairpins, there was most often a series of little shrines, of whitewashed brick or stone or cinder block, knee high, with a candle or a Madonna or plastic flowers inside, and letters scratched on the outside bearing the name of the deceased: "Raúl Anaya P., 12-5-62." Flew off this crazy height and into the great beyond. His Chevy's still down there because no junk man wants to risk his life winching it back up. You can see it if you get close enough to the edge...

The White Arrow was a glorified school bus, painted up, years before, to resemble a regular coach. It had been relegated by the forces of supply and demand to the hinterlands of Querétaro state, just north of Mexico City. From Querétaro City, the capital, to Ahuacatlán, high in the Sierra Gorda, was eleven extremely uncomfortable hours. The bus left once or twice a day, depending. To find its bay at the station, you asked at every counter until you came to White Arrow's: no one else had ever heard of Ahuacatlán. White Arrow, however, serviced two of them, Ahuacatlán de Guadalupe, and Ahuacatlán de Jesus. The clerk asked which I wanted. Barely able yet to pronounce Ahuacatlán by itself, I shrugged in resignation. It was in a high valley, I said, several hours away; that was all I knew. She chose Ahuacatlán de Guadalupe for me,and I hoped she was right. Riding the White Arrow required certain leaps of faith.

Another leap had to do with the tires. Because two were bald, two spares were tied to the roof, along with any other cargo that wouldn't fit through the door: trunks, crates, pieces of furniture, sacks of feed, lumber...even a casket. *"Is there somebody in that?"* I asked the bus driver, a tired-looking, bewhiskered man, when at last he appeared. *"I believe so,"* he said, flicking down his cigarette and staring at it. I waited for him to say more, but he didn't, just stared. I thought about that tired bus driver, about those bald tires, about that body, dying twice, as the Arrow took the sharp curves.

The first seven or eight hours were through poor farmland that gradually gave up and became desert. Then the desert took on contours: dunes grew out of the scrub-covered flatlands and then solidified into sandy foothills; these in turn yielded to full-scale, arid mountains of considerable grandeur, a landscape evocative of something between the Sahara and the moon.

I had felt safer on that part of the journey, the journey up: the old school bus engine strained to do even fifteen or twenty miles an hour on the steep grade, with obstacles and the need occasionally to stop and let off passengers conspiring to keep the driver from getting up a good head of steam. Where these passengers went was a considerable mystery to me—there were no settlements in sight at all, not a single house or lean-to. As far as I could tell the darkly tanned and deeply wrinkled old men and women with their bundles walked off into the middle of nowhere. Apparently somewhere in the vast rippled distance, from the deepest creases between parched piles of dirt and slate, water seeped out, and things could grow.

Up and up the bus climbed. The turns got tighter. We passed two shut-down mines which the old man next to me said had once produced mercury. Cut from the rib of one mountain, presumably with considerable effort, was a dirt soccer field, yet who was there to play on it? And if the ball were kicked out of bounds, what kept it from falling hundreds of feet? Near the top of our ascent, a painted sign advertised *"petróleo,"* and one next to it *"leña,"* or firewood, and there it was, stacked in tall cords...thick firewood, probably pine—where had it come from? As the Arrow finally wheezed through a mountaintop defile fifty feet deep, I realized we had reached the summit...and more. For as we began our descent, the more remote side of the range slowly began to turn green. Tall trees—live oak and eucalyptus—abounded; the ridge tops were rough with shrubbery and woolly with clouds, no longer bare; and sewn between woods on the mountainsides was an uneven patchwork quilt of tended fields. The summit, in other words, was also a sort of grand meteorological fence. On this side, water fell; on the other side, it did not. The land wasn't lush, but people could live.

The high valley we were descending, the Moctezuma River valley, had ancient human origins. When Hernán Cortés arrived in the 1520s, Ahuacatlán (literally "land of avocados") and the valley's other villages had for hundreds of years been home to the Otomí Indians. Though relatively near Mexico City—the ancient Aztec capital of Tenochtitlán, which was the Spaniards' first target—the Otomí were among the last peoples to be subdued by the Spanish conquistadors. Their inaccessibility and their fierceness, legendary in Spanish chronicles of the time, were two reasons, but they also were protected by their lack of organization: where Cortés had effectively paralyzed the Aztecs by imprisoning their ruler, Moctezuma, the same strategy was ineffective in dealing with the tribal Otomí. In the end, it was none other than Franciscan friars (and a large detachment of Spanish soldiers) who, in the 1690s, finally succeeded in subduing the valleys. The natives were forced—upon pain of death—into constructing the first links in a chain of missions that Father Junípero Serra eventually would extend up Mexico's west coast, all the way to present-day northern California. Impressive-looking Churrigueresque churches were one result. But a century of pain and death, memorialized by such reminders as the "Avenue of the Massacre" in a town we passed in the bus, and the ruins of cut-stone Otomí temples, in secluded forests unknown to guidebooks, spoke of the cost.

> The Spanish could not control the Apaches. For 150 years the Apaches chose warfare as a way of life. They captured horses from the Spaniards, mounted raids, and conducted guerilla warfare, hit and run style. They became experts at it. They wisely refused pitched battle. They had no bases which could be destroyed and they operated in bands. The Spaniards built a chain of *presidios* (forts) across northern Chihuahua to try to contain the raids but the Indians easily slipped past. Spanish settlers had to abandon their ranches; it was too dangerous to stay there.
>
> —Kal Müller and Guillermo García-Oropeza, *Insight Guides Mexico*

I wanted to go to Ahuacatlán because there was something missing, I had felt, in my travels with Mexicans in the United States. That something was a context—the missing pieces of family life, of women, of children, of animals, of town plazas, of *fiestas*. The Moctezuma valley area, including Ahuacatlán, was the home of the men whom I had driven to Florida, the home of Victor and Timoteo, who had accompanied Carlos to Los Angeles, of Mariano and others at the Martinolli ranch—including those who had waited in the orchard while I was looking for *coyotes* [smugglers]. From what I could tell, it was typical of many of the Mexican feeder villages to the

States: it had the poverty of southern Mexico, the remoteness that lent an extra Shangri-la luster to the image of the United States, the hard-scrabble agricultural base that took kids out of school at a young age, unprepared for any profession but enthralled by a get-rich-quick scheme called *El Norte*, the United States.

Lupe Sanchez had arranged for me to stay with the family of an old friend of his in Ahuacatlán, a former farmworker named Hilario Pacheco. It wasn't only as a favor to me: Hilario coordinated the work in the valley of an agricultural cooperative that the Arizona Farmworkers Union had helped to found. His job required visits to farmers not only around Ahuacatlán, but also in the twenty or so isolated *ranchos* that dotted the valley—and Hilario didn't like to drive the co-op's ten-ton truck on the narrow curvy back roads. Coming from a mountainous place myself, I rather did. And so was born our arrangement.

Soon we reached the valley bottom, and for the next half hour traced the route of the curving Río Moctezuma, hot air rushing in from the advancing night. We skirted a small hamlet, nestled deep in the valley and visible from a distance by the white dome of its large church, and stopped at an intersection on the edge. Few were around to see me descend from the bus, but those that were stopped to watch. No one would be there to meet me because they didn't know exactly when I was coming. Besides, one could spend a long afternoon waiting for the White Arrow.

I walked up to one older, straw-hatted man on the nearest corner. He looked down, pretending not to see me as I approached, but then at the sound of my *"Buenas noches"* was extremely polite and attentive. Yes, he said, he knew the house of Hilario Pacheco. He would take me there.

Concrete floor, gas range, long concrete countertop, and room for a table with four or five wooden chairs around it—Lupe Pacheco's kitchen was nicer than most. Poor Eustolia Romo across the road had only a dirt floor, had to keep a little cooking fire going all day long, breathe the smoke when she heated water. She smelled like smoke. How did she feel when the government gas truck came to town, and others lifted their empty propane tanks up to the highway for a refill? Perhaps Eustolia's sons would do well in *"Los Uniteds,"* and send something home to make life easier. Hilario certainly had. Though they had Lupe's brother to thank for the use of the house. He had left for Florida ten years ago, forsaking his inheritance for the chance of greater riches up north. He must have done all right, too, for they never heard from him, never had any word that he was headed home. Perhaps it was just as well—where would her family go if one day he showed up?

On the wall was their old AM radio, tuned to the only station it could be tuned to—500-watt XEJAQ, "Radio Happiness," in Jalpan, down the plains twenty-five miles away. The announcer was young Miguel Angel, son of her sister-in-law. Lunch hour was when he always did the requests and dedications received in the mail—often from as far away as Idaho. Lupe was not sure exactly where Idaho was, but she knew they grew potatoes there, and a fair number of young men headed there every spring, her husband's nephew Victor among them. The names stuck in her head, but the places were only vague imaginings—a vast cold treeless land of rich soil with potatoes popping up everywhere. On the edge of the farm, she saw the owner's house, his beautiful wife and children. Lupe's sister had a friend in California who sometimes sent to Ahuacatlán issues of a magazine called *House and Garden*. That was a fun Sunday morning—sitting at her sister's house and going over the pictures of the kitchens, the children's clothes, the surprising things they ate. Lupe had left Ahuacatlán only once—to have an operation in Querétaro City. It was that operation that had sent Hilario back to Arizona, the place he swore he would never return. They had needed money for the operation, and, in only a season and a half, Hilario had saved it. Querétaro was large and frightening, meshed, in her mind, with Hilario's absence and the experience of being in the hospital. Now she felt better, and was sure she would continue to if she stayed at home.

Lupe was thirty-three, but looked ten years older than an American woman her age. Most of the women in Ahuacatlán did, and it wasn't for lack of skin cream: childbearing started early, child rearing took up most of

I once met an old woman in Mexico who looked lonelier that anyone I have ever seen. She was a beggar woman in a slum market in Mexico City. The aisles of the market were covered with canvas; on either side of these tent aisles hung chickens and flowers and pineapples for sale. Within the transept of the market, against a stone wall, the old woman kept her anchor-hold.

Hair grew out of her nose like winter breath. Her reply to every questions was *no*. Nothing. Nobody. No husband. No sisters. No brother. Her only son dead.

If there was no one to claim her from the past, then she was unalterably separated from life. She lived in eternity. Even the poor neighborhood people, the poorest of the poor, could spare a few pesos for this mother of tragedy. People were in awe of her, for she was without grace, which in Mexico is children.

—Richard Rodriguez, *Days of Obligation: An Argument With My Mexican Father*

one's life. And when the husband was away—and in Ahuacatlán they were away a lot, making money—there were husband's duties, as well: taking care of the chickens and cow, managing the money, or lack of it, disciplining the kids, and handling relations with friends and neighbors. Vacations were when she got sick.

A laborer arrived from a *rancho* atop the mountain opposite Hilario's home. He carried in his arms a crate of small high-altitude peaches. They were from orchards Hilario had pointed out to me high on the mountainsides, on slopes so steep that every tree required a stone-rimmed terrace to survive—a project of the cooperative. They were the season's first, and the children cried out in delight—fresh, sweet fruit was hard to come by in Ahuacatlán. Our meal would have a fine dessert.

After receiving the peaches, Hilario sat back down at his chair on the porch next to the kitchen, surrounded by corn husks, and ate a peach without expression. His main work was with the cooperative, but in his spare time, almost as a hobby, he grew corn and small amounts of sugar-cane, coffee, and fruit. The sugarcane was mainly a treat for his kids to munch on—with his machete he had just cut down a single cane, sectioned it, sliced off its hard outer layer, and handed pieces to me and [his son] Juanito. We gnawed as Hilario returned to shucking the corn. He wasn't preparing it to be eaten on the cob; instead, the ears would go onto the roof, in a fenced-in area protected from birds, next to the coffee beans, to dry. Later, Lupe would grind the corn to mix daily with lime and salt as tortilla dough. Hilario didn't seem comfortable unless he was working: even in the moments before a meal, he shunned idleness.

Finally his daughter Lupita came out to tell us the meal was ready, and we walked past the partition to the kitchen. Soup, a chicken broth with noodles, was already on the table, along with plates of the ever-present corn tortillas. Tortillas, rolled into little scoops, were the primary utensils; the spoons, I had a suspicion, were mainly there as a courtesy to me. Next came rice, the rich brown chicken *mole*, and a small circle of white goat's cheese from a *rancho*, a few short white hairs attesting to its authenticity. A fresh batch of piquant salsa, ground that morning in Lupe's stone *molcajete*, was there to be added to anything, but tasted best with the rice. Cornelio twisted Hilario's arm until he consented to try Cornelio's cool white *pulque*; my arm needed no twisting. So many were there that only the males were seated, with Lupe running back and forth, keeping the stack of tortillas fresh and high, serving and clearing. Her sister-in-law, Rigo's wife, Conchita, stood by with baby Omar in her arms, and Grandma watched from the dark doorway to her room. Lupita pushed the colorful baskets that hung from the ceiling back and forth, on behalf of Omar, who would watch them for hours. The baskets were not only decorative but necessary for the storage of foods that appealed to crawling bugs. Lupita's older sister, Alicia, shooed out the chickens. Lupe served coffee and lemon tea, Cokes, and orange soda.

Cornelio poured us more *pulque*. Lupe presented us with a plate of the dry sugar-sprinkled pastry from the town bakery. Alicia cleared off more dishes, and carried them outside to wash in the tub. Juanito picked at his chicken and sipped his Coke with gusto.

Hilario decided we would take our coffee and peaches outdoors. *"Gracias, señora,"* I said to Lupe as we stood up from the table—immediately feeling silly. Though appropriate at home, it was an elaborate decoration here: people were not thanked for performing their duties. No one ever said it but me. It was just one of many things I had yet to learn.

Cornelio did not share his brother Hilario's strongly Indian appearance, or his reputation for strictness and self-discipline. His hair was wavy, his shirt collar open, his manner relaxed. The three of us sat in the shade of the large tree. Cornelio, to me, was a breath of fresh air; Hilario was trustworthy, sober, and responsible, but Cornelio was expressive and open, willing to discuss and joke about almost anything. I knew Hilario had spent many years in the States, but had not yet succeeded in getting him to talk about it. A proud man, he found his years on "the other side" to be demeaning, I knew. His fervent wish was that his son Juanito never be tempted, nor compelled to go there. That was one reason he worked so hard for the cooperative: if local agriculture could be developed to the point where it would support a living wage, men would not have to leave Ahuacatlán. That afternoon, though, with the prompting of Cornelio, the warm breeze, and the cool *pulque*, Hilario opened up a crack. I asked Cornelio about his time in the States.

"We left for the North in '49, the year father died, no?" he asked Hilario. Hilario nodded. He set down his drink and crossed his legs.

"Cornelio was eleven and I fourteen. Men had left Querétaro for other parts of Mexico for years back then, traveling to earn more money, but the States was still a new idea. In Texas the oil boom was starting, and there were jobs in that and in picking cotton."

"Well, we walked one hundred kilometers, from here to Xilitla, because there was no highway then, no bus. We took a bus to the border, crossed the Río Bravo, and found work in the valley, in Weslaco. The crossing cost us many humiliations—no, not from the *gringos*, from the other Mexicans—because we were so young and small and had no protector. The border towns can be very tough. We stayed there in Weslaco three years, sending money home to our mama. And then Cornelio left."

"I returned then because my maternal cousin, Antonio, wanted to sell me his delivery business," Cornelio interjected, somewhat defensively. "That way I was able to help Mama from closer by."

"Then, I was so sick of cotton—you know, they almost never pick it by hand anymore in the States—I was so sick of cotton I went with some friends to Oregon, to work in the onions," Hilario continued. "I did that for two years."

Hilario had been deported in 1954, during what I realized must have been the large sweep of illegal aliens—1.4 million of them—known as Operation Wetback. Besides being inconvenienced, he was deeply embarrassed by the episode. "To be handcuffed, put in a truck, have your name published in the paper—why, they treated me like a criminal! I did not go back until Lupe needed the operation." Cornelio, still delivering bricks thirty years later, had never gone back.

"No, I didn't save anything for myself, sent it all home to my mama," Hilario continued. "Ah, no, I take it back: I did bring home a souvenir...."

Hilario unbuttoned his shirt far enough to show a long wide scar on his shoulder. "You are lucky to live in a time when beer bottles have twist-off caps," he said. "A guy with a bottle opener in a Weslaco bar decided he didn't like me."

I was fascinated, as we talked, to learn of the history of what was for them an emigration to the States, of the patterns that had developed over time. Men from Querétaro, they told me, generally went to Arizona or Florida to work. Men from the state of San Luis Potosí, on the other hand, typically headed for California and Texas. And it did not end there. In Arkansas, picking tomatoes or planting seedlings for lumber companies, you found mainly workers from Michoacán; in Kansas feedlots, they came from Michoacán and Guanajuato. To California they also came from Guerrero, to Texas especially from Jalisco. In American cities the distribution of Mexican nationals seemed more random, but this order behind rural immigration patterns lent the phenomenon a completely different face from that presented in U.S. newspapers and magazines. This was less a random tide of desperate people than a traditional economic relationship, grown up over decades, between Mexican "hands" (the term bracero, used to describe Mexican immigrants in the early years, comes from the Spanish for "arm") and American growers. It was nothing for them to feel ashamed of, and they evidently did not.

There was a rapping outside my door. "Slee-ee-pyhead! Ti-i-ime to get u-u-p!" Waking his American was, it seemed, one of the great pleasures of Hilario's day.

"What time is it?"

"Late! Already very late!" I scrounged around for my watch. It was 5:30 a.m. The sun had not yet risen; roosters were only starting to greet the brightening sky. In half an hour or so, choruses of cock-a-doodle-doos would sweep over the town—but there had been barely a peep yet from the neighbors' big fighting cock, who seemed the village choral director. I needed a drink of water, badly...but the only water at Hilario's house came straight from the river. I groaned.

"Up yet?" said Hilario, cracking the door to get a good look at my puffy face.

"Sí, sí, I'm up!" I sat up painfully. Hilario was delighted. Americans acted so superior, but really they were soft. I was the proof. He grinned and gazed. It was not pleasant. "You can leave now," I said. "Shut the door, please?" Hilario grinned more widely, and shut the door.

My consolation was that Hilario really had a use for me. The night before, members of the cooperative had filled the bed of the group's ten-ton, three-axle, ten-speed truck with sacks of cement. Its destination was the *rancho* of Rincón de Pisquintla, where villagers would use it to construct a modest reservoir to store water from a small mountain spring, making possible the irrigation of otherwise unproductive land. The first hour of driving was paved highway, but the next two were dirt road—increasingly winding dirt road, that climbed high into the remote sierra. Hilario didn't like to drive, had no stomach for it. I thrived on it.

It was status to drive a big truck like this in the sierra—good ones were expensive and seldom seen. I felt powerful climbing up into the cab. Little kids waved; I tooted the horn. In the small city of Jalpan, down on the valley floor, we stopped for Hilario to buy oranges—the distributors made it this far, but not up to Ahuacatlán—and then soon it was back off the highway and into the mountains, *rancho* bound.

> Mexico greets its foreign arrivals with more grace than the United States greets its.
>
> "These are some of the nicest people in the world," said a retired American navy doctor [in Baja California]. "They are kind, they are generous, and they *work*. God, how they work."
>
> —Pete Hamill, "South of the Border," *Travel-Holiday*

The road was everything one would expect from a remote mountain road in Mexico—precipitous, curvy, full of surprises: a herd of goats around this bend, a muddy morass around that, a hairpin turn where you would least expect it, totally unmarked. Fortunately, Hilario provided verbal road signs, well in advance. We crept across two streams where the wooden bridges had been washed out. Hilario suggested I was being too nice to the livestock we encountered—if they couldn't get off the road, they were not meant for this world. And if they got hit, well, "Somebody will eat them soon," he assured me.

Ranchos were among Mexico's most remote locations. Typically they had only between twenty and fifty residents; almost never did they have electricity. Many could not be reached by automobile—you got a bus to let you off on a certain creek or ridge, and then you walked. Small mountain springs were often their sole reason for existence. Up these mountains, many had fantastic names: when we wanted to arrange a meeting, Hilario would pay for an ad to be broadcast on XEJAQ: "Attention, residents of Piglet, Big Peach, The Bats, and Saint Peter the Old! Meeting next Friday at the home of Rafael Ramos at sundown." Normally one person could be counted on to hear the message, and that person would be responsible for telling everyone else. The residents were generally interrelated, and family feuds had long and sometimes violent histories. Residents of *ranchos*, I had discovered at Martinolli's, often understood the world in different terms from the rest of us. I had asked a *rancho*-born student of mine in Phoenix how far he lived from Ahuacatlán.

"Eight hours," he explained.

"You must get tired of all that driving," I suggested. He looked very puzzled, and asked what I meant. "Just that, any time you need something, like radio batteries, you have to drive eight hours both ways."

"No, no," he explained earnestly. "We walk. Eight hours walking."

Hilario, in answer to my question, explained that parents in *ranchos* were among the most

Mexico's mountainous terrain and its rigid arid climate make it less than ideal for agriculture. Two mountain ranges run through the country, the north is largely desert, tropical jungles cover the south, and the soil of the Yucatán peninsula is paper thin. About half the country is considered too steep to cultivate, and more than 50 percent of the territory is arid, with another 20-35 percent considered semi-arid. Only about 15 percent of Mexico's 487 million acres are considered arable. Some 55 million acres are under cultivation, while 184 million acres are dedicated to grazing. The lack of water is the main impediment to intensive cultivation in Mexico.

—Tom Barry, *Mexico: A Country Guide*

eager anywhere to get their kids to emigrate to the States. "They see it as their big chance to get rich," said Hilario. "Their sons come home with fifty dollars, and it's the most money they've seen in their lives. Some parents nearly throw their kids out the door!"

The mountainsides were bushy, but not lush. Spectacular vistas opened up as we rounded one ridge, then the next. The broad mountainsides were different from those of my home in that they were cultivated—looking across any expanse, you could see the different-colored crops separated from each other by stone fences, dotted with faraway humans in straw cowboy hats and the stout oxen that helped them plow.

After passing several other settlements, we finally arrived at Rincón de Pisquintla. Only a few dwellings were visible to us, all of them made of wood or cane. Two had metal roofs; the others were thatched. There were a couple of old dogs. The air was wonderful, cool and fresh and full of butterflies. Men came out of fields, clad in *huaraches* and home-sewn clothes, to greet Hilario, and kids were sent to find other men. After a discreet interval wives and mothers asked Hilario for news of their sons in the north—had he heard anything? Hilario said I had been in Phoenix, and probably had more recent news—and then it occurred to me that probably I did know several of the men who belonged to these women. Talking with the wives, seeing the babies, the plots of beans and onions, was a revelation: up in the States, I had never appreciated that the men were...well, so important. On the ranch they seemed so single, and rootless—like random pieces of an unknown picture puzzle you found in a cabinet and were unsure what to do with. Here, suddenly, I saw how they were husbands, fathers, owners—missing pieces that would make a puzzle complete, prettier, a whole picture.

After the wives came younger men, just entering their teens. Approaching with extreme shyness and respect, they asked if I could get them jobs. No, I had to say, I wasn't an owner, I had worked alongside others from this town. Was there much work? Some, I said, not a lot, but some if you were patient. "University of Arizona," read the emblem on the t-shirt of one little girl.

By late afternoon we had the truck unloaded, and had been treated to chunks of quiote—the fibrous, sap-soaked inner core of the maguey cactus, round and white like a sliver of pineapple, chewed and sucked on as a pick-me-up. Cokes were served alongside, making the snack a bizarre combination of Otomí and Americana. Did I like it? a woman asked. Tastes a little like wood, I admitted—if you lied about these things out of politeness, I had learned, you were liable to get another helping.

"Wood?" Those who had understood me relayed the answer to those who had not. They thought it was hilarious. "Wood! Wood!" Their teeth weren't so good; you could tell when they laughed. One offered me a little piece of wood to chew on, so that I could tell the difference. We laughed about that too.

Rincón de Pisquintla was perched on a hillside; all afternoon I had been watching the colors of the land change as the sun moved across the sky. You could hear birds everywhere; no radio or TV noises diverted your attention from the life around you. But the sun began to set, and Hilario signaled it was time for us to leave. I was so pleased with the place, I wanted to spend the night. And I was annoyed when I started the engine—what a racket it made! how badly it stank!—and even more annoyed when a young man came running up with a big tape deck under his arm. He didn't look like anyone else in town. "I'm the teacher," he explained. He was from the southern Mexican state of Chiapas, on the Guatemalan border, assigned here to do his national service. He had run three miles from a neighboring *rancho* when he heard we were here. "Can you take me down with you?" We said sure, and fit him in front. I was filled with romantic thoughts about living in such a place. But the teacher wasn't. The bus to town—probably another White Arrow— hadn't made its weekly trips for the entire past month, he explained, and he was going crazy. His radio batteries were almost dead! He grasped the device with a fervor that made me realize he considered it his sole link to civilization. "Boy, am I glad to be out of there for a while!" he said, smiling broadly.

"No greater disaster has befallen Ahuacatlán since the Conquest," said Father Tomás Cano, transferring his heavy white vestments from his rounded shoulders to a wardrobe in the sacristy and wiping the sweat from his florid brow. He was a tall man, with close-together eyes that gave the impression of big cheeks. He walked through a door to his office and poured himself a glass of water from a pitcher on his desk. A ceiling fan turned slowly, and with questionable effect; it was hot in there. I had been waiting since he finished evening Mass to get his thoughts on emigration to the States.

"Please, have a seat," he said, pulling out a chair from under a table. There was a white cat on it. "Ah, *Gringo*, so that's where you've been hiding!" He shooed the cat away.

"*Gringo?*" I asked.

The father grinned a bit sheepishly. "It was named by some children," he said. "Because of its color."

"Did you mean that—about no greater disaster?"

"Yes! Though, of course, it is more complicated than that. It is mainly a great disruption, bringing with it much bad but also some good." He paused to finish the glass of water. "That is to say...it's, it's...say, do you know how to swim?"

"Excuse me?"

"I said, do you swim. It's late enough that the suds should be gone from the river, and the children will have left the swimming hole. It's so hot in here, there's nothing I'd like more than a swim."

The priest was a man of such importance in Ahuacatlán that I had not imagined he did things like swim. Out of respect, I had kept my sleeves rolled down and my collar buttoned high. But this sounded like a great idea.

"Sure—why not?" I said. He turned off the lights and fan and we exited through a side door. He didn't lock the door, I noticed—most doors in Ahuacatlán didn't even have locks. A tiny side street soon turned into a path along the river. The priest was in no hurry.

"Back to your question," he said. "Externally, yes—having men leave to work in the States benefits us. They send money home, and now we have better houses, clothing, highways, cars. More people can afford farm animals. The parts of life that you can quantify are better.

"But how much of life is that? I will say it again: not since the Conquest have we suffered such a disaster. And here is why. Seven out of ten households here lack a husband, a father—they're all gone, working somewhere else. Sure, maybe—maybe—their families have more money, but the family! The men come home once a year, they make their wives pregnant, and then they leave again. The wives get so frustrated; 'I married a man, not a letter, not a U.S. Postal Service money order!' one said to me. The children of these families have a character that is colder than normal.

"And, of course, terrible things happen. The men bring home venereal disease, from the prostitutes they have up there. We never used to have these diseases in Ahuacatlán; now—ask the doctor!—they're everywhere. Or, what's worse, the men never came home at all. They take a mistress up there, and get comfortable, and that's the last we hear. I think about two hundred never come home at all anymore. That includes the ones that die: my count is twenty-seven died in the past twenty years. Yes, they die in car wrecks, bar fights, farm accidents....

"That is why I have always said: This is a parish of widows and orphans. It is true figuratively, but also it is true literally."

The priest hopped over a log as we continued our way upstream toward the swimming hole. During the day the wide, shallow parts of the Río Moctezuma were dotted with women doing their wash, each crouched over large, smooth stones dragged into the river for that purpose. Their laundry detergent—and that of women all the way up the valley—was the source of the suds the priest had referred to; at midday the river sometimes resembled a moving bubble bath. But now the suds had been rinsed down into the Jalpan reservoir, and the river ran smooth and dark. Father Cano sat down a moment to rest.

"You know, I studied in your country for five years."

"Yes? Where?"

"Catholic University, in Washington, D.C."

I tried some English on him, but the priest had gotten a little rusty.

"Anyway, coming from the States, you will understand the desire to get ahead. It is called ambition, and it is a beautiful thing. But it is also the reason so many young people here want to leave. They all want to do the best they can, don't want anyone to be better than them.

"They hear their friends chatting—brothers, older boys who have been. Of course, even if they suffered fiascoes up there, the stories they tell are pure adventure. The younger boys see their new clothes, see how girls are attracted. To them it sounds like the Eternal Paradise! And besides, they think, only sissies stay behind. What can one who stays have to compare with a tale of crossing the border, eluding the FBI, even being in prison in the United States! The men take great pride in these things.

"So they leave school early and away they go. And six months, a year, or two years later, when they come back, they are disgusted at what they see. Ahuacatlán suddenly looks to them like a pigsty: livestock in the streets, no plumbing, dirt roads. They are ashamed. And this is the beginning of their inferiority complex—they think everything there is better. They see Americans as very high, themselves as very low. Of course, though, they can never be Americans, or even pass for them at their age—it's too late to learn English well enough. But many feel stupid because of it. And they are ashamed to be Mexican."

The father shook his head. "Ay, Teodoro, it's a crazy world, isn't it?"

"And getting crazier," I said.

"What is there to do, sometimes, but go for a swim?"

"Yes."

The swimming hole was just around the next bend. I was amazed as we got close: here was the Huck Finn swimming hole missing from my youth. The main pool went down about fifteen feet. One side was a wall of stone, with numerous diving-off spots; the other was flat and grassy, with two huge sycamores sprouting from the riverbank and arcing up over the deepest pool. As the priest would soon demonstrate, you could also dive off these.

It was dusk. Far above the rocky side of the river, the highway passed. Apart from the occasional whine of a truck, all was the rushing of the river. Without a word, Father Cano disappeared behind some shrubs, where he modestly disrobed; the next thing I heard was a great splash as his body hit the deep pool, and an "Ah!" as he came up for air. I hung my clothes on a tree and waded cautiously into a more shallow pool downstream, getting the feel of the pebbled bottom. This was the best bath you ever got in Ahuacatlán. It was also, I discovered, plunging all the way into the cool, dark water, one of the best swims you got anywhere.

Ted Conover grew up in Colorado and was educated at Amherst College and Cambridge University. He is the author of White Out: Lost in Aspen, *and* Coyotes: A Journey through The Secret World of America's Illegal Aliens, *from which this story is taken.*

Mexico, mad mother. She still does not know what to make of our leaving. For most of this century Mexico has seen her children flee the house of memory. During the Revolution ten percent of the population picked up and moved to the United States; in the decades following the Revolution, Mexico has watched many more of her children cast their lots with the future; head north for work, for wages; north for life. Bad enough that so many left, worse that so many left her for the *gringo*.

—Richard Rodriguez, *Days of Obligation: An Argument with My Mexican Father*

Tim Golden

Dancing the Goat

Ancient rituals continue just behind the mall.

P ast the Nissan dealership and Tehuacán Ford, just beyond the pastel-
colored tract homes going up on the edge of town, the Slaughter of
the Goats has begun again.

As they have at every harvest, the goatherds have brought their animals over the Oaxaca mountains to this market town, and the *matanceros*,
the butchers, have come from the nearby village of San Gabriel Chilac.
Each day for two weeks, or as long as the herd might last, they will fill
the courtyard of an old hacienda here with an ancient ritual of blood and
death.

On the first and last mornings of the slaughter, there is still a
dance—dancing the goat, the Indians call it. And each afternoon, as the
intestines hang from clotheslines and boys with wheelbarrows cart away
the severed heads, the goat killers rise up on their knees as their fathers
did, to pray at their chopping blocks for the Lord's protection.

But almost four centuries after it took root in what were then still
known as "the lands of the chieftains," the *Matanza*, as the ritual is called
in Spanish, has taken on an air of uncertainty. Some of the dancers have
begun to forget their steps, and no one seems to remember why one of
them holds a flaming chalice toward the sky. Some in the courtyard say
that this might be the last *Matanza*, or that at most there might be a few
more.

It has been six or seven years since the *matanceros* could slash the
necks of a thousand goats each day and let them stagger about the patio
bleeding until they died. Because of the protests of animal-rights cam-
paigners in Mexico City, 158 miles to the northwest, the killing is now
done with guns, thick black livestock pistols that leave neat holes in the
goats' heads.

Bloody as it remains, the business seems less violent to the men than
that of the rustlers who come out from the poppy and marijuana fields
not far from where the goats are pastured. The rustlers carry assault rifles
now; in a raid this spring, they shot two of the goatherds and left one of
them dead.

"We just do this to keep from giving up," says Inigo Garcia Peralta, a Huajuapan rancher who has brought his goats to Tehuacán for the last 44 of his 70 years. "We don't make money any more and what is it worth if they kill you?"

No one asks directly whether the ritual ought to continue right behind the new domed shopping mall, in a town that is trying to change its image, in a country that now has a free-trade agreement with Canada and the United States.

The challenge is more complicated than that.

There is the transport tax that the ranchers must pay because there is no longer enough open land to herd the goats from Oaxaca to Tehuacán, so they come by truck. There is sales tax on the meat and skins, income tax on any profits, and bribes to pay some of the health inspectors and highway police.

More important, goat-loin *mole* now cost about $10 a plate, more than poor people can afford for the spicy dish they have always eaten after the Matanza. Years ago, almost 100,000 goats were killed in a half-dozen slaughters in Tehuacán and the Oaxacan town of Huajuapan de León. Now, Mr. Garcia's slaughter is the only one left, and he will be lucky to kill and sell 6,000 goats.

There is little record of the history of the slaughter and some dispute over the prevalent notion that it supplanted rituals of human sacrifice that existed here before the Spaniards brought their goats and stockmen's guilds to the New World. But to view the slaughter as a way to butcher

One of the main reasons that true Mexican dishes are not available outside the country is the incredible amount of work and time that go into their preparation. A good *mole* sauce, for example, might take as long as a week to prepare and contain 30 ingredients or more. Special utensils and processes, such as the time-consuming and wearying grinding of corn with a *mano* and *metate* (stone hand roller and grinding stone), make it impractical to serve genuinely Mexican dishes in the US. In fact, most Mexican restaurants will only offer things requiring elaborate preparation on certain days of the week. Look for signs hanging in the window or on the door that say *"Hoy Mole"* (Mole Today) or the name of some other special meat.

—Carl Franz, *The People's Guide to Mexico*

metate

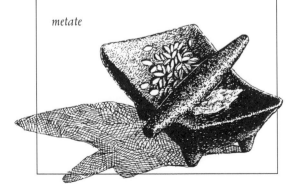

goat meat would seem to ignore the intensity and seeming symbolism of what takes place.

At the beginning, hooves scrape across the cement patio as young men drag the goats from their pens in twos, a horn in either fist. They swarm around the captains, men in coarse aprons and cowboy hats, and the captains drop their arms quickly, firing between the goats' eyes.

Older men wearing only shorts and t-shirts reach down and drive their knives into the goats' chests. Women with plastic buckets rush up to catch the blood, and the old men help them, holding the goats over their pails.

The younger men carry the animals away, dumping them across the patio in twitching piles of horns and legs and stained fur. For a while, the only sounds are the clacking and popping of the black guns and the thud of the goats being dropped on straw mats.

After a while, the frenzy gives way to an almost mechanical order. The least experienced men move across the first row of mats, carving off tails and ears. Behind them, the more expert butchers set to the harder work, scoring the bellies of the goats and then digging their bare heels beneath the skin to pull it off whole. For a long time, they say almost nothing to one another. When they do, it is Nahuatl, the language of the Aztecs and other Indian peoples of central Mexico.

On the patio's edge, a 69-year-old woman named Fermina Romero de Rojas watched the carnage the other day and was unimpressed.

"This is nothing," said the woman, who had come from nearby San Gabriel Chilac. "Each of us used to do 100, 150 heads every day. You did not have time to eat or sleep."

Beside Mrs. Rojas, her husband, Eusebio Rojas, 71, watched quietly.

"Before, they did not clean anything," he said after a while. "There wasn't any cement. It was the earth, and the earth consumed the blood."

Tim Golden is the Mexico bureau chief for the New York Times. *In 1987 he was part of the Pulitzer Prize-winning team at the* Miami Herald *for national reporting on the Iran-Contra affair. He also headed the* Miami Herald's *bureaus in El Salvador and Brazil.*

Some of us are appalled at the cruelty to dogs in Mexico, though they are skinny, yellow curs, poison-colored, and the shape of death. Mexicans are appalled at the harsh, piercing voices we sometimes use with our children. To them, *this* is the great cruelty.

—Kate Simon, *Mexico: Places and Pleasures*

RICHARD STERLING

Murderer's Eggs

Strange creatures can be found in the central desert of Baja California.

After leaving the paved road I had some trouble locating the arroyo. It was dusk and the features of the land were all beginning to look the same. I made rapid drives up two or three openings in the terrain only to encounter rock walls. Finally, in the last of the light, I recognized a distinctive portion of the skyline of jagged hills up ahead that could lead us through the arroyo and into a valley. Across that valley, another arroyo leads past the remains of a deserted, old *rancho*, then into a canyon where lay the long abandoned Mission San Borja, Lucretia Borgia's legacy to the New World.

I was traveling with Garrett Culhane and Matt Tully, two friends from school. Matthew is five foot, eight, with a beautiful physique and a perfectly silly-looking tattoo of a cherub and a crescent moon on his right shoulder. His shoulder-length hair and trim beard are both flame red. His hair is so thick and curly it looks like a 17th-century cavalier's wig. If he traded his gold-rimmed glasses for a rapier and a dueling pistol the picture would be complete. He's a fun guy, but he tends to forget that there is a tomorrow.

Garrett grew up on a ranch in the California Central Valley, but he looks like he stepped out of an Ian Forster novel about turn of the century England. He is tall, lean and angular with black hair and neat mustache. His jaw juts forward handsomely. His favorite cloth is tweed. He is cerebral and reflective and tends to preface his questions with "Well now, Richard, let me ask you something." He likes to have philosophical conversations that often become so convoluted he gets lost in them. He is also a first-rate mechanic.

Garrett and Matt were behind me in Garrett's rebuilt 1959 Willys jeep, panelled version. I led the way in my four-wheel-drive vehicle, the Argo. The normally clear skies were full of January clouds and a mist had risen from the ground. The sun had fully set and the darkness was so dense and so thick it was palpable. It gobbled up my headlight beams in mere yards. The recent annual rains had turned the dry water courses into gooey bogs and we would have to cross them in the dark. We crept along in low four-wheel drive, keeping in close radio contact.

We had been rolling for over an hour when Matt radioed "Argo, be advised we are overheating."

"Cause?"

"Unknown. Will keep you advised."

Within minutes he called again to say, "Argo, Argo! We've got to stop, we've got to stop, we're red-lining!"

"Ten-four," I answered. "I'm coming to help." I judged from the lights in my rear-view mirror that they were about forty or fifty feet behind me, so I cut the engine and hopped out and began walking toward the Willys. The mist was not uniform like a fog; it was a crazy mist, hanging in clumps and swirls with currents of clear air between them. It puffed up from the water courses and slid down hillsides and curled itself around the cacti and cirrio and other solid objects. It made the Willys seem much closer than it really was. I turned around and could no longer see the white form of the Argo.

When I reached the other vehicle the guys had the hood up, and in the reflected light of the headlamps I could see a stream of hot water drizzling down to the ground and making a big, steamy puddle. "Have you isolated the leak yet?" I asked.

"No," Garrett said. "It's almost dry now. We'll have to fill it up and try again. Let me ask you something, do you have plenty of water?"

"Five gallons. But from the look of that stream it won't get us back to the highway."

We filled the radiator and turned on the engine. Water gushed from a broken seam in the radiator's exit port. The damage could hardly have been worse. If it were a broken hose we might have fixed it, as we carried a few spares; but this situation required our removing the radiator and then having it repaired by a welder. The nearest welder was in Guerrero Negro. I would need a full day to get there, a day to have the radiator repaired, and a day to get back. I would have to take Matt with me in case I should have some breakdown; or

> Not many people are qualified or equipped to repair every possible break-down themselves while traveling. Whether you need a routine oil change for your new Ford or a complete overhaul for your aging VW, you'll want to select a mechanic and a repair shop with care.
>
> A typical Mexican garage is incredibly filthy, littered with junk parts, dark, smelly and filled with ragged kids casually smoking cigarettes as they wash strange metal objects in cans of gasoline.
>
> —Carl Franz, *The People's Guide to Mexico*

injury; or end up in jail; or who knows what. Garrett would have to keep his own philosophical company in the desert for the next three days. Happy New Year.

Somewhere in the mist a dog barked. "Was that a dog?" Matt asked.

"Must be a coyote," I said. "Got to be a coyote. No dogs out here." The dog barked again. In the headlamp beams a puff of drifting mist began to darken and take form. As it came near it assumed the shape of a man with rifle. A dog shape trotted alongside. When he was still a silhouette he stopped and hefted the rifle in the crook of his arm.

"*¿Quien es?*" he hollered. Who's there?

"*Amigos,*" I answered. "*Hombres que necesitan ayuda. ¿Quien es usted señor?*" Friends. Men who need help. Who are you, sir?

The shape paused. He said something to his dog, who then sat down and licked his chops. He came forward and with each step divested himself of mist. He came to within arm's length and stopped. He was a short, dark man, strongly built, with a curly beard. He was scruffy and dirty and lost-looking, and he eyed us with curiosity and delight, especially Matt's bountiful cascades of firehair. He thrust a stubby hand out to anyone who would take it and said, "*Manuel, me llamo Manuel. A su servicio, señores.*" I am Manuel, at your service, sirs. He spoke no English, so I translated introductions. He told us he was living in the ancient *rancho* a few miles from the mission. He lived alone.

"Why are you carrying the rifle?" I asked him.

"Because I thought you might be cattle rustlers. I have a few head and I thought you might be after them."

"Cattle rustlers, out here?" I asked.

"Who else would come here?" he shrugged. "Tell me, sirs. Why, in fact, are you here?"

We told him of our quest to San Borja, and then we told him of our trouble. He looked very excited and said, "Oh let me, let me." He took my flashlight and crawled under the hood, half his body disappearing between the V-8 engine and the radiator. He fingered the breach, then came up smiling. I told him it needed "*soldadura,*" welding. "Maybe not," he said, gesturing up the road. "At my *ranchito* I have a paste, an epoxy, that I mix together and use to repair metals. Maybe it can work to fix your radiator."

I translated this to the others. Garrett looked hopefully at Manuel and said, "Right now?"

"*¿Ahora mismo?*" I asked Manuel.

"Please, gentlemen, it's dark. It's no time to work, or to drive in the desert." Eagerly he said, "But I would be delighted if you would be my guests tonight. I can fix you some dinner. I can give you fresh eggs; I have chickens. You like coffee?"

"Hey, I'm for it," Matt said. "I'm starving." Matt is never not starving.

"How far is it?" Garrett asked. "Will we have to leave the Willys behind?"

The *rancho* was only about fifty yards ahead of the Argo. Manuel ran ahead. When we rolled up a few minutes later he was rousting his chickens for all the eggs he could find. "Come in, come in," he said with a sweeping gesture and a grin, as we walked into his kitchen. "Sit down. Be comfortable." His little house consisted of this room and a bedroom. It was lit by a kerosene lamp and candles, and at the sink he drew water with a hand pump. All was dirt and dishevelment but, putting a hand on his heart and a pious look on his face he said, "I have very little; but what I have I give with all my heart." Matt pulled a bottle of wine out of his jacket; Manuel glowed.

Manuel had collected six fresh, brown eggs, very large, and set about preparing them on his kerosene stove. "I have no tortillas, I hope you won't mind. I'll make you something similar to *huevos rancheros*. It's my own dish." He made a soupy *ranchero* sauce of onions, chili peppers, garlic, and tomato sautéed in *manteca*. To that he added cooked macaroni. He broke three eggs into the pan of sauce. The others he broke into another pan and fried them, again using *manteca*. The eggs in the sauce were poached semi hard; those fried were sunny side up and the yolks ran when cut. He served us each a fried egg and a poached egg, both covered with the macaroni salsa.

I pushed some of my macaroni over onto the fried egg. I cut the egg up and swirled it, letting the fat, yellow yolk coat the pasta. The pasta was still hot enough to cook the yolk into a tasty glaze. On the other side of my plate I cut up the poached egg and mashed the yolk into the piquant sauce, making it thicker and more savory. The *manteca* gave the whole dish a rich smoothness and produced a warm and satisfying full feeling in the belly. Matt poured the rosy red wine and we feasted. Manuel beamed and politely tried not to guzzle the Cabernet Sauvignon.

After dinner we decided that whiskey was called for and Garrett brought forth a bottle. Manuel was agog at his good luck. He had been living out there for months, he said, "with no comforts." Garrett poured healthy draughts all around and Manuel asked us to tell him our story. We described our lives to him, told him of work, of school, travel, war and peace. He followed each story with interest, he savored every detail.

He had been starving for human company and this was nourishment for him.

He became effusive with good cheer. "My friends," he said, suddenly inspired, "we have a custom where I come from. When men are friends, and they enjoy each other's stories and food and drink, they exchange *mustachios*." So saying he reached up to the corner of his mustache and, grabbing on to several whiskers, gave a snappy tug and yanked them out! Grinning, he held them forth between thumb and forefinger, the white roots like little flower bulbs at the ends of black stalks. "For you," he said. Not knowing what else to do we each took one, muttering a confused "*gracias*."

Manuel sat there grinning, looking at us each in turn, waiting for a response. With a shrug, Matt reached up to his mustache and ripped out a shard of hairs that made a sound like grass being pulled from the ground. "There you go, Manuel," he said, "and one for all of you, too," and he passed them around.

Garrett seemed to think the whole thing hilarious said, "Ha ha. And here's some for you," as he reached for both ends of his mustache and tore out his offering, sharing them with all. Manuel collected his mementoes and promised to keep them in a special place. I was so glad that I was the only clean-shaven member of this bizarre ritual of male bonding and said, "Damn! I wish I had a mustache!"

Lest this go any further and we start driving nails into our arms or slicing off bits of our flesh, I asked Manuel to tell us his story. He sat back for a moment and took a breath, as though gathering his powers. He requested a refill. Taking a sip, and rolling it on his tongue pensively, he began: "I'm here, my friends, for gold." We leaned closer. Taking another sip and gauging our interest he said, "I know gold. I know how to find it. It's here, my friends, in these hills. The Spaniards, they were no good at finding gold. They built the missions and found souls to save but they weren't good at finding gold. That's why it's still here," he whispered, "and I'm going to find it." He looked at his empty glass. Hands rushed to fill it.

He drew a lump of ore from his pocket and set it on the table. For a moment the only sound was breathing. "Look," he urged. "Look. If you know gold, you can see I'm going to be rich." We all leaned toward the quartzy piece of rock and peered into its interstices, as though it were a crystal ball, looking for a golden future.

"Let me have a closer look," I said. "When I was seventeen I worked in a gold mine." I picked it up and, turning it over said, "Mmm."

"Does it look like good stuff?" Matt asked as Manuel sat proudly looking on.

"Mmm."

"Well, what do you think? You think it's the real thing?" Garrett asked.

"Mmm."

"Good eh?" said Manuel.

"Uh...mmm...er...I can't tell. It's been a long time since I worked in the gold mine, and that was just during summer vacation."

Manuel took the ore and said, "I'll show you." He got up, a little woozily. Having been so long without "comforts" he was getting "comfortable" pretty fast. He dug through a wooden box and came up with a battered pair of binoculars. Looking through the big end he focused on the ore with the small end and said, "Here, look." We all looked. We saw nothing, but said nothing. We just nodded, not letting on that we didn't "know gold," and wondering how you could know it by looking through the wrong end of a pair of binoculars. Manuel helped himself to more whiskey.

The liquor coursed through him, and he waxed expansive as he described all the things he was going to do when he was rich, all the places he would go, all the women he would have; they would all be blondes. Then he suddenly changed the subject. "You see that saddle over there," he said, pointing to a ruined-looking pile of old leather. "Pancho Villa rode in that saddle. It belonged to him. You know Pancho Villa, the great general?"

"Oh yes," we all nodded. "Pancho Villa, the great general."

"He was from Sonora." Manuel told us. "I'm from Sonora, too."

It is a strange Mexican proclivity to tack the diminutive affix, ordinarily reserved for what is pitiable, lovable or cute, to the frightening and the truculant. Recall the fierce revolutionist Pancho Villa addressing his sinister-looking high command in a hortatory speech before a deadly engagement with the words: *"Amiguitos: Aquí vamos a morirnos todos..."* ("Little friends: We are all going to die here...")

—F. Gonzalez-Crussi, *The Day of the Dead and Other Mortal Reflections*

Lurching across the room he picked up his old rifle. I noticed that the butt was cracked and held together with electrical tape. He brandished it at us and said, "And this rifle was used in the Mexican revolution. It killed many men. Many men."

Matt looked like he was going to hide the whiskey, but I grabbed it and poured Manuel the stiffest drink his glass could hold. *"Salúd,"* I said. "Let's drink to Pancho Villa, the great general!"

Patriotically Manuel drank the health of the general, draining his glass. I refilled it.

"My friends," said Manuel, "I told you I'm from Sonora. You know why I'm now in Baja California?"

"For gold," we all said.

"Well, yes. But you know why I'm also in Baja California?" Cradling his rifle he sat down and eyed us all dizzily. Absentmindedly he reached into a pocket and pulled out a handful of bullets.

"Let's drink to Sonora!" Matt said. Manuel, rifle in one hand and bullets in the other, considered his glass. He put the bullets back in his pocket and drank to Sonora. I refilled his glass.

Manuel continued, "I'm here because I killed a man in Sonora. He was an Indian. I caught him cheating me at cards. I didn't have my famous rifle with me," he said, patting it on the breach. "So I killed him with my knife. He was a big man, but I'm fast, and my knife was big. I don't have the knife anymore because I left it in the Indian. Damned Indian," he muttered.

His rifle was getting heavy so he leaned it against a wall and turned his attentions to his glass which I kept full. "Yes, I had to run from Sonora. The police wouldn't get me because they're my friends. I had to run from the Indians! So I went to Sinaloa. And what do you think? I killed another Indian, over a woman! This time the police wanted to get me, so I ran away to Baja." His head drooping low, his face inches from the table, he murmured his last words of the evening: "And now I'm going to get rich and find gold."

He sank into a little heap of whiskey-soaked flesh. We laid him in his lumpy bed and covered him with his filthy blankets. We looked at each other and sniggered. Pancho Villa's saddle, a revolutionary rifle, two dead Indians, and a lost gold mine all in one night; we'd never heard whiskey talk so much.

The next morning Manuel was up and about, hung over and still drunk at the same time. After giving us his epoxy he kept get-

It is now commonplace to observe that the white men who toppled the Tontonac idols into the dust worshipped an equally false god—gold. Soon enough after the sack of the Aztec empire the tribes of Central and South America began making this charge themselves. And even Cortés, whose Christian piety cannot be doubted, may have suspected as much. His secretary Gómera records that in a message Cortés sent Moctezuma from here he asked for gold "because I and my companions suffer from a disease of the heart which can only be cured with gold."

—Frederick Turner, *A Border of Blue: Along the Gulf of Mexico From the Keys to the Yucatán*

ting in the way of things, so we dispatched him quickly and painlessly with a few more drinks. After making our repairs we set a big lockback knife, as a present, on his table and left him sleeping. About a week later, in Bahía de Los Angeles, we met Don Guillermo, who turned out to be *el Dueño*, the owner of the land Manuel occupies. "Was he kind to you?" Don Guillermo asked.

"Oh yes. He gave us dinner. And we gave him whiskey," and we all chuckled.

"You gave him whiskey?" Don Guillermo asked with visible concern.

"Uh...yeah. After all, he was very hospitable to us."

"*Señores*. You should be very careful who you drink with around here. Manuel can be violent when he's drunk. He's already killed two men, that we know of."

So, okay, Manuel is, indeed, a murderer. He has conducted two of his fellows out of this world untimely to the next. *Que vayan con Dios and Amen*. But when he follows them he will, at least, have left behind his single, humble contribution to the happiness of the living. His little culinary offering stays active in my recipe file, where it frequently satisfies the appetites of my friends and garners me much praise. It was no less a personage than Brillat-Savarin, the great 18th-century gastronome who said, "The discovery of a new dish does more for human happiness than the discovery of a star." Even if the telescope is wielded by a man with the curse of Cain, the discovery is a worthy one:

Murderer's Eggs

1/2 Spanish onion, diced
1 not-so-hot green chili pod, seeded and diced
garlic to taste, minced
6 oz. can tomato sauce
1/2 cup cooked (*al dente*) elbow macaroni or rigatoni
2 eggs
1 tablespoon cilantro, chopped
salt and pepper
manteca (You can use butter or olive oil and the result may be healthier but it won't be as satisfying.)

Sauté the vegetables in the *manteca* over medium heat till soft. Add tomato sauce, salt, and pepper. A dash of Worcester is good, too. Cook five minutes over low heat. Stir in pasta and cilantro. Push the pasta outward from the center, making a space for the eggs. Break the eggs into the pan and cover them with sauce, being careful not to rupture the yolks. Cover the pan, reduce heat to very low, and let the eggs poach three minutes or to desired doneness.

Richard Sterling is both a travel and food writer. He spends several weeks of each year dwelling in the hidden heart of Baja California, picking at its secrets and pursuing its gastronomic offerings. He is also the loser of the 1994 James Beard Foundation M.F.K. Fisher Distinquished Writing Award.

The menu may be more enjoyable than the meal; there's nothing I love more than reading garbled translations like "Dreaded meat with potatoes," "Eggs with Fool," "Fruit with ice cream—5 pesos, Fruit withnot ice cream—3 pesos," "Cheeselies," "Smack Pork Chops," "Black coffeecup—5 pesos," "Chicken Car Cold," and so forth.

—Carl Franz, *The People's Guide to Mexico*

MARY MORRIS

The Road to San Miguel

The author begins a new life in Mexico.

T here are only two ways to get to San Miguel. One is to drive north from Mexico City. The other is to drive south from Laredo. There is also a train but I only saw it once in the time I lived there, and it was two hours late. The road north from Mexico City is unremarkable—a superhighway to Laredo, lined with Pemex stations, auto parts shops, tire retailers. It is also lined with many foreign factories, such as John Deere tractors, Singer, Volkswagen, Pepsi, companies that find prices right and labor cheap south of the border.

If you are driving north from Mexico City, after about four hours you reach a turn. If you miss the turn, you can go straight back to America in about ten hours flat. But if you leave that main road and turn left, toward the west in the direction of San Miguel, as I did one summer in what seems now like a long time ago, you enter a different world. The kind of world you might read about in the works of Latin American writers such as Fuentes, Rulfo, García Márquez. Macondo could be out there.

You come to old Mexico, a lawless land. It is a landscape that could be ruled by bandits or serve as a backdrop for the classic Westerns, where all you expect the Mexicans to say is *"hombre"* and *"amigo"* and *"sí, señor."* It is a land with colors. Desert colors. Sand and sienna, red clay and cactus green, scattered yellow flowers. The sky runs all the ranges of purple and scarlet and orange. You can see dust storms or rain moving toward you. Rainbows are frequent. The solitude is dramatic.

You come abruptly to the high desert, where people travel on the backs of burros and everything slows down. Cacti are huge and resemble men in agony, twisted and wild; it is a trail of crucifixions.

I have a friend named Brenda Reynolds who was living in Mexico City, and it was Brenda who drove me to San Miguel the first time. She was preparing to move back to the States just as I was arriving, but she offered to take me to San Miguel, spend a night, and help me get my bearings. Brenda was one of the people who suggested San Miguel when I told her I wanted to live away from the United States for a while.

Brenda said it was a perfect place and that the weather was wonderful. I had heard other things about San Miguel as well. Americans who want to get away often go there. It is a place of exile.

I had grown weary of life in New York and had some money from a grant, so I felt ready for a change. With a terrible feeling of isolation and a growing belief that America had become a foreign land, I headed south. I went in search of a place where the land and the people and time in which they lived were somehow connected—where life would begin to make sense to me again.

When I arrived in Mexico City, Brenda served me black *zapotes*. A black *zapote* is a fruit somewhat like a giant prune which, when mashed with sugar and lemon juice, with the skin and seeds removed (an incredibly arduous task), tastes like something they'd serve in heaven. There is no comparable way to describe this dish except to say that it was the first thing I tasted when I arrived at Brenda's house in Mexico and I thought then that I had come to paradise.

This was before driving to San Miguel, before I traveled down that very dusty road with Brenda, laughing the whole way until we approached San Miguel. Then I grew serious, struck by the reality of the place to which I had come. As we twisted on those hairpin turns, a street sign appeared. It contained the silhouette of a full-bodied woman and beneath her the words *curva peligrosa*—dangerous curve.

I never saw pictures of San Miguel before I moved there, but I went with a very clear sense of what everything should look like, a cross between New York and my hometown and the island of Crete—exciting, familiar, and foreign all at the same time.

The Buddhists are right in their belief that expectation is one of the great sources of suffering. We try to direct the scripts in our heads and are miserable when we fail. We often wonder why things go better—parties, journeys, love—when we have no expectations. What I saw as we drove into San Miguel bore little relation to what I'd thought I'd find. A dusty town rose out of a hill, with a salmon-pink church spire and pale stucco buildings.

The driver closes the door of his bus outside the Querétaro station just as an old woman, dressed in the rusty black cocoon of perpetual mourning, shuffles frantically toward it, waving her shopping basket to catch the driver's eye. He opens the door and through her thin gasps learns that she has just missed her bus to Guanajuato. He lifts her onto the bus, and with much style and pleasure tears down the road to overtake her bus, terrifying by his speed, bulk, and confidence every other vehicle on the road. He and the old lady make it.

—Kate Simon, *Mexico: Places and Pleasures*

Buses were everywhere, idling near the center of town, sending up exhaust that would make me choke whenever I walked past. Their drivers shouted the names of destinations unknown to me—Celaya, Guanajuato, Dolores. Tortilla ladies and avocado ladies sold sandwiches near the buses as blind beggars and naked children, broken-spirited donkeys and starving dogs, filled the streets.

I was missing the fine points. Expectation does that to you: I missed the bougainvillea, the colonial buildings, the cobblestone streets. It is easy to miss all of that once the panic sets in. I only saw the dust and the donkeys and the strangers and a place that seemed so distant from anything I thought I could ever call home.

That night Brenda and I checked into a hotel where I drifted into despair. I had no idea how I was going to live in this place. I couldn't believe that I'd packed myself up and moved to a strange country where I barely spoke the language and didn't know a soul. My purpose seemed vague, and walking those streets for the first time, I told myself that I should just get back in the car and go home. We had dinner and strolled, hardly speaking. I was quiet, withdrawn, and Brenda, who has always respected my privacy, did not pry. Perhaps she suspected that something had happened to me before I left, but she did not ask and I didn't say.

In the morning we went to a hot spring nearby called Taboada, a place I would frequent on Sundays because the hotel there served a wonderful brunch. The Mexicans frolicked with their families, often fat, happy, splashing out of control, and I longed to be that carefree again. Afterward we drove back to the hotel and Brenda was ready to go. Like a scoutmaster sending a boy out on a survival training course, she left me with a Spanish-English dictionary, a few extra pens, and the name of the woman who ran the Blue Door Bakery, who supposedly had rooms to rent.

I was on my own. I had no idea what to do with myself. It grew dark early and I wasn't ready for bed. Instead I went out for a walk. The streets were dark and cobbled and smelled of garbage. I didn't know my way as I wandered through the back alleys and narrow roads. I passed restaurants with crowded tables and lighted rooms where families stared into the blue light of miniature TVs. Old women, grasping babies, sat telling stories and laughing on doorsteps. I searched for a movie house, a coffee shop with guitar music, but all I found were dozens of bars filled with men, and I wasn't ready to go into one alone.

I walked to the center of town, to a square lined with benches and trees, which in most parts of Mexico is called the *zócalo*, but in San Miguel is called the *jardín*, where an odd procession passed in front of

San Miguel, north of Mexico City, is quite simply one of the prettiest towns I've ever seen. (Pretty: to me, San Francisco and San Miguel are pretty; Paris and Venice are beautiful.) A hill town, it affords everywhere lovely views of rooftops and distant mountains, of narrow cobbled streets and tree-lined little squares—and churches, everywhere churches. Perched in the Bajío, the most Catholic center of colonial Mexico, San Miguel abounds in churches, all interesting and many quite beautiful. The main church, generally called the *parroquia* (parish church), dominates the landscape with its cluster of lacy spires around a taller, still lacier spire. This church, reputedly designed by an "ignorant" (this means Indian) stonemason who was inspired by postcards of gothic churches, has somewhat the look of Gaudi's Sagrada Familia, the church in Barcelona, another "ignorant" work.

—Alice Adams, *Mexico: Some Travels and Some Travelers There*

me. A circle of girls walked in the clockwise direction around the perimeters of the *jardín*, perhaps half the distance of a square city block. There were at least a hundred of them. And encircling them, moving counterclockwise, was a group of young men. Hesitating, I cut through their circle and sat down on a bench, where I watched as the single men and women of the town encircled each other on and on into the darkness in this ritualized form of courtship—called the promenade— which would occur every night at the hour when the birds came home to rest in the trees of the *jardín*.

They flirted and giggled and pretended to ignore one another, but as darkness fell, some wandered off, boy leading girl away to a more secluded spot in a darkened street, an alleyway. I imagined them whispering each other's names and thought of how far I was from someone who might whisper mine.

The church bells rang. From the steeple clock that seemed to rule over this town and mark the monotony of the days, I saw that it was only nine o'clock. I still had much of the evening ahead of me and no place to go. Then I noticed the people entering church. Toothless old men and corpulent women with babies wrapped in shawls shuffled in. Girls in miniskirts with white blouses held the hands of boys in green or cranberry polyester pants; others in blue jeans, black hair slicked back, lingered in the alcoves.

In this town of shrieking birds and promenading lovers, I could think of nothing else to do, so I went to church. I walked hesitantly into the large Gothic stone building and down an aisle toward the apse. Slipping into a pew off to the side, I sat beside a *campesino* family, the woman with a child suckling at her exposed breast, the children in freshly ironed shirts, the father, in a *sombrero*, keeping a toddler from running away.

I sat down with a blind man and with wide-eyed children, with the toothless, the ancients, the impoverished, the illegitimate mothers, the crippled, the drunk, the miserable, the lost. I prayed with the beggar who had no hands and with the woman whose eyes were empty sockets. I prayed with the contrite and the forlorn, with *los desdichados*—the unlucky, the misfortunate. I prayed until the tears came down my face and I was crying in that church on that Sunday night, my first night alone in Mexico, praying that the reason for this journey would be made clear to me, oblivious of the Mexicans who watched with troubled eyes, moved by my inexplicable grief.

The woman who ran the Blue Door Bakery did have rooms to rent and at dusk the next day she took me to see them. We drove down the hill away from the center of town. We left the cobbled streets with bougainvillea vines and turned up a dirt road lined with mud huts, garbage, diseased animals, children in tattered rags. When I asked where we were going, she replied, "San Antonio." And that was all.

She was a cold, calculating person whom I would simply call "the *Señora*" and who'd take only cash for rent. In the middle of these slums in the neighborhood called San Antonio, the *Señora* had built some town houses. One of them had been vacated recently, and she showed it to me. It had a living room, kitchen, and small patio on the ground floor. Two bedrooms upstairs. Upstairs the front of the town house had French doors and a small balcony, but the back wall had no windows. I should have suspected that someone was building a house on the other side but I did not. The sound of construction would punctuate my days. A small winding staircase went to the roof, where I'd read and do wash in the afternoons. From the roof I could see the sierra—the pale lavender hills and the stretch of high desert, the cactus, men, and wildflowers.

It was the only place I considered. "I'll take it," I said.

I should never have moved to the neighborhood called San Antonio if I'd known better. For that part of town was different from other parts. Very few Americans lived there. It was too far from the center of things. I would have to walk half an hour up a dusty hill to get to market. It was the poorest part; it was where the servants who served the wealthy lived and where others struggled just to get by. It was the dustiest, dirtiest place, where the Mexicans would call me *"gringita"* and my own mother, when she heard me describe it, would beg me to leave. I had no idea what I was doing when I moved into San Antonio. But I am grateful for the mistake I made.

I had come to Mexico with two suitcases and an electric typewriter, and the next day I brought them by taxi to my town house, whose name I noticed as I dragged my belongings from the cab: the *Departamentos Toros* (bull apartments). I am a Taurus and as I stood beneath the sign with the name of the apartment, I thought this must be a good omen, to move into a place named after my astrological sign. I spent the day settling in. But as dusk came, I realized I knew no one, was about a mile from town, and had no food in the house.

Climbing the winding stairs to the roof terrace, I saw the vast Mexican desert stretching before me, the sun setting in strips of brilliant scarlet across the horizon. The town with the pink steeple of the church seemed far away. I saw the birds—large, black, noisy birds—which every evening at dusk flew to the center of town to stand guard over the promenade. And then, as I'd do many evenings after that, struck by the prospect of the evening alone, I followed them.

I changed my clothes, put on a pair of walking shoes, and headed up the hill—a climb I'd never get used to. But I went to the place where the birds were going. It seems I have always followed the birds, or have wanted to follow them. The loud chirps, thousands of them, grew piercing as I approached the *jardín*.

The birds were bedding down for the night and the promenade was in process. I sat on a bench to watch. It is odd to sit in a place where you know absolutely no one. There was not a familiar face, not even the possibility of someone passing whom I might know. I was here a perfect stranger.

After awhile I got up and headed down a road. I paused in front of a bar lit in amber. Inside Mexican men drank and laughed. There were no Mexican women, but there were a few Americans, so I thought it would be all right. I went in and ordered a beer. I sat for perhaps half an hour, until it grew dark. People were all around me and I thought to myself how I should try to make conversation, but I found I could think of nothing to say. I was sure that someone would come up to me and say something like, "Been in town long?" or "So where'd you come from?" But no one did. I ordered another beer and nursed it slowly, realizing I did not want to go home. I watched the people around me. Mexicans laughing and talking with blond American women. Other Americans huddled in corners. One man, whom I'd later know as Harold, sat in his pajamas, which he wore when he went on a binge.

I took it all in, and then, at about ten o'clock, I walked home.

Mary Morris is the author of seven books, including Wall-to-Wall: From Bejing to Berlin by Rail, *and* Nothing to Declare: Memoirs of a Woman Traveling Alone, *from which this story is excerpted. She is also co-editor, along with her husband, Larry O'Connor, of* Maiden Voyages: Writings of Women Travelers, *an anthology of women's travel writing from the 18th century to the present. They live with their daughter in Brooklyn, New York.*

Machismo is the backbone of Mexican society. A knee-jerk reaction to any situation, this form of male arrogance is practiced the length and the breadth of the country with an assiduity that is breathtaking. Although as much of a cliché as the Sicilian Mafia, it has just as much relevance. Tourists don't escape it, neither men nor women. Try arguing with a bank clerk, after he has left you for 20 minutes to coo down the telephone to his girlfriend, and see his hackles rise in an instinctive macho response of aggressive defense. Mexicans don't like direct confrontation: on the other hand, requests for help are rarely refused. Apologetic references to a desperately ill wife/mother who needs to be rushed to the hospital are far more tactful (and standard) method of getting the clerk off the telephone.

Women will find that they can use sexism to their advantage. A double-headed serpent, machismo is sinuously attractive when its not unappreciable powers are turned full on. Chivalry goes hand in hand with peacock pride, and exaggerated manners are as much a facet of machismo as gross one-upmanship. It is no use arguing about splitting bills or finding your own way home. A Mexican has an instinctive courtesy which no amount of explanation of women's independence is going to shift, so enjoy it whilst it lasts (which is rarely beyond courtship).

—Katharine and Charlotte Thompson, *Cadogan Guides: Mexico*

DON STARKELL

Mad Dogs and Canadians

They used to say "only mad dogs and Englishmen go out in the noonday sun"—but they didn't know about these guys from Winnipeg.

We reached Progreso two days ago, and have been unable to move since, because of the punishing winds.

Within minutes of our arrival, a pleasant middle-aged woman, Señora Gladys Marrufo, appeared beside us on the beach among the many vacationers, and gave us a heaping salad plate and a couple of icy Pepsis. She was leaving the following day for her home in Mérida, but invited us to make camp in the veranda of a nearby beach house she was occupying. So here we've sat since, in relative comfort, with far more time than we need to shop and write and kibitz with the locals. The only thing we can't do is what we really want to do: paddle.

Yesterday at noon, Señora Gladys again brought us a fine Mexican meal: roast beef, rice, black beans, tomatoes, and radishes. Dana and I had just eaten a pile of tortillas from a local stand and were stuffed to bloating. So, after thanking our host, we quietly slipped the food under cover, to be enjoyed at suppertime. An hour or so later, Señora Gladys left for Mérida.

No sooner had she gone than a couple of men, also from Mérida, showed up and moved into the cottage—they told us they'd rented it. They were a doctor and an engineer, and were none too happy to see a couple of Robinson Crusoes occupying their veranda. But when I'd explained our situation, their attitudes did a turnabout, and they couldn't do enough for us: beer, food, anything we wanted. All afternoon it went on. At one point, the doctor proclaimed proudly, *"Soy Mayan,"* "I'm a Mayan," and he said a few words of his native language to prove it. They only stayed until evening, but before they left, the doctor pressed some money into my palm and told us to have a good meal when we got to Cancún.

The author and two of his sons set out to canoe—that's right, *canoe*—from Manitoba to the Amazon. By the time we join them here on the Yucatán coast, one son has gone home; Dana, 19 years old, remains.

—JO'R and LH

Today on the beach, I met a little boy who had enormous warts on his feet. He told me they'd been there for two years, and it was easy to see how much he hated them. I remembered treating Dana for warts many years ago and thought I just might have some of the treatment, Compound W, in my old medicine box. I looked, and, sure enough, there it was. I carefully painted the boy's warts, which were truly ugly, and watched them turn white as the compound dried. I gave him our little bottle and told him over and over how to apply the stuff and how often. If he follows directions, his warts will be gone in two or three weeks. It gave me a real kick to see him walk away with a big smile on his face, clutching his precious bottle.

Back on the Mississippi at Memphis, which now seems like ten years ago, I bought Jeff and Dana new Nike running shoes. There is now nothing left of Dana's but worn soles and a few strands of greying tattered canvas. Nonetheless, he wears them proudly, and everywhere he goes people comment on their astonishing condition. In a strange way, they seem to have become a talisman for him. Yesterday he left them on the beach, and when he returned half an hour later, they were gone, which threw him into distress. He ran around looking everywhere, and finally located them neatly wrapped in a plastic bag in a nearby trash can. Someone had apparently mistaken them for castoffs and, with the integrity of the beach in mind, had discarded them. Dana quickly laced them on to prevent another mistake.

Last night as we lay on our veranda two human shapes, a man and a boy, appeared out of the darkness. Dana recognized them as the proprietors of the shop where he'd bought tortillas earlier in the day. They'd brought Dana a present, a new pair of white Converse basketball shoes.

Later as we lay trying to sleep, Dana said quietly, "Why is it that some people are so kind?"

I thought for a few seconds and said, "Maybe it's because of the way you've treated them."

After a longish silence he said, "How can you repay them?"

"By passing on their kindness," I said, and there was no more conversation.

Mexicans are fiercely nationalistic, loyal, and proud of their culture. In spite of their poverty, Mexicans are remarkably generous. For their countrymen they provide a free educational system (83 percent of the populace is literate, according to government statistics). Similarly, travelers may find complete strangers stopping to help them. Big families will sometimes take in foreign visitors and treat them like royalty—feeding them and entertaining them and taking them along on their outings.

—Rebecca Bruns, et al., *Hidden Mexico*

Many people don't understand our trip and seem to feel that we're wasting two good years of our lives. But when I consider such things as the wonderful education Dana's getting, I privately rejoice that we're here. What's even more satisfying is that Dana understands and appreciates it all.

We got clear of Progreso on the 8th, but on the first day out advanced only ten miles into the wind. We spent the better part of our time hiding behind windbreaks on shore, to avoid being sandblasted to death.

We were getting severely frustrated and needed a new plan. So that evening we decided to try a night paddle while the winds were down. We've been out paddling in the darkness before dawn, but always with the knowledge that the sun would be up in an hour to show us our route. This was going to be different.

At about 2 a.m., we slid into the water and out to sea. Our only real guidance came from the stars and the direction of the waves. The trouble was that, in the dark, we couldn't tell a dangerous wave from a harmless one, and by the middle of the night we were paranoid about every black wave that came toward us. One would roll gently beneath the canoe, the next would smack us broadside and have us scrambling to keep our balance. By the time the wind drove us from the seas at about 8:30 a.m., we had come a creditable 20 miles and felt like conquerors.

It seems that our last miles on the Gulf will be won only if we can gather all our fighting resources and continue to outwit these phenomenal winds. So last night we went back out at 11 p.m. By 2 a.m., we had paddled seven miles under ideal conditions and were well past Yalcubul lighthouse. Then the moon went down, throwing our world into impenetrable darkness. I couldn't even see Dana's outline ahead of me in the canoe.

We had intended to paddle until daylight, but now, in our blindness, we would happily have settled for a safe landing. But we knew that the coast beyond Yalcubul was an unbroken line of high cliffs offering no welcome to the sightless paddler.

We had had only four hours of sleep back on the beach, and by 4 a.m. we'd grown so weary we were dozing off as we paddled. I'd drift off, awakening abruptly to Dana's sharp rebukes—"Do you wanta die? Do you wanta kill us both?" If only we'd had something to focus on, some headland or light. It wasn't long before both of us were in a semi-coma, thoroughly disoriented, and thoroughly lost.

At about 5 a.m., there was a bright flash of light in front of me, and a wall of palms emerged from the sea; I had begun to hallucinate. I now saw rock cliffs, then palms again. At one point, unable to stand it, I laid my head back on the stern deck, but was soon jolted upright by Dana's frenzied shouting. Back and forth we zigzagged—asleep, awake, asleep again.

After six hours of torment, the first hint of dawn appeared ahead. To our amazement, we were still moving east. I could see the shape of the guitar on the canoe deck, then the colour of Dana's shirt. By sunrise, we had gained new energy, and pushed on, now hoping only to get past the cliffs before the daytime winds forced us off the sea.

By the time we were safely ashore, it was 11 a.m., and we had been on the sea for twelve hours. We had come 38 miles, and our muscles and emotions were in pretty rough shape. So, too, are my hindquarters, which are rawer and more painful than ever. At about noon, I was carefully applying seven Band-Aids to the deepest of my abrasions, which won't scab over with the constant salt and friction. Dana's rump, too, is killing him, but he doesn't want Band-Aids on it, and I can't say that I blame him. For myself, I couldn't take the open sores any more.

For most of the day we lay around in a state of low-key anxiety, unable to stay awake, unable to sleep properly. We knew we couldn't take another night like the last one, but we were also more determined than ever to get over this last stretch of the Gulf. Another hundred miles will put us in Cancún, our gateway to the Caribbean; 400 miles will take us out of Mexico entirely and into Belize, our fourth country.

Near El Cuyo, Mexico, we are back to day paddling, though not really by choice. The night before last, we had our canoe dressed up and sitting with its bow in the shallows ready to go around midnight. But as the night wore on, it became clear we weren't going to get the weather break we needed to launch. We slept fitfully, and just after dawn the wind was still strong. Dana woke up and said, "Let's do three or four miles before it gets any stronger."

This sort of initiative had been rare from Dana—he's usually so cautious and I wasn't about to pass up the chance at a few miles. Without eating breakfast, we ploughed into the breakers, and by just past noon had covered 17 miles, every foot of which was gained with stupefying effort. We could barely take ten strokes without having to swing out to sea to avoid taking a giant wave broadside. One wave stood us right up on our stern, so that Dana was nearly twenty feet above me before he came crashing down. Time and again, he took powerful breakers in the chest and face.

We had another go this morning, but by 8 a.m. the seas were knocking us around so badly that we had to get off the water

Our skills are one thing, our tenacity another, our faith another—but I'm constantly amazed and dismayed by the amount of unadulterated luck that has affected our survival. Almost every day, we run into some appalling new circumstance that would seem to have the potential to finish us. *But we always scrape through.* This truly makes me believe that no one could ever duplicate our trip (I'd certainly never try it again myself); they could have our equipment and planning and willpower, they could have our faith and muscles and endurance, but it's impossible to believe that anybody could ever again have our luck.

The best news at the moment is that eight more miles on these horrible seas will put us behind Isla Holbox, the first of a chain of islands forming the north boundary of Laguna Yalahua, which should offer us pretty good shelter all the way to Cancún. The water is starting to show some green, and we dare to think it's because we're so close to the Caribbean.

We had a good day on Laguna Yalahua on the 17th and were expecting it to lead us tranquilly and triumphantly into the Caribbean yesterday. But the lagoon had other ideas, and by eight in the morning it had not only denied us the Caribbean but efficiently trapped us in what was surely the dirtiest circumstance of my canoeing career. As we headed southeast around the northern corner of the Yucatán, the water gradually decreased in depth until we were barely moving through 6-inch shallows of muskeg-like marsh.

When the depth reached three or four inches I jumped confidently into the water to do a little towing. But instead of landing on my feet I broke through the apparent floor of the lagoon and instantly was up to my armpits in slime—not to mention shock. What we'd thought was the bottom was nothing more than a fragile floating layer of tangled roots and lagoon debris. I laboriously dragged myself free of the suction and hoisted myself, stinking, back into the canoe.

Dana refused to enter the lagoon, as he still has open sores from our struggle months ago at La Pesca. So, after long deliberation, I propped myself on the stern of the canoe, supporting most of my weight with my arms, and did my best to push against the false bottom of the lagoon with my feet. Half an hour of this netted us one hundred yards but left me cursing with fatigue.

Eventually I discovered that if I entered the water cautiously and crawled around on all fours, as if I were on very thin ice, my weight was well enough distributed that the false bottom would support me. I could move ten or fifteen yards at a stretch without breaking through. So for the next half hour I crawled along crablike at the stern, pushing and grunting for all I was worth. Dana poled hard in the bow.

This, too, soon became too much for me, and I crawled back into the canoe, dripping muck. At this point, the sun was beginning to roast us, and we had no idea how far we were from navigable water. I was despondent. The only options we could see were to carry on or to go miles back along the lagoon and out around the headlands to the sea. We might have gone to shore, but the borders of the lagoon were little more than a tangled mass of mangrove roots and muck. And they were hundreds of yards away.

I now tried lying belly down on the stern deck of the canoe, head forward, and kicking into the muck with my legs, which were dangling behind. In effect, I was an outboard motor, and we were soon skidding across the swamp at our best pace yet. But the effort was stupefying—I could go barely two minutes without collapsing in a puddle of sweat.

Three and half hours of this took us into marginally deeper water, then quite suddenly into crystalline water some four feet deep. In spite of my weariness, I was quickly up onto my stern seat and paddling jubilantly. But it wasn't long before we were again in shallow water, then cut off completely by an impassable swampy landmass. Our only way out was to double back and try to escape through the mangroves to the sea.

We broke through a good mile of mangrove swamp and, as we emerged, the Caribbean appeared before us, as blue and calm as any body of water we could have hoped for. But what amazed us, as we paddled on to the ocean, was that it seemed to extend out for miles at no more than a foot or two of depth. We swung the canoe south, looking for anything resembling a camping spot. We had been on the water for ten hours. But mile after mile of paddling showed us nothing but more mangroves and swamp.

By 8:30 p.m., our world was dark. We were soon grounded in six inches of water half a mile from the thoroughly uninviting shoreline. Resigned to a night in the canoe, we poled a few yards to a tiny mangrove plant that was growing out here on its own. Using a half-rotted shoelace, I tied us up.

With great care, we laid our foam mattress across our equipment boxes and lay down beside one another on top of the canoe. The only way to keep from rolling off was to snuggle up front to back and hold on tight.

There we lay, one peaceful pea, one peaceful pod, hoping that tomorrow would bring us better luck.

The last miles into Cancún were a medley of ideal conditions: gentle seas, sugar-white sands, radiant turquoise waters.

As we paddled in along the waterfront, past the rows of hotels, we raised the flag for the first time since Texas. How proud we were, with our tarp and our flag and our bright orange canoe glistening in the sunshine. We beached the canoe in front of the elegant Camino Real Hotel.

We immediately took a bus from the tourist area into Cancún City to buy food. But as hard as we tried to obtain real groceries—rice and bananas and canned goods—all we could find were tourist treats at inflated prices. Someone told us to try Puerto Juarez, a more workaday town, which we'd passed in the canoe on the way in.

We went there by taxi and, an hour later, were staggering back to the Camino Real with enough groceries, I hope, to get us all the way to Belize City, two weeks down the line. Except for Tulum, the coast between here and Belize City is pretty well deserted, which will make groceries hard to come by.

We spent the rest of the afternoon beside the canoe, chatting with dozens of curious tourists: from France, from Germany, Cuba, the U.S., Venezuela. Many of them took photos of us, sometimes posed with their friends and families. We lapped it up like puppies.

During the afternoon, I walked out to Punta Cancún and for the first time saw the unprotected waters of the Caribbean. What we'd seen the day before

The dazzling white sand of Cancún's beaches is light in weight and cool underfoot even in the blazing sun. That's because it is composed not of silica but rather of microscopic plankton fossils called disco-aster (a tiny star-shaped creature). The coolness of the sand has not been lost on Cancún's ingenious promoters, who have dubbed it "air-conditioned". Combined with the crystalline azure waters of the Caribbean, it makes for beaches that are pure delight.

All of these delightful beaches are open to you because all Mexican beaches are public property. Several of Cancún's beaches are set aside for easy public access, but you should know that you have the right to walk and swim on any beach at all. In practice it may be difficult to approach certain stretches of beach without going through a hotel's property, but few hotels will notice you walking through to the beach in any case.

—Tom Brosnahan, et al.,
Mexico – a travel survival kit

was sheltered by islands and reefs, and was no real indicator of what we'd have to face further south. As I looked over the endless stretch of blue, my feelings were much like those I'd had on first seeing the Gulf back in Texas: smallness, aloneness, and outright fear. The waters here are deeper than any we've paddled, and will be nearly 900 fathoms by the time we reach Belize. The waves don't break; they just swell until they crash ashore.

Today, in the Cozumel Channel, we should never have been on the water. For eight hours, we survived fifteen-foot peaked waves, each one threatening to throw us into the sea, and ultimately against the high craggy rocks of the shoreline. Our fear was heightened by the presence of three wrecked pleasure boats at intervals along our route. We eventually gained land at a coral-ringed lagoon, but only by surfing in dangerously over a hundred feet of reef. Dana estimated that we'd cleared it by about eight inches.

We are now eighty miles south of Cancún, and our canoe sits on the beach in front of us in tatters—13 fractures and holes. We have survived the seas, if barely, but have not survived the treacherous coral reefs. This morning as we left the lagoon where we'd camped, we capsized on the same reef that we'd barely cleared yesterday coming in. There was no great damage, except that our equipment was soaked and our feet were pierced by sea-urchin spines.

Undeterred, we paddled south and were soon stroking along within fifty yards of another reef. Dana warned me several times that we were too close to it, but I told him not to worry. "Just keep paddling." Without warning, a massive wave rose to our left, bounced off the sea floor, and came at us like a train. Dana screamed the alarm, and I tried to swing the canoe to meet the wave. I managed two strokes, and the fifteen-footer hit us broadside, spilling us into the sea. Again we were scrambling to get out of our watery cockpits. Any delay and we'd be on the deadly coral of the reef.

We gained control, but with the canoe swamped we had no choice but to swim it over the reef to shore. As we worked our way in, we could see jagged coral protruding from the troughs of the waves. We edged up to it, hoping to pick up a swell that would wash us safely over it and into the bay beyond.

We picked up our wave, surfed in, and seemed almost clear of the reef when the wave turned suddenly to froth beneath us. We came crashing down on the coral, and our poor *Orellana* buckled and groaned. Dana and I found our footing and did everything we could to free the canoe. But with its weight of water it was too heavy to maneuver. For fifteen minutes we struggled to empty it and free it, each of us hollering with pain as our bare feet came down on the countless spiky sea urchins that inhabit the reef. But each new wave countered anything we were able to achieve and drove the canoe harder onto its bed of nails. How it crunched and groaned, and how I suffered with it!

When we'd all but given up and were simply standing on the reef beside the canoe, bemoaning our fate, another massive wave appeared behind us, lifted the canoe and tossed it into the tranquil waters inside the reef. We went with it.

As we unloaded ashore, I was misguidedly hopeful that we'd only been badly scratched. But as the equipment came out, the tale unfolded. Each time we removed a box, Dana would gasp, "There's a hole! There's another hole!"

In my optimism, I kept insisting they were only cracks. But with the canoe empty, I couldn't deny the evidence: thirteen punctures and serious fractures, one of them nearly twenty inches long. I'd never seen such a badly beaten hull. Nearly eleven months on the water, 4,800 miles, with no real damage; and now thirteen holes in fifteen minutes on the reef.

The challenge now was to make repairs, and I wasn't sure we had enough patching material. For hours I worked at it, straining my creativity to cut *exactly* the amount of fiberglass cloth needed for each mend. Any excess, and what little cloth we had would not go around. Never in my worst dreams had I imagined needing more than twenty or thirty square inches at one time.

Eventually I mixed our small supply of Mexican resin with hardening catalyst and applied it to the patches of cloth. The completed job was a mess. And no matter what I did, I couldn't get the resin to harden. Normally, it takes no more than a few minutes, but after several hours in the sun, the present batch was still soft. I babied it and cursed it and ranted at it. Dana sat quietly by, the anxieties of the day etched deeply on his face.

By suppertime, the resin had begun to stiffen, and we decided to test the work. I was afraid to look as we lowered the canoe into the water. The patches held. But then a puddle appeared in a spot I'd overlooked. Quickly I got the canoe back on the beach. With our last shred of material, I patched the fourteenth hole, and we left the canoe to dry for the night.

Whether we could get back over the reef in the morning without tearing my work to bits, I had no idea.

During the afternoon, Dana had grown increasingly moody. By early evening, he was thoroughly demoralized about our prospects. Several times, he abused me for my lack of caution. "The way you barrel ahead," he said at one point. "I'm starting to think this trip means more to you than our stinking lives."

As the evening wore on, I tried to cheer him up. I reminded him that on a journey this long, things were bound to fall apart from time to time.

"I know," he said, "but every day?"

"No," I said, "not every day." I had to admit, however, that things had gone badly since Cancún. The twenty-foot waves of the Caribbean were no place for a canoe.

As we lay under the stars in our sleeping shells, I said, "If we're going to come out of this, Dana, we're going to have to get our spirits back up." I raised myself on my elbow and looked at him. "Both of us," I said. "I can't do it alone. I need your support."

I lay there hoping for some positive response, but it didn't come.

If a graph were plotted of our emotional energy during the past few months, it would almost certainly suggest the ups and downs of a seriously afflicted psychotic. Outrageous peaks and valleys, with few plateaus in between.

At the foot of the cliff, on the southeast corner of the site at Tulum is a small but exquisite white bach outlined by gray rock and sloping easily into a limpid, multicolored sea. Despite the constant flow of sweating Cancún-trippers being marched up to the Castillo and then marched back down again, this beach is little used.

If I had to pick just one Mexican beach to be listed among the Great Beaches of the World, it would be this. To swim in these vivid seas, looking up at the exotic outlines of Tulum's Mayan temples, is to combine two of Mexico's greatest pleasures into a single experience.

—Ron Hall, "Great Beaches of the World," *Condé Nast Traveler*

When we got up the morning after our disaster, the sea was calm, and our spirits were high at the thought of reaching Tulum. We paddled off under near ideal conditions, and without a word about the previous day. Our chief concern was the patches—would they hold? Throughout the morning, I kept peeking beneath the tarp to see if there were any leaks. There weren't.

By 8:30 a.m., we had reached Tulum, and in no time were crawling over the Mayan ruins for which the city is famous. The great stone structures are officially closed to the public until 9:30 a.m., but because we came from the sea we were not blocked by the fences that prevent entry from land. We merely climbed up the rocky bank and for nearly an hour had the whole grand place to ourselves: the massive watch tower, the Castillo, the temple of frescoes with its depictions of Mayan life and mythology. The ruins are said to be some 1500 years old, and encompass 56 structures in all.

As Dana wandered on his own, I climbed the Castillo and walked along a narrow ledge that looks out over the Caribbean. I stood there marvelling at the view, which included perhaps a hundred square miles of green and turquoise water, as well as many miles of beaches and palms. Having arrived here by our ancient method of travel, and having suffered a near mythic array of tests and tortures, we seem to feel a particular affinity for this place and for the ancient Mayans who built it. As I stood on top of the wall, I swear I could feel a curious energy restoring something lost within me. I felt renewed, potent, optimistic. What a high!

By this time, the official gates were about to open (busloads of sight-seers were already lined up), and Dana and I were anxious to get back on the sea to make the most of our calm weather. We scrambled back down the bank and paddled off, feeling richly blessed by our ancient absent hosts.

Our only setback that morning came several miles down the coast when Dana realized he'd left his new Converse basketball shoes on a log beneath the ruins. Ah well, a little gift for the gods.

The two days since Tulum have shown us nothing but excellent paddling conditions. The sea life is our constant entertainment: sharks, giant rays, starfish, sea turtles, fish of all colors. This afternoon we were followed into a bay by no fewer than seven 4-foot barracuda. We see them frequently; they dart at our canoe, as if attacking, then veer off, undoubtedly daunted by the size of their big orange prey. This morning we saw what we think was a stork's nest—a massive pad of interwoven sticks and reeds—high atop the Herrero lighthouse.

This afternoon we had a stern reminder of who and where we are: as we came along the coast, we saw two severely mangled freighters driven hard onto the coral and left to the ravages of the sea. Tons of steel, tortured and twisted as if it were cardboard. And there we were in our little peanut shell of a boat, with its fragile fiberglass skin.

We paddled on to Ubero and are camped tonight on a quiet beach, doing our best to relax. Just down the way are hundreds of conch shells left by fishermen. I tried to find a whole one, but each has a sizable puncture where the fisherman has smashed it to break the interior suction so that the animal can be pulled out.

I'm afraid our health isn't the greatest just now. For one thing, we're still suffering from the sea-urchin spines we picked up in our feet on the reef back near Tulum. The spines are long and poisonous and can pierce to the bone if they hit at the right angle. All we can do is endure the discomfort and wait for our flesh to dissolve the calcium spines, which it will after a week or so. My hands, too, are suffering. I have a pea-sized open sore between the first and second fingers of my left hand. I've had it for days, and can't get it to heal, what with the salt and sand and the constant friction of the paddling. This morning, I could barely open my hand when I woke up. We're also sick to death of having salt all over bodies, but we can't afford to use our precious fresh water for bathing. Our clothes and bedding, too, are saturated with salt. Last night, I agonized for hours trying to find a sleeping position in which my sleeping shell wouldn't grind its load of salt into my various abrasions and bug bites.

On the brighter side, our radio is tuned to Belize City, and we're enjoying the English-language broadcasts (Belize is the former British Honduras). The announcer tells us that the U.S. destroyer *Connally* will be in port tomorrow. No mention of our own arrival in three or four days, ho hum.

We have now come nearly 5,000 miles, including 1,700 miles on the coast of Mexico. And I must say, as our Mexican experience winds down, that the people of Mexico have been more than kind to us. They have sheltered us and fed us and encouraged us. When we doubted we could continue, one of them got into the canoe with us and paddled nearly 400 miles. Others came to our rescue when we might have drowned, back at Alvarado. Not one of them has stolen from us or harmed us. They may even have prayed for us.

We feel deeply indebted to all of them.

Don Starkell is now permanently retired. In addition to his two-year canoe journey from Canada to Brazil, he has cycled from Winnipeg to Prince Edward Island, canoed from Vancouver to Ketchikan, Alaska, and hopes to fulfill a last canoeing dream: to paddle from Churchill, Manitoba, on Hudson Bay, through the Northwest Passage to Tuktoyaktuk, Northwest Territories.

Compadrazgo is a very important system of relationships between people who may otherwise have no formal connection. It is easiest to compare with the godparent relationship in other societies, though two peope may become *compadres* without involving children. Anything of importance can lead to new *compadres*: marriage, birth, buying a new house, a business deal, a close friendship, and so on. We have a friend who acquired a *compadre* when he managed to save up the money for a new pickup truck.

Compadres are supposed to support each other in times of need (though they often don't). This tightens the social structure, especially in poorer communities. *Compadres* are often on quite different social and economic levels, however. This is another type of bridge, usually based on mutual respect. A businessman, for example, who accepts an employee's invitation to be his *compadre* upon the birth of a child, is now more than an employer, he's a shirttail relative.

You'll often hear people refer to each other as *compadre* (also *compa*) and *comadre* or *comadre* María, *compadre* Pancho, etc. Once the relationship is entered into this title replaces the person's name or is added to it. Dropping *compadre-madre* is impolite.

Compadre and *comadre* are frequently used among younger people who are actually not *compadres*, but just good friends.

—Carl Franz, *The People's Guide to Mexico*

GERMAINE W. SHAMES

Mexican Mating Calls

The author raises the eternal question: is love amphibious?

Once I had a lover—let's call him Juan—whose English was, at best, rudimentary. But Juan spoke the universal language like a master. On his silvery tongue, even the most garbled expressions took my breath away.

Juan and I met in Mexico, his country of birth, my temporary residence. Land of the *piropo* (verbal tributes to feminine charms), of long songs and laments, Mexico was the perfect setting for a storybook romance, and Juan, as I said, was well-suited to the role of Don Juan.

"My love, my heart, my life," he'd croon, looking deep into my eyes with a fiery gaze that made my heart smolder, "I love you with every breath I take, I can't live without you. You are the queen of my existence, and I your slave."

Whether or not I believed Juan, I can't really say. So dazzled was I by his declarations of love, so mesmerized by the burning look that accompanied them, discernment failed me. Juan made me feel desired, cherished, worshipped. His words entered my bloodstream like an elixir and made my heart cha-cha-cha. In love with Juan's verbiage, I let it work its magic and asked no questions.

Life with Juan was all-day siestas and all night fiestas, serenades at my balcony, roses at my doorstep, and Juan pinned to my ear, cooing his inimitable Mexican mating calls.

"My nightingale, my heaven, my saint," he'd tell me, letting the words trickle down my earlobe like warm honey. "I love you with every beat of my heart. You're part of my very being, as essential as the air I breathe. If you left me, I swear I would die."

Leave Juan? I supposed I might one day, but I was in no hurry. Life as Juan's *novia* (sweetheart) was sweet indeed. As long as the nectar in Juan's tongue continued to flow, I saw no reason for our idyll to end. Latin courtships might last months, years, long enough for me to soak up volumes of Juan's odes and oaths.

"My light, my soul, my treasure," he'd whisper endlessly, growing bolder, drawing me closer, so close I could see the facets in his eyes glow like hot coals. "I love you more than I love myself, more that your own mother loves you, more than—may the Virgin forgive me!—more than God Himself could ever love you. I swear I would die for you."

Fortunately for most Juans few loves are ever actually put to the test. No doubt, my Juan banked on not having to make good on his claims. He was only telling me what I wanted to hear, after all: words of love.

But, as fate would have it, circumstances intervened—drastic circumstances—that thrust my very life into his hands. I'll explain.

One weekend Juan took me to a small seaside resort outside Playa Blanca where we intended to spend a few quiet days romancing to the rhythm of the waves. The setting—white-hot sands, placid sea, a caressing breeze—had all the promise of a sultry summer daydream. Shortly after our arrival, however, a nasty storm blew in, and the tide rose like a waterfall in reverse.

For two days Juan and I kept to our sweltering hotel room, glued together by our own perspiration. Whatever the mosquitoes spared of me, Juan nibbled at unceasingly, until every pore of my body stung. By day three—the last of our little holiday—raw, dehydrated, half-incinerated, I decided to have a swim come what may.

> *Mientras dura, vida y dulzura.*
>
> While life yet lasts, laughter and molasses.
>
> —Mexican proverb from *Folk Wisdom of Mexico*, edited by Jeff M. Sellers

Out I ran to the beach with Juan calling after me, "My love, the sea, she's mean. Don't go!"

He was right. I was no match for the waves, and they had their way with me. Tossed about like a dummy, suctioned down into the drink again and again, I quickly felt my fight give out. I was drowning.

"Help me, Juan!" I screamed. My mouth filled with brine each time I opened it. "Help me! Help! Help...!"

"Sweem, *mamacita*, sweem!" Juan cried back.

"Help!" I cried desperately, a dozen times, a hundred, though Juan had no doubt heard me the first time.

"Sweem, *por Dios* (for God's sake): Sweem!" he repeated, matching me yelp for yelp.

The poor man was beside himself, clearly. He ran up and down the beach, weeping, wailing; he tore his hair, waved his arms, fell to his knees...and never so much as wet the tips of his toes.

When a wayward wave finally heaved me onto the beach where he waited dry and safe, I couldn't help but feel sorry for him. Not meaning to, I had exposed him; his words had been so much flotsam.

But Juan showed no signs of embarrassment. To the contrary, his face lit up and he shed tears of joy.

"My goddess, my angel, my adoration...," he cooed, riveting me once more with his searing gaze as he led me away.

Germaine W. Shames has written from five continents—soon to add a sixth—on topics ranging from dual-cultural romance to volcanic trekking. Her byline appears in such periodicals as Diversion, *the* Oakland Tribune, *the* Rotarian, *and many others. she was last spotted skydiving—in tandem with a burly Kiwi—over New Zealand's Southern Alps. Her mother wishes she would meet the All-American boy and settle down.*

"Mexicans learn to love so quickly and easily, no matter how unlovable we may be," I say. "Some of us learn to love them in return, without reserve. We *gringos* are so much slower, so much more fearful. We might call it love, but to us it's more like taking hostages."

—Carlos Amantea, *The Blob that Ate Oaxaca & Other Travel Tales*

REBECCA BRUNS

City in the Mist

The old ways live on in San Cristóbal de las Casas, mountain city of the Maya.

T he driver said he'd taken this road 5,000 times before, but that was small comfort as the tires screeched around every curve and the asphalt in places crumbled away to nothing. We were on our way out of the mountains of San Cristóbal de las Casas to the rain forest. The morning mist of the highlands, hovering over corn patches as gilded as the inside of Santo Domingo church, gradually sank into steam. Waterfalls frothed down fern-choked cliffs.

Finally, four hours along, we turned into a parking lot on the edge of the most beautiful Mayan ruins in Mexico: Palenque. Temples and palaces as sun-bleached as bones, with the jungle clawing at their backs, towered toward a faint smudge of moon. Every stone felt as alive as the leaves. In this mystical sense, Palenque is a fitting ancient counterpart to San Cristóbal, modern-day capital of the Maya.

Over the years, San Cristóbal de las Casas has quietly become a favorite of adventurous travelers in Mexico. Its cobblestones and austere cathedrals radiate a glow, an ethereal quality that I attribute to the magic of the rainbow-garbed Maya who still inhabit these mountains. Mexico's two seed cultures—indigenous and Hispanic—share the streets here more than anywhere else south of the U.S. border.

The town hides in the remote highlands of Chiapas, the southernmost state in Mexico, next door to Guatemala. In fact, a

M exico was shaken to its roots on January 1, 1994, when Maya rebels calling themselves the Zapatista Army of National Liberation took control of San Cristóbal de las Casas and several other towns in Chiapas. Their protest wasn't new, but a new chapter in an ongoing history of deprivation at the hands of the governing powers and *ladino*, or *mestizo* (Spanish speakers of mixed races), settlers. The army responded with massive firepower and many lives were lost before the government agreed to peace talks with the rebels to consider their grievances. The area may have a military presence for some time and the situation could remain unsettled, part of the tragic history of Mexico's poorest region.

—JO'R and LH

271

visit here is a great introduction to Guatemala's Indian-rich society. The problem is that San Cristóbal has no airport, nor any deluxe hotels. This may explain why fewer Americans go there than do Europeans, who seem less concerned about convenience and luxury while soaking up Mexico's history.

I went to San Cristóbal for the fourth time recently, renting a car in Tuxtla Gutiérrez, the booming, homely capital of Chiapas, and driving east into the southern Sierra Madre. It took me two hours to crawl up the dizzying fifty-mile slope; along the way I remembered a terrifying skid that had almost spun me off the hairpin road five years before in rainy weather. As I climbed out of the valley in which Tuxtla sits, the mountains rippled into a lush panorama splashed with pines and wild-flowers, a foretaste of Mexico's only rain forest and the ruins of Palenque down in the Chiapas lowlands.

For all its beauty, Chiapas is the poorest, least developed state in Mexico. It has the country's largest concentration of Indians—more than 1 million, living in pueblos around the market city of San Cristóbal. I saw their shanties teetering on high ridges with million-dollar views. Indians trotted along the road, doubled over with babies or loads of sticks bound to their backs. Stalls of their weavings blazed in scarlet and psychedelic pink against greenery steeped in a dense mist that made me feel as if I were riding into the clouds.

At 7,000 feet, San Cristóbal almost touches heaven. Its 460-year-old lanes, barely wide enough for a car, zigzag between rows of close-packed houses. As I trundled past a man painting a wall sunflower-gold, I felt a rush of excitement. Everything seemed as familiar as an old friend: the steep sidewalks, the rubble-heap churches with weeds sprouting from crevices like hairs from a mole, the white-gloved cops tweeting their whistles.

Yet everything was busier than I remembered. San Cristóbal had about 25,000 people when I first visited in the '70s, but now has some 100,000. Big tour buses lined the woodsy zócalo. Blue-shawled Indians waved clay dolls at tourists. There are now twenty-odd hotels, making up in charm for what they lack in luxury. Having no reservation (rooms are seldom full except in summer, the balmiest season), I hunted for a good inn with a fireplace, a near necessity in the winter.

I prowled the fountained courtyards at the Posada Diego de Mazariegos, generally considered the town's finest inn. I admired the decaying 16th-century façade and the caged macaws at the Hotel Santa Clara, occupying the city's oldest building. I parted the big glass doors of the Hotel Ciudad Real, fondly remembering its leafy, covered patio and the cozy quarters where I'd stayed years ago. I overlooked what I later decided was the best room in town, an upstairs chamber at Na-Bolom named Jatate, with a molded hearth and a view of the estate's primeval garden. But in the end I settled again into my old standby, the Hotel Español, and nursed a fire every night in my room

As dusk fell that first day, the aroma of wood fires began to creep over the red-tile roofs. Crossing the square, I wandered through the red-and-white arcade where baskets of macaroons, sugar cones, peanut brittle, and glazed fruit seethed with bees, which a vendor was plucking off with tongs and putting into a humming plastic bag.

In front of the hulking cathedral, built in 1538, *elote* vendors were roasting corn on the cob over fires, like holy offerings, and the popcorn vendors were setting up their machines to dispense *palomitas* (little doves). In the onset of moonlight, the cathedral's chipped, sun-bronzed face cooled to ghostly rust, blue, and albino-yellow. Its massive wooden doors, studded with medieval knobs, opened onto a brilliant interior supported by immense lily-white columns. Outside, under the stars, I studied the statues on the façade; they were enduring eternity in their niches after four centuries of pigeon snow and the leprosy of time, which had eaten away their hands and eyes. Only one, a pious friar, still had both his hands clasped in prayer, always on the outside looking in.

San Cristóbal feels like the self-contained kingdom it once was. Founded in 1528 by Diego de Mazariegos, perhaps the only conquistador in all Mexico with a statue still standing in his honor, the town was first called Ciudad Real (Royal City). With its noble colonnades and courtyards, it must have lived up to its name. Until 1892 it reigned as capital of Chiapas, at that time a feisty empire under the umbrella of Guatemala. For its errant autonomy, Mexico punished the town in the late 1800s, ultimately wresting Chiapas into its fold and transferring the capital to Tuxtla. Ciudad Réal was renamed after its patron saint, Christopher, and the first bishop of Chiapas, Fray Bartolomé de las Casas.

The bishop came onto the scene in 1545, rattling the rafters of tradition. He was aghast at the abuse of the *indígenas,* whom the Spanish had enslaved. De las Casas fired off protests to Madrid and made the local politicos fume until Spain finally freed the Indians.

Since their long mistreatment, most highland Maya have avoided integration with the Hispanic populace. They've maintained their own costumes, crafts, festivals, forms of worship, and language (nine dialects of Mayan). Tourists often patronize the Maya as a rare endangered species, and many *mestizos* of San Cristóbal still scorn them as dirty primitives without education or domestic plumbing.

But the good bishop—*el padre de los indios*—has three modern-day successors who care about the Indians as much as he did. Gertrude Duby Blom, Sergio Castro, and Mercedes Hernández have all found a way into the Indians' closed society and their understandably cautious hearts, and have helped preserve their dignity, even their survival.

Long ago, as a young journalist just starting out, I interviewed Blom at Na-Bolom (Mayan for "House of the Jaguar"). That great walled *hacienda* on the eastern edge of town looked as forbidding as a monastery outside, but was a 22-room dream of bougainvillea, art, and artifacts within (a tour of it is a must).

Blom, a stately but short-tempered Swiss, was 76 at the time, and was the expatriate grande dame of Chiapas. As she led me to her room, I felt nervous and intimidated by her formidable reputation. Her black-and-white photos of local *indígenas*, especially the Lacandón Indians—the only remaining pure jungle Maya in Mexico—plastered the walls of the *hacienda's* library, museum, and four patios. The pictures had a classic, splendid look: mist rising around dugout canoes, stern long-haired leaders chomping hand-rolled cigars. The intimacy of these shots was achieved because the Indians trusted her as a friend, not someone whose photos would steal their souls. In the early 1950s, she and her husband, the late anthropologist Frans Blom, turned Na-Bolom into a Mayan study center. Both northern Europeans, they'd met in Chiapas and had fallen in love through their common love of the Indians.

Our interview went poorly. Blom snapped at me and answered my bungled questions fussily. I escaped with embarrassment and relief.

Swiss efficiency notwithstanding, Na-Bolom has its surprises. Awakened by what sounded like gunshots at 5:00 one cold morning, I listened, intrigued, to the strains of live *mariachi* music outside my window. When curiosity overcame my better judgment, I pulled a blanket around my shoulders and padded through the dark patio to the street entrance. There the night watchman intercepted me. "What's the noise?" I asked him.

"¡*Cohetes!*" he exclaimed, thrusting both arms upward like a firecracker exploding. Behind him, seven *mariachis* lined up under the streetlamp as though posing for a record cover. The watchman explained that the firecrackers and lively tunes were a signal to the townspeople that a procession to the church was about to begin. Sure enough, as I watched, entranced, men, women, and children appeared in little groups. When a sizeable crowd had gathered, they picked up their flowers and instruments, fired off a few more *cohetes*, and filed up the hill to the church.

—Joyce Gregory,
"At the House of the Jaguar"

Now she is more than ninety, and when I met her again recently she approached with a cane, wearing a fantastic collar of huge lavender crystals set in silver. I reminded her of our first interview so many years earlier. She blinked behind thick glasses and smiled like a child, saying sweetly, "It must have been before you were born." She sat for a moment, then got up to fetch some coffee. A staffer confided, "She can't relax. She's never calm."

Seeing her suddenly with admiration rather than self-conscious fear, I realized her edgy toughness comes from an internal fire. It has pushed her to help preserve the dwindling race of Lacandóns (now numbering four hundred) and, in the last ten years, to save the shrinking Chiapas rain forest. As she said in a film on her work, *La Reina de la Selva* (Queen of the Jungle), "My life is full of lost battles, but the spirit of the fight is still in me."

> Trudy Blom passed away in 1993.
>
> —JO'R and LH

One day during lunch at Na-Bolom, I found myself staring at a Lacandón family at the far end of the table; their mahogany faces, with tilted eyes and straight noses fused to their foreheads, were living Mayan sculptures. They'd come to town for medical attention and were staying at Na-Bolom. Blom's doors are always open to the Lacandóns, whom she visits, despite her age, several times a year in the jungle.

I saw others on a one-day side trip to Palenque, close to where the Lacandóns live. They stood in the parking lot of the 1,500-year-old ceremonial site, wearing baggy white robes and shoulder-length hair, selling

Palenque ruins

bows and arrows made with parrot feathers. I felt they should have been inside the temples, among the glyphs and stucco sculptures and stone galleries that ramble over a broad plateau.

From the jungle came the muted shriek of howler monkeys. I climbed to the tops of so many pyramids that my knees quivered and my eyes were drunk from scanning oceans of trees where miles of unexcavated ruins still lie buried. Then I descended into the Temple of the Inscriptions. Its steep, perspiring steps lead deep down to the only known tomb in a Mayan pyramid, the elaborately carved funeral chamber of Lord Shield Pakal, ruler of Palenque. I remembered a similar experience, wriggling through the long, claustrophobic passage in the Pyramid of Cheops to get to the pharaoh's sarcophagus at its heart.

Even more than Palenque's majesty and wilderness, its acknowledgment of an afterlife is what, to me, sets it apart from other Mayan ruins, where pyramids merely raised temples closer to heaven. Palenque, instead, symbolizes the city of night, where the dead await rebirth. Wandering the grounds, I wondered if the Lacandóns will have a rebirth or if they're doomed to die peddling souvenirs in the parking lot of past glory as the forest vanishes around them.

Logging has wiped out nearly eighty percent of the Indians' homeland. But, thanks in part to Trudy Blom's efforts, a recent state law forbids the cutting of any more tropical trees. Today Blom focuses on reforestation, distributing up to 40,000 trees a year from her nursery. "Whenever I feel desperate," she said, "I plant a tree."

The same passion shines through in the private museum of Sergio Castro. Every evening between six and seven, Castro opens the plain metal door to his residence at 32 Avenida 15 de Septiembre. The receiving room mimics a little Mayan church, decked in Christmas lights and rows of stoic, coal-blackened statues whose vaguely sinister air is quickly dispelled by the animation and warmth of the curator. Like a gamin cowboy, in boots and jeans and a red bandanna tied pirate-style over his bald spot, Castro welcomes guests who, by word of mouth, have heard about his fine costume collection. The museum is free, though offerings of money, pens, even aspirin, stuff the donation box.

After migrating from the rich northern city of Chihuahua, Castro discovered his true calling: to help the Indians of Chiapas improve their lot. "My work is not a devotion," he said. "It's my *obligation.*" Supported by grants from a French institute and, occasionally, money from his father, he has poured thirty years of his life into helping the Indians grow crops, build schools, and develop good sanitation; he treats epilepsy, burns and colds, does minor surgery, and never charges a penny. Instead, the

Indians thank him with their handiwork, mostly costumes, which now fill three big rooms of his house.

huipil

Some of those items are commonly worn by Indians around town, but others are found nowhere else: lavishly embroidered *huipils* (overblouses); police "uniforms" with lace-up sandals, carved staffs and ribbon-strewn hats; an ingenious palm-leaf raincoat; "monkey man" carnival attire; a dusty heap of violins, flutes, guitars, drums, and monkey-skull *maracas*; a bachelor's robe with a discreet opening for the benefit of prospective brides ("No show, no buy," explained Castro). All the items are arranged according to village. After toiling in the fields of San Juan Chamula all day, Castro opens his costume museum and conducts tours in English, French, Italian, or Spanish (he speaks three Mayan dialects, too). That he finds the time for all this, and for his own family of six as well, is a lesson in the miraculous energy generated by a giving heart.

Over the years, I've visited the best known Indian pueblos—San Juan Chamula, Zinacantán, and Tenejapa—but I wanted to try a guide this time, for more insights. Notices all over town for a "shamanistic tour" led by Mercedes Hernandez caught my eye. Hoping it wouldn't be too hokey, I found myself in the *zócalo* one morning with a dozen or so other travelers. Hernandez, short like her friends the Indians, and thirtyish, appeared in a pink-and-white *huipil* with a thousand-watt smile on her broad, brown face, pleased at the turnout.

Two vans sped us off to San Juan Chamula, a twenty-minute ride from town. On a hillside overlooking the village's famous church, Mercedes described some regional ironies ("Chiapas wins prizes for export-quality coffee, but here we drink Nescafé") and the complex politics and religion of this poor community of 100,000 Indians. "It is here"—she pointed to her head—"that the Indians were destroyed by the Spaniards, and we are still paying for it." That the Chamulans have kept their own identity after centuries of battering is amazing.

One of their slow-dying ways is a virulent sexism: two wives to every man, no shoes for the women (their feet are coarse and as hard as truck tires), and utter subservience (a woman must always walk behind a man). "Because of machismo, I don't move here and marry a Chamulan," Hernandez explained. "Here the women call getting married 'committing suicide.' Many are delaying marriage these days because they make their living with handicrafts. The men think I'm a pretty crazy woman," she said with a grin, "but they accept me."

Hernandez is that rare case: a liberated Latina. She understands the Indians, having faced prejudice herself from those who resent the fact that the city's top guide is a woman. Married once, she had a son, then was abandoned by her husband. She hasn't remarried. "I can tell when men want to take advantage of me," she said. "Sometimes I get depressed to think I may be alone the rest of my life. Then I snap out of it and keep going."

As she led us down into the village with a red-and-white umbrella, like a Mexican Mary Poppins, she smiled and waved, greeting everyone by name, gossiping with the women selling bananas and shawls. Their faces, normally flat and shut, lit up with a fondness and trust seldom attained between *indígenas* and *mestizas*.

We began our tour at a town official's house. Past the leaf-ruffled doorway, candles lit a crude altar supporting terra-cotta bulls, upon whose backs copal incense burned; we were asked to leave a coin on the altar. The lady of the house opened a bottle of *posh,* a local cane liquor so potent that fourteen of us could not finish the jigger of it that was passed around.

That was just the appetizer. The real drama lay inside the nameless church on the square. Appearing innocently Catholic—white stucco with carefree aqua trim—it contains a world as pagan as voodoo. After paying the town authorities, we timidly entered the dim church. Instead of holding pews, the cement floor was scattered with pine needles and hundreds of glittering candles awash in the eerie drone of chanting. We sat in one corner like mute initiates into the other-worldly workings of the cosmos, stirred by the weird casting of spells over Cokes and chickens.

"Souls and churches are Spanish," Hernandez told us. "Shamans talk about invisible, cosmic energy." Shamans of both sexes ("God isn't macho in choosing *curanderos*") do ritual cleansings (*limpias*) to remove villagers' negative energy ("what we call depression").

The *limpias* looked like a lot more fun than therapy. Near us a shaman in a murmuring trance was running eggs over a woman's arms and braids to absorb her bad energy. Next he sprayed *posh* from his mouth onto her head, passed a live chicken over the candles, and ended by sharing a spiked Coke with his client, the idea being to burp out the problem.

"Those nasty Indians *drink* in church," the Mexicans of San Cristóbal have complained, not realizing that *posh* is to a shaman what wine is to a priest. The Indians take their rituals so seriously that if anyone dares shoot photos in their church, it's said they'll smash the camera and put the offender in jail. According to several published accounts, two foreigners were executed in the mid-1980s for violating the photo ban.

This deep sensitivity to picture-taking cropped up everywhere. I drove with some Europeans to Amatenango, a village of superb potters. At one home, a teenage Indian girl gave a lesson in molding a dove to a Swiss woman who fumbled bravely and hilariously with the clay. But warm as the villagers were, they allowed no photos. It's only respectful to ask permission. Some Indians will say yes if you ante up a dollar, but don't insist.

You can see the Indians of every major village at San Cristóbal's daily market. Each morning, except on Sunday, they bring in goods to sell and trade. Squat mothers nursing babies grip turkeys by the legs. A father and son, two midgets in pink, lick tiny four-color ice cream cones. Stands, manned by Indians with tan, chapped faces and gold teeth, glisten with yellow *pepinos* and huge pineapples. Long-ribboned hats and butterflies flutter up a cobbled walkway whose roof of hanging clothes resembles stained glass.

I reeled through this kaleidoscope searching for the candle market, finally deciding to let

I rummaged through my bookshelves and found a book of star maps, Menzel's *Stars and Planets*. Unfortunately, this book printed the south and north views of the sky on two separate pages, so I had to find some tracing paper and place it over the page showing the north sky. I drew it and then shifted the tracing paper to the south page and joined both sides of the sky together. I drew in Scorpius and the North Star and then looked at the result. My heart jumped into my mouth. There it was. The Milky Way stretched south to north from Scorpius past the North Star. The Wakah-Chan was the Milky Way.

When I presented this new insight at my next seminar, one of my graduate students, Matthew Looper, contributed yet another critical idea to the growing pattern. While I was telling the class about the Wakah-Chan World Tree being the Milky Way, I heard him murmur from the back of the crowded seminar room, "That's why he entered the road." His words exploded like a lightening bolt in my mind. The great image of Pakal's sarcophagus at Palenque shows him at the moment of his death falling down the World Tree into the Maw of the Earth. The expression the ancient Maya used for this fall was *och bih*, "he entered the road." The road was the Milky Way, which is called both the *Sak Be* ("white Road") and *Xibal Be*, "Road of Awe," by the Maya. Pakal enters this road in death.

—Linda Schele, with David Freidel &
Joy Parker, *Maya Cosmos: Three Thousand
Years on the Shaman's Path*

myself get lost. A few minutes later I stumbled into an alley choked with dangling tapers, some as big as bludgeons. Nearby stalls were heaped with quartz-like copal incense whose aroma underscored the pungent scent of the whole town. A vendor called the crystals tears of the copal tree. "When the tree is cut, it cries sap."

The delights of the market spill into the surrounding streets. On Avenida Utrilla I found a surprising amber workshop (*taller de amber*) at Plaza Sivan. Its artists, using the crudest equipment, carve amber from northern Chiapas into dainty, first-rate miniatures—a jaguar devouring a woman, a spider featuring a tiny real incarnation of itself frozen in the amber—and honey-toned jewelry. On the street of *artesanias*, Real de Guadalupe, you can spruce up your ethnic look with garish blouses, patchwork vests, baggy skirts, and woven sashes galore.

Of all the city's bazaars, the plaza around Santo Domingo and La Caridad (Our Lady of Charity) is most dazzling. Weavings flood the stones with hues of berries and wine in the shadow of the old cracked churches. Indian women sit hopefully before their wares, calling "*Qué va a llevar?*" ("What'll you take?"). You feel like a heel unless you buy some of the incandescent goods so lovingly made by hand.

The mood changes utterly in the gloomy, 16th-century basilica of Santo Domingo. Its gaudy baroque interior and gold-leaf-encrusted pulpit brought to mind a decadent carousel, and its musty oils of martyrs made paradise seem a grim destination. Why do so many old Latin churches reek of such suffering? I preferred the simple, sunlit interior of nearby La Caridad, where 34 bouquets of carnations and tuberoses exhaled a garden's fragrance. By contrast, a bloody Jesus laid out in a glass coffin in Santo Domingo reminded me of a macabre Prince Charming and sent me hurrying outside for fresh air.

Santo Domingo's decorative pink facade, as light as wedding-cake frosting, concealed within its curlicues the Hapsburg emblem of a two-headed eagle and the imperial coat of arms of Carlos I, King of Spain. I also confess to liking the bronze statue of Captain Diego de Mazariegos outside Santo Domingo. I know, he's an evil conquistador, but somehow the way he surveys the rooftops of the town from his pedestal conveys a sense of real pride in his little corner of heaven.

I left San Cristóbal in an icy, crystalline rainstorm that evaporated about halfway to Tuxtla. A stunning rainbow out of a children's coloring book arched across the mountains. I drove through its prism of pale Mayan pinks and blues, and as I dropped into the humid valleys it faded like something divine in the higher distances.

Rebecca Bruns wrote frequently for Travel & Leisure *during her career, and was a co-author of* Hidden Mexico. *She was also an accomplished pianist and painter. She traveled all over the world, but had a special love for Mexico, where she died of cancer in 1994.*

Some of the best-informed, most capable, faithful, knowing, cynical, polite, energetic, interesting guides are the little boys aged eight to fourteen who haunt the railroad and bus stations of small towns and the highway entrances. Sometimes they are dreadful birds of prey, pushing, mauling, pulling at you for the pleasure and profit of carrying your bags. Mostly, they gather around more gently, trying to outcharm each other. Whomever you choose—the one with the saddest, most opaque black eyes, or the whitest smile, or the showiest collection of English words, or the hungriest look—he will teach you, if you want to learn, something of the children of Mexico. He may make witty, skeptical comments but never complain. He will wait and wait for you and never feel the need to be patient; he just is. He has many fine antennae which search out your mood with fine delicacy: if you want silence he will be quiet, if your mood is loquacious he will babble away. You need never tell him that you're displeased with him; he'll know by the tone of your voice and the set of your face, no matter how well you think you're dissembling. No matter how hurt he is—and he is, like all Mexicans, extraordinarily vulnerable—he will not cry or display injury; his is a built-in stoicism, painted over by a winning smile and fine manners. He will never ask you for anything to drink or eat, although he may be quite hungry. If you offer him food or drink he will accept it gravely, eat it slowly, in small, delicate bites, as if he weren't hungry and it didn't matter whether he was fed or not.

—Kate Simon, *Mexico: Places and Pleasures*

ROBERT B. COX

City Under Grass

Nestled in the hills of Veracruz, the lost city of Cuajilotes begins to emerge.

The canyon of the Bobos River opens between two knolls at the edge of a pasture crowded by lethargic Brahma cattle. A thin gauze of mist hangs a hundred feet below us near the green floor of the valley, where the river twists into sight, bends, and recedes toward the point where it joins with the Nautla River and proceeds to the Gulf of Mexico.

The weak afternoon light and the sheer walls of the canyon make the ruins in the river valley appear flat and two-dimensional. No stone surfaces are visible: the fallen city of Cuajilotes appears to be nothing more than a series of miniature tufts of symmetrically arranged vegetation. From this elevated perspective it's easy to understand how this Mesoamerican metropolis, known simply as *las ruinas* to the ranchers who guide their cattle through the valley and the citrus farmers whose groves speckle the hills of Veracruz, was overlooked by the rest of the world for centuries.

We follow a goat path that zigzags down the steep mountainside. As we approach *las ruinas*, the outlines of grass-blanketed pyramids become clear, rising more than 60 feet above what was once a vast plaza.

Little is known about Cuajilotes' past. Published reports of the site's discovery in 1992 suggested that it might have been a trading post serving the ancient cities of Tajin and Teotihuacan. One archaeologist posited that Cuajilotes may have included the garrison post from which Aztec warriors dealt the invading Spanish their first defeat. Mentioned in a conquistador's journals, that Indian fortress was never located.

The ruins were "discovered" only a few years ago when spotted by some Yankee rafters on the Bobos. The adventurers took photos of the site and gave them to S. Jeffrey K. Wilkerson, an archaeologist in the United States. Word of the discovery soon spread, sparking the exploratory zeal of archaeologists throughout the Americas.

We approach the ruins from the south, where the steep canyon meets the valley of the river. The city's largest temple rises from a thicket of briars, vines, and vegetation so dense it is virtually impossible to scale. On either side of the main temple, five smaller mounds—probably temples—flank the central plaza, which is crowned to the north by the rectangular edge of a ball court. The main plaza is about 300 yards long and is punctuated by the remains of what appear to have been three smaller temples or altars.

As we attempt to climb a pyramid, two blue-green parrots swoop from the dense leaves of a tree growing from the pasture that envelops the main temple. They squawk discordantly as they flit across the plaza and out of sight. Along the northern edge of the site, a cowboy rounds up a few cattle. Man and horse are dwarfed by the enormous grass-covered pyramids behind them.

Besides a few local ranchers, today we are the only people in the lost city. We wander for hours from temple to temple, speculating about those who built and lived in Cuajilotes. For now, the ruins can only be reached by foot, horseback, or raft, but soon the Mexican government will begin an extensive excavation and restoration project. We wonder what the valley will look like when it is filled with tour buses and Chiclet vendors.

When the afternoon's light drizzle turns to a steady flow, we hike back up the steep ravine to the pasture where the Brahma still sulkily graze. We make our way across the field toward a rutted path used by citrus farmers that will lead us to the main road back to the hill town of Tlapacoyán.

At the pasture's gate we meet a man tying a bundle of hay to the back of his horse. Assuming from our appearance that we're not locals, he asks what we think of the ruins. We tell him we are amazed that such a place could exist for so long without recognition. He agrees, and we talk about what will happen to the neighborhood now that *las ruinas* are known throughout the world.

The rancher, who owns land close to the valley and lives in a concrete-block house at the end of the dirt road, is optimistic. Once the citrus path is paved, he tells us, he intends to build a lot on his land across from the pasture leading to Cuajilotes. Before we leave, he insists we take some grapefruit from a tree on his future car park. We pick three. "Take more," he smiles. "This tree may not be here when you come back."

Robert B. Cox writes about travel when he isn't in New York writing about money.

The history of Mexico is the history of man seeking his parentage, his origins. He has been influenced at one time or another by France, Spain, the United States, and the militant indigenists of his own country, and he crosses history like a jade comet, now and then giving off flashes of lightning. What is he pursuing in his eccentric course? He wants to go back beyond the catastrophe he suffered: he wants to be a sun again, to return to the center of that life from which he was separated one day. (Was that day the Conquest? Independence?) Our solitude has the same roots as religious feelings. It is a form of orphanhood, an obscure awareness that we have been torn from the All, and an ardent search: a flight and a return, an effort to re-establish the bonds that unite us with the universe.

—Octavio Paz, *The Labyrinth of Solitude and Other Writings*

CAROL CANTER

Time Travel with My Daughter

*There's no going back to the old days, but the glory of the present
is right in front of our noses.*

It was a spur of the moment decision to spend four nights in
Zihuatanejo with my seven-year-old daughter Nicole before going on
to Club Med Ixtapa. There was no time for reservations, and my husband, busy at work, couldn't join us. But this was my chance. I could
make a leisurely return to the tiny jewel of a fishing village I had discovered in 1967, when I was footloose and fancy free, and share it with my
child.

Zihuatanejo has changed tremendously in twenty-five years. It is no
longer a town with one mud street where pigs run free. But the beaches
remain powder white and the water turquoise, warm and gentle. With
the addition of its upscale sister resort—Ixtapa—Z or Zihua, as it's affectionately called, has boomed to a population of more than 25,000.

The roads are paved now, the cruise ships call, and an airport serves
this two-in-one destination. Shops, galleries, and hip restaurants, such as
Coconuts, exude an international flair. And yet, amidst this modern
resort, fishermen still ply their trade, weaving nets on the municipal
beach and bringing home their daily catch. The market is colorful, the
sunsets brilliant.

My daughter and I flew from San Francisco to Zihuatanejo direct.
The trip was a far cry from 1967, when the journey to Zihuatanejo from
Acapulco meant seven hours of bumping along rutted roads in a Jeep and
singing songs to keep from feeling sick. Yet, even at the international airport, with credit card and daughter in hand, I still had the sense of
adventure, like old times, that comes from not having a reservation, from
arriving with no definite plan.

I wanted to stay on La Ropa—the expanse of white sand that curves
around Zihuatanejo Bay for two picturesque miles—which sports a range
of hotels, most being funky and affordable. A small shuttle van from the
Catalina/Sotavento, sister hotels that have been recommended to me
over the years, was parked outside. We hopped in, joining two other
American women my age. We quickly became a *simpatico* quartet.

At the Catalina, Nicole and I found a large room with tile floor, bright Mexican weaving, and a large bougainvillaea-lined patio overlooking the sea. The fourty-year-old Catalina, Zihuatanejo's oldest hotel, is built into the cliffs above La Ropa beach. That meant plenty of stairs and gorgeous views. Nicole and I immediately headed down to play in the surf.

That night, we joined the two women we had met on the van for dinner at the hotel. The food was good and reasonably priced; the view was worth the price of the air fare. Nicole became one of the group, happy to have new friends and not seeming to mind being the only kid.

A timely and marvelous developmental leap had occurred on the plane ride down. My daughter had gotten hooked on a "chapter book" and read nonstop throughout the flight. This meant that for the first time since motherhood, I found myself able to make real headway in a book of my own. This continued the next day as we lay side by side on the beach reading, stopping only occasionally as Nicole updated me on the latest twist or turn in *The Baby Sitters' Club*. We swam and played in the water, sipped milk from young coconuts, and read—the kind of total relaxation I had come to believe was mutually exclusive when traveling with a child.

We ate dinner at Elvira, the tiny restaurant on the beach just below our hotel. We knew the fish was fresh because two women were filleting a huge sailfish on a wooden table right out-

T he Aztec emperor, Moctezuma, set a precedent for Mexican seafood lovers when he established a system of runners from Tenochtitlán (Mexico City to us) to the Gulf of Mexico. Life for these relay teams must have been like perpetual Olympic Games, with the runner's baton substituted by red snappers, fresh mangrove oysters and steamer clams.

The tradition continues, though the runners have been replaced by fast trucks. *Mariscos* (seafood) are extremely popular and towns of any size, even far from the coast, will have at least one seafood restaurant.

Because of these fast trucks, many refrigerated and others using ice, there's rarely any worry about being served something spoiled or overripe. If you're in doubt, however, don't eat it. This is especially true when eating seafood from street vendors.

As a general rule I only eat street vendor's seafood when within sight or smell of the ocean. Even then I avoid the less prosperous stands (which can't afford to throw anything away if it's marginal) and prefer to eat seafood before the heat of the afternoon. Most *mariscos* are delivered early in the morning and several hours out of water or ice is more than enough to reduce their flavor and increase the chance of spoiling.

—Carl Franz, *The People's Guide to Mexico*

side. We watched in fascination as they removed the bill, the sail, and the bones, turning a seventy-five-pound trophy into what would soon become a succulent feast.

Before we had a chance to order, an American angler entered with his wife and friends. They took the big table next to ours, and it slowly filled with other guests. When a Mexican family with three children joined them, we learned the sailfish we had seen outside was the fishing enthusiast's catch of the day. The father, Alfonso, had taken the Americans ocean fishing that morning on his boat, so he and his family had been invited to share the bounty.

The meal began with *ceviche*, a raw fish cocktail marinated in lots of lime. Next came the *dedos*, strips of the white fish lightly breaded and fried—my daughter's favorite. Each course was served on huge platters, which were circulated generously to include our table.

Alfonso spoke a little English; his wife and children spoke none. The family looked uncomfortable in the midst of a boisterous, if good-natured, group of Americans. Meanwhile, Nicole opened her bag of markers and began to draw, a strategy she adopted long ago to get through long meals monopolized by too much adult conversation. She and Alfonso's girls, ages six and eleven, kept eyeing one another. Finally, Nicole asked me if she could invite them to draw with her. I spoke with the mother in Spanish, and she answered enthusiastically "¡Sí!".

And that is how a friendship without words began in Zihuatanejo. I was used, occasionally, to translate, but the children communicated well on their own—drawing, jumping rope, and doing cartwheels on the beach. The girls' brother ultimately joined in on the fun.

By midnight, the feast drew to a close, but not before much *cerveza* was downed and plates piled with French fries and grilled sailfish fillets gorged upon. Topping off our meal were ice cream and *plátanos fritos*, fried bananas.

It was time for us to head upstairs to the hotel, but the kids were not ready to leave one another. We finally pulled them apart with pledges of another chance to play. Alfonso promised to come by with his boat the next day and find us on La Ropa.

I had offered to photograph his boat, *Rebelde* (Rebel), in late afternoon, when he would take us for a ride with his children. But by the time he came, the winds had picked up and he could not bring the boat close to shore. Yelling across the surf, we arranged to rendezvous the following day at Las Gatas.

Las Gatas, a perfect palm-fringed crescent beach, sits at the end of a peninsula jutting west from La Ropa. We headed there the next day by launch from the municipal pier, Zihuatanejo's nerve center, where wind-surfing, snorkeling, deep-sea fishing, and other excursions can be booked. Boats called *pangas* make the ten-minute crossing all day. It's a lot easier than hiking or horseback riding over rough terrain with kids to reach this isolated beach.

Before boarding, we spent some hours in town shopping, outfitting Nicole in inexpensive, colorful Mexican cottons. We grabbed a *paleta de coco*, a fresh fruit ice bar of coconut, and another made of cantaloupe, and set off for Las Gatas.

Twenty-five years ago the deserted beach of my dreams, Las Gatas has since sprouted some half dozen *palapa* (thatch) seafood restaurants. Crowded and no longer pristine, this Polynesian-looking beach is nonetheless a captivating retreat. The swimming here is gentle for young ones, thanks to an underwater system of barriers built long ago by a Tarascan King to protect his baby princess during her daily swims—or so the story goes. Tiger sharks were kept out of Las Gatas for the sake of the princess, but Nicole likes to think of this haven as "Princess Beach."

Just before the last *panga* back to Zihuatanejo was scheduled to arrive, Alfonso's *Rebelde* appeared. We rode up the coastline toward Ixtapa, where we surveyed the new construction—a three-hundred-slip marina, new homes, a restaurant on the water. As we sped along, the warm sea air caressed our skin, but Nicole was crestfallen. Nora and Maritza had not come.

"Why don't you come home with me to visit them?" Alfonso asked. "But my house is *muy feo* (very ugly) for we are poor" he quickly added.

"*No importa*," we replied. It didn't matter.

We joined him in a taxi to the other side of town—the back side of the resort—a classic *barrio* with corrugated tin-roofed shacks, pigs and chickens in the streets, barefoot kids playing ball.

No one was home, so Alfonso dispatched a teenage boy on bicycle to fetch the family. Some fifteen minutes later, Alfonso's wife and three kids appeared in the distance, on the crest of a hill. Returning from a party, the girls wore pastel green and blue dresses. The moment they saw Nicole they ran downhill to greet her. Somehow that scene is etched in my memory, as if in slow motion—two olive-skinned beauties running to my child, their new friend, hair and dresses blowing in the balmy perfumed air, the sky aflame with sunset.

I watched Nicole happily at play, so at home with Nora and Maritza that she wanted to stay behind while I went off to dinner. It was then that I realized my love of travel was already alive and well in my daughter. No barrier would stand in the way of her coming to terms with the diverse world around her. I also understood then, with a slight ache in my heart, that this moment signaled the future—a lifetime of long-distance calls and letters from a globetrotting child whose very nearness I cherish.

Carol Canter is a writer who lives in Oakland, California. Ever since climbing to a mountaintop shrine in Japan's back country with baby Nicole on her back, she has found traveling with her daughter to be an enlightening experience.

If you're a single parent or married but traveling without your spouse, be prepared to prove that the other parent has given permission for the kids to travel with you. Your children will not be allowed into Mexico otherwise.

Married couples and divorced, separated, or never married couples on good terms can meet this restriction easily. The parent staying home simply visits a notary public and obtains a notarized letter stating that he or she agrees that it is okay for the children to travel to Mexico with the other parent.

Other single parents face more red tape, these requirements help prevent a disgruntled parent battling over custody from transporting children across the Mexican border to hide them from the other parent.

If you do not have sole legal custody of the children and cannot convince the other parent to provide a notarized statement, you will not be able to take the children into Mexico. However, if you do have full custody, you can present to authorities a copy of the custody papers.

If you have no contact with the other parent or have no idea where that parent is, you will need to go to court to obtain full legal custody. Another possibility is to have a notary public draft a letter declaring that you are the sole parent of the child and that you have no contact with the other parent. Finding such a notary public may prove difficult, though, because he or she must be willing to take that immense responsibility.

To provide letters okaying travel into Mexico, notary publics will need to see proof of identification for each family member—driver's license, passport, or birth certificate—plus a copy of the court document providing proof of child custody, if applicable. When traveling to and within Mexico, keep these same documents, as well as the notarized letter, handy. You will need to present them at the airport or at the border, and you may need to present them during your visit.

—Deborah Haeseler, "What Single Parents Need to Know," *Parents' Press*

DONALD G. SCHUELER

The World Tree and the Praying Girl

A vehicle breakdown in the bush leads to a moonlight discovery.

I spent a couple of days easing the van and myself over the stony back-roads around Ticul, touring the *casas grandes*—the *"haciendas"*—that once housed, at least for a few weeks each year, the owners of the region's *henequen* plantations. The oldest of the *haciendas*, with their long, cool galleries and Moorish arches, were stopovers for Stephens and his companions, Dr. Cabot and the artist Frederick Catherwood, on their journey from Mérida to Uxmal. At Mucuyche, I took a dip in the *cenote* where the men had bathed, and admired the fine Moorish gate where the doctor had shot a circling hawk "to the astonishment of the gaping natives." But most of the *haciendas* were of more recent vintage, impressive beaux arts villas with wide stairways and towering façades, built by nouveau riche *hacendados* during the great *henequen* boom at the turn of the century. Although two or three of these grand dwellings have been restored by private owners, and a few

> In the early 1840s John Lloyd Stephens, an American lawyer, wrote the best-selling *Incidents of Travel in Central America, Chiapas, and Yucatán* and *Incidents of Travel in Yucatán*, books still very much worth reading.
>
> —JO'R and LH

others are minimally maintained as schools by the *ejidos* that have replaced the old plantations, most are abandoned and in ruins. In their weedy courtyards I parked the van, then prowled their gutted interiors, meditating on the transitoriness of it all under the suspicious eyes of browsing goats. Even in their fallen state, these buildings could be dauntingly impressive—Ozymandian monuments to the vision and the vanity of the *hacendados* who built them.

Yet, imposing as they were, I finally decided that none of the ruins I visited in the vicinity of Ticul could quite match those of Uayamón, far to the south in Campeche.

No rain had fallen during my northward journey, so the window of my van's rebuilt hatch door still carried on its dusty surface three full sets of smeary handprints and two half sets. I had only to glance at them in my rear-view mirror to remember the excursion to Uayamón, and Anita and her family. And the strange little adventure that had befallen me when, alone, I had revisited the great *hacienda* by moonlight.

Actually, none of the prints on the glass were Anita's. The three complete sets belonged to her sister-in-law, Lupe's wife, and two young buxomly attractive nieces from Escárcega who were visiting her at the time. The half prints at the corners of the van were mine and her nephew Jorge's. Anita, who had problems with her back as well as her foot, had appointed herself rear guard, carrying the girls' white high-heeled shoes and emitting empathic little grunts and gasps as we pushed the van slowly onward.

We had been returning from the picnic excursion in my van, which I had just reclaimed from the mechanic's shop, when a light on the dash-board flashed on, warning us of what proved to be a slow leak in the oil tank. I, like a fool, hadn't stocked a reserve can of oil, so there was nothing for it but to stop and switch the engine off. The track we were traveling was barely wide enough to allow for the passage of a single vehicle, so if another car came along—which might happen five or six times in a day—it would have been effectively blocked.

I felt awful. Up until now, we had had a pleasant time of it, exploring the ruins of the *hacienda*, eating oranges and cookies on the weed-choked grand stairway, and taking each other's pictures in the gallery. And so, because the preceding hours had passed so agreeably, it seemed that much more a rotten shame that I should have stranded these good people in the middle of nowhere, with night coming on.

Wonderfully, however, Anita and her family had reacted to the situation with far more grace than I did. They treated the whole thing as something of a lark. The women, all in their white Sunday finery (except Anita, in blazing red), piled out of the van, took off their shoes, and, laughing and joking, joined Jorge and me in pushing the van forward along the stony track, while up front, short-legged Lupe both pushed and steered. By sheer luck, our strength had lasted long enough to get the van to one of the road's infrequent wide spots, where a byway led to a deserted *milpa*.

I decided not to take the chance of leaving the van unguarded through the night. Anita had fretted about *bandidos* and Jorge had offered to stay with me; but I eventually convinced them all that they must try to reach the paved road, a good two miles away, before darkness fell.

Lupe said that he and Jorge would return with a wrecker first thing in the morning. Then, with many waves and backward looks, they finally left me.

Which is how I got to see Uayamón by moonlight.

I had come ill-prepared for this misadventure. Normally, the van would have been adequately stocked with vodka, cigarettes, and Off!; but this was supposed to have been an afternoon's jaunt, not a camping-out. An orange, a roll of toilet paper, and three cigarettes remaining in the pack were the only necessities aboard. It was hot—impossible to shut the windows—and by midnight, what with a swarm of tormenting memories stirring in my mind, and bloodthirsty mosquitoes humming in my ears, I had had it. The way I was feeling, if *bandidos* wanted to steal the damned van they were welcome to it. Provisioned with the still-uneaten orange and my lone surviving cigarette, I headed back along the moonlit track to Uayamón, serenaded along the way by the voices of a million tree frogs.

In due course, I passed the landmarks we had driven by in blazing daylight, now appropriately spectral and bleached-looking, every moon-washed masonry plane a bluish white, everything else a bluish black. First came an impressive private railroad station set beside the narrow gauge tracks on which miniature trains once carried both freight and people, the only automated means of travel in this part of the Yucatán until not so long ago.

Beyond the tracks, barely visible in the heavy shadows of the trees that crowded in on them, were the shells of several stone and stucco outbuildings, not as large as *quintas*, but well proportioned and still handsome despite their gutted state. Anita had said that these were once the quarters of the "*esclavos*," the slaves. But she was surely wrong about that. Such substantial dwellings would have housed the *hacienda's* overseers and factory foremen. The Maya workers would have lived in stucco shanties and thatched

The next day, when I asked the bus driver to drop me off on the highway next to a sign that said TUZIK, 3KMS, he shrugged as if to say "It's your life," stopped the bus and let me down. After he'd disappeared over the horizon, I was left in silence. A fly flew by, making a nice demonstration of the Doppler effect. I looked around at the flat landscape. Not another sign of human habitation. A lizard scurried across the baking pavement. A collared aracari—a toucan—winged purposefully overhead. I remembered reading that certain birds acted as scouts for the *balambob*, the lords, the jaguar spirits of the forest, and wondered what *separado* gods were monitoring my approach.

—Peter Canby, *The Heart of The Sky: Travels Among the Maya*

chozas—as they still do. To me, for whom the preservation of fine old buildings seems almost as worthy a cause as the preservation of wildlife, it was a difficult thing to understand: how at Uayamón and most of the other *ejidos* that were once *haciendas*, the workers, who could have easily made the outbuildings if not the great houses themselves, comfortably habitable, had chosen not to do so.

That afternoon, when we overshot the overgrown side lane leading to the *hacienda*, we had inadvertently ended up at the hamlet where the *ejido* workers lived. It was mid-afternoon, and the settlement lay in a somnolent trance. It was a dreary-looking place, the small huts baking in the sun around a large communal square-*cum*-grazing ground. The only inhabitants in view were two short, brown, weathered-looking women, standing in the middle of the shadeless dusty square, wearing white cotton *huipiles* and brown *rebozos*. Anita had acknowledged their existence just sufficiently to ask directions to the *casa grande*. They had acknowledged hers just barely enough to point us back the way we had come.

It was weird, that minimal exchange, and the way everyone else in the van fell silent and kept their eyes averted from the *ejido* and its women, as though they were embarrassed by the sight of them. This was my first small experience, though it would hardly be my last, of a cultural separation that still exists in Mexico, not so much between Indians and *mestizos*, although there is enough of that too, as between the urban middle class and the rural workers. Actually, the distinction is a little more complicated than the obvious one between city mouse and country mouse. There are gradations, of course, as the studies of a number of social anthropologists have made painstakingly clear. But the basic demarcation is between those who feel at ease in the 20th century—that is, the modern technological world—and those who do not. In the United States, where even people who live on remote farms and ranches are, in effect, exurban residents of an urban high-tech world, this particular type of class apartheid has pretty much faded out. But in Mexico, where the impact of technology-and-all-that-goes-with-it is still a recent phenomenon concentrated largely in the cities, the effect has been the opposite: it has tended to intensify the traditional differences, especially marked in Hispanic countries, between cosmopolitan town and backward country. I doubt that those differences were consciously present in the thoughts of Anita and her family; but they were there. On this easy-going picnic afternoon, with a *norteamericano* in their company they just didn't want to be reminded that the place where we had dead-ended—these thatched hovels and these Indian women with their impassive faces—represented everything that they regarded as still benighted in their country. Not to mention, of course, everything from which they, thanks to Anita and Lupe's fierce Lebanese mother, had escaped.

They were glad to escape now. As soon as the *ejido* community was out of sight, everybody fell to talking and laughing at once. I too put the strained awkwardness of the moment out of my mind—until that midnight, when I retraced my way to Uayamón. Then I remembered the distancing, impersonal look the two Indian women had given Anita and the rest of us, denying us every bit as much as my friends had denied them, and it occurred to me that this habit of rejection, long ingrained in the conservative minds of rural people, might at least partly explain why the *ejido* workers refused to inhabit those roomy satellite dwellings at Uayamón much less the *casa grande* itself. They allowed the buildings to decay for the same reasons that they had allowed the jungle to dismantle the great palaces and temples of their own vanished priests and kings a thousand years ago: because these marvelous structures, which they had given their lives and labor to build, represented a state of civilized consciousness that had been systematically denied to them. Ancient and modern, the cultural trappings that had once set their masters' lives apart were still beyond reach of their aspirations or even their envy. Even derelict, the *hacienda* and all its trappings rejects the humble *campesinos*. They sense this, I think; they know they could never be at home where they were never welcome.

At Uayamón, however, there is one exception to the general state of not-so-benign neglect. During the afternoon visit, I had noticed that the chapel at the right side of the grand staircase was the one part of the *casa grande* that the people of the *ejido* had, after a fashion, maintained. The

Amidst the noise and fumes of Mexico City, there is a quiet square where the modern Foreign Ministry building and a sixteenth-century Spanish Colonial church look onto the remains of the pre-Hispanic pyramids of Tlatelolco. The government has named it the Plaza of Three Cultures to venerate Mexico's mixed-blood heritage, or *mestizaje*. In front of the church, a plaque carries these simple but moving words: "On August 13, 1521, heroically defended by Cuauhtémoc, Tlatelolco fell into the hands of Hernán Cortés. It was neither a triumph nor a defeat: it was the painful birth of the *mestizo* nation that is Mexico today."

Yet, the birth pains of the new *mestizo* race are not over. More than 460 years after the Conquest, neither the triumph of Cortés nor the defeat of Cuauhtémoc has been properly assimilated, and the repercussions of that bloody afternoon in Tlatelolco continue to be felt.

—Alan Riding, *Distant Neighbors: A Portrait of the Mexicans*

bell was missing from the small belfry arch, but the facing wall was freshly painted. The door was locked, but peering through the window grill,
we had been able to see most of the stark, shadowy interior. A plastic
crucifix and a faded picture of the *Cristo* in a brown wood frame hung
behind a simple altar table. There were a few chairs, and the floor had
been recently swept. The one cheery touch was a strand of gilded tinsel
wrapped around the iron frame of the ceiling lamp. Otherwise, the effect
of the place was to project the impression that if God dwelled here, He
was under house arrest.

I could understand the way a *campesino* might feel about Uayamón,
but there was no way I could share that feeling myself. Certainly not
now on this beautifully luminous night. The raised central building was a
chiaroscuro masterpiece of light and shadow: the three huge Palladian
arches and their supporting columns reflected the moon's reflected radiance as though they were its source; while behind them the gallery
hoarded darkness as a miser hoards gold. The wide, grassy quadrangle
below the central stairway was drenched in an almost phosphorescent
light. On one side it was flanked by the remains of the huge plantation
factory and storehouse, and on the other by a long, narrow building that
had perhaps been used as carriage house and stables. Their utilitarian
functions notwithstanding, these buildings had been ambitiously built to
conform to the grandiose effect of the *tout ensemble*. As I advanced from
the *entrada*, the details of their façades—archways, lintels, cornices,
steps—stood out in bold moonlit relief against the yawning openings
that had once been wide doors and windows. Only at the corner of the
quadrangle where the *casa grande* and the factory were almost joined was
this symmetrical etching of skeletal white on black interrupted by a total
darkness—the shadowy mass of a huge ceiba tree billowing upward into
the clear sky like a thunderhead.

Viewed from the near distance, the *hacienda* appeared to be spookily
deserted but intact, the very sort of place that some well-bred Hispanic
vampire might have chosen for a good day's sleep. But I knew from the
afternoon's explorations that there was no way he would have got one.
Uayamón was gutted: the sun had barged brutally through doorless
doorways wide enough to admit a sixteen-wheeler; through gaping holes
in the walls that sprouted gardens of ferns; through the shredded plaster
still clinging to ceilings twenty-five feet high.

I had fretted about all that while the sunlight was busily ransacking
the place. But now the decay seemed natural and inevitable. I fit into it
comfortably like a figure introduced into a Piranesi drawing to indicate

the scale. Moonlight and desolation were the perfect match for my present mood.

Even back when I had enjoyed a healthier frame of mind than any I had experienced lately, I had always been romantically susceptible to *Gone with the Wind* syndromes. As a small boy, I had fought back tears when Vivien Leigh had to eat raw turnips because the Yankees had looted Tara. In college I was the one who sympathized more with the *Cherry Orchard's* evicted aristocrats than with the old servant they absentmindedly left behind. And now, here I was, smoking my last cigarette on the rubble-strewn gallery of moonlit Uayamón in the middle of the froggy, bug-ridden night, getting into it again, bestowing on this lovely, lizard-haunted wreck, as might Prince Charming if he had kissed a really dead princess by mistake, an imagined but almost palpable sense of the decorous life it once harbored, the pleasant family gatherings, the house parties and fiestas, the flirtations and small domestic dramas that, according to Señor Sansores, had still been enacted here only fifteen or twenty years earlier.

I welcomed this hazy communion with a sadly but safely vanquished world. It was somehow comforting to indulge a painless nostalgia for the loss of something that had never been mine to lose.

So then: this was the otherwhere in which my mind was roaming when the girl materialized from out of the shadow of the ceiba tree. The ceiba was that something extra; the perfect prop

---

The names of the ancient trees are as important as their appearance. The hieroglyphic name of the bejeweled and bemirrored World Tree was *wakah-chan*. It was written with the number six prefixed to the phonetic sign *ah* and the glyph for "sky," because the sounds of *wak*, the word for "six," and *ah*, are homophonous with the word *wakah*, meaning "raised up." The name of the tree literally meant "raised up sky." The Classic texts at Palenque tell us that the central axis of the cosmos was called the "raised up sky" because First Father had raised it at the beginning of creation in order to separate the sky from the earth. Each World Tree was, therefore, a representation of the axis of creation.

—David Freidel, Linda Schele, Joy Parker,
Maya Cosmos: Three Thousand Years on the Shaman's Path

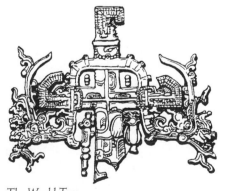

The World Tree as depicted on the sarcophagus lid of Lord Pakal

to set the scene. The tree was sacred to the ancient Maya—it was the central support holding up the world's sky-roof—and out here in the country, some of their descendants still believe it possesses magical properties. One such belief holds that it is the dwelling place of the x-*tabai*, a sort of Maya Lorelei who destroys unwary mortals. Anita, when we had passed under the tree that afternoon, had excitedly revived some of her half-forgotten childhood fears: "At Umán, when I was little, oh, I was afraid the—how you say?—witch? would come down from the branches at night and get hold of me." She had grabbed her elbows and hugged herself nervously. "I no like that! No sireee."

I, of course, was not afraid of the x-*tabai*. I knew perfectly well that there was a real girl down there. She was wearing a white dress and cradling something flat and silver-tinted in her arms. But her sudden appearance was so melodramatically improbable that, for as long as it took me to stop blinking my eyes and holding my breath, I couldn't help but wonder if she might be real to me the way the wife of an octogenarian friend of mine was real to him. The woman had been dead for almost ten years, but when he was in one of his fugue states, he still held the door for her whenever the three of us went out for a little walk.

By the time I had gotten over that sort of uncertainty, the girl—I was sure she was young, even though her face was shadowed—had come forward, moving toward the right side of the central stairway. There, the roof line of the chapel blocked my view, but I knew she had slipped inside it. I was surprised at how quickly she accomplished this. There was no rattling of a key, no sound of squeaking hinges. Evidently the door, locked that afternoon, had been unlatched by someone before she arrived.

I sat up there on the gallery for what seemed a long time—ten minutes, maybe—being careful to brush the mosquitoes away rather than slap at them. I bounced the still-unpeeled orange in my hand, and listened to the heartbroken, thrice-paired cry of the tinamou, a rather large but demure bird that I had never heard calling except at dawn or dusk. All the while, the curiosity that had killed the cat was killing me; and finally I gave into it. Helped by the brilliant moon, I picked my way down the steps, maneuvering them a good deal more quietly than I had on the way up. When I touched ground, I moved out a considerable way into the quadrangle, not wanting my shadow to fall across the open chapel doorway, then circled around to the large, grated window through which I had peeped that afternoon.

I'm not sure what I expected. An assignation? Or maybe some sort of secret rite? After all, ever since the days of Bishop Landa, Catholic authorities have been scolding Mexican Indians for not keeping their pagan superstitions and the true faith as separate as they should. As it turned out, the reality was somewhere in between an assignation of a sort, and a secret rite as well; but orthodox enough in its intense, off-hour way. The girl was kneeling on a white handkerchief she had spread on the tiled floor. Two large votive candles, of a sort commonly available in Mexican churches, burned on the altar. Also on the altar was a silver-tinted picture frame, faced toward the picture of Jesus on the wall above. The girl's face was tilted in the same direction. Jesus was calmly gesturing toward his bleeding, thorn-encircled heart, exposed against his breast as though an ancient Maya priest had had a go at it.

I assumed she must have come from the *ejido* settlement; but although I could see no more of her face than the left ear and an angled view of her cheek and chin, she didn't seem the type of a *campesino's* child. She was very slender, long-necked, and, as best I could judge, fairly tall; and her hair, under a small, lacy, white cap, was short and waved, maybe even permed.

Whoever she was, there could be no doubt about the intensity of her devotions. Her attention was absolutely fixed on the picture of Christ. Her hands, hanging limply at her sides rather than lifted in prayer, suggested, not laxity or just plain tiredness, but a touching defenselessness; as though to signify that she were quite at the Savior's mercy.

It was this vulnerability, not meant for me to see, that made me realize I was doing something wrong. Until I reached the chapel window, it had seemed a natural-enough impulse to want to know what the girl was up to; and it had been exciting and suspenseful, sneaking up on her as I had done. But now I felt guiltily conscious of being an emotional voyeur, spying on someone who had innocently bared her heart just as Jesus had bared his. Chastened, I made haste to slink away; but before I did, acting on some obscure, propitiatory impulse, I left the orange on the windowsill—although I knew she would almost certainly not notice it.

I passed under the ceiba tree and then kept close to the walls of the old factory until I was clear of the quadrangle. At the *entrada*, I broke into a run, and kept on running until I reached the van.

For what was left of the night I slept soundly, awakening only when the wrecker showed up soon after first light, with Lupe and Jorge aboard. Even before it came to a full stop they had jumped out, grinning, the one waving a thermos of coffee, the other a pack of cigarettes.

Occasionally I still think about the girl. I hadn't needed to see the face in the turned-away photo to guess what she was praying for. The problem must certainly have been serious to warrant the absolute privacy of that late-night rendezvous with Jesus. Perhaps the fellow didn't love her as she did him, or maybe the parents were objecting to the match. But whatever the obstacle, I want to believe that Jesus of the Bleeding Heart answered her prayer. How could he not? How could he not have been charmed and touched, and perhaps a little amused, by someone who had brought him her beloved's picture just to make sure there wouldn't be any mix-ups when he granted her her wish?

Donald G. Schueler also contributed "Temple of the Jaguar" in Part I and "Roberto and the Permanent Revolution" in Part IV. These stories are from his book, The Temple of the Jaguar: Travels in the Yucatán.

At its best and worst, Mexico is tolerant. Spanish Catholicism bequeathed to Mexico an assumption of Original Sin. Much in life is failure or compromise. The knowledge has left Mexico patient as a desert, and tolerant of corruptions that have played upon her surface. Public officials tread a path to corruption, just as men need their whores. *No importa.* Mexico manages to live.

The intimate life, the family life—abundant and eternal—is Mexico's consolation against the knowledge of sin.

—Richard Rodriguez, *Days of Obligation: An Argument with My Mexican Father*

PETER CANBY

Lost in the Lacandón Jungle

The author joins a scientific expedition into the Lacandón rain forest, where he quickly discovers that the jungle has a mind of its own.

Twilight arrived around five o'clock, and soon thereafter the birds and insects began their crepuscular rounds. Overhead an oropendola, a huge oriole-like bird, began to sing, its trill sounding like water dripping into a pool from a great height. Archie slapped a mosquito, examined it, and announced that it was from the genus *Anopheles*, which carries malaria.

A light rain began to fall. I pulled the plastic over my mosquito net and, exhausted, got into my hammock. I dozed off while listening to the popping sound made by huge drops of water falling onto the jungle leaves. An hour or two later, however, I suddenly awoke to the sound of a large animal prowling in the underbrush. It was closest to Pancho and Elías who, having refused hammocks, had built themselves a bed of palm fronds and draped their sheet of plastic over it. I heard them talking nervously among themselves. Suddenly, they switched on their flashlight. The animal, whatever it was, froze.

"Nacho," Elías called out in a nervous voice, *"aquí los tigres no comen la gente, verdad?"* "The jaguars around here don't eat people, right?"

Nacho got out of his hammock and swept the forest edge with his flashlight. Nothing. Five minutes later, after we were all back in our hammocks, the creature got up, a mere ten or fifteen yards away, and ambled off into the forest.

From the size of the animal and the way it moved, the consensus was that it had been a jaguar. I lay back in my hammock and thought about these large cats. Once found from Argentina

Expedition members include José Luis Patjane, a surgeon; Ignacio "Nacho" March, a wildlife biologist and expedition organizer; Archie Carr III of the New York Zoological Society; and Tom Ensign, a video cameraman from Bellingham, Washington. Perhaps the expedition's most important member K'in Bor, a Lancondón Maya with an intimate knowledge of the rain forest, had to pull out at the last minute, leaving the group without a guide.

—JO'R and LH

to Arizona, jaguars are the largest cats in the world after lions and tigers. Although in the Lacandón they seldom exceed 120 pounds, in parts of the Amazon they grow to 300 pounds and almost six feet in length. Their curiosity is legendary, and they are said frequently to follow people in the jungle without the humans' knowing it. In his book *Los Mamíferos de Chiapas* (*The Mammals of Chiapas*), Miguel Alvarez del Toro, the dean of Chiapas mammologists, describes being awakened in his hammock one night by the sensation of hot air blowing across his face. He opened his eyes to see a jaguar peering at him through his mosquito net. With this strange image in mind, I fell back to sleep.

The next morning we set out east in search of the elusive Río San Pedro. After we'd walked for an hour or two, Nacho stopped and examined some hoofed tracks.

"Collared peccaries," he said, referring to a species of native American wild pig.

I knew that Nacho was doing his master's research on peccaries, and I asked if these were the pigs he was studying.

"No, they're not," he answered. "There are two kinds of peccaries in the Lacandón: collared and white-lipped. I'm studying the white-lipped."

"How are they different?"

"The collared peccary is a small, adaptive animal that lives in a wide variety of habitats from Arizona all the way down through South America. The white-lipped is something else. The white-lipped grow to as much as a hundred pounds and have sharp tusks. They travel in herds of up to several hundred and only live in the deep forest. It's rare to see a herd, but they can be extremely dangerous. If we come across one, make for the nearest tree."

"Both collared and white-lipped peccaries are members of the old family Tayassuidae," Archie added. "They split off from the Old World pigs some twenty million years ago, after one of their ancestors trotted across the Bering Strait. It's an interesting case of parallel evolution. Up until the Pleistocene, the period of the ice ages, there were a half-dozen peccary species knocking around the New World, including a long-legged peccary. But the Pleistocene was

white-lipped peccary

304

a tumultuous period during which a large number of North American mammals—including the New World elephants, New World horses, and the saber-toothed tiger—became extinct. The Pleistocene winnowed out the peccaries until only the present species survived."

"What are the differences between the Old World pigs and the peccaries?" I wondered.

"There are morphological differences," Archie said, "such as scent glands and the ridge of coarse hair that bristles off peccaries' backs, but there are also behavioral differences, most notably, in the case of the white-lippeds, herding behavior."

Was the white-lipped peccary the so-called *jabalí*, the wild boar of Central American forests?

"*Jabalí* is the term used in Spain for the Old World wild boar," Nacho answered. "People use the word *jabalí* for white-lipped peccaries for the same reason that they use the Spanish words *tigre* for jaguar and *león* for puma. The Spanish saw everything in terms of their own experience. I prefer the word *peccary* to the word *jabalí*. The word *peccary* is derived from a Carib Indian word."

Nacho's point made me think of how jarring to the Spanish was the intellectual shock caused by the flora and fauna of the New World. The Bible was the source of most European knowledge of the natural world in the 15th and 16th centuries. In *The Colombian Exchange*, Alfred Crosby observes that the Bible explained "the heavens, earth, angels, plants, animals, and men." Most particularly, the Bible told the story of the Flood and of Noah's Ark, on which, Europeans believed, the breeding stock for all animal life had been preserved. That was fine for Europe and for limited parts of Asia and Africa known to Europeans. They contained a limited number of species. But how to explain the myriad creatures of the New World? How to explain iguanas, anteaters, jaguars, tapirs, and tree sloths—creatures that, says Crosby, by their very existence "called into question the entire Christian cosmogony"?

On a practical level, the Spanish got around this problem by simply treating the New World as a religious renegade. The Spanish crown equipped the conquistadors with a document that they were legally obliged to read to the Indians before engaging them in battle. The document, the *requerimiento*, reiterated the Bible-based view of creation and erected on it a legal and logical superstructure that essentially glossed over the huge differences between the Old and New Worlds. It began (as translated by William Gates in his 1937 edition of Landa's *Relación de las Cosas de Yucatán*):

God, our Lord, One and Eternal, created heaven and earth, and a man and a woman, from whom you and I, and all the people of the world, were and are descendants. But because of the multitude thus begotten out of them in the past five thousand and more years since the world was created, it was necessary that some should go to one place and others to another, and divide into many kingdoms and provinces, since in one alone they could not sustain themselves...

The *requerimiento* reminded the Indians that God had made Saint Peter "lord and superior of all the people in the world," and threatened to destroy them if they did not submit to the "Catholic kings of Castile." The point of this document, which was addressed to Indians but might as well have been addressed to the whole of New World life, was a stated refusal to understand, a public reiteration of the biblical explanation of creation in the face of a teeming strangeness that it could not explain. On some functional, administrative level the *requerimiento* must have proved satisfactory. It is always easier to deny than to understand. But on a more profound level, it did no more than paper over the gaping hole that the discovery of the New World had torn in the European world view. Unable to reconcile the fauna of the New World with the Biblical stories of Noah's preservation of all life, subsequent European theologians were forced to postulate all sorts of heretical theories of multiple creations, which, as Crosby points out, were not fully ironed out until Darwin's time.

Around midday we reached the river again. It was now about fifteen yards wide and a beautiful, clear shade of green. Fish two feet long were cruising its submerged sandbars.

"At least here we have fishes and water," said Nacho in charmingly fractured English. "We won't die, and that is important."

That night we camped on a bluff above the river. While we were sitting around after dinner, Elías suddenly asked if there were *duendes* in the United States.

"Of course there aren't," answered Nacho impatiently.

"A friend of mine saw one on a sandbank along the Lacantún," Elías observed.

Pancho nodded in grave agreement.

I asked what a *duende* was.

"The *duende* is something you hear about throughout Mesoamerica," Archie answered. "He's a little bearded man with his feet on backwards who travels with peccary herds. What happens is that someone goes out hunting peccaries and doesn't come back. His friends go out looking for him and find him wandering aimlessly in the forest. He's been enchanted by a *duende*. He's lost all sense of time and space."

I thought about *duendes* and this association with peccaries. Nacho had already told me that white-lipped peccaries only live in large unbroken tracts of tropical forest; and to me this made the white-lipped peccaries seem like something the Germans might call a *Waldgeist*, a "forest spirit." Alvarez del Toro claims that when peccary herds accidentally stumble out of the forest—into a ranch, for instance, they become disoriented and confused. Inside the forest, by contrast, white-lippeds have a system of trails that connect their favorite eating grounds and a strict order of travel: young and middle-aged pigs in front, females with sucklings in the middle, the best males and females next, and finally the oldest pigs. The peccaries even use mudbaths in hierarchical sequence, and there are persistent, although probably apocryphal, stories of a reddish-colored peccary leader. There was something beguiling in all this, the hint of a seductive, parallel, *duende*-ruled world that might tempt you to forget your own.

I looked over at Pancho and Elías. Their fears hadn't been eased by Nacho's scoffing. For the first time I noticed that they were more nervous about our situation than we were.

The next day, afraid to stray too far from the river, we hacked our way through reeds, vines, and what looked like lush walls of house plants. By the end of the day, exhausted, we stumbled to a halt under a huge straight-as-an-arrow mahogany rising directly from the river bank. As we were making camp, the sky darkened and thunder began to roll. No sooner had we tied down our plastics than the wind gusted violently. Suddenly we heard a loud tipping of branches and tearing of vines, and then an earth-shaking crash as a tree hit the earth on the other side of the ridge we had just crossed. A moment later, another tree smashed to the ground just out of sight across the river.

I looked apprehensively at the mahogany above us, but there really wasn't anywhere to go.

"It's going to be a long night," I said.

"Why?" Nacho said. "This is nothing."

Just then the wind gusted and there was a loud crack overhead. I jumped under a small tree, my hands over my head. Nacho landed on top of me. A log-sized branch fell just where we'd been sitting.

"I'm going to get rid of that guy up there," Nacho said. "I told him to drop it directly on the fire."

We took the next day off. In the morning I lay listening to the roaring of a group of howler monkeys in some nearby trees and thinking of

It was at Yaxchilan that I had my introduction to howler monkeys. My companions had warned me of these monkeys' eerie nighttime howls, but the first time I woke up to the sound my flesh crawled nonetheless. Actually, "howler" doesn't do them justice—it's more like an amplified Darth Vader roar, raspy and threatening, followed by staccato grunts. The first night at Yaxchilan, I lay wide awake in my tent, rationalizing that the reason they sounded so close was because they had to pass our tents to get from the forest to the river.

—Joyce Gregory, "In Search
of the Lacandón Maya"

how strange it was to be in the middle of the rain forest. Although we kept ourselves busy, we could all feel the looming presence of the forest around us. It was not entirely comforting. Two days of slashing through thorns and vines had left me with the sensation that the forest was resisting our entry. We were bulling our way in, and already the forest had exacted a price. We'd lost our sense of distance. End-of-the-day debates over how far we'd traveled elicited wildly varying estimates. Although we knew we were still on the San Pedro, only two days out we no longer knew where.

As the howlers swung off through the tree tops, two scarlet macaws took over, squabbling raucously overhead while an invisible toucan croaked away across the river. When a large and very noisy crested currasow flew to a branch over the water and began to cluck incessantly, I decided it was time to get up.

José Luis was already in the river taking his morning bath. Suddenly, he let out a shout. He was surrounded by a school of minnows and one of them had bit him on what the Mexicans call the *huevos*. Archie, who has a doctorate in tropical aquatic ecology, ambled to the riverside, peered at the little fish, and pronounced them tiny relatives of the piranha.

"In Costa Rica they get big enough to eat the ticks off cattle. Ranchers drive their herds into the streams so that the fish will clean them off," he said.

Archie spotted one of the larger fish that we had seen cruising the sandbars the day before.

"*Brycon guatemalensis*," he said, "commonly known as the *macabíl*. It's a fish that subsists on the fruit and flowers that fall from the trees."

We decided to go fishing. We had hooks and line and, after breakfast, scattered into the forest in search of reed poles. When Nacho returned, however, he was carrying not a pole but a basketball-sized termite nest.

"This is the way the Lacandóns fish," he said. "They break up termite nests and throw pieces into the river. It whets the fishes' appetites."

But since the *macabíles* seemed to be the largest fish in the river, we took Archie's suggestion and baited our hooks with dried fruit. I began with a dried apple. It attracted no interest. I switched to an apricot, which attracted only slightly more. However, the prunes worked like a charm, and soon we had a string of a dozen fish, the largest of which we made into a soup. As I sat eating, a *macabíl* head loomed up out of my bowl. Archie noted its heavy rounded teeth, which he said were designed to crack open seeds and nuts. Taking my cue from the New England taste for cod tongues and cheeks, I pried off its powerful jaw muscles and ate them. They were delicious.

The land finally began to rise after we left camp the next day, our fourth under way, and despite the constant recurrence of vines and *jimbales*, we began to get patches of respectable high jungle. Tracks ran everywhere, including the three-toed, dessert-plate-sized tracks of the tapir. We hadn't seen much wildlife, however—not many mammals anyway, a scarcity that Nacho attributed to the fact that in the rain forest ninety percent of mammals are nocturnal.

Still fascinated by white-lipped peccaries, I asked Nacho if they, too, were nocturnal.

"They're both diurnal and nocturnal," he responded. "They follow their own schedule."

White-lipped peccaries have few enemies beyond jaguars and man— and because a peccary herd is so dangerous, even jaguars are leery of them. Alvarez del Toro reports that a jaguar takes a peccary by shadowing the herd until it can pick off a straggler. It then leaps into a tree with its prey. The peccaries respond by going into a frenzy, surrounding the tree and attacking and destroying anything they can find, including, sometimes, each other. The jaguar typically waits them out in the tree, although this can take a day or longer.

Nacho suddenly froze at the bottom of a muddy brook. The ground was covered with fresh peccary tracks.

"I smell peccaries," he said.

I didn't smell a thing. I assumed that Nacho was putting me on. But as I listened, I began to hear a peculiar scuffling and snapping in the distance. We put down our packs and crept to the top of a ridge in front of us. From the ridge top the scuffling mixed with a low grunting and a knocking that sounded like the wooden percussion blocks in an orchestra.

"Those're their tusks clacking against their molars," Nacho said. "It's a big herd, white-lippeds, and they're headed our way."

Thanks to the thick underbrush, the peccary herd was still invisible, but the sounds emanated from a wide arc of jungle directly in front of us. We decided to split up and approach the herd from its two flanks. Archie, José Luis, and Elías went one way, Nacho, Pancho, and I, the other. So eager were we to see the pigs that we abandoned Tom, fumbling, trying to get his video camera unsheathed.

As we split up, Nacho reminded us to keep a tree in mind in case the pigs charged.

We crept forward until we could make out a few of the peccaries rooting around on the forest floor. They were broad-shouldered, torpedo-shaped creatures. Their snouts were pink, their noses white, and the rest of their bodies black. A line of spiny bristles stood in a ridge along their backs. No sooner did we catch sight of the peccaries, however, than the peccaries caught sight of us. Pancho, Nacho, and I scrambled into the lower branches of our chosen trees, but when the pigs edged nervously away, we climbed down and followed. Just then the peccaries noticed Archie and his group, did a mass about-face, and stampeded back toward us. The forest reverberated with hoofbeats and tearing shrubbery. I looked around. The tree I had just descended was ten yards behind me. The next one I'd been aiming at was at least five yards ahead—in the direction of the charging peccaries. Out of the corner of my eye I spotted a closer tree, its trunk about a foot in diameter at the butt. It was wound with a thick vine, and its top was obscured by the foliage above. Not a very big tree, but not having a lot of choice or time, I leapt for it anyway. No sooner had I gotten a few feet off the ground than the whole tree crumbled. I collapsed in a heap on the forest floor, dead branches showering all around me. Fortunately for me, the noise was tremendous. In the end, the peccaries may have been more frightened than I was. They'd surely seen a lot of strange creatures in their lives—jaguars, snakes, caimans, God-knows-what-else—but I doubt they'd ever seen a gringo journalist fall out of a rotten tree. For a moment longer the forest was filled with a confused thrashing and crashing. Then they were gone.

I picked myself up off the ground. Nacho came over, eyes glowing.

"That's an orgasm for me," he said.

"How many do you think there were?" I asked.

"At least eighty."

"Have you seen a herd like it before?"

"To see a herd of white-lipped peccaries is a very rare occurrence," he said, still beaming. "I've seen only one other herd in my life, near Bonampak, and it was only half the size of this one."

The pigs left a powerful musty odor behind them, like too many people locked in a small room. Nacho offered a granola bar—a considerable bribe, given our stores of food—to anyone who could find peccary scat for his studies. The only thing we turned up, though, was a freshly killed, scoured-out armadillo carcass.

"A jaguar or a puma probably got it last night," Nacho said.

When we turned to pick up our packs, I realized that in the process of pursuing the peccaries, I had completely lost my sense of direction. I clutched instinctively at the compass around my neck, but quickly realized that it was useless. The compass could tell me which way was north, but not how to get back to the gear. I was seized with an irrational panic. The forest had already robbed us of our ability to gauge distance. Now it was threatening our sense of direction as well. I looked at the wall of uniform green around me and thought of the twin components of our navigation—the compass and the river valley—realizing what a flimsy construct they were. As I did so, I had a vision of a *duende*, his feet on backward, galloping away.

The river had remained our touchstone. Every day we cut away in search of high ground and every night we returned to it. As long as it was there, we knew we were headed in the right direction. Two nights after we saw the peccaries, we returned to the river only to find that it had fragmented into a half-dozen streams of similar size wandering in a westerly direction across a swampy plain. Our maps were no help. They showed the San Pedro as a single channel all the way to its source near Indio Pedro. We had a choice of either following our compasses in the northwesterly direction we knew we wanted to follow, or staying with what we hoped was the main channel of the river. Since we did not really know where we were on the map, a compass course seemed the riskier of the two choices. We chose the river.

But following the now-braided river valley meant contending with more swamp, so we decided, at Archie's suggestion, to speed our progress by dividing into two leap-frogging groups of three machetes each. Tom was granted dispensation in order to continue taping. While one group cut, the other rested, then carried their packs to the trail head and took over the cutting.

I worked with Archie and Elías. Our machetes rang, each with its own tone, and as Archie cut he sang the song of the Jabberwock:

'Twas brillig, and the slithy toves
Did gyre and gimble in the wabe;
All mimsy were the borogoves,
And the mome raths outgrabe.

"Beware the Jabberwock, my son!
The jaws that bite, the claws that catch!
Beware the Jubjub bird, and shun
The frumious Bandersnatch!"

Elías listened, uncomprehending, to the extraordinary cadences. When Archie had completed the rest of the poem, Elías paused for a minute and then said, *"Archie está alegre. Alegre en su corazón.* Archie is happy. Happy in his heart."

The swamp seemed to guide us backward into the heart of the forest. Woven spiders' nests spiraled irresistibly inward to the dark underside of rotting logs. A group of angry red army ants were looting the larvae out of a wasp's nest. A humming that sounded like an electrical generating plant in the distance originated from a bees' nest. Around midday we came upon a troop of spider monkeys in the top of a huge tree supported by dinosaur-fin buttresses. A group of four adults, two carrying babies, and one adolescent, they chattered and screamed, shook branches, and threw sticks.

"Oh, estan muy bravos, muy enojados," Elías said. "They're very brave, very angry."

New World monkeys are considered remarkable for their uniformity, at least when compared to the monkeys of Africa, motherland of primates. Primatologists think that all New World monkeys are probably descended from a small population of African monkeys who migrated to South America during the Eocene, forty or fifty million years ago, perhaps on a floating island. They believe this to be the case both because the fossil ancestors of South American monkeys are strikingly similar to then contemporary African species, and because South America, which originally calved off from Africa, was then much closer to Africa than to North America. If African monkeys did cross into a monkeyless New World during the Eocene, it might have been their last chance to get aboard. The two continents continued to drift apart for tens of millions of years thereafter, until South America finally arrived at its present proximity to North America. During all this period, South America developed on its own, in biological isolation from the rest of the world, including North America. Such creatures as tree sloths, armadillos, and the true anteaters existed in South America and nowhere else.

Although made and broken several times earlier, the present land bridge between North and South America was made some three million years ago, and an exchange of species began that continues to the present day. Not only the monkeys but many other animals as well worked their way northward into the unbroken belt of tropical forest that once covered the Lacandón, the Petén, and the southern Yucatán peninsula. Among the most successful of the northward-bound South American migrants was the porcupine, which made it all the way to the Arctic.

A short while after we left the spider monkeys, Archie came across some fresh tapir tracks and, next to them, a pile of dung that looked just as if it had come off the stable floor. I remarked on the similarity to horse manure.

"That's because the horse and the tapir are closely related," Archie said. "In the fossil record, the horse was a tiny three-toed creature that browsed, like the tapir, on leaves. As it evolved, two of its toes shrank and the third enlarged into the hoof."

Of all the animals we might have come across in the forest, I most wanted to see a tapir, although I knew it was unlikely because the tapir is notoriously shy. A tailless, thick-skinned animal that grows to six hundred pounds, the tapir—at least Baird's tapir of Central and South America—is nearly amphibious. When threatened, it makes directly for water. Alvarez del Toro says it sometimes sleeps there, with only its long nose visible above the surface. Up until the period of Pleistocene extinctions, the tapir was widely distributed in the tropics, but now only three species survive, three in Central and South America and one in Malaysia. Because its habitat is disappearing so quickly, Baird's tapir is an endangered species.

When we caught up with Nacho and his crew, he told us that they were sure they had heard a tapir crashing off into the underbrush, although they hadn't actually seen it.

"The Lacandóns call the tapir *caxir tzimin*," Nacho said, "which means jungle horse. They believe that tapirs were the horses of the ancient Maya and that the ancient Maya kept them tethered by their tails. The ancient world came to an end when Kisin, the Earthlord, created a terrible earthquake. The tapirs were so frightened that they ran off without their tails."

Struck by all the strange creatures we were now encountering, I asked Nacho what he felt was distinctive about the fauna of the Lacandón.

"We don't know enough about it to say," he answered. "But it seems clear that the Lacandón is a place of Pleistocene refuge."

"Pleistocene refuge?"

"During the lowering of global temperatures that accompanied the ice ages, the tropical flora and fauna that until then had been found across wide sections of the globe survived in only relatively small pockets. This means that in places such as the Lacandón ancient species have survived that are extinct elsewhere."

As I picked up my machete and prepared to cut off into the swamp, I tried to imagine what this meant in terms of the forest we were traveling through. For one thing, I knew it meant that the process of evolution, broken in the temperature latitudes by the ice ages, had continued unabated in rain forests. In that sense places like the Lacandón serve as repositories of the accumulated possibilities of life on earth. Since climate change—perhaps even radical climate change—is a given in the future, the ability of the earth to make the necessary adjustments might well depend on the degree of preservation of its biological heritage. It struck me that the ignorance which has allowed the destruction of the forests is not significantly different from the ignorance epitomized in the Spanish *requerimiento*. Just as the Spanish confused their own cosmogony with truth, so have we confused the needs of our industrial society with the needs of the earth itself.

There were times, sitting in the god-house at Nahá, when I could almost touch the frail thread that intertwines all living things in the forest, from the lowliest bed-louse to the noble jaguar. In the wake of these glimpses I began to understand how each synthetic object we admit into our lives nullifies a bit of our souls, and removes by that much our purchase in the natural order. In Nahá I saw this process at work in K'in Bor, K'in Garcia and Young Mateo. The weight of their freedom—however diminished—is becoming too great for them, and so they erect barricades of plastic gadgets that symbolize their passage from one way of life into another, and further their apprenticeship in the occidental laws of supply and demand.

—Victor Perera and Robert D. Bruce,
The Last Lords of Palenque: The Lacandón Maya of the Mexican Rain Forest

For three days we wandered across the swamp, until the river channel we were following had shrunk to a small, meandering stream. At that point we gave up on it and decided to cut north across the braided river system until we hit either the main river or the rising ground that would indicate the eastern edge of the valley that held Indio Pedro. At the end of the day we finally located high ground consistent with the valley edge we'd been looking for. Although we weren't sure how we would find Indio Pedro, we hoped that in the next day or two we'd come across some sign of human habitation that would lead us there.

That night, exhausted, we camped between the swamp and the unexplored ridge above us, right on top of what looked like a game trail. Nacho had some sections of vine strapped to the back of his pack. He chopped them up and brewed them in water to make cups of reddish, slightly sweet tea. After dinner, owls hooted and whistled. José Luis recognized one that he said subsisted on fruit bats. Just after darkness had fallen and we got into our hammocks it rained briefly and thereafter the forest was filled with the popping of raindrops and a mysterious snapping of twigs.

Around nine, Archie was up pointing his flashlight into a tree. Some creatures were making what sounded like loud Bronx cheers. Archie couldn't see them, but decided they were kinkajous. No sooner had he gotten back into his hammock than three or four coatimundis decided to raid the camp. Long-nosed, long-tailed members also of the raccoon family, they squealed and snarled for an hour, vociferous in their indignation at finding us blocking their path. After they finally left, I heard the low grunting of a herd of white-lipped peccaries passing in the distance.

At three I woke to the sense of a very large creature passing fifteen yards from my hammock. It was moving like a tank, brushing aside large branches and snapping small logs underfoot. Inside my hammock, inside my mummy bag, I felt like a trussed chicken in a rotisserie. My mouth went dry and my palms grew wet. Reason flew out the window. If this was a jaguar, I was cooked. I grabbed my flashlight, groped for the edge of my plastic canopy, and pointed the beam in the direction of the noise. The light from the flashlight's little AA batteries barely dented the night, nor did it frighten off whatever beast it was, which continued on its cumbersome way. I saw Elías and Pancho's light go on. It was some consolation to know that no matter how spooked I was, they were spooked a hundred times over. I called out, asking if they'd heard the animal. Pancho answered that they had.

Pancho's English had been coming along nicely. He had begun to speak in memorized sentences rendered in cadences not unlike those used by automated directory assistance telephone operators.

"Peter," he called out.
"What?" I answered.
"Be careful," he warned.

The rising ground put us in good spirits, and we spent the next day in relatively open terrain, alert for signs of Indio Pedro. On our second day, however, the drainage of the irregular ridge we were following suddenly reversed. Instead of running west toward where we imagined Indio Pedro to be, the streams we passed were running east. The answer to this puzzle became apparent toward the end of the day, when we came down off the ridge, traversed a dense swamp, and emerged, blinking like pupfish, on the banks of a wide river. The water was clear and quiet, the banks lush and draped with heavy fruit-bearing foliage. Parrots whistled and squawked from high trees. We made camp, set aside thoughts of caimans, and swam. Afterward we worked on a theory to explain the anomalous river. We decided we'd overshot Indio Pedro and had traveled both farther north and farther east than we'd imagined. This was the Lacanjá, the next river east of the San Pedro. There was nothing else of its size. It flowed down from the Lacandón village of the same name. Lacanjá, Nacho told us, meant "serpent water" in Lacandón Maya.

After the initial elation, however, I began to wonder. The river was so wide and so beautiful

---

Once more I am in the spell of the story-teller, as Chan K'in's eyes range over ours, drawing us in. Freed of my note-taking compulsion, at least for now, I become absorbed in the puppet-play of his hands, in the rising and falling of his voice as his tale unwinds between heaven and earth. I catch only a few words, but his voice carries me back to the beginning, to the dawn of jaguars and men:

A Lacandón farmer becomes so enraged at the animals that keep raiding his *milpa* he finally lights incense to Akinchob, the god of maize and protector of farmers, and asks to be changed into a jaguar, so he can chase the animals off. But when Akinchob accedes to his request, the farmer/jaguar sees the animals as his kin, and instead of eating or chasing them off, he takes pity on them. "You poor people," he says. "You must all be hungry. Come in, come in. I have plenty to eat in my *milpa*. I am just lying in wait for some damn animals that have been stealing my corn so I can eat them."

"Of course," explains Chan K'in, "the farmer did not realize that he was now an animal himself, and that other animals looked like his companions, whereas humans would now look like animals and he would have eaten them."

—Victor Perera and Robert D. Bruce, *The Last Lords of Palenque: The Lacandón Maya of the Mexican Rain Forest*

that it seemed as if there should have been someone on it. I half expected to see a dugout canoe filled with happy Lacandóns come around the
bend and lead us out of the jungle. Having formulated the thought, I
realized that what was really bothering me was the feeling that we had
all agreed too readily on our location. Perhaps it was easier to do that
than to admit that we didn't really know where we were. I took stock of
our situation. We were now ten days out, and although we were getting
low on staples ranging from sugar to cigarettes, we still had five days of
food left. Pancho and Elías were a problem, however. They'd not only
become convinced that we didn't know where we were going (a not
unreasonable conclusion), but they'd eaten their twelve days of lunches
within the first week. When I'd asked them why, Elías had answered that
they'd been dying of hunger.

"With you *gringos* it's different," he'd said. "You're used to not eating.
But we're accustomed to three good meals a day."

I had to laugh at this formulation. But we'd been breaking off bits of
our diminishing stock of granola bars ever since to share with them at
lunch.

I spent a tormented night. Sand flies small enough to get through
the mesh of my mosquito net feasted on me until dawn. When I got up,
complaining, Nacho looked up from his cup of coffee and blandly told
me that sand flies were the carriers of leishmaniasis, "chiclero's disease," a
protozoan infection that caused persistent face ulcers and, left untreated,
could lead to death through secondary infection.

Nacho was studying the map, revising our route. Directly across the
Lacanjá the map showed a long ridge, the Sierra Cojolita, which paral-
leled the river and eventually passed directly behind Bonampak. It
seemed clear that if we could stay in the narrow corridor between the
ridge and the river, it would be impossible to get lost. Bonampak, more-
over, was not far—although how far was a question, since we didn't
know where we were on the Lacanjá.

After breakfast we walked
upstream until we came to a
large tree that had fallen
most of the sixty or seventy
feet across the river. We covered the last six feet with a
pole-and-rope bridge and then
gingerly, with our packs unbuck-
led, in case we fell, traversed the
river. The far bank was covered

jaguar

with a mangrovelike swamp, which we cut through until the ground began to rise toward a ridge. Praying silently that this was, in fact, the Sierra Cojolita, we turned northwest.

The ridge was a welcome change. Not only were its slopes open, but the summit consisted of a remarkable uplifted band of stone that ran 320 degrees northwest—our revised direction of travel—in a line straight enough to have come off an engineer's board. Five or six yards wide, this stone band arched over hilltops, dove under streams, and always reappeared on the other side. The most extraordinary thing about this ridge, however, was that it wasn't entirely natural. Although covered with leaf mold and broken by trees, we could easily see that it had been built up and that its edges had been squared off with cut stone. My sense that we'd arrived in an area that should have been populated hadn't been entirely misplaced. It had been populated—a thousand years ago. Somehow, we'd stumbled onto a *sacbe*, an ancient Maya road.

Discovering this road gave rise to conflicting emotions. On the one hand, we knew that we were in a sector of the jungle that had once been considered habitable, and that the road presumably led somewhere. On the other hand, where did it lead? To Bonampak? Or to the ruins of some undiscovered city where we would all starve to death among crumbling temples and broken *stelae*? Ultimately, as long as the road took us in the direction we thought we should be traveling, it didn't seem to matter. Like the trip itself, it was a gamble.

As we proceeded along the ridge, the contrast between the road and the surrounding wilderness made me think of the supposed incongruity of the Classic-era Maya having raised a civilization out of the rain forest. In Western European thought, civilizations are supposed to arise in the dry lands, preferably those of southwest Asia. According to the formula, rain forests are only suited to the crudest slash-and-burn agriculture. The academic logic has therefore been that *milpa* agriculture, the basis of the Maya civilization, is too simple a productive unit to have supported a superstructure of any sophistication.

Even setting aside the question of raised-field agriculture, it was clear to me that the idea of *milpa* agriculture as unsophisticated was based on ignorance. In his doctoral study of traditional Lacandón agriculture, the ecologist James Nations discovered that instead of simply burning a patch of jungle, planting corn for a few years, and then moving on—the cliché view of jungle farming—the Lacandóns took a much more complicated approach that both mimicked the ecological complexities of the surrounding forest and took advantage of the peculiar dynamics of forest disturbance. Immediately after burning, the Lacandóns protected the soil by planting root crops and fast-growing trees. Then they planted their corn. Rather than stopping with the corn, however, the Lacandóns proceeded to plant more than eighty different food and fiber crops in a sequence dictated by the flowering of natural species in the forest. In order to reduce the possibility of the spread of plant-specific diseases, these crops, which included beans, sweet potatoes, onions, pineapple, chili peppers, bananas, cotton, and tobacco, were grown in isolated bunches. They were also grown in layers, with plants at different levels above the soil and roots at different levels in the soil, thus creating ecological niches to which each plant was best suited. By the time the field was exhausted the trees had grown high enough to form what the Lacandóns call a *pak che kol*, a "planted tree garden," containing cacao, citrus, rubber and other trees, and shrubs; it would not only serve as an orchard but would also attract wild animals, thus making the recuperating *milpa* a source of game until it was ready for cutting and burning again.

The forest through which we were walking was at last the beautiful high jungle we'd been hoping for. On the second night after crossing the river, we camped next to a small stream that splashed down over a series of descending rim pools. Huge mahogany trees soared overhead, giving the jungle an open, airy quality. Along the stream banks we found two cacao trees, their yellow-green, grapefruit-sized fruit growing directly out of the trunk.

"*Cacao silvestre*, wild cacao," Nacho noted, "although it's not clear whether the cacao found in the Lacandón is native or introduced by the ancient Maya."

I watched as Pancho and Elías ate the pulp of a fallen pod, carefully spitting out the seeds, which contain the stimulant theobromine.

In the morning, after we left camp, we ran into another troop of spider monkeys. Again, they shrieked and threw branches at us, one of which narrowly missed Tom and his camera.

This raucous demonstration is the same that spider monkeys use to repel jaguars, their primary predators. But this behavior stands in stark contrast to the way the monkeys behave in the face of the still-more-menacing harpy eagle, the world's largest eagle. The harpy eagle is a canopy dweller that drops down on its prey from above. When the monkeys detect its presence they go stony silent, and their silence is understandable. With its double-crested head, huge hooked beak, and seven-and-a-half-foot wingspan, the harpy eagle is a primeval bird, a throwback to another era. The female is larger than the male, grows to twenty pounds, and can handle prey the size of a small deer.

Later that day, Archie, Elías, Tom and I were resting at the trail head when Pancho arrived and told us that Nacho and José Luis had unknowingly stepped over a fer-de-lance. The snake was a small one, about fourteen inches, coiled on the trail. This was unwelcome news, since we had to go back over the same section of the trail to retrieve our packs. Eyes glued to the ground, we walked until we reached the packs, then turned and started forward again. Archie lagged behind, however, and after we'd been walking for a few minutes, he stopped and yelled out that a fer-de-lance a foot long was in the trail right in front of him. Either we, too, had walked directly over the snake or it had been lurking by the trailside. As we walked on, a third possibility occurred to me. A six-foot female fer-de-lance gives birth to as many as sixty or seventy foot-long young. The young are potentially as toxic as the adults; if we had threaded our way through the aftermath of such a birthing, we'd been lucky. The action of a fer-de-lance's toxin is hemolytic, which means that it destroys red blood cells and breaks down the walls of the blood vessels. Victims die from massive internal bleeding. Although José Luis had serum in his kit, we couldn't count on its effectiveness.

That afternoon we camped by the side of a winding, fish-filled river. After we'd strung the hammocks, we sat down to discuss our situation. Our lunches were long gone, and after the next morning's breakfast, only one dinner and one breakfast would remain. In an attempt to explain our nonarrival at Bonampak, we'd been recalculating backward the point at which we'd crossed the Lacanjá. It was clear that this no longer made sense, and, although no one believed our navigational theories any longer, no one had better ideas to propose. Our maps were useless except for the increasingly futile exercise of trying to force the unruly landscape to correspond to map features. Basically, we were lost. Our only consolation was that we knew we'd been traveling in a consistent direction, a direction that we knew would eventually bring us out. When and where was another question. The jungle that had resisted our entry now seemed to be resisting our exit.

fer-de-lance

We discussed ways of surviving after the food ran out. Fishing seemed the best possibility, but we'd run out of dried fruit, and over the course of the preceding two weeks Pancho and Elías had lost seventeen of our twenty fish hooks.

Someone had the idea of converting a hammock to a fish net, and Nacho pointed out an evil-looking plant with a swollen root bulb and thorny vines that he said was *barbasco*, a plant used by the Lacandóns, and indeed by indigenous peoples throughout South America, to poison fish. Archie said that *barbasco* contained the same compound as rotenone, a commercial fish poison.

After our discussion ended, I lay back in my hammock. The afternoon was achingly beautiful. A tinamou whistled plaintively in the distance. A ray of light shone through a filigree of palm fronds over the camp and pierced the smoke of our fire before exploding in a pool of burning jade in a corner of the river. The uncanny beauty enhanced my perception of how much more dangerous the forest suddenly seemed. Earlier in the trip, when we thought we knew where we were, when we'd had plenty of food and plenty of time, the forest had been a strange and menacing presence, but still something on the periphery, something on the edge of our consciousness. Now it seemed both more powerful and more animate. I thought of the linguist Bill Hanks's "principle of verticality." The Maya, he said, didn't speak of walking "in" the forest, they spoke of walking "under" the forest. This was because they viewed the forest as a dangerous place, equivalent to being in the underworld. The sacred directions didn't exist in the forest. Therefore things weren't ordered, didn't have their place. As a result, humans were at the mercy of everything from snake bites to the ubiquitous and dangerous *balam* spirits. We were going to have to become a lot more observant, experience the forest on a different level, acknowledge its power. We'd be lucky if it let us go.

That night I slept as if I'd been drugged. I had a recurring dream that I was borne aloft in a bower of vines. It was supremely comfortable. All night long I felt myself falling backward into darkness.

After we set out in the morning, we found a marney tree. We gathered and ate its sweet, coral-colored fruit, then discarded the pits, although I'd read that they were famine food for the Lacandóns. The Lacandóns pound the pits into a paste, rinse it to get rid of its bitterness, and make the resulting dough into an oily tortilla.

We were still following the *sacbe*, as we had been for the last four or five days. It continued its northwesterly course, rising and falling with the terrain, until, late in the morning, it arrived at a small temple, fifteen feet square. The temple's sharp corners protruded from under a thin layer of leaves and soil. Everywhere, worked stone erupted from the jungle floor. Just where the temple appeared, however, the ridge ended, as did the *sacbe*.

In front of us rose a steep mountain, the largest we'd seen by far. For the first time on the trip, cicadas were singing. This mountain was definitely not on the map—at least not where we had located ourselves. We decided to climb it and see if we could get a view. If the river was still to our west, we might be able to get a glimpse of it. If there were more mountains to the west, we were lost.

It took an hour and a half of hard work to reach the summit. On the top, looking for a ridge from which we'd be able to see the surrounding land, I found a piece of snakeskin lying on a rock ledge. It was five feet long and clearly only a fraction of the snake that had shed it. Archie thought the skin was from a boa. I hoped it wasn't from a bushmaster, a snake that grows to twelve feet, the largest poisonous snake in the Americas.

The view, when we found it, was not encouraging. We were surrounded by mountains—although to our west, over a ridge or two, we thought we could make out a valley. Dissension, building for days, broke out. José Luis, normally taciturn, wanted to bolt north through the mountains in the hopes of reaching a road that we knew was somewhere in that direction. Pancho declared that although he trusted our compasses, he had no faith at all in our maps. He and Elías suggested that it was time for us to split up, for each to go on his own. Archie assured them that if they did this, they'd die. Eventually Nacho brought us around to his position: despite the intervening mountains, we should change our course from northwest to due west and try to reach the valley that we thought we could see in that direction.

It was Elías who spotted the cut sapling. Graying with age, its top had been sliced off with a machete. One cut sapling led to another, two cuts into three, and three into the faintest signs of a trail—the first we'd seen in fourteen days. Over the next ridge the trail became more distinct. Like a torrent gaining force, it pulled us down the mountain. Elías was in the lead. After twenty minutes he stopped and pointed to a young tree that had been cut off six feet above the ground.

"Now I know we're getting close to a settlement," he said. "These are the poles we use to make our roofs."

The path became wider, its shoulders sprouting with yellow flowers. We crossed a newly planted coffee grove, passed a banana tree, and finally arrived at a recently burned-over *milpa*. A child's dress hung forlornly from a scarecrow frame.

Elías reached down and picked up a piece of sugar cane. He chopped it with his machete and handed me a section. I peeled and began to chew. My mouth gradually filled with the fermented taste of raw cane sugar. It was delicious beyond anything I could imagine. I was struck with the mastery over plants that this farmer had demonstrated and felt something of the awe that hunting people throughout history must have felt for the powers of agriculturalists.

The path led us across a maze of streams bridged by fallen logs, and finally to the edge of a wide green pasture in which a dozen skinny horses were grazing. Two hundred yards away, a line of thatched huts crowned a ridge. Indian women in bright clothing emerged and stared, their hands nervously stroking their jaws. Beyond, a rooster crowed. We all sat down on the edge of the pasture, while Nacho went ahead to negotiate. I leaned back on my pack, felt the soft afternoon breezes waft over me, and marveled at a fat half-moon hanging low in the open blue sky.

Peter Canby also contributed "A Walking Witch" to Part I. Both stories were taken from his book, The Heart of the Sky: Travels Among the Maya.

In Mexico my father had the freedom of the doves. He summoned the dawn. Each morning at 5:30, my father would climb the forty steps of the church tower to pull the ropes that loosened the tongues of two fat bells. My father was the village orphan and it was his duty and his love and his mischief to wake the village, to watch it stir; the pious old ladies bending toward mass; the young men off to the fields; the eternal sea.

—Richard Rodriguez, *Days of Obligation: An Argument with My Mexican Father*

PART IV

In the Shadows

PETE HAMILL

Where the Air Was Clear

*Mexico City is one of the world's largest and most polluted cities,
but there is hope for the future.*

When I first came to Mexico City, I wanted to stay forever. The year
was 1956. I was 21, a student on the GI Bill, a half-formed product
of the tenements of Brooklyn. To be sure, I was not completely raw.
I'd grown up in the shadows of the towers of Manhattan; as a sailor, I'd
seen other American cities. But Mexico City was magical.

The magic of that time lives within me still. Say "Mexico City" to
me, and in memory I am walking into the cool morning in the clear, thin
air of the high mesa. The shopkeepers are hosing the sidewalks of the
Avenida Melchor Ocampo. The sky is a scrubbed blue. Trees rise high
above the street, green and lush as they take the first rays of the sun. I
turn a corner, and away off in the distance to the southeast I can see the
two great volcanoes, Popocatepetl and Iztaccihuatl. The light is brilliant.
My blood tingles. I whisper, Nothing will ever be this good again.

I was as wrong as all 21-year-olds are wrong, of course; the world is
full of good places and astonishing people. But this was true: Mexico
City was never as good again as it was that blessed year in the 1950s.

That year there were about 3.5 million people in the city the Aztecs
called Tenochtitlán ("Place of the Cactus"). The traffic was so light there
were no stop signs on the Paseo de la Reforma, the broad and splendid
boulevard that serves as the city's major northeast-southwest axis; drivers
merely hit the horn and prayed for clearance. On most other major
streets, trolley cars still shaped the traffic pattern.

The air was so exhilarating that we walked everywhere then. The
balance of people, work, place, and climate was matchless. We knew it,
but so did the Mexicans. A year later Carlos Fuentes published his first
novel, a panoramic, multilayered equivalent of a Mexican mural. The
subject was Mexico City. The title was *Where the Air Is Clear*.

At the end of that magical year, I had to go home. But across the
decades, I've kept returning. I have seen the changes and the growing
catastrophe. In 1964 a few of the old places were gone—a small, noisy
cantina, a bookstore, a restaurant where I used to have squid in its own

> "**A**nd some of our soldiers even asked whether the things that we saw were not a dream.... When we had looked well at all of this, we went to the orchard and garden, which was such a wonderful thing to see and walk in, that I was never tired of looking at the diversity of the trees, and noting the scent which each one had, and the paths full of roses and flowers, and the many fruit trees and native roses, and the pond of fresh water.... Of all these wonders that I beheld, today all is overthrown and lost, nothing left standing ...."
>
> —Bernal Diaz del Castillo, a soldier of Cortés, describing Mexico City in 1519

ink. Many of the streetcars had vanished too, replaced with buses that coughed black exhaust fumes along the 14 miles of the Avenida de los Insurgentes. I noticed more people on the noontime streets and more beggars in the Zona Rosa, but it was still basically the city of the mid-1950s.

I was back in 1968, on the eve of the Olympic Games. For the first time, my eyes teared when I walked out of the airport. The city was jammed that year, the streets denser, the traffic slower, louder, more bad tempered. These were people drawn by the Olympics, I thought; when the Games ended, they would go away. They didn't. I still loved the city, but in the mornings, I could no longer see the volcanoes.

The capital had grown into a megalopolis of nine million human beings, sprawling south out of the federal district into the state of Mexico. Arriving by airplane, I could no longer see the town; it was hidden under a urine-colored smog. By the late '80s it had the worst air pollution in the world.

I didn't see the volcanoes again until the fall of 1985. On the morning of September 19, an earthquake smashed into the city, measuring 8.1 on the Richter scale. As many as 10,000 people were killed; 56,000 buildings were destroyed or damaged; and half a million people were left homeless. For a few days, everything stopped: work, factories, all traffic except emergency vehicles. At night the city was eerily silent. But after the huge aftershock, after the smoke of the fires had blown away and the dust of the broken buildings had settled, something extraordinary happened. People on rescue teams paused in their work and looked up, and there, blue and clean, was the sky. And away off, serene and majestic, their cones white with snow, were the volcanoes.

A week later, when traffic resumed and the factories opened again, they were gone. A year later, birds were falling dead out of the poisoned air.

I spent the winter of 1987 in Mexico City, editing an English-language daily newspaper, and began to understand the problem. Statistics weren't very reliable; some reporters suspected that the government was holding back details to avoid frightening its own people or scaring off tourists and investors. But the known facts were appalling. About 4.3 million tons of contaminants were emitted into the air every year—a pound and a half a day for every human being in the megalopolis. On an average day the air was polluted with 600 tons of particulate matter, much of it fecal dust, which led to widespread salmonella and hepatitis infections, particularly among infants. Respiratory infections also were common. On 80 percent of the days of the year, the air contained unacceptable levels of ozone.

In addition, about 40 percent of the people were living without a sewage system. Wandering through the so-called *ciudades perdidos*—"lost cities"—on the outer perimeter of the city, I saw garbage rotting in the streets and kids hunting rats for sport. There was no running water in most houses and only scattered electrical service. I visited several huge mountains of garbage, including the notorious Santa Fe dump on the southwestern edge of the city, where platoons of the city's 15,000 organized garbage pickers, called *pepenadores*—most of them women and children—scavenged through rotting meat and fruit, dead dogs, broken furniture, plastic bottles, old dolls, and plump cats. The stench was sickening.

But even the corrupt odor of the city's enormous dumps was overwhelmed by the general contamination. Everybody knew where that contamination was coming from: on each weekday, burnt gasoline rose from 2.5 million automobiles, 200,000 buses, 35,000 taxis, and many additional thousands of trucks. Together they accounted for 70 percent of the pollution. The rest came from the city's 30,000 factories. On a

---

From the window of an aircraft, I catch the sight of the huge, sprawling metropolis. Mexico City! In adamantine prose, Alfonso Reyes, peerless master of Spanish letters, once called the valley of Mexico "the most transparent region of the air." A quick glance from my observation post quickly dispels the illusion in the poetical conceit. A thick cloud of toxic fumes hangs over the entire city, traversed by the waves of local broadcasts that warn of the dangers of the atmospheric levels of ozone. Over twenty million people, close to one-third of the entire population of the country, form the vibrant, teeming, cruel, tender, affable, and desperate mass of humanity before my eyes. The metropolitan area is known by the abbreviation D.F., for *Distrito Federal*. With a touch of that cruel humor that characterizes the natives, they are prompt to point out that the initials really stand for *Defiéndete*—"Defend youself."

—F. Gonzalez-Crussi, *The Day of the Dead and Other Mortal Reflections*

---

regular basis, international levels for sulfur dioxide, carbon monoxide, lead, and suspended particles were surpassed. Just breathing was said to be the equivalent of smoking two packs of cigarettes a day.

There were no simple solutions. To begin with, nobody could change the facts of geography. At 7,500 feet above sea level, Mexico City is located in a vast natural bowl surrounded by a wall of mountains, some of which rise another 5,000 feet into the thin air. The air contains 23 percent less oxygen than at sea level; auto engines must work harder, producing twice as much hydrocarbon pollution and carbon monoxide.

Everywhere, man has wreaked havoc. When the Aztecs founded the city in 1325, most of the valley was covered by a shallow saline lake and its surrounding lagoons, marshes, and forests; today the lake is completely gone, the forests felled, the marshes drained, the valley covered with houses and factories, asphalt and concrete. During dry periods, great clouds of dust, heavy with bacteria and excrement, rise to blanket many square miles of shantytowns. The built-up city spread from 45 square miles in 1940 to 483 square miles in 1990, with a present population density twice that of the New York metropolitan area, four times that of London. Seventy percent of the trees have been destroyed in the past 30 years, thus removing a desperately needed source of oxygen. One new city, Nezahualcoyotl, didn't exist when I was a student; it now houses 3 million human beings. On its bald streets there are almost no trees.

New York and Tokyo have shown that large urban populations can exist under certain conditions. But Mexico City is one of the world's few major cities that is not on a mighty river or an ocean; no fresh wind travels down river valleys or comes whipping in from the sea. The city is locked into what geographers call a closed hydrologic system: wind velocity is less than 3.4 miles per hour, too weak to propel a flow of clean air across the choking valley; the slowness of the wind actually traps some contaminants in the air.

Although Mexico City, at 19° 25' N latitude, lies within the Tropics, its altitude puts the average mean temperature at 65 degrees Fahrenheit. In winter, the upper air is colder, and the warm, seething soup of polluted city air can't even escape into the atmosphere. These thermal inversions are scary. With direct sunlight blocked, the days are dark, all color muted. You feel nauseated, indoors and out. You have steady headaches, feelings of drowsiness, and occasional dizziness. As the inversion continues, day after day, the psychological pressures can be worse. From the first morning glimpse of the unmovable roof of filthy smog, you feel smothered, convinced that you will never again feel healthy, never again see the sky.

Air isn't the only problem. Water is almost as bad. The city requires 177 cubic feet of water every second. This can't be completely supplied from local wells and pumps, so an elaborate system of pumps, canals, and tunnels carries water from rivers, springs, and wells on the far side of the surrounding mountains. Some water travels almost one hundred miles and must climb two thousand feet or more. This is not a one-way problem. The city's sewage also must be carried away. None of this is easy. Because of the old lakes, the subsoil of the city is a spongy compost, five parts water to one part solid. Even the "solid" parts are often volcanic ash and lava, which turn into a grainy porridge during extended rains. That is why earthquakes can be so devastating; the 1985 shock caused a great rolling movement—forward, then backward, then forward again—like water sloshing in a bathtub. Tall buildings were heaved first in one direction, then in another, until they snapped.

As pumps have sucked groundwater from below, some parts of the city have begun to sink as much as ten inches annually. Sidewalks crack; underground pipes break apart, wasting millions of gallons of fresh water or allowing raw sewage to seep into the ground. In the city's famous Chapultepec Park, the water table has dropped drastically. Trees assaulted by pollution above ground are also being starved for water from below. No wonder many of them are dying.

There are two obvious causes of the city's environmental calamity: overpopulation and the internal-combustion engine. Mexico City now contains almost one-fifth of the country's 84.5 million citizens, and more arrive every day by bus and on foot. There is some evidence that internal migration to La Capital has slowed from the late-1980s peak of one thousand arrivals daily. Many of the nation's poor are now heading farther north, to the rim of *maquiladora* assembly plants stretched along the border with the United States. With the North American Free Trade Agreement that demographic shift is likely to intensify. But even if the city's borders were sealed tomorrow, the pressure of too many people would be extraordinary. Mexico's birthrate is down to 1.9 percent, but half the city's population is under 18, and every year another 300,000 children are born. In addition, advances in education, medicine, and health have extended the lives of millions; in 1940 the average life span was about 40 years; today it is more than 60. Population growth might slow, particularly among the middle class, but it will not end, and it is unlikely to be reversed.

There were other forces at work in the making of the catastrophe. For the growing middle class, Mexico City was virtually the only destination. It was the peak of the symbolic Mexican pyramid, the psycho-

The city represents posture and hypocrisy to the average Mexican. The average Mexican imagination will weigh the city against the village and come up short. But the city represents the only possibility for survival. In the last half of this century, Mexicans have abandoned the village. And there is no turning back. After generations of ancestors asleep beneath the earth and awake above the sky, after roosters and priests and sleeping dogs, there is only the city.

—Richard Rodriguez, *Days of Obligation: An Argument With My Mexican Father*

logical imprint that so deeply shapes the Mexican character. As it had been since colonial days, the city was the nation's political and bureaucratic capital. It was the communications capital, too, the headquarters for the country's publishing, music, film, and television industries. If you wanted to be a singer or an editor, a movie star or the president, you had to be in Mexico City.

By the mid-1970s almost everyone realized that something terrible was happening. Anarchic growth had to be tamed, and with the discovery of vast petroleum reserves during the post-OPEC boom in oil prices, it seemed that Mexico could at last choose both jobs and the environment. Javier Caraveo Aquero, a young Stanford-educated urban planner, was asked to create a master plan to clean up the city. With a small, passionate staff, he went to work.

In 1979 the 182-page plan was ready. The megalopolis would be divided into nine "service concentration centers," each, in effect, a self-sufficient city. Each would have its special employment base: a light, nonpolluting industry or business or bureaucracy. Each would contain a commercial district, leisure centers, and residential areas. Within each minicity there would be self-contained transportation systems, with shuttles that went to other areas of the megalopolis. The government would plant 119 million trees to increase the oxygen supply.

The plan was brilliant. Everybody said so. Yes, it would cost billions. Yes, it would need time—at least a generation—to have an effect. But in the end, Mexico City could be saved. The plan was accepted by the city government in 1980, and a series of hearings to deal with specifics took place over the following year.

One problem was immediately obvious: the unwillingness of various bureaucracies to surrender their own narrow powers. Because there were overlapping responsibilities in competing agencies, the infighting was brutal. The power of bureaucracies to obstruct movement is immense in any country, and even more powerful in a "controlled democracy" like Mexico; hacks will do anything to hold on to their own jobs.

Sometimes the most difficult problem of all in Mexico is getting reliable information; the hacks don't want to give their bosses accurate measurements of their own failures. On environmental matters, they don't want to provide hard evidence of the calamity that most citizens know has already engulfed them. In analysis of the master plan, delay, obfuscation, and deliberate vagueness became the order of the day.

In Mexico City such bureaucratic tensions are even stronger because the mayor is appointed. He is called *el regente*—the regent—and he serves a constituency of one: the president. Too often, city developments such as highways or extensions of the metro are approved behind closed doors, without public hearings. Trying to bring about genuine change, supported by the people who are most affected by it, is further complicated because the adjacent state of Mexico—an inseparable part of the megalopolis and the location of much of the polluting industry—does have an elected governor and must raise its own revenues. The result is that two separate local governments, with two separate tax bases, are trying to solve what is essentially one problem.

In the usually docile Mexican media, the master plan was discussed in great detail and with much passion. Some newspapers even went out and did actual reporting, instead of dutifully printing government handouts, and more columnists and intellectuals began calling for the election of the mayor as an important first step.

And then all the sound and fury became irrelevant.

In 1982 world oil prices collapsed, and so did the Mexican economy. When Miguel de la Madrid became president at the end of that year, all government energies were directed toward preventing default on the enormous debts owed to foreign banks. With 80 percent of its budget picked up by the federal government, Mexico City itself was bankrupt, unable to pay almost three billion dollars in debts. Without vast amounts of money, no master plan could be

The *lucha libre* is a purely Mexican tradition. Every neighborhood has its ring where masked wrestlers go on stage to enact predestined fights of good against evil. Everyone in the audience knows who is going to win but the stadium will ring with whoops of enthusiasm time after time as the bad guy goes down. Winners become national heroes. Superbarrio, a former *lucha libre* victor, has gone on to champion human rights, exhorting his numerous supporters to use condoms to prevent the spread of AIDS and campaigning against pollution. These Robin Hood figures symbolize all the hopes and aspirations of the people, which they themselves prefer not to voice for fear of disappointment.

—Katharine Thompson and Charlotte Thompson, *Cadogan Guides: Mexico*

executed. The 1985 earthquake both underlined and deepened the crisis. Who could worry about the 21st century when families were living in tents?

And so Mexico City muddled along, imprisoned in a shroud of pollution and fatalism. The rich began wintering near their sequestered money, in Miami or Aspen. Others established second homes in Cuernavaca or Tepoztlán, saying they needed to clean their lungs on weekends. During the day, people held handkerchiefs to their faces as they walked the streets. A few lonely souls continued to protest.

In 1988 Carlos Salinas de Gortari became president in the closest election in Mexican history. His Institutional Revolutionary Party (PRI) had been in power since the 1920s but was shocked by the returns. Among other setbacks, the PRI received only 28 percent of the vote in Mexico City and lost every election district there. One reason was the government's failure to deal firmly with pollution. The problem was, in fact, getting worse: a 1990 World Bank study showed that the city was three times as noxious as in 1986, with lead levels in the blood of the average citizen four times higher than for a resident of Tokyo.

In his first year, Salinas moved to repair the political and ecological damage. He appointed a young technocrat named Manuel Camacho Solis as the new mayor of the city. Under De la Madrid, Camacho had served as minister of urban development and ecology; if the PRI was not yet prepared to allow the election of the mayor, it at least chose a first-rate man to deal with the city's enormous problems. He began to make immediate changes. The huge March 18 refinery, sprawling over 430 acres north of the city, was closed. It would be replaced by parks. Said Salinas, "Let's plant trees where today there is nothing but pipelines."

Camacho played a major role as peacemaker in the 1994 Chiapas uprising and its aftermath.

—JO'R and LH

In November 1989 the mayor also started the "Day without a Car" program, using color-coded stickers to force motorists to leave their cars home one day a week. The colors were determined by license plate numbers. "*Hoy no circula,*" was the order: "Today don't drive." Violators were fined about $115—a month's pay at minimum wage, the heaviest traffic fine in Mexican history—and had their cars impounded. The program applied to commercial vehicles too (but not taxis) and took 500,000 vehicles off the street every weekday. The air became noticeably cleaner.

On many days residents could see the volcanoes. Some government studies insisted that pollution had been reduced two percent from the year before, although ozone levels remained significantly higher than Mexico's own standards. But the program did give many people hope. "It's remarkable for such an anarchic city, especially one with a history of apathy and individualism," said Louis Manuel Guerra, director of the Institute for Ecological Research. "It marks a turnaround in the consciousness of the people."

As Mexico's economy improved, however, cars became more affordable. This made it easier for some to circumvent the law, particularly those who didn't want to use the city's excellent but overcrowded metro, which was handling 5.3 million riders every day. The rich already had more than one car; now the middle class started buying second cars, an estimated 600,000 of them. These were often oil-burning heaps (the average age of a Mexican car is between 8 and 12 years) that began thwarting the brief period of progress. Between 1988 and 1991 gasoline consumption increased 30 percent, according to the Los Alamos National Laboratory. Some ecologists fear that if the free trade agreement with the United States and Canada is an economic success, an expanding Mexican middle class could add several million more automobiles to the city. That would make gas masks a new growth industry.

Camacho also overhauled the city's bus system, replacing or refurbishing the fleet of 3,500 city-owned buses by March 1991. Taxis that had been built before 1985 were taken off the streets. Trucks were ordered to convert from gasoline to LPG (liquefied petroleum gas). Diesel fuel was desulfurized. From November 1992 on, all buses and trucks entering Mexico City from the provinces were forced to undergo emissions testing.

In the spring of 1992, in spite of all the reforms, Mexico City was subjected to the worst ozone pollution ever recorded. The maximum level acceptable by international standards is 100 points. On February 6, 1992, the Mexico City ozone level reached 342 points. It was 332 points on February 10 and an incredible 398 points on March 16. Factories were ordered to cut production 50 to 75 percent. Schools were closed. Citizens hid behind closed doors or wore masks.

Then the ozone levels dropped by 120 points. The factories reopened. Citizens went back to forcing leaded fuel into unleaded tanks or removing the catalytic converters. Life, such as it is, went on.

The office of the mayor is at the top of a flight of worn stone stairs, past a heroic mural inspired by the triumph of the 1910 Revolution. The hallways and anterooms are full of the players in the city's drama: thickset, blocky women in peasant clothing; lawyers and engineers in tailored suits; tall men from the northern provinces with elegantly tooled boots, high-crowned cowboy hats, and fierce mustaches; cops, reporters, secretaries. They exchange petitions, requests, and demands, approvals and denials in a ceaseless ritual of need and reward.

From his office, Manuel Camacho Solis presides as mayor of Mexico City, *el regente* of the Federal District. Princeton-educated, touted as a future president, Camacho is part of the Salinas generation of technocrats who are trying to bring Mexico into a prosperous 21st century. They honor the country's revolutionary past and its bruised idealism, but they resist ideology and sentimentality. They are, above all, pragmatists. They are for whatever works.

"Dealing with the problems of Mexico City is quite complex," Camacho says, seated at a long, polished conference table. "Everything happens here.... Here you see, to a certain extent, the result of what's happening all over the country. The problems of other places come to Mexico City. But it's nice to know that those problems can be solved. Although there are many conflicts and tensions, finally it is a country that can talk. And can bring about agreements that can become policies."

Camacho compares the problems of Mexico City with those of other large cities in the Third World and is encouraged. "In so many cities of the world, there are so many cleavages—so many things that don't seem to have any solutions," he says. "Here there are many problems, but we don't have so many deep cleavages. And people think there are solutions to the problems. That makes a big difference."

Like all Third World countries (and certain areas of countries of the so-called First World), Mexico must deal with the conflict between jobs and the environment. "The only argument that really works," Camacho says, "is to reduce the cost in jobs while improving the environment. If one follows a policy of losing jobs then one will not have the possibility of financing the control of pollution. And then other problems might grow so fast they might become more important—problems of .social unrest, for example. What's the best mix? The best mix is the one that protects most of the jobs while cleaning up the environment. And if something doesn't have any possibility of solution, then one must pay the price in jobs—but those are the exceptions.

"It's extremely difficult to create new jobs. It can take decades to create one hundred thousand jobs, five hundred thousand jobs. So if you destroy jobs, then you will not have the jobs and you will have all of the pollution."

The ideal solution for all cities would be replacing the internal-combustion engine with some nonpolluting alternative, but that seems impossible for now. Still, Camacho has worked hard to control the automobile. "We have to reduce its attractiveness," he says. The costs of parking and fines have been increased. Public transportation has received a high priority: new subway lines are being built, comfortable and secure buses are coming on line. And he is proud of the progress of the past three years: the reduction of lead, sulphur dioxide, and carbon monoxide in the air. "We're now concentrating on ridding the air of particles," he says. "And we must deal with ozone. We are making progress."

He admits that population growth is a problem but has no faith in master plans. "I don't think it's possible to have master plans for population control in any city of any underdeveloped country or less-developed country," he says. "Remember all those plans for Cambodia? Well, even with a dictatorship like the Khmer Rouge it didn't work. If you have freedoms in a country, it's impossible to think that the size of a city can be controlled. Of course, we are doing some things. You can make decisions about where to grow, where not to grow. You can stimulate regional development. But a master plan for controlling a city like ours cannot be done anyplace in the world."

Camacho was encouraged by the 1990 Mexican census, which, although it was disputed by some critics, showed that the population was actually smaller than most people thought: about 15.5 million. The growth rate was 1.85 percent, adding about 300,000 people a year. "That's still too high," Camacho says, "but the trend is going down." He also said that as municipal services—water, electricity, schools, hospitals—have been extended to the city's poorest sections, the birth rate has

> As we finished our lunch and came back downstairs and out onto the square, all the vendors were out in full force, with *rebozos* and baskets, armloads of jewelry— down to the smallest, inevitable enchanting, tiny children with their Chiclets. (I have never seen anyone buy these Chiclets, but surely someone must?) These children, these vendors of Chiclets, are sometimes alone, or as often a dark young mother trails along with wares of her own, some necklaces or leather bookmarks. The mothers are young indeed, fourteen or fifteen, they look to be. I would guess that the accompanied little children are firstborns; with second, third, and god knows how many more children, the mothers must, of necessity, give up on such surveillance; those later children are the ones out selling on their own. And what tired, sad, nearly defeated faces those young women have, their brief girlhoods and the moment of romance already over, years of labor and childbirth, more labor and more childbirth almost inevitably ahead.
>
> —Alice Adams, *Mexico: Some Travels and Some Travelers There*

decreased. "There is a direct relationship between poverty and population growth," he says. "In attacking the worst poverty we have done in three years what usually takes fifteen."

There are many projects ahead. One is to convert to the use of natural gas as quickly as possible (there are two basic problems: finding spaces for distribution and establishing absolute safeguards against calamitous accidents). The universities are being encouraged to expand degree-granting programs in environmental studies. He reached out to the city's environmental groups, too, understanding that theirs is a basically adversarial relationship but welcoming ideas and criticism. The Salinas government also arranged for almost one billion dollars in credits from Japan to help transform the city's environment. Camacho remains optimistic. But he must also live in the city he governs. I asked him how he deals with the pollution himself.

"Someone gave me an air filter as a present, for my house," he said, smiling dryly. "But I had it put away. I didn't think it would be just for the mayor to have better conditions than the rest of the people.... And it would be a very bad lesson for my children. At the same time"—he laughed out loud—"those things don't work."

The year 2010 will be the hundredth anniversary of the outbreak of the Mexican Revolution, the crucible from which modern Mexico was born. I asked Camacho what kind of city the capital would be then. He paused, glancing around his high-ceilinged office, and answered: "I think we will have a city that will show the world that under the most adverse conditions, the inhabitants were able to agree upon long-term policies necessary to make the city of 2010 viable. A city that would not have been viable if decisions had not been taken in the 1990s. And also, with all the problems, the city will not be as big as was predicted." He paused. "I'm doing everything I can so that it will not be a paradigm of urban disaster; it will be a paradigm of how under adverse circumstances people can find a way to live together. And be part of government. To do things right. Not to lose what has been acquired in the past."

He smiled and shrugged. "I plan to be living here in the year 2010," he said. "Probably my children will be living here, too. I've never thought about leaving."

Pete Hamill also contributed "A Healing Place" in Part II.

Ivan Restrepo is a genial scholar of garbage who directs a government-financed institute for ecological research called the Centro de Ecodesarollo. In 1985, in Chapultepec, the city's most popular public park, Restrepo and his center mounted an exhibit on the subject of garbage. A tent, designed by an artist, had a long, dark entrance, filled with giant illustrations of microbes and garbage-related pests, from which the public emerged into "the world of garbage." One of the exhibits, Restrepo said, was "the most gigantic rat we could find."

Dr. Restrepo was telling his story in one of Mexico City's best restaurants, and he interrupted himself briefly to order roast kid, guacamole, and a *millefeuille* of poblano chilies and cream. "It was huge!" he went on, gesturing descriptively. The rat, one gathered, must have been about the size of a large cat. "It weighed almost eight pounds. But we had a problem. We began to realize that the rat was dying on us. It wasn't used to the nice, healthy pet food, or whatever it was, that we were feeding it. So we went out and collected fresh garbage for it every evening. Kept it happy. And that was important, because thousands and thousands of people came to see the garbage exhibit, and the rat was the absolute star of the show."

If *capitalinos*—the residents of Mexico City—flock to an exhibit on garbage featuring a giant rat, it is because the subject is never very far from their minds. The problem of waste disposal may be only one of the the critical aspects of the city's ongoing public-services emergency, but it is certainly among the most visible. One of the world's three largest urban conglomerates, the city never had a proper service infrastructure to begin with and has been growing too much too fast for too many years.

—Alma Guillermoprieto, *The Heart that Bleeds: Latin America Now*

KATE SIMON

La Bruja and the Mushroom

Indigenous people have used hallucinogenic plants for centuries. For others,
the effects vary from tranquility to terror.

The road out of Mexico City takes us into the mountains and then
pours into Puebla, a city gathered tight on itself, as reclusive as a bitter man. On to Cholula, blistered with churches, and through
scraped hills to Tehuacán a spa of shaded streets and family hotels whose
dining-room shelves hold arrays of vitamin pills and digestive aids.
Shortly out of Tehuacán, the road becomes rough rock and dusty pits;
the vistas of dry scrub flow into the dark maw of the encircling mountains; the bump and sway of the
car, the taut, hunched back of the
driver, impose silence on the
party of six. Everyone seems to
be alone with his anticipation—
curiosity, fear, hope—of the
effect of the hallucinogenic
mushrooms.

It is night when we reach the
village, shapeless and anonymous
in the dark, lit by just enough
street lights to indicate the
unpaved main street which leads
to the hotel. The hotel is in the
one stubborn mold of most
Mexican rural hotels: large, bare,
white-washed rooms, two or
three hooks forced into the wall
to hold clothing, one bare uncovered light bulb, weak and half
blind, hanging from the center of
the ceiling, two or three or five
tired beds, and one thick tumbler
on the windowsill.

In its externals this experience is a
"Mexican" one and belongs among
Mexico's uncommon possibilities, but it
is definitely not recommended. Borders of
physical and mental safety have not been
clearly defined, nor is the dose prescribed
by an Indian woman who has been taking
them all her life necessarily the optimum
amount—if there is such a thing—for the
unaccustomed body and psyche. Perhaps
other reporters of the effects of hallucinogenic mushrooms have been luckier or stur-
dier; they seem to have experienced only
the glorious visions. Our group suffered
inordinate anguish, each in his own way
as abysmally black and suffocating as the
earlier, perfect happiness had been
supremely, vaultingly beautiful. It is not a
thing to do alone or lightly or without some
recognition of what one's own body and
mind can tolerate.

—Kate Simon, *Mexico: Places and Pleasures*

341

After breakfast the next morning, we explore the village. It is fairly large, and though the evidence may not be apparent to foreign eyes, it is quite prosperous, the center of coffee-growing in the surrounding hills. The shopkeepers—some of them bake, shoe horses, and mend shoes under one low-pitched roof—and the growers are *mestizos*, while much of the labor is Mazateco. The latter are small, neatly designed people, golden-skinned and, for mountain Indians, extraordinarily affable. Their speech is quite unlike the Aztec tongue spoken in most of the area; it sounds rather like Chinese, running a scale of nasal sounds and glottal stops. Like a number of Indian groups they are polygamous in a casual system of picking up, dropping, and changing women. The men wear blue jeans or chino pants and cotton shirts, like workers elsewhere, but the women are beautifully showy. They spend much of their time embroidering bright designs of birds, flowers, and vines on rectangles of coarse white cotton.

The village is voluble and hospitable, very different from the usual closed, guarded mountain village. (It was suggested by one of the party that this extraordinary mood was a result of a light, constant diet of "happy" mushrooms. A less exotic reason may be that coffee is a good crop and the village eats fairly well, not depending on sparse stands of mountain corn.) It is a lovely place. The wooden, steep-roofed houses and the winding green-lined paths lurch and roll into each other in appealing illogic; gardenias and hibiscus well over the earthen steam-bath cribs which stand at the sides of the road; bird of paradise shafts flame through beds of broad, green-gray elephant ears; roses spill into the paths, and gaudy vines sing across the houses. The large town square holds an uninteresting church whose interior is dominated by a plump Italianate Christ very unlike the gaunt, tormented figure of Indian churches. From the town hall dangles a loudspeaker which alternates music and announcements in Mazateco—except for times of the day and days of the week, for which Spanish is used. Mazatecan thinking seems not to include time concepts, and it may be more than a coincidence that timelessness is one of the prime ingredients of mushroom intoxication.

Strolling through the village, our eyes fixed on its vividness, our minds and vague emotions moving around the prospect and mystery of the mushrooms, we were approached two or three times by men who, in the voices of stolen goods or prohibition liquor, offered us mushrooms. "Strong, fresh magic mushrooms, picked this morning. Meet me at my house in an hour and I'll have them for you."

We visited the house of one of the men, who told us something about the mushrooms. They could be taken anywhere, there was no ritual place; one could sit up or lie down, it didn't matter. The mushroom dream seemed to answer a number of purposes: it would discover the seat of an undiagnosed disease or malaise, it would reveal places, bring one close to distant people, disclose the whereabouts of lost or strayed objects. Usually, when the "secret" disease is found, one goes to a "curer" for alleviation; the mushroom savant is merely a diagnostician, a primitive psychiatrist who makes the "journey" with his patients as companion and guide, warding off evil, helping and encouraging along the way. However, our host, better educated than most Mazatecos, a man of considerable though untrained scientific curiosity and an independent thinker (he believed strongly in monogamy, for instance), had tried the mushrooms for curative purposes. His wife had been suffering from T.B. of the bone, he said (but never said who made the diagnosis). He had cut her arm to the tubercular bone, poured bits of mushroom into the open wound, and bound it. She displayed the scar proudly. It was large but smoothly healed, and she seemed fine and hale, smiling happily at us with all her gold-rimmed teeth—a symbol of her husband's love and prosperity. The man had also treated other members of his family with the mushrooms and the whole large, attractive brood survived, seemingly robust and contented. He assured us that he used the mushrooms sparingly, only when the illness was grave, and always, he added, he took the mushrooms along with his patient. He then showed us the four varieties of local magic mushrooms which grew in the area. They looked like ordinary, putty-colored mushrooms, but there trembled an aura of magic around them: folk tales still felt but not remembered, witches' brews, toadstools, Alice's shrinking-and-growing mushrooms. They melted together with the sudden strangeness of standing in a Mazateco house ruled over by a grinning old cigarette-cadging grandmother in a beribboned *huipil*, babies with black cherry eyes staring out of hammock cradles, the soft singsong of the women's speech, the flat, impenetrable stares of the children clustered at the doorway, the being very far from our accustomed language and safeties. We said nothing but were already preparing fear.

Our intermediary for negotiations with the *sacerdotista* (the gatherer and priestess of our mushrooms) was the proprietress of the hotel, a stout alert *mestiza* matron who was singularly knowing about Americans and dollars. The first asking price was outrageous, as usual, the test for determining the degree of gullibility or eagerness of the buyer. We made a counter offer, which was rejected (supposedly by a messenger from the priestess herself) on the shrewd ground that we didn't need the mush-rooms, but were simply taking them for *"gusto,"* or kicks; therefore, the price to us should be high. Toward evening, we arrived at a sum. We were told to be ready at about ten or eleven o'clock that night.

We are called for and enter the big, bare dining room of our hotel. All the tables but one have been pushed to a far side, the one arranged as a crude altar near the entrance to the kitchen. The proprietress, her daughter, her sister, and two of our group who had refused the mush-rooms are seated on chairs across the room from a long straw mat stretched along a wall. The only light comes from a candle on the improvised altar which also holds a brazier of burning carbon and four half gourds which obviously contain our portions of mushrooms. The Indian woman kneels near the door, the girl who will later guide her home kneels behind her, both in the posture of the patient, endless wait-ing of the Indian women. The old woman has the face of an aged mon-key with deep-set blank eyes under high-curved prominent brows. Two black wings of hair wipe across her low forehead. She is dressed in a dirty white *huipil* which hangs loosely from her meager shoulders. Her thin dark hands float like disembodied claws in the misty white of her lap. It is impossible to guess her age, but she is old, even for a society where women age rapidly. As one stares at her, trying to see more than the dim light permits, she becomes all her female ancestors kneeling and waiting, impassive, neither alive nor dead, not quite flesh, not quite stone.

Not knowing what to expect or what is expected of us we move rather aimlessly, like children in a new class, waiting to be directed by some authority. We are told that the two men are to place themselves at a distance from the two women, but on finding out that we know each other only two days or so, the priestess says (in Mazateco translated into Spanish by the landlady) that we might all lie on a long straw mat, decent space between us. While we arrange ourselves, making nervous little jokes, the old woman prepares the mushrooms—a matter of pour-ing some sugar water over them, we are told, to help reverse or slow up reactions. She then pours some *copal* (incense) over the carbon into the brazier, and as the sweet smell and smoke come toward us, one remem-bers Bernal Díaz's description of Indian emissaries passing braziers of copal over Cortés' clothing, and the sight of saints' images in Indian churches being caressed by the same incense from the same kind of bra-zier. The act is pleasing; it has a certain antique authenticity, an overture to mysteries.

The copal brazier is soon brought to us and we each make ceremonial gestures of washing and warming our hands in the smoke. Each bowl is then held over the brazier for a moment and is handed to us. We are ready to take the "journey."

We stare into the bowl prepared by the woman we had begun to think of as the *bruja*—witch. In the semidark we can't see the color of the fluid surrounding the mushrooms but we recoil from the imagined dirt in it and the memory of the dark little claws which handled the mushrooms. Each bowl holds four mushrooms (we check with each other), possibly of the four different types, although the two small mushrooms look alike, as do the two large ones. While we eat the mushrooms, gagging with disgust and fear all the way, the *bruja* eats hers slowly, ruminatively. We can get ours down only by swallowing sips of the gritty water with large pieces of mushroom; not chewing, not biting, just tearing off chunks and swallowing them whole. The rubbery, slimy stems are the most difficult and the stomach keeps rising like a large fist to push them out. We lie down on the mat to wait for the effects. The room is now totally dark and quiet.

The *bruja* begins to make the slow, inhaling whistle sounds of shaman drawing disease out of a body. The whistles change to a chant in low and high voices in swift alternation, almost close enough to be a duet. The low voice alone emerges, an inhuman grunting, rooting sound, then the duet again. In a mixture of Mazateco and Spanish, the woman invokes Christ, the Virgin Mary, and a long list of saints (Saint Eulalia and Saint Euphronia figure prominently) and asks them to protect us from ill or evil. Her chant is, for a while, quite simple and pretty, and then changes to a high nasal Oriental plaint. Now the low grunts again, back to the simple folk song, back again to the high and low voices. This goes on for fifteen minutes or so while we watch for the beginnings of hallucination. They come: lights, lines of glacial blue passing in a constant shift and flow of designs; line drawings made by illuminated icicles on a deep, blue field, changing in slow, stately motion. Our limbs and heads are becoming heavy, our jaws feel anesthetized, we have the stiff, tingling lips that follow novocaine injection. Disgust and apprehension are gone. The large noble tempo carries richer and richer patterns and tonalities, colors glow like the depths of gems or layers of stained glass—perfectly lit, always in harmonious, beautifully balanced combinations. The colors and patterns begin to arrange themselves in series: one group combines with utmost felicity variations of cream, orange, lemon yellow, and ocher; another, deep red and purples around small areas of deepest emerald green. Sometimes the patterns appear as light clusters,

I n Mexico color is everywhere, from riotous tumbles of hot pink bougainvillea to heaped piles of market fruits—the brown skin of the *mamey* acting as a foil to its delicate pink flesh, the proclamatory puce and psychedelic green of the *pithaya*, the reds, greens, yellows, browns, and blacks of the chili peppers. A green cactus-leaf salad is thrown into relief by strips of bright red chili, sprinkled with white cheese. The dark, rich chocolate brown of the *mole* sauce doesn't just happen to be that color but is the product of 32 ingredients and hours of careful combination. Parched landscapes are brightened by the sharp splash of a flame tree or the soft lavender of jacaranda.

The Mexican has an innate, audacious sense of color, form and texture. Natural, bright dyes from pomegranate seeds, marigold flowers and cochineal are used to color wool and woven together into elaborate shawls and textiles, worn by all the indigenous Mexicans who haven't yet been seduced by the fluorescents.

—Katharine and Charlotte Thompson,
Cadogan Guides: Mexico

sometimes as mosaics, and for a long, luxurious period, there move before us the most opulent pieces of jewelry, whose designs we desperately try to remember, but there are too many. We contain the colors and lights and are contained by them; a thousand years have passed and are passing. Our universe is moving designs in endless space and time and yet outside of space and time.

It seems simultaneous, as a number of our reactions do (possibly in response to time spans dictated by the drugs in the mushrooms, or maybe one of us triggers off reactions ripening in the others), but at some point, without saying so directly, we all find that we don't like being alone in the immense, strange beauty. We begin to call each other—"Where are you?"—trying not to say, "where am I?" We reach for each other's hands, offered and taken with gratitude, a gift of kindness for kindness needed. The sexual impulses which had concerned the *bruja* do not seem to exist. We are too young for adult sex, swimming in an amniotic prenatal world, and at the same time, aware of its fantastic unsuitability for the adults we also are—gentle, very old, and lost.

Someone speaks of feeling entirely weightless, bodiless, yet the drunken body insists on being felt. Someone complains of intense nausea, which the *bruja* says she will cure. The nausea does leave in one, but reappears, and again disappears, and continues in intermittent waves (a common result of mushroom eating, we discover later). One woman complains of terrible, clamping pain in her head, her usual response, she explains, to uncertainty and fear. The Indian woman, who seems to be taking the "journey" particularly with her, says that the headache is symptomatic of a secret disease, which she will unearth. We have the impression that she continues to chant for a while, but we are too much interested in each other to listen. (Is this a response to fear or is it a return to innocence, to purity unstained by disappointment and mistrust?) We reassure each other, hold each other's hands. As the designs roll on, in inexorable large harmonies, we pull toward each other with words of almost maternal concern, having to break out of the splendid isolation in which we are drifting. If we are good, kind children and considerate of each other, nothing will happen, we will not be lost.

Someone calls out, "Evil seems so far away." He is answered, "I don't know what evil is." For one of us, the subject is so remote that it deserves neither thought nor words. Another is in the hideous presence of imminent evil, and she turns and twists trying to escape it.

The woman who had had the headache now insists that her bladder will not be denied relief any longer; this anchor, her body, reminds her that she is earthbound and must stay earthbound. The other three, with great patience and in gentle tones, as if to a very young child, explain why she can't go to the bathroom: the light coming in the door will break into the visions; the sensation is false, only the effect of the mushrooms; wouldn't it be better to concentrate on the colors instead? They would all love to help but they are much too drunk, they say. The sufferer insists, laughingly, that their observations are reasonable but make no difference to the basic fact. And they all laugh and continue to laugh in radiant full voices, lovely children dancing in a summer shower. The laughter is a river of gold and they ride it wittily, charmed with each other, enchanted with themselves, radiant with all the gifts and beauties.

The old woman makes herself heard, saying that she and her chosen companion are in a most beautiful country. Relief is expressed among the spectators; the American's headache and nausea followed by fever had frightened them. They begin to reassure each other—"She'll be all right; she'll be fine"—and go on to explain that they had seen people leap and shriek and run in uncontrollable flights from anguish. The American woman seemed for a while to be headed that way.

One of the men, still laughing, breaks in to say that nightclub comics might do well to distribute mushrooms to their audiences, and we embroider on this theme, glittering, inventive, audacious.

Between bouts of laughter and love, we *know* that we are coming into full control of our situation, that we can move in and out between reality and the color worlds at will, by the simple act of concentrating with open eyes on what *is*. It is a little surprising, but of no significance, that a man coming toward us is eight feet tall and moving from a very high place sharply downward. We are still in control, invincible, flowers of grace, shining with affection, laughing shimmering music, incandescent. A woman calls out, "I feel all-powerful, but what's much better, I don't want to use any of my power," a kindlier god than any yet devised. A shadow moves over the gleaming world which is oneself; the small, cold sliver of judgment which pierces the visions warns: this is an echo of infantile omnipotence suddenly returned, too magnificent and mad.

There has been enough of glory for two of us. One retreats to nausea, is taken out and put to bed; one woman, muttering that she can't bear any more, please, please, take her to bed, is led out. One woman and one man, still rolling in the waves of laughter, stay on. By this time, the candle has been relit and the pair are lying on the mat talking and laughing luminously, swinging in great arcs from the bright, loving conversation to rhythmic seas of jewels and lights. The woman asks to be conducted to the bathroom, and assuring the man that he is not to worry or feel alone and she will be back, she floats and stumbles out of the room, supported on either side by the two spectators. When she returns to the big room, her partner is still lying on the mat, roaring over a private joke. He is aware of her return, opens his eyes to greet her, and shuts them quickly with a grimace of pain. The red of the wall is too red, the color has changed, its brilliance is insupportable. Her assurance that the wall has not changed makes him easier. He opens his eyes, asks her to sit down: "Let's talk." She is afraid to sit down, it was so difficult getting up before. She tries to persuade him to go to bed and offers him her hand to help him up. She can't pull hard enough, loses her balance, and almost falls on him. They break into laughter again, making exquisite jokes about each other's drunkenness. She turns to her gracious audience and explains in extraordinary fluent Spanish that they are playing a classic drunk scene. She translates carefully: "You're drunk." "You're drunker." "No. I know I'm drunk but you don't, which shows that you are drunker"; then turns to her partner, who is enjoying the act inordinately. Between bursts of laughter he tells her that they would have made a great vaudeville team. Inspired by this judgment, the laughter of the audience, and the spotlight that the candle casts on her shadow weaving against the blood-red walls, the woman turns to the spectators again and tells them that they are witnessing a rare performance, a fine demonstration of ancient, universal vaudeville, older than Dionysius. Her Spanish is flawlessly supple, her accent classic, of the academy. The audience is beautiful soft shadows floating in exquisite arabesque designs like the music of flutes.

Suddenly, she is drowning in nausea and drunkenness. She makes one more effort to get the man up; she doesn't want to leave him alone, the red wall may frighten him again, but he is invulnerably cocooned in his laughter and can't be reached. She asks to be taken to the bathroom, where she vomits eagerly and lustily, knowing that getting rid of the mushrooms will take her out of her awesome private universe. (Some idea flashes by about the Hebrews fearing to use the name of God, something about Moses not wanting to see God, or was that Krishna? Something about religious revelations which were too large and blinding.)

Eagerly, she awaits the return to the familiar. It doesn't come, though; surely the visions and unsteadiness should go now that she is rid of the mushrooms. Standing on the balcony outside her room, the goddess cloak slipping from her shoulders, she looks up at the sky. The stars are heads of glowing pearl, linked by dancing paths of sparkling diamonds pulsing against deep-blue velvet. The woman describes the sky to the girl who helped her. The girl says that the stars are very dim and few and asks the woman to describe some nearby leaves. They look completely natural. Out, away up, are the directions of magic.

As she looks at the sky, her chest becomes constricted; she cannot breathe and knows she is going to die. It must be done with dignity, no hysterics, but can't quite be managed alone. She asks the girl to stay with her a little longer, saying only that she is having difficulty breathing and apologizes for keeping her up so late. She waits for death, knowing that the witch has put a curse on her, had given her poisoned mushrooms to eat. Her invocations were false, she had really called down evil, like the uninvited fairy at the happy feast.

Death is slow in coming. She tells the girl that it must have been a long, cold night for her, probably frightening, and suggests she go to bed. The girl leaves and the woman is alone. The others have been in bed for some unmeasurable time, the "witch" had been conducted out and up the road by the Indian girl, the landlady and her relatives have retired to their houses. She is alone with a hideously gorgeous sky, the witch's poison in her chest, the poison of Sleeping Beauty's spindle in her heavy arms, the wicked stepmother's poisoned apple in her throat. Now she is no longer so much afraid of dying as of meeting the dead. Her mind opens a little dark tree-covered path at the end of which stand two small figures, shrouded, shapeless. She quickly closes them off, but knows they're waiting and who they are. They hate her because she couldn't keep them alive, because they have no one to take care of them in the black quiet place since she abandoned them. They will be unbearable. From their desiccated, frightful heads will come reproaches and loathing, and she will have to see and hear them forever.

Out of the unbearableness rises the voice of the woman: "This is silly. I'm reliving fairy tales and Bela Lugosi movies. I am a fairly sane adult bothered by the altitude, drugged and drunk, nothing more." She comforts herself with the common answer to agony: "It will pass." But the little girl is stronger. She clings, strangles; like a huge amoeba, she engulfs and swallows the woman. "I *am* poisoned and cursed, the dead are coming for me. If I don't go to bed," she thinks slyly, "they won't catch me. If I stay awake and alert I'll be able to run away from them." The grotesque sky beats down; terror tightens around her. She wants her mother with every sinew; every pore is begging, every bone is stretched in supplication. Somewhere in her chest she hears a deep wail and feels a thick emptiness of desperation and loss.

The woman takes over and convinces the little girl to go to bed, but the little girl won't let her undress. "In case I have to run from death it's better to be fully dressed, sweater, shoes, and all." She turns, sits up, lies down in bed, violently hyperactive, afraid of sleep and death. The woman in the next bed is awake, and they talk in frantic explosions of remembering, conjecturing, evaluating experiences. Between attempts at rational speech the other woman moans that she is wrapped in anguish, she cannot move, and during occasional lapses into sleep, screams, "No, no! Don't! Don't! Please don't!" When awakened (and movingly grateful for her partner's presence), she cannot describe or explain what she is experiencing but keeps repeating that she is trapped in anguish and insupportable guilt. She has been somewhere she shouldn't have been, has seen things she shouldn't have seen, lived with something abysmally evil. She is sure they might have died or gone mad and cannot understand how they escaped.

She falls into a quiet sleep finally and her partner realizes that her own fear of the dead and death are gone: she can undress and get under the covers, and does. She looks around her. The chair standing in the faint dawn light coming through the open door (the other woman had insisted that she leave it open, her escape hatch, though she couldn't move if she wanted to) is throwing off fast-moving swirls of color whose rhythm is audible. The skirt hanging from the bedpost makes a downward swishing sound as her eyes move along it. The sleeping woman's muttering voice makes color patterns. Everything seen is heard in a parallel rhythm, everything heard is translated into vision. An old anesthetic dream, never entirely forgotten, confronts her again; sounds arrange themselves in a ring of light moving in a tormenting circle, blinking on and off in a steady rhythm of sickening blows. As she frantically searches for a way out, a great voice comes from all directions, embedding her in a black nest of sound, and says, "You are thinking that this must end, if only in madness. That's not necessarily so and now you're thinking if not in madness, it must end in death. How do you know death is an end? That it isn't interminable torture like this? How do you know that 'an end,' with which you console yourself, means anything at all?" It doesn't, she is convinced, as before, that the voice is right. It must be; it is the voice of God of childhood, Who sees everything and forgives nothing, the God Who makes you collect all your fingernails and bits of hair—no matter where they may have been discarded and forgotten—when you die. It is the God of the eternal purgatory promised Joyce as a school-boy.

Hanging like loathsome rags on this dream are other experiences of tangled sight and sound, and terror: the deafness of high fever; watching a schoolmate anesthetize a cat which they had both caught; Poe's cat screaming from its wall tomb; mashed, decaying bodies of cats in street lots. Recoiling from the murky well of remembering, unable to sleep, she stares and listens intensely, trying to dispel the noise of the closet angles and the patterns of color made by the early-working voices outside. The fears and guilts gather into a strangling knot. Is this tangling of the senses the promised punishment for the forbidden titillations and explorations of childhood? Is this what they meant when they said you were an odd child? Painfully bright are the beautiful designs which now sing whether the eyes are open or shut, suffocating, inescapable, rushing through the body as if it were a sieve.

Do something practical and helpful. There hasn't been a sound from the room above, where the men are staying—not a stumble, the creak of a bed, a shoe dropped. The woman begins to worry about them and finds it a great pleasure. She reaches for her clothing, examines each piece with drunken care, puts her slip on over her pajamas, her brassiere on top of that, and very proud to have thought of it, a large sweater. The woman in the next bed awakens and dissuades her from going upstairs. "They're all right. The stairs are slippery and you'll fall and break your neck and I won't be able to help you. I can't move." She does not want to be alone, the rest is rationalization. The woman in the peculiar costume returns to bed and they talk, the other repeating periodically, like the refrain of a ballad, "I'm so glad you're here. I couldn't have borne it alone."

Gradually, terror ebbs, washed away by short periods of sleep with insignificant dreams. The sight-sounds well back, but with less frequency, and the woman is lost in admiration of the crude, now silent chair and the band of daylight standing mute in the doorway, plain, cold, and thin. She runs out to look at the world from the balcony. The sky is dull and heavy, gray mist drags along the gray-green hills, the elephant ears in the corner of the garden lie flat and gray, the boards of the balcony and the bathhouse are wet gray, the rocks in the path are gray. The air is cold, like gray steel. She goes back into the room and her friend asks, "How does the world look?" She sings, from her toes: "Like its old, ordinary, dull, beautiful self." She is still drunk, still assailed by chills and fever, but nothing bothers her. She lies on the bed, wallowing in the pleasure of being back; her blood sings and dances; she is in love with the whitewashed walls, the hooks in the walls, with the creeping cold and the lumpy bed, with her moaning companion, with her untangled self, and with the troublesome, imperfect world she knows.

Kate Simon wrote several books in her career, including New York: Places and Pleasures; Italy: The Places in Between; A Renaissance Tapestry: The Gonzaga of Mantua; *and* Mexico: Places and Pleasures, *from which this story is excerpted.*

As far as tourists are concerned, it all boils down to this simple fact: drug laws are now being vigorously enforced in Mexico. Ironically, penalties for possession and trafficking are often harsher in Mexico than the U.S. As pressure mounts for the country to clean up its act, Mexican cops and judges are taking a much harsher line than in past years.

Possession of even small amounts of mild drugs like marijuana and mushrooms runs the risk of terrifying jail sentences. Forget about bribes; although the *mordida* is still alive and well in many levels of Mexican life, the "bite" can no longer be depended upon to save your neck. The word I've picked up in recent years is that travelers are now being jailed for minor drug offenses that used to be settled with a "golden handshake." Corruption certainly won't be eliminated soon in Mexico, but the days are over when virtually every offense was open to "negotiation."

—Carl Franz, *The People's Guide to Mexico*

DONALD G. SCHUELER

Roberto and the Permanent Revolution

Driving the back roads of Quintana Roo, the author muses on Mexican politics, and gets perspective from a local hitchhiker.

If you can imagine the liberal and far-left wings of the Democratic party controlling all three branches of government in the United States, at both the federal and state level, *for seventy years*, you might have some conception of how things operate south of the border. What you end up with is a government of, for, and by bureaucracy. Huge government agencies, all dependent on a single more-or-less socialist political party, all underfunded and overstaffed, almost all corrupt to varying degrees, control every aspect of the country's political and economic life. Unlike more totalitarian regimes, however, this bureaucratic system is not overtly oppressive. Democratic forms are carefully maintained, "equality" is celebrated, and opposing candidates within the PRI [*Partido Revolucionario Institucional* or Institutional Revolutionary Party], the dominant governing party, often have genuinely different platforms. Private enterprise is tolerated for the good and sufficient reason that it is the only viable sector of the nation's economy. And even within the bureaucracy itself, individual administrations sometimes beat the odds, gallantly initiating sensible programs, accomplishing some good things. Yet, in principle and in practice, it is against the interests of the central government—that is, the PRI—to encourage its own agencies, or the unions, or the *ejidos*, or business whether private or government-controlled, or even private non profit organizations like *Amigos de Sian Ka'an* [a conservation group] to run their own shows and do too good a job of it. That sort of initiative fosters independence of action—a desire to break away from government control altogether; and that is the last thing that the PRI and its huge party-controlled agencies want to see happen. Therefore, new initiatives are deliberately discouraged if they in any way challenge federal authority. Better that the *ejidos* should remain in debt peonage to the national banks, that the whole economy should operate on a colossal workfare-welfare system, that the nation, which is as rich in resources as the United States, should remain chronically poor, than that this unwieldy one-party bureaucratic system should be modified, much less dismantled.

The instructive thing is that the system does work, in the sense that it successfully perpetuates itself. Most of Mexico's citizens are in some way dependent on it. There is no need for death squads or a KGB or anything like that. A certain amount of carefully rationed protest is allowed. And if any dissatisfied wheel in the collective machinery squeaks loud enough—for example, a big labor union demanding a pay raise—it gets a bit of what oil there is to go around. For the rest, intimidation works wonders. If the enterprising *campesinos* on an *ejido* try to sell their produce without going through the government middleman, the debt to the national bank comes suddenly due. If a businessman supports an opposition party, his income tax is ruthlessly audited by the same tax collector he's been paying off for years—which means that he faces potential bankruptcy, since Mexican income tax levels are deliberately maintained at levels too high for anyone to actually pay. And of course, if a worker in a government agency should make any waves at all, he wakes up one morning without a job. There are no directives from on high, no official policy, concerning all this. Powerful bureaucrats and politicians at the grassroots level take care of their own troublemakers.

After leaving the *cantina* and getting through the military checkpoint at the road junction, I turn right, meaning to drive only a few miles on the northern half of the coast road before turning

As Mexicans everywhere analyze the lessons of the surprising indigenous insurrection that rocked Chiapas in early 1994, they must decipher a complex social fabric of race and class divisions, historic injustice, religious conflicts and a political system attempting to straddle the First and Third Worlds.

"The Mexican theater has collapsed," said Amado Avendano Figueroa, the editor of the small daily newspaper *El Tiempo*, in the quaint colonial tourist town of San Cristóbal de las Casas, 55 miles from Ocosingo. "They had a very pretty and artificial stage, but the Indians came along and tore down the marquee, destroyed the panorama, and are showing us the reality—the other Mexico that really exists down underneath."

The Zapatistas, the vanguard of a nascent indigenous rights movement here, are demanding good land for thousands of peasants shunted off to the harsh Lancandón jungle to make room for agribusiness and grazing.

—Thomas Long, "Social Fabric Fraying in Wake of Mexico Peasant Uprising," *San Francisco Examiner*

back and heading inland. I have scheduled myself to reach Chetumal before nightfall.

But then I see this man at the side of the road, signaling that he wants a lift. "Ooopf!" he exclaims as he climbs in, "you are my savior, *Señor*. I never would have made it with my sore feet. If I had to walk the whole way, I would have been crawling on my hands and knees!"

This is Roberto, a thick-set *mestizo* of about forty, with a dapper little mustache, angry eyes, and the smile of a cartoon shark. Right off, I misdoubt that his feet are all that sore. Also right off, I decide that I like him. He is good company for the duration of a sunny afternoon drive, though not, perhaps, for much longer than that. His wife, he tells me, divorced him years ago, and I can understand why. He has opinions about everything and everyone. Except when they concern himself, they are invariably uncharitable, but in the course of delivering them, he is entertaining and sometimes informative. Life is the villain he loves to hate; but he rails against its inequities with such gusto that one could almost envy him his discontent. By comparison, my own misanthropy seems anemic and insincere.

He was born on this coast, but he has been around, enduring one horrible job after another: as an underpaid seaman, visiting many ports, none of which he liked; as an underpaid worker for a timber company in Tabasco ("It was terrible. Sometimes I would be working up to my waist in mud!"); and most recently as an underpaid handyman for a Texas businessman who owns some of the beachfront up ahead of us. Of this man, Roberto says, "He was always getting angry at the men he hired. They didn't show up on time or they didn't work hard enough to suit him. So one day when they were clearing a landing strip he lost patience and started doing the work himself. I told him it was all right to work hard, but he shouldn't work *too* hard, not down here; but he wouldn't listen. So he got heat stroke or something! He could hardly breathe." Roberto chuckles delightedly, savoring the memory. "They had to fly him back to the States. He almost died!"

Although not fanatically devoted to the work ethic himself, Roberto deplores the lack of it in others. When a battered truck full of cheerful looking Maya passes us, heading the other way, he says, "You see those fishermen? All drunk. They are on their way to get more beer, or anything they can get their hands on. It's disgusting. They work four hours a day for eight months, only it's more like four months because the weather isn't always right. They catch maybe sixty lobsters a day if they're lucky. The lobsters and the conch are how they earn their money. And as soon as they have enough, they buy liquor and get drunk! They smoke the grass, too. It's a normal thing with the Maya. The *chicleros* do it, they do it, the father, the son, they all do it. What? No, they don't grow it. They get it in Chetumal. Four months of the year they go there to live. What do they do? Nothing! They live off the government. The government lends them money for new nets, power motors, and then they never pay it back. Why should they? It's the way things are down here."

He goes on to give the government a few licks for controlling people's lives the way it does. But when I ask him if he would like to see the *ejido* system dismantled, he looks skeptical. "If that happened," he says, "the Maya would need another type of boss, a *patrón*, to take the government's place. They won't work hard on their own." He pauses and then, in a rare moment of self-deprecation, admits, "Even I don't work as much as I should if someone doesn't make me."

I tell him that that is the way it is everywhere. Nevertheless, it occurs to me that, cynical as he is, Roberto may be onto something. Privately, if not publicly, every invader or immigrant from temperate zones always has and always will complain about the sort of indolence that Roberto speaks of. Of course, it is a truism that everybody everywhere who thinks he is possessed by a work ethic tends to lament its absence in everybody everywhere else. But even taking that into account, it is also a truism that what we Westerners, and some Eastern peoples too, describe as a work ethic has never existed as a concept among the great masses of people in most tropical Third World countries. Undoubtedly, environmental considerations are a partial explanation for its absence. In the tropics there is no winter to survive; and the natives have better sense than to get out in the noonday sun like mad dogs, Englishmen, and workaholics from Texas. The Maya for example, rarely store surplus from a good year in anticipation of a bad one; they don't even pick it from the stalks until they are ready to use it.

But I suspect that there is a more important explanation for the work ethic's failure to take root in equatorial lands. It has to do with the fact that, throughout the millennia, the people of these regions have never known anything but a collective—tribal—existence, combined with servitude. They can and do work hard when they have to, the women especially; but most of them can think only in terms of getting by, not of getting ahead. I see the same pattern all the time in the south among the descendants of black slaves and white sharecroppers.

The habit of mind may help to explain why Mexico's "permanent revolution" has been so successful in its weird, bumbling way. The "revolutionary" rulers, the politicians and bureaucrats, may be corrupt, incompetent, exploitative; but they adequately fulfill the quasi-paternalistic functions of the old *patrón*, and before him the Spanish priests and landowners, and before them and after them all the *jefes*, the local chiefs. Indeed, the more I think about it, the more I suspect that the revolutionary upheavals that occur with such regularity in other Third World countries come about not because the dictatorial or oligarchical governments in power are oppressive, per se, but because they fail to honor the ancient contract that has always cemented the relationship between master and slave, *patrón* and peon, chieftain and tribal serf: the tradeoff between work (but not too much work) on the one hand, and a subsistence living (but not much more than that) on the other.

Donald G. Schueler also contributed "Temple of the Jaguar" to Part I and "The World Tree and the Praying Girl" to Part III. These stories are from his book The Temple of the Jaguar: Travels in the Yucatán.

I had the ruins in Cempoala to myself. The only sounds now were the muffled buzz of battered car mufflers from the town and the dry clacking of the palm fronds, but these seemed suddenly inconsequential in a vast silence. Octavio Paz has called that silence "prehistoric," and said that it is the ultimate ruler of Mexico. It is a silence, he says, that wells up out of Mexicans' profoundly felt understanding that everything that has happened in their country—the Conquest, the Revolution, even the ancient kingdoms like this one—is evanescent, chimerical. What is real is only the land itself, which broods over all.

—Frederick Turner, *A Border of Blue: Along the Gulf of Mexico from the Keys to the Yucatán*

PETER LAUFER

Beans or Luxury in a Tijuana Jail

*There are many reasons to avoid trouble that lands you in a Mexican jail,
not least of which is, once in, it's hard to get out.*

Americans stand out in the crowds on Avenida Revolución in Tijuana
as conspicuously as the street-corner donkeys that are so curiously
painted to look like zebras. The vendors bark their wares at the *gringos*; the cabs cruise by slowly, the drivers yelling.

"Taxi?" asks still another cabbie.

"No," is the answer.

"You want women?" is the next question. It is easy to get into trouble
in Tijuana. Trouble is one of
Tijuana's most profitable industries.

South from the tourist strip
that hugs the international fron-
tier, the nightclubs and trinket
stands give way to upholstery
shops, car dealers, and a residential district. There, miles from the
tawdry downtown but still within
sight of the hills of San Diego
County north of the border, La
Mesa Penitenciaria waits for the
unlucky, including plenty of
Americans.

"I had a car accident." Keith
Prohaska doesn't mind his name
being noted. He has been locked
up in La Mesa for three weeks,
charged with drunk driving and
destruction of private property:
the parked cars he hit. But he

From the border you can share a cab for
five bucks a head or you can walk along
the Tijuana River, where you will see
broken bottles and young men asleep on the
grass. It is more fun, perhaps, to approach
Revolución with adolescent preconceptions
of lurid possibility. Marrakesh. Bangkok. For
this you will need a cab. In the first place,
where is he taking me? In the second place,
cab drivers still offer male passengers
cualquier cosa as a matter of form.

For all that, you are deposited safely
when the cab driver announces, with a dis-
tracted wave of the hand, "El Main Street."
El Main Street is what you'd expect of the
region's fifth tourist attraction, after the San
Diego Zoo, Sea World, some others. A
Mexico ride. A quick shot of the foreign.
Unmetered taxis. Ultramontane tongue.
Disney Calcutta.

—Richard Rodriguez, *Days of Obligation:
An Argument With My Mexican Father*

talks like a prison veteran: "You learn real quick, Spanish is not the language here. Money is."

We are standing around the noisy open yard inside La Mesa; I am meeting the handful of Americans held in the Baja California Norte state penitentiary. Keith still sounds dazed when he speaks of his sudden confinement. "I had several drinks at dinner. I don't know how long I've got here." He is already disgusted with his own government. "The American consul is absolutely useless. All they do is call home collect and give us vitamins."

Alex Hines is a little more than a third of the way through his seven-year sentence for possession of one gram of marijuana and contributing to the delinquency of a minor. "It was just seeds," he complains. "If I had killed somebody I would have been out already." For almost two of his years inside La Mesa, Alex's wife and two young children lived in the prison with him. "Oh yeah, my wife was here. Every day she'd go out, go to the store, shop, do what she had to do, do laundry, whatever, come back in. We'd walk around the field."

A counterfeiter joins the group, a U.S. marine serving five years—he's been in eleven months so far—and allows that life isn't so bad for him, considering he is in prison. "There are certain benefits you can't get in the States: women and bottles."

Another marine agrees. "This is a better jail than jail in the States. Let me put it this way: If you've got the money, you can get anything you want."

"Except out," interrupts Phil Trembley, who says he has been locked up for a year, and then looks at his watch and adds, "and eleven days." The charge is homicide, but Phil has not yet been tried, let alone convicted and sentenced.

The high walls of La Mesa don't keep the outside world away from the convicts, they just keep the inmates away from the outside world. Guards armed with rifles crouch on top of those walls, looking sinister in their blue jeans, t-shirts, and baseball caps. There is something especially threatening about their lack of official uniforms, a reminder that the authority they represent does not necessarily answer to a government that controls them. They look like free-lance toughs, adding to the sense of whimsical justice that pervades the Mexican legal system.

One guard is on the ground at the front gate of the prison, working alone. The gate is a far cry from the sophisticated automatic barriers complete with detection equipment protecting prisoners in Canada, France, and Germany. At La Mesa, it's just a swinging door in the chain-link fence. The gatekeeper casually cradles a machine gun and watches over a steady stream of visitors coming and going, deciding who comes in and who doesn't, decisions based as much on deals and bribes as on legalities. Any searches of the visitors are cursory operations. That's why inmates can buy just about anything they want or need inside the prison.

A small clutch of Mexicans is outside the gate, mostly women, talking rapidly, gesturing, passing parcels. Inside, the yard is full of prisoners and a blaring loudspeaker barks orders, announcing visitors and calling individual inmates.

Behind his office, in an open alleyway leading to the yard, the new warden has collected La Mesa's American inmates, all eager to talk. Their stories come fast, tumbling out all at the same time, all rejecting the American government as worthless to their causes. None of the inmates know when they are getting out of La Mesa, but all agree that they are being treated better than most other inmates because they are Americans with money.

We walk into the yard, which looks like a stage set for a small, poor Mexican village. The inside of the actual prison wall is difficult to see. In most places it is covered by what the Mexican inmates call their *caracas*, private quarters referred to as "houses" by the Americans. And indeed they are houses, tiny but adequate private rooms actually built onto the prison's walls. For an American with images of American style prisons as a reference point, these private homes inside the walls are disorienting. Furnished with shag rugs and TV sets, equipped with padlocks controlled by the inmates, they bring to mind children's clubhouses more than prison cells.

"I did all of this," one of the marines says, proudly showing off his studio apartment, barely larger than his bed. An English-language San Diego television station is coming in loud and clear on the black-and-white set. "I did all of this, even the wiring." Where did he get the wire and the connectors and the electrical outlet? "A hardware store delivered it."

Some of the houses are on a second floor, complete with balconies, barbeques, and a sweeping view of the nearby San Diego hills.

"At first it was really scary," says Alex Hines, the inmate serving seven years for marijuana possession. "But then—I dunno—I haven't been in touch with friends of mine or the normal way a person is supposed to live. Just being locked up in here, it's just like, hard. It's bad."

But soon he learned to deal with his new routine. "I get up, eat, go with a few other Americans who are in here, you know, we just talk. That's about it. Watch TV. Listen to the radio. Walk to different places back and forth in here, to different cells people are living in in here. And that's about it. And then go eat, go to sleep, and occasionally, like when I have visits here, like when my wife's here and stuff, we go eat and, you know, everything else you could probably do on the outside."

Alex's house sports two bedrooms, a bathroom, and a kitchen. He has room for a couch and apologizes for the mess, but the Mexican woman prisoner who cleans for him hasn't arrived this day from the women's side of the prison. From his smile and wink, it is clear she performs other services for Alex, too, when his wife isn't visiting or living with him. We run into his "maid" later in the women's section of the prison. They hug and hold hands while we talk. The guard escorting us hoots over the hand-holding; Alex just smiles. Cooking, cleaning, and prostitution are the most common options available to the women inmates for making money in the prison economy.

The women live in a separate wing of the prison, but mingle with the men as they go about their daily business. Carol, one of the American women in La Mesa, sits on her cell floor chewing a pear as we talk. "Stay out of Mexico," is her advice. "Especially if you have tattoos. They saw my tattoos." Carol is accused of robbery, a charge she denies. So far, she has been locked up for eight months of pretrial detention.

"They don't do much of anything to help," she says of the U.S. consular officials. "They just ask what's happening. I'd like them to give us a lawyer from over there. These lawyers are jokes."

Carol looks tough and seems in her element sitting on the cell floor. "I'd done a robbery," she says as she explains her history in Tijuana. "I got out, went back to the U.S., came back here to drink with some friends of mine. I was only here three days." Then she was picked up for robbery again.

"I've been hit because I wouldn't cop to the robbery," she tells me in a resigned voice. "I'm waiting to go to court to see how much money they want. It all works out to money."

"It's pretty well set up," Alex says proudly about his house. "You'd be surprised, this is like no prison at all. This is like, they just take me off the street, and they put me in another world, but far away from everyone else. And I have to get along with all these people in here." Getting along with his neighbors is important for self-preservation. He tells stories of stabbings and killings in La Mesa. "I never thought about death until I came here," he says. But on the high-rent side of the prison where his and the other Americans' *caracas* are scattered, life is relatively quiet. The really nasty fights and fires usually occur across the yard in the maximum security section of the prison, or where the poorest prisoners share unlocked cells. "Where I live, it's fine. It all depends on how you're set, financially. If you've got a lot of money you can do anything here."

Alex Hine's *caraca* cost him about five hundred American dollars to secure and furnish. For the duration of his sentence, it's his. And he didn't need to come up

> I f you should encounter legal troubles with public officials or local business people anywhere in Mexico, you can contact La Procuraduría de Protección al Turista (Attorney-General for the Protection of the Tourist). English-speaking aides are on the staff at each attorney general's office. There's an office in every state capital and in some other cities as well.
>
> —Tom Brosnahan, et al.,
> *Mexico – a travel survival kit*

with all of the money up front. The prison administration takes time payments for the house. Alex and the other inmates either buy what they need from the outside, get it from visiting friends and relatives, buy it through the prison marketplace, or do without. Nothing is free. Even the routine beans and rice from the prison kettle require a payment to the guards.

Mordidas, these daily expenses, are called, literally "little bites." Everything carries a price: blankets, cots or the more comfortable beds, showers, and, of course, illegal recreation like drugs, alcohol, and sex. The guards provide the goods, take a cut for themselves, and augment the warden's salary with his percentage. This controlled, market-driven economy keeps prison costs low for the government, and makes the job of guard and warden appealing because there is plenty to be made for those who know how to use the system. Mexican and other Latin American politicians point with some pride to their prison systems, saying that because they approximate life on the outside they are a more humane method of incarceration and better prepare inmates for their return to open society than the greater isolation of North American penal communities.

Prisoners with no money sleep outside in the yard. Even one of the unbarred barren cells, known as the Tanks, costs twenty-five cents a night. Women with babes in arms mingle with their men in the Tanks and throughout the prison. Only the most incorrigible are locked up behind bars in the cellblock called *Las Tumbas*, the Tombs.

Radios blare pop music throughout the prison yard, competing with the official announcements coming over the loudspeakers. A couple of smiling men sashay by flirtatiously, their faces heavily made up, their cheap women's clothing ill-fitting.

"If you're a clean person, you can stay clean," explains one of my guides as we pick our way through the rougher and dirtier neighborhoods of La Mesa, "If you're a pig, you can live like a pig." A guard tags along as we tour, but he just smiles; he doesn't censor the commentary, nor does he keep me from seeing the entire complex. "The guards are really good people," says Alex. "Once you're in here, it's okay." He smiles, "There's a problem getting out." The guard smiles, too. He struts a bit, in stylish uniform and dark glasses, looking cool and comfortable. He's clearly feeling just as at home as Alex.

The Americans order out to Tijuana restaurants or grocery stores for their food, or eat at one of the restaurants in the yard owned and operated by inmates. These are actual private eateries. Coming into La Mesa for the first time, it takes some getting used to, these restaurants and the private apartments. The jail doesn't appear to be a penal institution as much as a walled city. I expected to find miserable prisoners and dirty facilities. I expected to hear horrible stories of abandonment and abuse from the Americans I found detained in Mexico. But the commercial village environment is an odd surprise.

The open-air restaurants are complete with hand-painted signs, just like those seen out in the streets of Tijuana. *Cantina*, announces one restaurant's brightly colored signs. Up on the makeshift wall is a listing of ham-

---

I t all began with a knock on the door of Room 1924 of the Hotel Stouffer Presidente.

When Alex Argueta opened that door three years ago, the resort developer from Tucson, Arizona, found four federal judicial policemen telling him he had a problem with a car registered in his name. But this, he says, was a ruse. The police really wanted to talk about his dispute over a bank loan. Although it would have been a minor civil matter in the U.S., Mr. Argueta quickly found himself behind bars. In the headquarters of the federal attorney general, he says, he listened to a man being beaten in the next room, and was told he would be beaten, too, if he didn't answer some questions.

He answered them. But still he languished for 16 months in the infamous *Reclusorio Preventivo Norte* as his case wound through Mexico's courts.

Mr. Argueta was never convicted of a crime.

If you think dealing with the U.S. legal system is vexing, try tussling in Mexico. Despite the enthusiasm over trade with Mexico, dozens of Americans are finding, as he did, that when a cross-border deal sours, they risk entering a labyrinth where their investments can be wiped out by bureaucratic blockades, mercurial magistrates, or worse.

—Diane Solis, "In Mexico, a Dispute Over a Business Deal May Land You In Jail," *Wall Street Journal*

burgers, fries, and other menu offerings. The counter, too, is restaurant-issue Formica. Commercial bottles of catsup are set out with the meals, along with restaurant-style napkin dispensers. Inmate customers and guards sit on red Naugahyde-covered swivel stools. A juke box pumps tunes out into the yard. For a minute it's possible to forget that this is a dangerous, dirty prison.

In the prison kitchen, where the inmates without the money to buy better meals get their food, the huge cooking tubs are bubbling with lunch. "Every fucking time," says a Mexican inmate in English when he sees me taking notes, "beans and rice. Every fucking time, beans and rice." Alex and my other American guides point to the beans and rice with disgust and say they never eat the prison food.

We pass the bakery with its giant earthen oven, and the furniture shops, where exquisite parquet tables are produced along with other traditional Mexican folkcrafts. Private concerns contract with the warden to use the pitifully underpaid convict labor to make the appealing handicrafts hawked for bargains in the stalls on the tourist-rich Avenida Revolución. This prison labor is a reality to consider when buying souvenirs in Tijuana. All the prisoners, including the Americans work—making pennies a day—unless they spend a few more pennies to bribe themselves out of their appointed jobs. Even roll call, *lista*, can be slept through; all an inmate must do is spend twenty-five cents "buying your count." There is a handball court, a movie theater (the pictures are always in Spanish), and a basketball court full of men shooting hoops.

Alex Hines and his colleagues are making the best of their bad situation at La Mesa, but the sometimes acceptable conditions do not mean that these Americans are happy. "I'm never going to come back to Mexico again," says Alex, musing about his release. "Never." And he goes back to a game of Risk with his friends, dreaming of taking advantage of the prisoner-transfer treaty between the United States and Mexico. It's not that he would necessarily prefer to serve out his time in a U.S. prison. But once back north of the border, he could apply for parole, and he knows that few U.S. parole boards would keep him locked up seven years for the crime of holding one gram of marijuana.

Presidents Ford and Echeverría negotiated the prisoner-exchange treaty. Military and political prisoners cannot take advantage of it, nor can inmates locked up for violating immigration laws. And once Americans accept a transfer, the Mexican conviction remains on their records; the right to appeal is lost. Those who serve out their sentences in Mexico can come home with a blank record in the United States. But, since the treaty was ratified, for thousands of Americans it's been a reprieve from the bizarre and dangerous conditions in which too many unfortunates find themselves trapped far from home.

Peter Laufer is an award-winning radio correspondent and author of Iron Curtain Rising: A Personal Journey through the Changing Landscape of Eastern Europe *and* Nightmare Abroad: Stories of Americans Imprisoned in Foreign Lands, *from which this story is excerpted.*

I have spent years exploring the canyons and river floors and hillsides of Tijuana—hillsides where plywood and rebar combine with vigorous colors (called, variously, Tijuana Pink, Tijuana Green, and Tijuana Blue), to make *colonias* filled with the most original housing. Rather than being confusing and depressing, this do-it-yourself building encompasses variety and originality in design and execution which gives it a warmth and humanness so far beyond any of America's rigorously zoned corpseyards called "suburbs." The streets are filled with life; each tiny house can be a store or place to take in laundry, to do repair, to clean, mend, cook, fix. Automobile tires are used for steps, crates for outhouses, hard-beaten earth for floors, any available material for ceiling or wall. I once saw a dozen fine blue-and-white Coldwell Banker signs—a large real estate combine north of the border—making up the sides and roof of a shack in Rosarito.

Most of these homes have no water, no electricity, no sewage. "The Calcutta of the Americas," some have called it; but like Calcutta, amidst the poverty and garbage are children everywhere, and dogs and chickens, and people, people of every hue, every culture, people grappling with an inhospitable land but, in all the poverty, a ceremony, an individuality, a life—a rich life of the streets and interaction of neighbors that is so alien in those prim and sanitary cities to the north.

—Carlos Amantea, *The Blob That Ate Oaxaca* & *Other Travel Tales*

RICHARD RODRIGUEZ

The Evolution of *La Frontera*

The lure of the North has changed the Mexican village.

In 1991, President Bush proposed the establishment of a free-trade consortium among North American "neighbors." In fact, the new idea derived from old Mother Mexico. It was Mother Mexico, after all, who long ago mocked the notion of a border on the desert.

The United States shares with Mexico a two-thousand-mile connection—the skin of two heads. Everything that America wants to believe about himself—that he is innocent, that he is colorless, odorless, solitary, self-sufficient—is corrected, weighed upon, glossed by Mexico, the maternity of Mexico, the envy of Mexico, the grievance of Mexico.

Mexicans crossing the border are secret agents of matriarchy. Mexicans have slipped America a darker beer, a cuisine of *tú*. Mexicans have invaded American privacy to babysit or to watch the dying or to wash lipstick off the cocktail glasses. Mexicans have forced Southwestern Americans to speak Spanish whenever they want their eggs fried or their roses pruned. Mexicans have overwhelmed the Church—eleven o'clock masses in most Valley towns are Spanish masses. By force of numbers, Mexicans have taken over grammar-school classrooms. The Southwest is besotted with the culture of *tú*.

But Mexico was fooled by her own tragic knowledge of relationship. The desert is a tide. How could Mexico not have realized that tragedy would wash back on her, polluted with *gringo* optimism?

A young man leaves his Mexican village for Los Angeles in 1923. He returns one rainy night in 1925. He tells his family, next day he tells his village, that it is okay up there. The following spring, four village men accompany him back up to L.A. They send money home. Mothers keep their sons' dollars in airtight jars, opening the jars only when someone is sick or someone is dying. The money is saturated with rumor.

Thus have Mexicans from America undermined the tranquility of Mexican villages they thought only to preserve. The Mexican American became a revolutionary figure, more subversive than a *Chichimeca*, more subversive than Pancho Villa.

In the 1970s, President Luis Echeverría invited planeloads of "Chicano leaders" to visit Mexico with the apparent goal of creating a lobby for the interests of Mexico modeled on the Israeli lobby. Perhaps the Chicano was the key to Mexico's future? The Chicano, after all, defied assimilation in the United States, or said he did. The Chicano sought to retain his culture, his mother tongue. In the 1980s, the government ministry in Mexico City announced a policy of reconciliation (*acercamiento*) regarding Mexican Americans.

By the 1980s, Mexican Americans were, on average, older, wealthier, better educated than the average Mexican; we also had fewer children. In the 1980s, the proud house of Mexico was crumbling, the economy was folding, the wealthy of Mexico had begun their exodus, following the peasant's route north. Along the border, Mexican towns inclined toward America and away from Mexico City, and from the North came unclean enchantments of the *gringo*—the black music, the blond breasts, the drugged eyes of tourists.

How much is the gum?

Mexico worries about her own. What influence shall she have? The village is international now. Most of the men have been north; many of the women, too. Have seen. Everyone has heard stories.

Mexico cannot hold the attention of her children. The average age of the country descends into adolescence. More than half of Mexico is under fifteen years of age. What is the prognosis for memory in a country so young?

For Mexico is memory...

Richard Rodriguez is an editor at Pacific News Service, *an essayist on the* MacNeil/Lehrer NewsHour, *and the author of* Hunger of Memory: The Education of Richard Rodriguez, *and* Days of Obligation: An Argument with My Mexican Father, *from which this story is excerpted. He lives in San Francisco, California.*

As we drive the last miles, I think on the pilgrims who have preceeded us, and those who will follow. Some of them will look out, as we have, to see the great mysterious peaks of the Sonoran Desert at sunrise. They might be moved, as we were, by the boulders of the Rumoroso; like us, they may wonder at the singular violence of geology that extruded a rich crop of stones which, in a million years of rains, have turned rounded and golden.

All of those who come on this journey may be passing through Via Dolorosa, the highway paved with hope and fear. It is, as well, one rich with timelessness, born of these golden boulders cast out of time. With the countless tiny crosses at the side of the road, we know, too, that some of the wayfarers have left part of their beings among the stones.

—Carlos Amantea, *The Blob That Ate Oaxaca* & *Other Travel Tales*

WILLIAM LANGEWIESCHE

The Border

There is little joy along the boundary where Third and First Worlds meet.

The boundary between the United States and Mexico is in places, merely a trace in the dirt. Its permeability is famous. In the cities the boundary hardens into a steel fence to keep northbound immigrants out, and it does not work. In the open desert it dwindles to three strands of barbed wire to keep cattle in, and it works better, at least for the cattle. For more than half its length the border is the Rio Grande, a small, swimmable river. Given all this, what is most surprising about the boundary is its power to divide. For slightly more than a century it has cleaved the North American continent, and now it separates rich from poor, First World from Third World, with no Second World in between. Without ocean, high mountain, or other natural barrier, it is largely a human construct.

The twin cities of El Paso and Juárez, with a combined population of two million, mark the midpoint of the border. This is where the Rio Grande, having flowed due south from its origin in the Rockies, snakes through a gap in the desert mountains and turns southeast. It is also where the two halves of the boundary join: to the west the line runs crisply across the deserts; to the east it rides a more ambiguous midchannel course through the curves of the Rio Grande.

The U.S.-Mexican border is of course wider and more intricate than a simple boundary line. Defining it is a problem that concerns members of a group called the Association of Borderlands Scholars. I have met only a few of them, but I have read their papers.

What is the border? The traditionalists confine themselves to the fifteen or so sets of twin cities that straddle the line. Seven million people provide ample material for study.

Others feel less constrained. They refer to a "zone of influence" perhaps sixty miles wide on either side. With one simple assertion they double their population base. And why not? If they stretch a bit farther, they can include Tucson, which is a nice city.

The other day I met a North American. He is a Mixteco Indian from the State of Oaxaca in Mexico. Part of the year he works near Stockton, California; otherwise, he lives in his 16th century village, where his wife watches Venezuelan soap operas. This North American is trilingual. His first language is the ancient tongue of his Indian tribe. Spanish is his second language. He also has a working knowledge of California English.

—Richard Rodriguez, "The Mexican Peasant
is the True North American,"
The New York Times

Diehard regionalists emphasize the similarities of language and interests, and talk about a unified border region as if it already existed. Some speak of a third nation, and call it MexAmerica. The radicals among them are ready to draw up new boundaries.

Finally, global thinkers go all the way. In Mexico they point to the explosive growth of the north, the recent U.S.-inspired economic reforms, and the corruption unleashed by drug smuggling. In the United States they point to immigration problems, industrial decay, and unlawfulness. They say the border encompasses all of both countries.

The border is a word game.

It is also grimy, hot, and hostile. In most places it is ugly. The U.S. side is depressed by the filth and poverty in Mexico. On the Mexican side the towns have become ungovernable cities, overrun by destitute peasants, roiled by American values. The border is transient. The border is dangerous. The border is crass. The food is bad, the prices are high, and there are no good bookstores. It is not the place to visit on your next vacation.

Neither the United States nor Mexico wanted this intimacy. The boundary was drawn after a two-year war of conquest, during which U.S. troops invaded northern Mexico and occupied Mexico City. By the terms of the Treaty of Guadalupe Hidalgo (1848) and the subsequent Gadsden Purchase (1854), Mexico was forced to cede the northern two-fifths of its territory—a national tragedy it has not forgotten. The role of U.S. business in the exploitation that eventually led to the Mexican Revolution added to the resentment. For these reasons and others, anti-Americanism has long been a strong element of the Mexican national character. This has changed somewhat, but only recently, and—despite the new political rhetoric—unsurely.

The United States has less complex emotions: we would have preferred a second Canada on our southern flank. To put matters simply, the current move by Mexico and the United States toward some degree of economic integration—under the terms of the North American Free

Trade Agreement, which would tear down trade barriers—is an attempt to create, eventually, a more prosperous and stable Mexico. It is also a recognition of the fact that the border is no longer remote and no longer a buffer against our chaotic southern neighbor. Quite the opposite: growth on both sides of the border has physically bound the countries. Mexico's problems inevitably become ours.

It was morning in San Ysidro, California, and the air blew cool with an ocean breeze. San Ysidro is the southernmost district of San Diego, where the city presses hard against Tijuana. I stood at the border fence while six boys came over the top. The fence here is a welded steel wall, and it supported their weight easily. The boys wore jeans, t-shirts, and sneakers, and carried no luggage. The last one balanced on top and watched his friends dashing north toward a Kmart. He was thin, red-haired, and clearly disgusted by their haste. He glanced at me, seeking eye contact. I guessed he was twelve or thirteen. He wanted me to understand that he was unafraid. To prove it, he turned and dropped through a full backflip, ten feet down into the United States. He landed beside me with a thump and a grunt. In Spanish I said, "What's happening?" He answered, "Not much," and ambled off into the city.

In places the fence is new, and reinforced. Not everyone is athletic enough to go over the top. Enterprising Mexicans dig holes underneath it, and charge a dollar for each passage. Along older sections they also hack right through the steel. I watched a woman squeeze through a gap, careful not to tear her dress. A quarter mile inland the U.S. flag

The U.S. erects metal fences, hires 10,000 Customs and Immigration people just to keep the Mexicans south of the border—and it's all ass-backwards. These fences should be turned round the other way. Any Americans seeking to enter Mexico should be given deep (and painful) examinations, with seven-day visas, no extensions, forced to ante up a $25,000 bond swearing that we will not inflict our plague of needs, hungers, angers, hurts and wants on the gentle and good people. We should be required to pledge understanding that our psychic and emotional violence will not be tolerated south of the Rio Grande, that any American coming here and foisting off his brutalism on the innocents of this land will make him subject to fines and immediate banishment north of the border.

The Great White Plague, carrying with it all our desires, our malaise of our form of love, our fantasy of "civilization." We bring it along with us like a curse, to ruin the innocents of this dry and dusty and wounded earth.

—Carlos Amantea, *The Blob That Ate Oaxaca & Other Travel Tales*

flew over the official port of entry. The "port" is, in fact, two gates—one Mexican and one American—big, boastful structures that span the north-south freeway. Together they tally fifty million crossings every year, and claim to be the busiest border point in the world. Southbound traffic slows but rarely stops. Northbound traffic backs up for hours. In 1991 U.S. gatekeepers blocked some 52,000 fraudulent entries, but for every unauthorized foreigner they turned back, perhaps twenty others hit the fence. The Immigration Reform and Control Act of 1986 was meant to solve that problem. The gatekeepers still cling forlornly to it. "The law should have worked," they say. But California beckons, and the immigrants feel neither reformed nor controlled.

Border scholars believe that half of all illegal entries into the United States occur here. The immigrants choose San Diego not just because the crossing is easy (it is easy everywhere except in the harshest deserts) but because it is convenient. Three million people live in San Diego and Tijuana, and another fifteen million live in Los Angeles, to the north. The hustle is relentless. Even in recession there is opportunity. Ambitious workers from all over Mexico and Central America come to Tijuana by bus. Tijuana is the sort of Mexican success story that free-trade proponents promise: tourism has been supplemented by industrial development; the city claims full employment and factories that hire at seven dollars a day. Still, many of the new arrivals keep going. They are met at the bus station by "coyotes," smugglers who can lose them into California cities. In California they can find friends and family. They can find work at five dollars an hour.

The boundary here is a fourteen-mile stretch from the Pacific through brushland and city streets to the first desert mountain. In daylight the immigrants trickle across the fence; after dark they hit it in waves, and come by the thousands. The San Diego sector of the Border Patrol has 800 agents, by far the largest concentration anywhere on the border, and they only touch the flow. If this is a war zone, it has its recurring battlefields—places like Dairy Mart Road, McDonald's, Denny's, the borderland motels. The earth is hard-packed, and scarred by polished trails.

The morning's calm was a form of exhaustion. From the port of entry I walked along the fence, past the boy who had backflipped, to the point where the Tijuana River flows in from Mexico. The Tijuana River is an open sewer. After it enters the United States, it turns west and runs parallel to the boundary, between massive levees. An indignant San Diegan instructed me to "go look how the Mexicans pointed that river at us!" But the river was once a natural flow, and it still approximates its original short course to the ocean.

A bulldozer was clearing brush from the banks. Brush makes good cover, especially at night. Some congressmen believe that clearing it away and installing bright lights, thereby "sanitizing" the border, will reduce illegal immigration. But I watched a family cross within a hundred feet of the bulldozer. The father led, followed by four children and the mother. They balanced on old tires that had been laid across the shallow river like stepping-stones. After the family left, the bulldozer eased into the current and pushed the tires onto the south bank. I thought the tires should have been piled on the north side. The man on the bulldozer probably figured it made no difference.

Later I watched as a young man shepherded across a group of stocky, dark-skinned women. Wearing plastic bags around their legs, they bunched together and waded shin-deep through the filthy water. On dry ground again, they stooped and peeled off the leg protectors. The bank was littered with hundreds of these bags; vendors sell them on the south side for a dollar a pair, rubber bands included. The guide told the women to wait, and he scrambled up the levee to scout for the Border Patrol. He stood near me, breathing heavily, and checked the neighborhood. We did not speak. He beckoned to his group, and they started up, bent forward against the slope. Suddenly a green Border Patrol Bronco drove onto the levee, and accelerated toward us. The women retreated to the river. The guide took two steps down the levee and stood his ground. The Border Patrol agent stopped above him and didn't bother to get out. He was a burly man in a green uniform and a felt cowboy hat. My presence seemed to make him uncertain. He backed away and parked below the levee in a field. The guide returned and squatted comfortably. He seemed amused.

The Border Patrol is the uniformed law-enforcement branch of the Immigration and Naturalization Service. It deploys about 2,800 agents along the U.S.-Mexican border. Texans are heavily represented. Border Patrol agents have had various names for the people they catch. They used to call them wetbacks, even in dry country. Responding to the times, Washington encouraged the use of the term "illegal aliens." After critics objected to "illegal," Washington compromised on "undocumented." This was one change too many for the Border Patrol agents, who are not inclined to chase fashion.

Ninety percent of the people they catch are Mexicans. The other ten percent are "OTMs," which stands for "other than Mexicans," and means mostly Central and South Americans. The distinction is important, because OTMs cannot be shipped to Mexico; they must be flown home. Deportation is a serious setback for them; it may be months before they can return north. Mexicans move faster. They waive their right to a hearing, take the INS shuttle to the border, and if the night is young, turn around and come right back. The official estimate is that half or two thirds get through, but in the long run the real numbers are higher. Anyone who tries will eventually succeed.

Border Patrol agents simply do their job. One said to me, "Catch'em, write'em up, back to Mexico. Catch'em, write'em up, back to Mexico." In fiscal year 1991 they wrote them up 1,077,000 times. This number should not be confused with the number of aliens; the Border Patrol acknowledges that it includes people who have been caught more than once in a fiscal year. What it does not mention is that some are caught twice in a fiscal night. Still, the figures are not complete nonsense: they measure the labor performed by the agents and give a rough accounting of the flow.

In the afternoon I drove through the eerie flatland where the Tijuana River meanders its last five miles to the ocean. Few people live here, though the real estate is cheap. This is the war zone at its most dismal. There are killings, rapes, robberies. Placards with skulls and crossbones warn of contamination. The river is diseased, and the stench of sewage is inescapable. Coastal winds stir clouds of fine-grained fecal dust, making you want to cover your face when you breathe. There is a sod farm, a nursery, and a stable that advertises horse rentals. At an abandoned ranch house a hand-painted sign reads NO MAN'S LAND.

The boundary runs just to the south, along low hills that slope down into Tijuana. All day the crowds gather at the fence. By late afternoon you see hundreds out there, dark lines of people waiting for the sun to set. Vendors sell them drinks and tacos. Where the fence is torn, they swell through it and stand inside the United States. Border Patrol agents square off against them in a few scattered trucks, radios crackling, hoping that their mere presence will serve as a deterrent. They face a near riot every afternoon, and they keep a safe distance. For the city toughs who jeer at the agents and sometimes throw rocks, the fence is a shelter.

At dusk the line crumbles. Down in the flatland, a group of men and women hurry across Monument Road. They emerge suddenly from Smuggler's Gulch and disappear without a trace into the bushes. You wonder if in the twilight your mind has tricked you, but then you see another group, and another. The night turns black under ocean clouds, and fills with immigrants moving north. A dog barks viciously. A helicopter circles low in the distance, probing the land with its spotlight. The port of entry glows to the east. There are no birds, crickets, or frogs.

You hear the muted roar of the cities, and the crunch of footsteps on gravel.

Two miles away, along Interstate 5, the first wave sweeps across the freeway. Interstate 5 starts at the port of entry and heads north, through downtown San Diego and Los Angeles. It is lit, but the immigrants hide in the shadows, waiting for a gap in the traffic. Some misjudge the speed of the oncoming cars; since 1987 more than 150 have been hit and killed. California has lowered the speed limits and installed flashing yellow lights above warning signs. The warning signs show figures immediately recognizable as immigrants—they run, they hold hands, the women wear scarves. But people drive fast in San Diego, rarely under seventy. A local driver said to me, "Gee, those poor Mexicans. You know who I'm more concerned about?"

I thought, Let me guess.

He said, "The people who hit them. When you run out on the freeway, you make a choice. When you're driving the freeway, you have no choice. You go straight ahead or into the cars next to you."

"You could slow down," I suggested.

"They're causing people to have accidents," he said. "We ought to build a fence."

Most of the people who run onto the freeway go all the way across and melt into the city at San Ysidro. But others stop halfway, along the freeway's concrete median strip. The median is neutral ground, where the Border Patrol will not chase them. By midnight several hundred people have gathered there, under the glare of overhead lights. They wait with their guides for prearranged rides, or rest before moving on. They sleep, eat, play cards. I have watched them dancing. Some may have made love, or given birth. At dawn you see those who are stuck, afraid to move on. Like any neutral ground, the median can be a trap as well as a haven.

William Langewiesche is a pilot and author who writes regularly for The Atlantic Monthly. *This story is excerpted from his book,* Cutting for Sign, *published by Pantheon Books. His next book will be about the Sahara.*

Tecate is the last town between Tijuana and the border. Our passage is almost done. Before us there is a truck—one of the many noisy, overloaded, about-to-tip-over trucks, so ubiquitous in Mexico. It is heavy with flowers, thousands of carnations of a particularly delicate mauve. With each lurch of the truck, a few dozen of them sprinkle down before us onto the highway, circle about in its wake. Many trucks must have gone before us because the roadway and its edges are littered with hundreds of these mauve carnations. They roll merrily across the asphalt, come to rest in the center, and atop the weeds and trash at the side of the highway.

A floral highway. They are greeting us, aren't they? Those who have gone before are laying a carpet of flowers for those of us to follow. In the pearl light of the Cóndor Mesa, the golden mountains behind us, the fresh landscape: we're being glorified with blossoms out of our days.

—Carlos Amantea, *The Blob That Ate Oaxaca & Other Travel Tales*

PART V

The Last Word

CHARLES BOWDEN

Vaya con Dios

The present is paramount in Mexico.

The first man was called Head of a Cow, Cabeza de Vaca. He and three companions walked six thousand miles, beginning around Galveston, Texas, and blundered into the place we now call the Southwest in the United States, the Northwest in Mexico. Since then of course, many have followed in his footsteps as explorers, settlers, prospectors, missionaries, conquistadors, vagabonds, scientists, and tourists. I doubt that any person has ever penetrated the country as deeply as Cabeza de Vaca and I wonder if anyone ever will. The blood price for such a journey is high, very high.

While many people are said to have conquered America, Cabeza de Vaca was conquered by America. He began with different intentions. His grandfather had taken the Canary Islands, enslaved native people, and set his stamp upon that land. Cabeza de Vaca was raised in a household staffed with slaves from this sacking. When he arrived in this New World, he was second in command of an expedition to seize Florida, find gold, spawn empire. The men starved, and became lost and in time, their number was pared from several hundred to finally four souls huddled on the Texas coast. By this time they wore no clothes, had been the slaves of the Indians, had learned the languages, and knew how to survive off the land. They had been slowly stripped of the Old World that adorned their bodies and much of their souls. They were three Spaniards and a Moor from the coast of Morocco and they began to walk toward Mexico.

The cold they did not feel, nor hunger either. And to the native Americans they met along the way they seemed like holy men, like healers. They were reluctant to try and effect cures. One of their number felt he was not clean enough, not free of sin enough to have such powers. But the people they met insisted and so they tried, and many were healed. Soon they traveled with hundreds in their entourage, with entire villages giving them food and shelter and objects of power—arrowheads made of turquoise, magic gourds, special pelts, copper bells. The four companions walked naked at the head of this procession, walked across

Texas, walked across southern New Mexico, walked across southeastern Arizona, dove into Sonora.

They escape time. We are fated to live almost every moment of our lives in the future tense, in anticipation of things we will do, things we will achieve, people we will become. The past for us is a vast barren that pulls at us from behind, a place we know by reputation. But we do not live there. The present, it hardly exists, the briefest flickering as we stride ahead, our minds focused on our becoming, becoming, becoming. But the future, it justifies all our acts, occupies all our days and nights, and feeds all our lusts. We will be.

Cabeza de Vaca escaped into the present in his six thousand miles of trudging, in his years on the trail. He became perhaps the only one of our number ever to truly live in America. His world became bizarre yet normal. In central Sonora, natives offered him six hundred deer hearts. Of course, he shared this bounty with everyone. He and his companions always shared. And so while they kept plunging on toward their Mexico, two things happened. One, they were always exactly wherever they were, healing, sharing food, talking, and learning from the Indians. And they were remade from whatever they were into something that had probably never been before: people from the Old World who have been devoured by the New World.

Finally, in northern Sinaloa, they came upon the Spaniards. Their compatriots did not recognize these naked men at the head of a column of natives as their fellow citizens. The Spaniards were slavers, and had devastated and depopulated much of Sonora. They wished to make Cabeza de Vaca's entourage into slaves, also. They envied his friendship with the natives and their respect for him. Cabeza de Vaca forbade the slavers to act and denounced their activities. The Spaniards argued. They tried to convince the Indians that the four men they were following were just like themselves and not special or different men. The Indians rejected this argument out of hand.

> The Indians paid no attention to this.... They replied that the Christians lied: we had come from the sunrise, they from the sunset; we healed the sick, they killed the sound; we came naked and barefoot, they clothed, horsed, and lanced; we coveted nothing but gave whatever we were given, while they robbed whomever they found and bestowed nothing on anyone.
>
> Alvar Núñez Cabeza de Vaca
> *Adventures in the Unknown Interior of America* (1542)

Of course, these moments passed. When the four men arrived in Culiacán, they still found clothes unbearable to wear and Cabeza de Vaca preferred the ground to a soft bed. By the time, in the summer of 1536, he arrived in Mexico he was wardrobed by Hernán Cortés, the great conqueror. And from his lips escaped stories that became the seven cities of gold, and launched the greed that became the Coronado expedition of 1540. The man conquered by America slowly freed himself, and became again a Spaniard with a sword. But not quite. He was later sent to South America, led an expedition into Paraguay, and was returned to Spain and prison for basically being too kind to the Indians.

We are left with his brief book, *Adventures in the Unknown Interior of America*, the first and best book ever written on the place that still has no common name, that dry hot region called Southwest or Northwest, depending on a person's national background. His little yet profound book ends in the tropical forest that blankets southern Sonora and rolls on into Sinaloa, a place described by Cabeza de Vaca as "no doubt, the most prolific land in all these Indies. It produces three crops a year; the trees bear a great variety of fruit; and beautiful rivers and brimming springs abound throughout. This land, in short, lacks nothing to be regarded as blest."

We look again, our eyes weary with centuries of life here, our hearts heavy with centuries of plundering. We have fabricated a world so dense with objects and demands that we need national parks and official wildernesses as sanctuaries from its fangs and talons. We tell each other at times that we have lost touch with something that truly is life. We spend most of our time on tomorrow and hardly notice today. We look into the forest and wonder what might be there. We hesitate.

A faint memory tugs.

Yes.

Christina's world is different than we remember it from the Andrew Wyeth painting. She has no limp this time and she is not crawling toward the big house with yearning radiating from her limbs. Instead, she rises at 3 a.m. and grinds corn on the *metate* for tortillas. The black stone is embedded in her *cocina* right next to the wood fire, where small limbs from the forest crackle in the hours before light. Her face is round, the teeth perfect and white, the smile seeming to come without effort. Her five children still sleep, as does her husband. They will arise when the tortillas are made and the coffee bubbles over the flames. She is a woman and she is about her work in the hours before the sun touches the sierra and the world begins again. Her dress is shiny and a brilliant blue.

Corn ground, tortillas made, coffee poured, her man eats, packs some more in his *bolsa*, and is off for the sierra to cut *leña*, wood for the fire, and to look for some cows that have failed to come home. A kitten rubs against Christina's leg as he leaves in the gray light. Then the children rise, eat also, and move down the dirt lane to the highway and walk into a nearby town for school. The oldest is fifteen, and Christina, her years are hard to measure—perhaps on her face, thirty-five years, perhaps since her birth date, thirty. Now she goes out into the cool air of morning.

The cows must be milked in their wooden corral near the house. Then she goes down to the wash where a bucket dangles over the village's ancient well and she hauls load after load of water to the stock. The day is now on and she pours herself a cup of coffee, and goes to the portals facing the *milpa* and the wash below, and enjoys the sounds of the forest coming alive. Over her head, the *perico* squawks and she grabs a pole, hoists it up, and the bird hops aboard. The wings have been severely clipped—Christina's mother captured the parrot, trimmed its feathers, and gave it to her as a gift—and the markings show it to be a white-fronted parrot. The bird climbs on her shoulder, nuzzles against her hair, and nibbles at her ear. In the brown field below the *chapotes* are in leaf, the big trees a welcome sign of green in the endless brown of the *campo* as it awaits the rain. In a week or two or three, *las aguas* will fall, the ground will go wet, life will quicken, and the corn will be planted. Another year will truly begin.

The neighboring hills are being scrapped as more and more of the forest is felled by the village for the planting of the buffel grass. Wood also disappears for the cook fires, for the pottery making, for the brick making, for all the warmth that life requires. No one knows the age of this village but its bones and bloodlines testify that it is Indian in origin and winds back into the mists of time. Christina sips her coffee, a young piglet snores at her feet, the parrot chatters in her ear. In the kitchen hangs the haunch of a deer—a fellow villager brought it down off the sierra—and she will cook it today, slow boil it over the wood fire. After that goes in her kitchen, she will put three quarts of milk in her *bolsa* and walk into town and sell the milk. Then...it hardly matters. The days manage to flow ceaselessly with things to do. Christina sleeps but five hours each night and never rests in the heat of the afternoon.

Ah, Christina's world, if she only knew. There are many conferences about Christina's world now, meetings all over the world concerned with the rapid disappearance of the tropical forest, coalitions dedicated to stopping the people of the world from eating the world. These groups meet in fine buildings with climate-controlled air. There are no wood fires at these gatherings and the deer is not in the stew pot. That's the rub, the thing we come back to always after enjoying the beauty of the forest, after being fascinated by the intricacy of the forest. The people of the forest who are eating it root and branch, they to a man, woman, and child are very poor, and they consume very few things of this earth, not nearly as many things as the people who attend the conferences in very distant locations. And yet, their way of life now seems suddenly lethal to all of us. There are so many people now and the earth itself, it does not grow but seems to shrink. So we have this meeting, produce these papers, consider these problems, and we always seem to wind up telling the poor they take too much and they look at us, and know they have very little and we have very much.

There will be an answer to this problem—we have no doubt of that. The forest will be gone, dead in a generation if something is not done, and Christina's world of subsistence, babies, cook fires, and deer in the pot will die also if the forest dies. Or we can intervene through some plan, and, armed with money and rules, try to save the forest and then also, the poor will perish if we take away their only source of food, warmth, and home. So we hesitate because the choices become hard and we do not like hard choices. Even worse than a hard choice is the nature of the decision facing us. Not only will Christina have to change...we must change also. And we are not used to this, not experienced at all in giving up some of our comforts, in curbing some of our appetites. But we will, but we must or....

For Christina, these concerns do not matter this morning. The sun is up, the parched corn is ground, the tortillas are made, the cows milked and watered, the deer is slow-cooking in the pot, the parrot is nibbling at her ear and chattering. She smiles, she smiles so very easily. She will not sleep for fifteen hours but this does not matter either as she looks out at the field ready for the rain and enjoys the calm of God's world under the dark brow of the sierra.

Charles Bowden also contributed "The Wedding and the Land" to Part I. These two stories are from his book, The Secret Forest, *published by the University of New Mexico Press.*

Books for Further Reading

We hope *Travelers' Tales Mexico* has inspired you to read on. A good place to start is the books from which we've made selections, and we have listed them below. We've also included some of the better general guidebooks, because they're worth reading. The guidebooks have annotated bibliographies or sections on recommended books and maps.

Abbas. *Return to Mexico: Journeys Beyond the Mask*. New York: W.W. Norton & Co., 1992.

Adams, Alice. *Mexico: Some Travels and Some Travelers There*. New York: Simon & Schuster, 1990.

Amantea, Carlos. *The Blob That Ate Oaxaca & Other Travel Tales*. San Diego: Mho & Mho Works, 1992.

Barry, Tom. *Mexico: A Country Guide*. New Mexico: Inter-Hemispheric Education Resource Center, 1992.

Bowden, Charles. *The Secret Forest*. New Mexico: University of New Mexico Press, 1993.

Brosnahan, Tom, John Noble, Nancy Keller, Mark Balla and Scott Wayne. *Mexico – a travel survival kit*. Hawthorne, Victoria, Australia: Lonely Planet Publications, 1992.

Bruns, Rebecca, Dave Houser, Jan Butchofsky, Richard and Donna Carroll. *Hidden Mexico*. Berkeley: Ulysses Press, 1992.

Canby, Peter. *The Heart of the Sky: Travels Among the Maya*. New York: HarperCollins, 1992.

Coe, Michael D. *Breaking the Maya Code*. New York: Thames and Hudson, 1992.

Conover, Ted. *Coyotes: A Journey Through the Secret World of America's Illegal Aliens*. New York: Random House, 1987.

Conrad, Jim. *On the Road to Tetlama: Mexican Adventures of a Wandering Naturalist*. New York: Walker and Company, 1991.

Cummings, Joe. *Baja Handbook*. Chico, California: Moon Publications, 1992.

Davies, Miranda and Natania Jansz. *Women Travel: A Rough Guide Special.* London: Rough Guides, Ltd., 1990.

Franz, Carl. *The Peoples Guide to Mexico.* Santa Fe: John Muir Publications, 1992.

Freidel, David, Linda Schele, and Joy Parker. *Maya Cosmos: Three Thousand Years on the Shaman's Path.* New York: William Morrow & Company, 1993.

Gonzalez-Crussi, F. *Day of the Dead and Other Mortal Reflections.* New York: Harcourt Brace & Company, 1993.

Harris, Richard and Stacy Ritz. *The Maya Route: The Ultimate Guidebook* Berkeley: Ulysses Press, 1993.

Harrison, Jim. *Just Before Dark: Collected Nonfiction.* New York: Houghton Mifflin, 1992.

Harvard Student Agencies. *Let's Go Mexico.* New York: St. Martin's Press, 1994.

Langewiesche, William. *Cutting for Sign.* New York: Pantheon Books, 1993.

Laufer, Peter. *Nightmare Abroad: Stories of Americans Imprisoned in Foreign Lands.* San Francisco: Mercury House, 1993.

Mallan, Chicki. *Cancún Handbook and Mexico's Caribbean Coast.* Chico, California: Moon Publications, 1993.

McDonald, Paula. *Crossing the Border Fast and Easy.* Phoenix: Borderline Associates, 1992.

Morris, Mary. *Nothing to Declare: Memoirs of a Woman Traveling Alone.* New York: Houghton Mifflin Company, 1988.

Müller, Kal and Guillermo García-Oropeza. *Insight Guides: Mexico.* Singapore: APA Productions Ltd., 1993.

Nelson, "Mexico" Mike. *Mexico from the Driver's Seat: Tales of the Road from Baja to the Yucatán.* Oak Park, MI: Scrivener Press, 1991.

Paz, Octavio. *The Labryrinth of Solitude and Other Writings.* New York: Grove Press, Inc., 1991.

Perera, Victor and Robert D. Bruce. *The Last Lords of Palenque: The Lacandón Maya of the Mexican Rain Forest.* Boston: Little, Brown and Co., 1982.

Riding, Alan. *Distant Neighbors: A Portrait of the Mexicans.* New York: Vintage Books, 1989.

Rodriguez, Richard. *Days of Obligation: An Argument With My Mexican Father.* New York: Penguin Books, 1992.

Rogers, Steve and Tina Rosa. *The Shoppers Guide to Mexico*. Santa Fe: John Muir Publications, 1989.

Schueler, Donald G. *The Temple of the Jaguar: Travels in the Yucatán*. San Francisco: Sierra Club Books, 1993.

Sellers, Jeff M. *Folk Wisdom of Mexico*. San Francisco: Chronicle Books, 1994.

Sienko, Walter. *Latin America By Bike: A Complete Touring Guide*. Seattle: The Mountaineers, 1993.

Simon, Kate. *Mexico: Places and Pleasures*. New York: Harper and Row, 1988.

Starkell, Don. *Paddle to the Amazon*. Rocklin, California: Prima Publishing and Communications, 1989.

Steinbeck, John. *The Log From the Sea of Cortez*. New York: Viking Penguin, 1986.

Thompson, Katharine and Charlotte. *Cadogan Guides: Mexico*. London: Cadogan Books Ltd., Connecticut: The Globe Pequot Press, 1991.

Turner, Frederick. *A Border of Blue: Along the Gulf of Mexico from the Keys to the Yucatán*. New York: Henry Holt & Company, 1993.

Wauer, Ronald H. *A Naturalist's Mexico*. Texas: Texas A & M University Press, 1992.

Whipperman, Bruce. *Pacific Mexico Handbook*. Chico, California: Moon Publications, 1993.

Wright, Ronald. *Time Among the Maya: Travels in Belize, Guatemala, and Mexico*. New York: Grove/Atlantic, 1991.

Glossary

ayate	type of carryall/bag/tote
barranca	ravine
barrio	area, neighborhood
bolsa	bag, sack
bruja	witch doctor, shaman
calle	street
camino	road
campesino	peasant
cenote	deep water-filled sinkhole
cerveza	beer
ciudad	town or city
cocina	kitchen
colectivo	minibus or car which takes passengers along a set route
compadre/comadre	Godfather, godmother, close friend, relative
ejido	collective farm granted to landless peasants after the Mexican Revolution
frijoles	refried beans
gente	people
hacienda	farm or ranch
huevos	eggs; slang for testicles
huevos rancheros	traditional egg dish served on tortillas with beans and salsa
huipil	traditional piece of clothing consisting of a white overblouse with delicate emroidery around the neck and bottom
ídolo	idol

Lacandón	region of rain forest on the eastern slopes of the Chiapas highlands. Inhabited by Maya known as "Lacandóns"
ladino	person of mixed Indian and non-Indian blood
mestizo	person of mixed Spanish and Indian blood
metate	shallow stone bowl with legs, used for grinding corn and other food
milpa	plot of land used to grow corn, beans, squash, and other crops
mordida	literally "little bite," a small bribe paid to bureaucrats or policemen
palapa	thatched roof shelter, often found on beaches
panga	traditional high-bowed fishing skiff
pescado	fish
pox	Chiapas moonshine. Pronounced "posh"
pulque	slightly alcoholic milky drink made from the maguey cactus
quinto	country house
rancho	ranch or small farm
refresco	cold drink
refritos	refried beans
tienda	shop or store
traje	traditional Indian clothing
vaquero	cowboy
zócalo	central community open-air plaza

Index

Acknowledgements

Enduring thanks to Wenda Brewster O'Reilly, Andrea, Noelle and Mariele O'Reilly, Paula McCabe, Timothy O'Reilly, Susan Brady, Raj Khadka, Edie Freedman, Jennifer Niederst, Linda Sirola, Allen Noren, Maureen and Kerry Kravitz, and John McLean, to whom we also say with much love, *vaya con Dios*. Thanks also to Sean O'Reilly, Anne O'Reilly, Van Deren Coke, David White, Deborah Perugi, Patti Polisar, Kathleen Kenny, Cindy Collins, Paula McDonald, Lee Foster, Dave G. Houser, Jan Butchofsky, Dave Bartruff, Steve Bly, Cynthia Hunter, Ken Rice, Desmond O'Shaughnessy Doyle, Martin Pray, Dottie Furman, Harriet Bullitt, Alexander Voronin, Jeff Brady, Tobi Richards, Adrienne LeFarge, Marcia Kegel, and Trisha Schwartz. And last but not least, to the families of those who must endure our company, bad jokes and flatulence at the end of the book process.

"Serenading the Future" by Alma Guillermoprieto excerpted from *The Heart That Bleeds: Latin America Now* by Alma Guillermoprieto. Copyright © 1994 by Alma Guillermoprieto. Reprinted by permission of Alfred A. Knopf, Inc.

"Crossing the Linguistic *Frontera*" by Joel Simon reprinted by permission of the author. Copyright © 1994 by Joel Simon.

"Temple of the Jaguar," "The World Tree and the Praying Girl," and "Roberto and the Permanent Revolution" by Donald G. Schueler excerpted from *The Temple of the Jaguar: Travels in the Yucatán* by Donald G. Schueler. Copyright © 1993 by Donald G. Schueler. Reprinted with permission of Sierra Club Books.

"Welcoming the Spirits On Janitzio Island" and "Getting Wired in Oaxaca" by Jeff Greenwald reprinted by permission of the author. Copyright © 1994 by Jeff Greenwald.

"A Routine Night in Veracruz" and "Road Warrior" by Frederick Turner excerpted from *A Border of Blue: Along the Gulf of Mexico from the Keys to the Yucatán* by Frederick Turner. Copyright © 1993 by Frederick Turner. Reprinted by permission of Henry Holt & Co., Inc., the Robin Straus Agency, Inc., and the author.

Acknowledgements

"Sometimes A Shave" by Richard A. Cole reprinted by permission of the author. Copyright © 1994 by Richard A. Cole.

"In Nahuatl it Means Butterfly" by Anthony DePalma reprinted from the November 18, 1993 issue of *The New York Times*. Copyright © 1993 by The New York Times Company. Reprinted by permission.

"The Flamingos of Celestún" by Ronald D. Goben reprinted by permission of the author. Copyright © 1994 by Ronald D. Goben.

"The Hills of Guanajuato" by Jenny Lenore Rosenbaum reprinted by permission of the author. Copyright © 1994 by Jenny Lenore Rosenbaum.

"Riding the Rails in Sonora" by Carol Pucci of *The Seattle Times* reprinted by permission of the author. Copyright © 1994 by Carol Pucci.

"Diving with Hammerheads" by Scott Doggett reprinted from the February 7, 1993 issue of the *Los Angeles Times*. Reprinted by permission of the Los Angeles Times-Washington Post News Service and the author. Copyright © 1993 by Scott Doggett.

"Golden Guadalajara" by Bart McDowell reprinted from the September/October 1991 issue of *National Geographic Traveler*. Reprinted by permission of the author. Copyright © 1991 by Bart McDowell.

"Finding Frida Kahlo" by Alice Adams excerpted from *Mexico: Some Travels and Some Travelers There* by Alice Adams. Copyright © 1990 by Alice Adams. Reprinted by permission of Simon & Schuster, Inc.

"*Se Habla Español*" by Joyce Gregory reprinted by permission of the author. Copyright © 1994 by Joyce Gregory.

"A Healing Place" by Pete Hamill reprinted from the December-January 1992 issue of *Travel-Holiday*. Reprinted by permission of International Creative Management, Inc. Copyright © 1992 by Pete Hamill.

"The Underground World of the Yucatán" by Richard Bloom reprinted by permission of the author. Copyright © 1994 by Richard Bloom.

"Up the Volcano" by Reed Glenn reprinted by permission of the author. Copyright © 1994 by Reed Glenn.

"In the Land of Avocados" by Ted Conover excerpted from *Coyotes: A Journey Through the Secret World of America's Illegal Aliens* by Ted Conover. Copyright © 1987 by Ted Conover. Reprinted by permission of Random House, Inc. and Sterling Lord Literistic, Inc.

399

Acknowledgements

Georges Borchardt, Inc. for the author. Copyright © 1992 by Richard Rodriguez.

"The Border" by William Langewiesche originally appeared in the May 1992 edition of *The Atlantic Monthly*. From *Cutting For Sign* by William Langewiesche. Copyright © 1994 by William Langewiesche. Reprinted by permission of Pantheon Books, a division of Random House, Inc.

Additional Credits (arranged alphabetically by title)

Selections from *A Border of Blue: Along the Gulf of Mexico from the Keys to the Yucatán* by Frederick Turner reprinted by permission of Henry Holt & Company, the Robin Straus Agency, Inc., and the author. Copyright © 1993 by Frederick Turner.

Selection from *A Naturalist's Mexico* by Roland H. Wauer reprinted by permission of Texas A & M University Press. Copyright © 1992 by Roland H. Wauer.

Selection from "An Irishman In Guanajuato" by Desmond O'Shaughnessy Doyle reprinted by permission of the author. Copyright © 1994 by Desmond O'Shaughnessy Doyle.

Selection from "Artists Find a Home in Puerto Vallarta" by Ron Bernthal reprinted by permission of the author. Copyright © 1994 by Ron Bernthal.

Selection from "At the House of the Jaguar" by Joyce Gregory reprinted by permission of the author. Copyright © 1994 by Joyce Gregory.

Selection from *Breaking the Maya Code* by Michael D. Coe reprinted by permission of Thames and Hudson. Copyright © 1992 by Michael D. Coe.

Selections from *Cadogan Guides: Mexico* by Katharine & Charlotte Thompson reprinted with permission from Cadogan Books Limited, London House, Parkgate Road, London, SW11 4NQ, and The Globe Pequot Press. Copyright © 1991 by Katharine & Charlotte Thompson. Published in North America by The Globe Pequot Press.

Selection from "Cities of Silver" by Gully Wells reprinted from the November 1992 issue of *Condé Nast Traveler*. Courtesy *Condé Nast Traveler*. Copyright © 1992 *Condé Nast Traveler*.

Selection from *Coyotes: A Journey Through the Secret World of America's Illegal Aliens* by Ted Conover reprinted by permission of Random House, Inc. and Sterling Lord Literistic, Inc. Copyright © 1987 by Ted Conover.

Acknowledgements

Selection from *Just Before Dark: Collected Nonfiction* by Jim Harrison reprinted by permission of Houghton Mifflin Company. Copyright © 1992 by Jim Harrison.

Selections from *Let's Go Mexico* by Harvard Student Agencies reprinted by permission of Let's Go, Inc. Copyright © 1994 by Let's Go, Inc.

Selections from *Mexico – a travel survival kit* by Tom Brosnahan, John Noble, Nancy Keller, Mark Balla, and Scott Wayne reprinted by permission of Lonely Planet Publications. Copyright © 1992 by Lonely Planet Publications.

Selections from *Maya Cosmos: Three Thousand Years on the Shaman's Path* by David Freidel, Linda Schele, & Joy Parker reprinted by permission of William Morrow & Company, Inc. Copyright © 1993 by Linda Schele, David Freidel, & Joy Parker.

Selection from *Mexico: A Country Guide* edited by Tom Barry reprinted by permission of Inter-Hemispheric Education Resource Center, Albuquerque, New Mexico, and Tom Barry. Copyright © 1992 by Inter-Hemispheric Education Resource Center.

Selections from *Mexico: Places and Pleasures* by Kate Simon. Copyright © 1988 by Kate Simon. Reprinted by permission of HarperCollins Publishers, Inc. and International Creative Management, Inc.

Selections from *Mexico: Some Travels and Some Travelers There* by Alice Adams reprinted by permission of Simon & Schuster, Inc. Copyright © 1990 by Alice Adams.

Selections from "Mexico: The Devil's Piñata" by Lee Foster reprinted by permission of the author. Copyright © 1994 by Lee Foster.

Selections from *Mexico from the Driver's Seat: Tales of the Road from Baja to the Yucatán* by "Mexico" Mike Nelson reprinted by permission of T.G.P., Inc. and the author. Copyright © 1991 by T.G.P., Inc.

Selections from "Mexico's Copper Canyon" by Elías Castillo reprinted from the Spring 1993 issue of *Great Expeditions* magazine. Reprinted by permission of the author. Copyright © 1993 by Elías Castillo.

Selection from "Nobody Retires to Mexico" by Martin Pray reprinted by permission of the author. Copyright © 1994 by Martin Pray.

Selections from "Of Spyhopping and Firkydoodeling: Whale Watching In Mag Bay Remembered" by Kent Madin reprinted from the Winter/Spring 1994 issue of *Adventure West* magazine. Reprinted by permission of SKI WEST Publications, Inc. and the author. Copyright © 1994 by Kent Madin.

Acknowledgements

Selections from *The People's Guide to Mexico* by Carl Franz reprinted by permission of John Muir Publications. Copyright © 1992 by Carl Franz.

Selection from *The Shopper's Guide to Mexico* by Steve Rogers and Tina Rosa reprinted by permission of John Muir Publications. Copyright © 1989 by Steve Rogers and Tina Rosa.

Selections from *The Temple of the Jaguar: Travels in the Yucatán* by Donald G. Schueler. Copyright © 1993 by Donald G. Schueler. Reprinted with permission of Sierra Club Books.

Selection from "Treasures of the Sierra Madre" by Guy Trebay from the November 1990 issue of *Condé Nast Traveler*. Courtesy of *Condé Nast Traveler* and the author. Copyright © 1990 by Guy Trebay.

Selection from *Time Among the Maya: Travels in Belize, Guatemala, and Mexico* by Ronald Wright reprinted by permission of Grove/Atlantic, Inc. Copyright © 1991 by Ronald Wright.

Selection from "What Single Parents Need to Know" by Deborah Haeseler, copyright © 1993 by Parents' Press. Reprinted with permission.

Selection from *Women Travel: A Rough Guide Special* edited by Miranda Davies and Natania Jansz with Alisa Joyce and Jane Parkin reprinted by permission of Rough Guides, Ltd. Copyright © 1990 by Miranda Davies and Natania Jansz.

About the Editors

James O'Reilly and Larry Habegger first worked together as late night disc jockeys at Dartmouth College in New Hampshire. They wrote mystery serials for the San Francisco Examiner in the early 1980s before turning to travel writing. Since 1983, their travel features and self-syndicated column, "World Travel Watch," have appeared in magazines and newspapers in the United States and other countries. James was born in Oxford, England, raised in San Francisco, and lives with his family in Leavenworth, Washington and France; Larry was born and raised in Minnesota and lives on Telegraph Hill in San Francisco.

About this Book

The cover design of *Travelers' Tales Mexico* is by Edie Freedman; cover photograph by Van Deren Coke. The cover art was created in QuarkXPress 3.3 and Photoshop 2.5. Color separations were done by Best Gagne.

The travel stamps were created in Aldus Freehand 3.1 and Adobe Photoshop 2.5. The stamp illustrations were created by Edie Freedman and David White, with some help from the Dover Pictorial Archive.

Interior design is by Jennifer Niederst. The pages were produced by Karla Tolbert and Jennifer Niederst using QuarkXpress 3.3 in a Macintosh environment. Kathleen Kenny provided production assistance. The fonts are Adobe Birch and Weiss. Jeff Robbins created the Weiss Bold Italic and Birch Italic fonts using Fontographer software and Adobe original fonts. The illustrations are by David White; maps are by Deborah Perugi. Patti Polisar provided photo research (for illustration source material) and proofreading.

TRAVELERS' TALES

Watch for these new titles

We hope you enjoyed your journey while reading
Travelers' Tales Mexico, the second book in our new series.

Look for these other Travelers' Tales:

Thailand
India *(Nov. 1994)*
France *(early 1995)*
Hong Kong *(early 1995)*

Explore the "Travelers' Center" on the Internet

The *Travelers' Center* is the first interactive guide to the wild world of
travel on the global Internet. Initially an online service produced
for *Travelers' Tales*, the *Travelers' Center* has quickly blossomed into
a one-of-a-kind online resource that serves as a guide and
focal point to all the travel-related information
scattered about the Internet.

In addition to these important Internet resources, the *Travelers' Center*
also features an exclusive collection of up-to-the-minute electronic
dispatches from travel writers on the road: authors and reporters
like Joe Cummings, Tony Wheeler of Lonely Planet Guides,
and Jeff Greenwald, Bill McMillon and Eric Hansen.

If you would like more information about the *Travelers' Center*,
send email to **travinfo@gnn.com**. The *Travelers' Center* is produced by
O'Reilly & Associates' Global Network Navigator™ (GNN).